How to Prevent Genocide

How to Prevent Genocide

A Guide for Policymakers, Scholars,
and the Concerned Citizen

John G. Heidenrich

Westport, Connecticut
London

Library of Congress Cataloging-in-Publication Data

Heidenrich, John G., 1963–
    How to prevent genocide : a guide for policymakers, scholars, and the concerned citizen
/ by John G. Heidenrich.
        p.   cm.
    Includes bibliographical references and index.
    ISBN 0–275–96987–8 (alk. paper)
    1. Genocide—Government policy.   2. Genocide—Prevention.   3. Genocide—Moral
and ethical aspects.   I. Title.
    HV6322.7.H43   2001
    179.7—dc21   00–064962

British Library Cataloguing in Publication Data is available.

Library of Congress Catalog Card Number: 00–064962
ISBN: 0–275–96987–8

First published in 2001

Praeger Publishers, 88 Post Road West, Westport, CT 06881
An imprint of Greenwood Publishing Group, Inc.
www.praeger.com

Printed in the United States of America

The paper used in this book complies with the
Permanent Paper Standard issued by the National
Information Standards Organization (Z39.48–1984).

10 9 8 7 6 5 4 3 2 1

Copyright Acknowledgments

The author and publisher gratefully acknowledge permission for use of the following material:

Excerpts from personal correspondence with Ernest W. Lefever, letter dated September 5, 1998, used by permission.

Excerpts from personal correspondence with Joshua Muravchik, letter dated September 8, 1998, used by permission.

Excerpts from Ronald Reagan's speech, reprinted as "The Work of Freedom . . . An Unending Challenge," *Washington Times*, December 14, 1992, p. E-1, used by permission of the *Washington Times*.

Excerpts from Sandline white papers, "Private Military Companies: Independent or Regulated?" and "Should the Activities of Private Military Companies Be Transparent?" on the Sandline International website (*www.sandline.com*), used by permission.

Excerpts from Tim Spicer, "Why We Can Help Where Governments Fear to Tread," *Sunday Times*, May 24, 1998, used by permission of Sandline and the *Sunday Times*.

To Raphael Lemkin and Raoul Wallenberg

Contents

Preface

This book took me more than seven years to write. Most of it was written in the last decade of the twentieth century, the bloodiest, most genocidal century in recorded history. In its last decade—the first of our post-Cold War era—blatant campaigns of genocidal violence were inflicted in Europe's Balkans, in central Africa, in Kurdistan in the Middle East, and in Southeast Asia. Consequently, I had to revise and update this manuscript many times, even as I attempted to make it as timeless as possible. The result is a book that is not a history text, though it draws upon history, not a report, though it draws upon reports from many disciplines, a book that is designed for the layperson, the specialist, and the policymaker.

My career began in the last years of the Cold War, as a military analyst for the Pentagon's Defense Intelligence Agency (DIA). I went into intelligence work because I wanted to fight tyranny, and there was no tyranny more global and more powerful during the Cold War than Communism. Most of my time was spent assessing the then-uneasy military balance in Europe between the Soviet Union and the West's NATO alliance. Later, during the Gulf War in 1990-1991, I served as an expert on the Iraqi Army, producing crisis reports for the Secretary of the Defense and the Chairman of the Joint Chiefs of Staff, among other readers. I was very deeply involved, but I still greeted the ends of the Cold War and the Gulf War with enthusiasm, believing, as many people did in the early 1990s, that a better world would soon emerge. A world free of Communist obstructionism in the United Nations and without Soviet troublemaking around the globe. A world where the United States would stand preeminent, its values of constitutional democracy and free enterprise spreading globally to encourage a better life for literally billions of people.

That world has emerged, believe it or not, but the "New World Order" has clearly not been orderly—as global television audiences in the early Nineties saw for themselves, watching daily broadcasts of the violent disintegration of the old Yugoslavia. What they saw was the unwelcome return to Europe not only of war but of genocide, the deliberate mass murder of civilians, including women and children, murdered for representing a different religious or ethnic group. Genocide is no stranger to Africa, unfortunately, but in 1994 its magnitude in Rwanda was almost unprecedented—as was global news coverage of it.

I watched those horrors of the 1990s with as much frustration as revulsion, because I knew they could be prevented. But the Great Powers did not believe that genocidal violence was an immediate danger to their own vital national interests, and so they were unwilling to expend enough of their own military resources and domestic political capital to stop it. And yet, at the same time, none of them would have strenuously objected if *someone else* had forcibly intervened to stop the genocide in Bosnia-Herzegovina and Rwanda. There was a need, therefore, for an alternative "third party" force for this purpose, an idea publicly proposed in 1993 by Sir Brian Urquhart, one of the pioneers of UN peacekeeping and its director for many years. This idea was also endorsed, in a little noticed speech, by former President Ronald Reagan.

I took up the challenge of developing this idea and, in 1994 and 1995, it was the focus of my graduate studies at Harvard University. Today, I am intellectually indebted to my professors of that time, including Stanley Hoffmann, an eminent professor of international relations; Brian Mandel and Kalypso Nicolaidis, two very popular professors at Harvard's John F. Kennedy School of Government; the Right Honorable Shirley Williams, a former high-ranking member of the British Parliament; Erich Goldhagen, an extraordinary authority on genocide, himself a Holocaust survivor, and the proud father of Daniel Jonah Goldhagen, author of the best-selling book *Hitler's Willing Executioners;* Abram and Antonia Chayes at the Harvard Law School, both of them having previously held high positions in the U.S. Government; the Reverend J. Bryan Hehir at the Harvard Divinity School and today that school's dean; and, at Tufts University's Fletcher School of Law and Diplomacy, the eminent professor Robert Pfaltzgraff, founder of the respected Institute for Foreign Policy Analysis. While each may not agree with everything I have written in this book, I could not have written it without the benefit of their insightful teachings.

The United States Institute of Peace is an independent, nonpartisan federal institution created and funded by the U.S. Congress to strengthen the nation's capacity to promote the peaceful resolution of international conflict. In 1996 the Institute awarded me a research grant to investigate the idea of a UN "legion" for humanitarian intervention purposes—but with the condition that I also research alternatives to such a force. This condition seemed reasonable enough to me, and so I agreed. Little did I know (and, I suspect, did anyone else) how daunting this condition would turn out to be.

For to determine those alternatives, I had to first decide what the prime mission of a UN "legion" ought to be. I decided that it should be genocide prevention; indeed, I had already suggested as much to the Institute when I applied for my grant. Yet such a mission, such a goal, meant that this book would have to examine the nonmilitary alternatives of diplomacy, economic pressure, covert action, and nonviolent resistance. It would have to explain the causes of genocide, how to detect its clues, as well as the respective roles of ideology, politics, propaganda, and publicity. It would have to explain the roles of international law, international organizations, even international relations in general. It would have to address the controversial issue of humanitarian intervention, its criteria, its ethics, and its differing schools of thought. All this and more, it would have to cover, explained at an intellectual standard acceptable to experts from many disciplines, and yet still be readable by the most important reader of all, the common citizen. Only gradually did the sheer enormity of this challenge dawn on me, after the grant had already been approved and issued. The U.S. Government was expecting, and deserved, a good return on its investment. So I pressed on.

I soon became acquainted with a remarkable association that, today, I am honored to be a member of, the Association of Genocide Scholars. Dedicated to the study and prevention of genocide as a phenomenon, the Association's oldest members are the most eminent scholars in genocide studies today. Many head their own institutes, most affiliated with major universities. They helped me immensely. I, regretfully, have space enough here to thank only a few by name: Frank Chalk, the Association's President as I write this and, with Kurt Jonassohn, co-director of the Montreal Institute for Genocide and Human Rights Studies; Helen Fein, the Association's first president, currently director of the Institute for the Study of Genocide; Roger W. Smith, another past president, currently a professor at the College of William and Mary; Israel W. Charny, editor-in-chief of the *Encyclopedia of Genocide* and executive director of the Institute on the Holocaust and Genocide, in Jerusalem; Barbara Harff, a brilliant professor at the U.S. Naval Academy, and Ted Robert Gurr, director of the Minorities at Risk Project. Other scholars deserving of mention with this august list include Rudolph J. Rummel, Professor Emeritus at the University of Hawaii, Ervin Staub at the University of Massachusetts at Amherst, and Gregory Stanton, the founder of Genocide Watch among his many accomplishments. One of my great hopes is that two Association members whom I have a very high respect for, Steven L. Jacobs and Jim Fussell, will soon write biographies of Raphael Lemkin, a man whose personal efforts almost single-handedly produced the Genocide Convention in 1948.

For further information, literally hundreds of research centers and similar organizations were contacted all over the world. Many were quite helpful and I thank them all. Space constraints preclude a full listing here, but I especially thank the Netherlands Institute of International Relations *Clingendael*, the Carnegie Commission on Preventing Deadly Conflict, the Interdisciplinary Research Program on Root Causes of Human Rights Violations (PIOOM) based at Leiden University, and International Peace Brigades. As this manuscript developed, copies of it were kindly and constructively reviewed by the U.S. Army's Institute of Peacekeeping, the RAND Corporation, the Lester B. Pearson Canadian International Peacekeeping Training Centre, and countless individuals. Officials of the UN's Department of Peacekeeping Operations were interviewed. My thanks to them, as well as to the many other organizations and individuals who assisted this project.

Of the many ideas expressed in this book, I cannot claim to have originated any; I merely brought these ideas together into a single volume and, I hope, explain them here clearly and accurately. Since I did not originate these ideas, I would be remiss if I did not mention at least a few of the people whose writings and words had a profound influence: Chester Crocker, Romeo Dallaire, Eva Fogelman, Alison Des Forges, Erich Fromm, Edward R. Girardet, Samuel Huntington, Edward Luttwak, John A. MacInnis, Andrew Natsios, Samuel and Pearl Oliner, David Owen, Barry Posen, Adam Roberts, William Starr, Brian Urquhart, and of course Raphael Lemkin. I thank them all and apologize to anyone else whose name ought to appear here but, because of my own oversight, does not. I also apologize if my book has misrepresented any ideas, facts, or concepts. The responsibility for that is mine alone.

Among the notables who asked to see an early version of this manuscript was Elliot Richardson. Years earlier, as the U.S. Attorney General during the Nixon administration (one of four administrations he served in), Richardson resigned rather than obey Richard Nixon's order to fire Archibald Cox, the Watergate Special Prosecutor. Richardson later wrote a book he entitled *Reflections of a Radical Moderate*, published in 1996. He wrote on many subjects, including of his own favorable interest in the UN "legion" idea proposed by Brian Urquhart. It was in late 1999 that Richardson mailed me his personal request to see my book's most recent draft. Sadly, his letter did not reach me until early 2000. Elliot Richardson died on December 31, 1999.

Another notable who also asked for a draft copy was David J. Scheffer, the Clinton Administration's Ambassador-at-Large for War Crimes Issues at the U.S. State Department. Scheffer worked directly for then-Secretary of State Madeline Albright. His office, after requesting this manuscript twice, received a copy in mid-1998. Later, at a conference at the U.S. Holocaust Memorial Museum (which also received and favorably reviewed a draft copy), Ambassador Scheffer told me that his own copy had not left his desk for days because he kept turning to different sections of it for reference. He also asked for my permission to photocopy portions to circulate among his staff.

It was the start of an important relationship. Scheffer soon became the head of the Clinton Administration's new genocide early warning system, initiated by Clinton himself on the fiftieth anniversary of the Universal Declaration on Human Rights. I personally persuaded the Ambassador that this new system needed daily reports of genocidal clues and war crimes reported by the news media and non-governmental organizations. So, beginning in the Kosovo War and lasting until December 2000, under a contract paid for by the Central Intelligence Agency, I provided those reports via a private company called Open Source Solutions (OSS), Inc., serving as its Senior Analyst for Genocide & Instability Warning Issues. For those two years I helped the State Department track war crimes in Kosovo, the Congo, Chechnya, East Timor, and dozens of other places. Scheffer's office, in turn, directly assisted the international war crimes tribunals for Rwanda and the former Yugoslavia. When the United States signed the Rome Statute in December 2000—an important step in the formation of an International Criminal Court to try genocide-related offenses—David Scheffer himself penned the signature. This book includes the relevant events of those two years.

I thank the U.S. Institute of Peace for its patience and I am grateful to those who helped persuade the Institute to fund this project, including professors Bruce Russett at Yale University, Michael Doyle at Princeton, and Kosta Tsipis at MIT. I recently received a very kind note from Elie Wiesel, the Nobel Peace Prize laureate and eloquent Holocaust survivor. "An impressive piece of work," he said of this book, adding that he believes it will "surely elicit discussion and comment."

I especially thank my family and friends who, over the years, supported me in so many ways. Even something as ordinary as a sympathetic ear meant so much to me—and, I suspect, was not always easy to provide, having to listen to my woes and frustrations year after year.

Of everyone who helped me, my highest praise goes to two remarkable people. Randall Forsberg is executive director of the Institute for Defense & Disarmament Studies in Cambridge, Massachusetts. One of the founders of the Nuclear Freeze Movement in the early 1980s and, later, an arms control advisor to American presidents from both parties, Randy was also my primary advisor and mentor through most of the research and writing of this book. It was through her institute that the U.S. Institute of Peace funneled my research grant, saving me from the headaches of administering it. Later, when I went from research to activism by helping the U.S. State Department track genocidal situations, I was taken under the protective wing of Robert D. Steele, the President of Open Source Solutions, Inc. A former CIA case officer and a Marine, an entrepreneur, and a dedicated patriot, Robert believed so passionately in the importance of this book that he insisted I use the company's considerable resources to ensure its completion and publication. The final cost in money and manhours was not insignificant. Randy Forsberg and Robert Steele are two of the most generous, selfless, visionary people I have ever known. They will call this praise an exaggeration, but it is not; they deserve every word, and more. They gave me a chance when others would not. More than once I tried their patience, but their commitment to my success never wavered. One might think that their respective backgrounds would put them at opposite political poles, but to me this shows how much common political ground exists when people commit themselves to opposing genocide.

As I write these words at the beginning of the twenty-first century, I cannot confidently predict the future of genocide prevention. President George W. Bush has declared, "We should not send our troops to stop 'ethnic cleansing' and genocide in nations outside our strategic interest." Such a policy is not necessarily unreasonable, since U.S. troops should not be sent everywhere and anywhere to fight every injustice and right every wrong. But a hesitance to intervene with U.S. troops must not become an excuse to, in effect, do nothing—if only because, when left to fester, today's problems of "nonstrategic" human security too often become tomorrow's much larger problems of national security. To preclude such crises, the United States needs to promote early constructive efforts to prevent genocide in places that are not necessarily in America's "strategic interest"—and sometimes this means deploying a military-style police presence to safeguard local political moderates, fragile democratization, and civilized tolerance. If U.S. troops will not perform this type of peace enforcement, someone else must. Fortunately, the American people are more generally aware of the problem of genocide than ever before; hopefully this greater awareness will not dissolve into passivity or apathy. Though international instruments such as the United Nations and the Genocide Convention entered today's millennium with as much controversy as popularity, there is a general recognition that international instruments, though flawed, are nonetheless indispensable in today's world.

In summary, the future is wide open, waiting for us to create it. If we do not, if we display only apathy, then the future belongs to those who would employ terror, coercion, and mass murder for the sake of power and materialism. If, however, we act to encourage universal values such as compassion, tolerance, and freedom without impunity, our future could be bright indeed. My hope is that this book, as well as you the reader, will help make that future at least a little better than our past.

Abbreviations

ABC – American Broadcasting Company

ACRI – African Crisis Relief Initiative

AFSOUTH – Allied Forces Southern Europe (a NATO acronym)

AGS – Association of Genocide Scholars

APC – armored personnel carrier

ASEAN – Association of South East Asian Nations

CARE – Cooperative for Assistance and Relief Everywhere

CIA – Central Intelligence Agency

CIS – Commonwealth of Independent States

CIVPOL – Civilian Police (a UN acronym)

CNN – Cable News Network

CS – tear gas

CSI – Christian Solidarity International

DNA – deoxyribonucleic acid

DRC – Democratic Republic of the Congo

ECOMOG – ECOWAS Monitoring Observer Group

ECOWAS – Economic Community of West African States

EO – Executive Outcomes

ERRF – European Rapid Reaction Force

EU – European Union

FEWER – Forum for Early Warning and Early Response

FFCD – full, final, and complete disclosure

FM – field manual

Gestapo – Geheime Staatspolizei (German: "Secret State Police")

GEWS – Genocide Early Warning System

Gulag – Russian: "Chief Administration of Protective Labor Camps"

HRIC – Human Rights in China

ICC – International Criminal Court

ICRC – International Committee of the Red Cross

ICTR – International Criminal Tribunal for Rwanda

ICTY – International Criminal Tribunal for the former Yugoslavia

IFOR – Implementation Force

IMF – International Monetary Fund

INTERFET – International Force in East Timor

INTERPOL – International Criminal Police Organization

ISG – Institute for the Study of Genocide

KDP – Kurdistan Democratic Party

KFOR – Kosovo Force

KGB – *Komitet Gosudarstvennoj Bezopanosti* (Russian: "Committee for State Security")

KLA – Kosovo Liberation Army

Laogai – Chinese: "Reform through Labor"

MIGS – Montreal Institute for Genocide

and Human Rights Studies
MIT – Massachusetts Institute of
    Technology
MP – Military Police
MSF – *Medecins Sans Frontieres*
    (French: "Doctors Without
    Borders")
NATO – North Atlantic Treaty
    Organization
Nazi – *Nationalsozialistische Deutsche
    Arbeiterspartei* (German: "National
    Socialist German Workers Party")
NGO – non-governmental organization
NKVD – *Narodnyj Komissariat
    Vnutrennih Del Volk* (Russian:
    "Committee for Internal Affairs")
NLW – non-lethal weapon
NTV – An independent Russian
    television network
OAS – Organization of American States
OAU – Organization for African Unity
OCHA – Office for the Coordination of
    Humanitarian Affairs
OHCHR – Office of the UN High
    Commissioner for Human Rights
OSCE – Organization for Security and
    Cooperation in Europe
OSINT – Open Source Intelligence
OSS – Office of Strategic Services
P-5 – Permanent Five of the UN
    Security Council
PAO – Public Affairs Officer
PDD – Presidential Decision Directive
PfP – Partnership for Peace
PHR – Physicians for Human Rights
PJC – Permanent Joint Council
PLA – (Chinese) People's Liberation
    Army
PMC – private military company
POW – prisoner of war

PRC – People's Republic of China
PSYOP – psychological operation
Psyops – psychological operations
PUK – Patriotic Union of Kurdistan
RFE/RL – Radio Free Europe/Radio
    Liberty
SA – *Sturmabteilung* (German: "Storm
    Troopers")
SACEUR – Supreme Allied Commander
    Europe (a NATO acronym)
SAS – (British) Special Air Service
SFOR – Stabilization Force
SHIRBRIG – Stand-by Forces High
    Readiness Brigade
SS – *Schutzstaffel* (German: "Protection
    Squad")
U.K. – United Kingdom of Great Britain
    and Northern Ireland
UN – United Nations
UNAMIR – UN Assistance Mission in
    Rwanda
UNDP – UN Development Program
UNHCR – UN High Commissioner for
    Refugees
UNICEF – UN Children's Fund
UNIDIR – UN Institute for Disarmament
    Research
UNITAF – Unified Task Force
UNOSOM – UN Operation in Somalia
UNPROFOR – UN Protection Force
U.S. – United States
USA – United States of America
USMC – United States Marine Corps
USSR – Union of Soviet Socialist
    Republics
VOA – Voice of America
VX – A specific type of lethal gas
WFP – World Food Program
WMD – weapons of mass destruction

1

What Is Genocide?

During the 90 days that began on April 6 in 1994, Rwanda experienced the most intensive slaughter in this blood-filled century we are about to leave. Families murdered in their home, people hunted down as they fled by soldiers and militia, through farmland and woods as if they were animals. . . . It is important that the world know that these killings were not spontaneous or accidental, [that] they were most certainly not the result of ancient tribal struggles.

We in the United States and the world community did not do as much as we could have, and should have, to try to limit what occurred in Rwanda in 1994. And we're still not organized to deal with it.

— U.S. President Bill Clinton, 1998

In the five years after the Berlin Wall came down, the word *genocide* was heard far more often than in any five years of the Cold War.

— Harvard Professor Samuel P. Huntington
The Clash of Civilizations and the Remaking of World Order, 1996

There is a legal difference between war and genocide. Wars are supposed to be fought only between armed forces. Genocide is inflicted upon the largely defenseless. In war, to preserve at least some civilized conduct, there is the concept of the *noncombatant:* infants, children, expectant mothers and women generally, the elderly, the infirm, civilians in general, and even some military personnel, including military physicians, medics, and prisoners. International law declares that anyone who wages war must actively try to avoid harm to noncombatants. Genocide, by contrast, is utterly contrary to international law, because its victims—no matter how innocent—are targeted intentionally.

War perpetrates killing. Genocide perpetrates murder.

A CONTROVERSIAL DEFINITION

Today the word *genocide* is used so frequently to express hyperbole that the average person might be surprised by the word's actual definition. Some believe that the word should describe almost any persecution of almost any category of humanity—a very broad definition that has included the atomic bombing victims of Hiroshima and Nagasaki, the sufferers of female genital mutilation, and abortions for birth control. Some people want a more selective definition; not used, for instance, to describe the African slave trade (without belittling that centuries-old nightmare), but legitimately used to describe the decimation of indigenous peoples and their native cultures. Still others believe that the word's definition should be narrowed to denote only the most methodical, factory-efficient campaign of mass murder ever inflicted, the Holocaust.

Even the word's international legal definition is controversial. Article III of the Convention on the Prevention and Punishment of the Crime of Genocide defines the crime as:

any of the following acts committed with intent to destroy, in whole or in part, a national, ethnical, racial, or religious group, as such:
  (a) Killing members of the group;
  (b) Causing serious bodily or mental harm to members of the group;
  (c) Deliberately inflicting on the group conditions of life calculated to bring about its physical destruction in whole or in part;
  (d) Imposing measures intended to prevent births within the group;
  (e) Forcibly transferring children of the group to another group.

Notice in this definition that the targeted groups—national, ethnic, racial, and religious—do not include political and socioeconomic groups. This is because in 1948, when the definition was negotiated, various delegations (including one from the Soviet Union, at that time ruled by Joseph Stalin) asserted that political and socioeconomic groups are too nebulous to define in legal terms, so those groups were simply not included. Consequently, whenever a government has committed mass murder without discriminating according to nationality, ethnicity, race, or religion, that government has not committed "genocide" as international law defines the crime, even if its victims number in the millions.

In Cambodia in 1975-1979, the Khmer Rouge followers of Communist leader Pol Pot murdered people for "political" reasons as inane as for simply wearing eyeglasses. The Khmer Rouge, being Communists, wanted to eliminate all bourgeois intellectuals—and they assumed that any Cambodian who wore eyeglasses must be one. In their effort to socially re-engineer Cambodian society using terror and killing, later dramatized in the motion picture *The Killing Fields,* the Khmer Rouge murdered an estimated 1.7 million Cambodians out of an original population of only 7 million. In per capita terms, the Cambodian nation suffered the worst mass murder ever inflicted upon a population by its own government.[1] Yet according to the international legal definition of genocide, the great majority of those victims were not victims of "genocide" because they were killed according to a purely political, not a racial, criteria. The only exceptions were Cambodia's ethnic minorities.

Should it be legally acceptable to massacre, say, 999 people for reasons of nationality, ethnicity, race, or religion—but only upon the 1,000th victim, or whatever threshold number is chosen, does a "genocide" exist? The delegates to the Genocide Convention could not agree on a number, so they left the question open. Consequently, if an ordinary gang of thugs kill a person simply because that person belongs to a particular nationality, ethnicity, race, or religion, that one murder is, legally speaking, an act of genocide.

Today, in deference to the Convention's limited definition of *genocide*, some scholars prefer to use the term *politicide* to describe political mass murder, or *democide* to describe mass deaths caused by any deliberate means, including willful neglect, avoidable famine, forced labor, or direct massacre.

Someone who devised a more conceptually useful definition of *genocide* is the man who coined the word. His name was Raphael Lemkin, a Polish scholar of international law and a secular Jew. In World War II, after Poland was invaded by Nazi Germany, Lemkin fled to the United States and became an advisor to the U.S. War Department. In 1944 he published a book he entitled *Axis Rule in Occupied Europe: Laws of Occupation, Analysis of Government, Proposals for Redress.* In it, he described the enormity of the atrocities the Nazis and their Fascist partners were inflicting on the European continent—atrocities so savage, so widespread, and yet so integrated into a monstrous whole that Winston Churchill remarked, "We are in the presence of a crime without a name."

Lemkin gave the crime a name. By combining the Greek prefix *genos* (which means *nation, tribe,* or *group*) with the Latin suffix *cide,* from *cidium* ("to kill"), he constructed the word *genocide.* Lemkin wrote:

The crime of *genocide* involves a wide range of actions, including not only deprivation of life and also devices considerably endangering life and health: all these actions are subordinated to the criminal intent to destroy or to cripple permanently a human group. The acts are directed against groups as such, and individuals are selected for destruction only because they belong to these groups.

Mass murder does not convey the specific losses to civilization which can be made only by groups of people united through national, racial or cultural characteristics. . . . We can best understand this when we realize how impoverished our culture would be if the peoples doomed by [Nazi] Germany, such as the Jews, had not been permitted to create the Bible, or give birth to an Einstein, a Spinoza; if the Poles had not had the opportunity to give the world a Copernicus, a Chopin, a Curie; the Czechs, a Huss, a Dvorak; the Greeks, a Plato and a Socrates; the Russians, a Tolstoy and Shostakovich.[2]

It is this deliberate destruction of a people and of their ability to freely contribute to human civilization that makes genocide more than a crime against any particular people, but indeed a *crime against humanity*—because literally all of humanity suffers the loss. To illustrate this, Lemkin quoted the following Nazi account of how the library of the Jewish Theological Seminary in Lublin, Poland, was destroyed by the Nazis in 1939. Those perpetrators declared:

For us it was a matter of special pride to destroy the Talmudic Academy, which was known as the greatest in Poland. . . . We threw out of the building the great Talmudic library, and carted it to market. There we set fire to the books. The fire lasted for twenty hours. The Jews of Lublin were assembled around and cried bitterly. Their cries almost silenced us. Then we summoned the military band and the joyful shouts of the soldiers silenced the sound of the Jewish cries.[3]

The destruction of that great library was a loss suffered by all humankind, not only by the Jews of Lublin, nor even of all Poland. It was an act of genocide, even though no one was killed. Lemkin explained:

Generally speaking, *genocide* does not necessarily mean the immediate destruction of a nation, except when accomplished by mass killings of all members of a nation. It is intended rather to signify a coordinated plan of different actions aiming at the destruction of essential foundations of the life of national groups, with the aim of annihilating the groups themselves. The objectives of such a plan would be disintegration of the political and social institutions, of culture, language, national feelings, religion, and the economic existence of national groups, and the destruction of the personal security, liberty, health, dignity, and even the lives of the individuals belonging to such groups.[4]

Instead of ending his word with *cide*, Lemkin could have paired *genos* with *cidio*, a suffix that means "total destruction" or "extermination." Indeed, for a short time the word *genocidio* was the preferred term of international law. In late 1945, at the postwar Nuremberg Trials, several captured Nazi officials were indicted by the Allies for having perpetrated various crimes during the war, including:

Intended and systematic *genocidio*, that is, extermination of racial and national groups of civilian population in certain occupied territories in order to destroy certain races and layers of nations and peoples, racial and religious groups, in particular Jews, Poles, Gypsies and others.

It was the world's first legal indictment for the crime of genocide. Later, in 1948, Lemkin helped to draft today's Genocide Convention; its emphasis upon safeguarding national, ethnic, racial, and religious groups reflects his ideas. But Lemkin's concern for the well-being of national groups went far beyond the bare physical existence of their members; he also wanted to protect their political, social, and cultural institutions. Lemkin died in 1959, but if he had lived to witness some later debates over whether horrors such as the Cambodian "killing fields" deserved to be called "genocide" or not, he would have probably argued that such debates neglect what he wanted to do: use international law to oppose mass atrocities.

The United States signed the Genocide Convention during the presidency of Harry S. Truman, announcing it would interpret the Convention's key clause of "with intent to destroy, in whole or in part" to mean a *specific* intent to destroy in whole or in *substantial* part. The United States defined *substantial* as "a part of a group of such numerical significance that the destruction of loss of that part would cause the destruction of the group as a viable entity within the nation of which such group is a part."[5]

For the United States, signing any treaty is not the same as ratifying it. The Genocide Convention, despite being signed in 1948, was not ratified by the U.S. Senate until 1986, finally encouraged by President Ronald Reagan as well as Senate Majority Leader Robert Dole. The Senate also voted 93 to 1 to direct the President to seek a new treaty provision to cover political mass murder. To date, however, the Genocide Convention remains unaltered.

THE BLOODIEST CENTURY

The phenomenon of genocide is not new: It is mentioned in writings as old as the Bible's Book of Deuteronomy (7:1-6). Despite such distant beginnings, however, the most genocidal century yet recorded in human history is uncomfortably recent: the twentieth century.

In the Boer War of 1899-1902, waged in what is today South Africa, British colonial troops adopted a counterinsurgency strategy used years earlier by Spanish troops in Cuba: Those British troops herded Dutch-descended Boer (Afrikaner) civilians into prison-like camps, along with many of the Boers' African friends and servants, causing tens of thousands to die of starvation and disease. The Spaniards had called their own camps *campos de reconcentración.* The British shortened the term to *concentration camps.* Decades later this notorious term earned its present connotation from the Nazis.

Racist forms of nationalism often intertwine with genocide, especially in modern times. In 1915-1916 in Turkey, at that time called the Ottoman Empire, a secular nationalist dictatorship known as the "Young Turks" tried to racially solidify that long-troubled empire by using the First World War as a pretext to massacre the empire's Armenian Christian minority. Aside from a few places with a sizable foreign presence of diplomats and journalists resided, almost the entire Armenian population of the empire of perhaps 2 million was deported into the desert. Vast numbers starved to death or were murdered along the way; estimates range from 600,000 to more than 1 million. Most survivors did so by escaping into neighboring lands.[6] Throughout the rest of the twentieth century, various Turkish governments denied even the existence of this genocide. But the evidence for it is overwhelming. In 1915 the U.S. ambassador to Turkey, Henry Morgenthau, Sr., called it "a campaign of race extermination" in a report back to Washington. His successor in 1916, Abram Elkus, agreed, calling it an "unchecked policy of extermination through starvation, exhaustion, and brutality of treatment hardly surpassed even in Turkish history."[7] Denials of its existence only obscure the fact that, during its perpetration, many Turks, including a few Turkish governors, bravely opposed it—at great personal risk.

Eventually the "Young Turk" regime was overthrown and a Turkish court later tried and convicted its three highest leaders, in absentia, for perpetrating the Armenian genocide. In 1926 the founder of today's Turkish Republic, Mustafa Kemal Ataturk, acknowledged both the massacres and their perpetrators in an American newspaper, declaring:

These left-overs from the former Young Turk Party, who should have been made to account for the millions of our Christian subjects who were ruthlessly driven en masse from their homes and massacred, have been restive under the Republican rule.[8]

While some contemporary historians note that German colonial troops in South-West Africa, now called Namibia, systematically destroyed a tribe called the Hereros in 1904-1905, killing as many as 30,000 men, women and children,[9] the Armenian genocide has nevertheless become remembered as the first major genocide of the twentieth century. But what lesson, if any, does the Armenian genocide teach? In a speech he delivered in 1939, just before he launched Nazi Germany's invasion of Poland, Adolf Hitler revealed what he had learned. With a tone of future vindication, he asked: "Who still talks nowadays about the massacres of the Armenians?" [10]

Hitler's regime directly mass murdered an estimated 17 million human beings before and during World War II—and caused millions more to perish through wanton neglect. The noncombat victims of the Nazis included some 5 million Poles, primarily intellectuals; at least 6 million Soviet civilians and captured prisoners of war, most of them starved to death; nearly 800,000 Serbs, most butchered in atrocities inflicted by the Nazis' Croatian allies; hundreds of thousands of Roma (Gypsies); and, most notoriously, some 6 million Jews— including 1 million Jewish children.[11]

These numbers are immense in part because the Nazis used a few abstract racial definitions, formulated by the Nazis themselves, to condemn entire *races* of human beings to death. Nazi ideology asserted that Jews, for example, were not merely a different religion but literally a different species, a bastard race biologically inferior to "normal" human beings, a form of social vermin so dangerously malignant that all Jews—*all Jews*—had to be exterminated, including their offspring. Jews therefore suffered the Nazis' most methodical methods of mass murder, what the Nazis called their "Final Solution to the Jewish question." Those methods included mass shootings, burning victims alive, deadly torture, hideous medical experiments, starvation, working victims to death in concentration camps such as Buchenwald, Bergen-Belsen, Dachau, Ravensbruck, and Mauthausen, or gassing the victims—crowded together and naked—in the factory-efficient human extermination complexes of Auschwitz-Birkenau, Chelmo, Sobibor, and Treblinka.

Today's Jews refer to this nightmare time as the *Shoah,* more commonly as the Holocaust. Although the murder tally of Nazism was later exceeded by Communism's, Nazism piled up its tally much faster—and had further intended to exterminate other categories of people after exterminating the last Jew. Even today, the Holocaust remains the most systematic, most industrialized genocide ever inflicted, in many ways rendering it unique, so unique that any comparisons to it risk belittling how monstrous the Holocaust actually was. However, since no other genocide remains so widely known and well documented, this book will make references to the Holocaust to illustrate some crucial points. Without cheapening its horror, we must learn some preventive lessons from it.

Joseph Stalin perpetrated more mass murder than Adolf Hitler, albeit over a longer reign. In the 1930s Stalin subjected the Soviet Union's own Communist Party and the Red Army to the *Great Purges*, a deadly "purification" of those institutions through mock trials, imprisonment, forced labor, and executions. According to the once-privileged sources of Andrei Sakharov, the famed Soviet physicist and dissident, more than 1.2 million Soviet Communist Party members —half of the party's total membership—were arrested between 1936 and 1939. Only 50,000 ever regained their freedom. Some 600,000 were shot. Most of the rest died in forced labor camps.[12]

Yet even before the Great Purges, an estimated 7 million well-to-do Soviet peasants, the so-called *kulaks,* were executed or intentionally starved to death in a campaign officially called *collectivization,* ordered by Stalin to reshape Soviet agriculture. Another 12 million Soviet citizens died in a network of forced labor camps collectively known by the Russian acronym GULAG, many of them from the physical toil of satisfying Stalin's relentless drive to rapidly industrialize the Soviet Union. Others were murdered more quickly, their deaths shrouded in official secrecy. Typical was a mass grave outside the city of Minsk, concealed until the late 1980s. In Stalin's time Minsk had fewer than 1 million inhabitants, yet his regime managed to concoct enough reasons to fill the mass grave with 200,000 victims.[13] Overall, between 1924 and 1953, Stalin's regime is estimated to have murdered at least 20 million people.

Mao Zedong's regime in China may have been even worse; the official execution records are incomplete. What is known is that during Mao's "Cultural Revolution" in the 1960s and 1970s—when China suffered near chaos from a regime-encouraged terror campaign meant to make the population as fanatically Communist-minded as possible—some 2 million Chinese were killed. Worse was Mao's rule in the 1950s, when several million died, either from avoidable famine or mass execution. Countless others were imprisoned in the *laogaï,* a network of forced labor camps. The overall death toll from Mao's rule from 1949 until 1976 is estimated at more than 27 million.

The ideologies of Nazism and Marxism-Leninism were not the only ones used to justify genocide in the twentieth century. Baathism, an atheistic pan-Arab ideology espoused by Iraq's Saddam Hussein among others, was used to justify killing the Iraqi Kurds among other groups. Genocide was also waged in the name of anti-Communism. In Guatemala and El Salvador in the 1980s, tens of thousands of innocent people (especially from native tribes) were murdered for being the supposed sympathizers of Marxist guerrillas. In the mid-1970s, the armed forces of Argentina abducted and murdered at least 9,000 Argentines suspected of being Communists, a reign of terror known as the "Dirty War." In Indonesia vast numbers of suspected Communists were slaughtered during a few months in late 1965; estimates range from 80,000 to over 1 million killed. Many political independence movements, from Bangladesh to Bosnia-Herzegovina, were also attacked with genocidal campaigns.

No one knows how many people in total died from genocide in the twentieth century, but some estimates for the years between 1900 and 1988 were compiled by Rudolph Rummel, the professor who coined the word *democide*. Rummel's chillingly comprehensive estimates, published in 1994 in a book entitled *Death by Government*, generally exclude war-related deaths unless caused by methods now considered criminal under the Geneva Conventions; therefore his estimates include the Allies' aerial bombings of civilian populations in World War II, including the atomic bombings of Hiroshima and Nagasaki. He wrote:

In total, during the first 88 years of this century, almost 170,000,000 men, women and children have been shot, beaten, tortured, knifed, burned, starved, frozen, crushed, or worked to death, buried alive, drowned, hanged, bombed, or killed in any other of the myriad ways regimes have inflicted death on unarmed, helpless citizens and foreigners. The number of dead could even conceivably be near a high of 360,000,000 people. This is as though our species has been devastated by a modern Black Plague. And indeed it has, but a plague of absolute power and not germs.[14]

What is the cause of this plague? What is its solution? Rummel concluded:

Power kills; absolute power kills absolutely. . . . The more power a government has, the more it can act arbitrarily according to the whims and desires of the elite, and the more it will make war on others and murder its foreign and domestic subjects. The more constrained the power of governments, the more power is diffused, checked and balanced, the less it will aggress on others and commit democide. At the extremes of power, totalitarian communist governments slaughter their people by the tens of *millions;* in contrast, many democracies can barely bring themselves to execute even serial murderers. . . . The way to end war and virtually eliminate democide appears to be through restricting and checking power, i.e., through *fostering democratic freedom.*[15]

Fostering democratic freedom using free elections, individual rights and social tolerance is certainly a laudable policy, but what can be done when a genocidal regime is already in power? The last decade of the twentieth century, when more people lived under democratic governments than ever before, still witnessed plenty of genocide.

Ethnic Conflict in Bosnia-Herzegovina

Bosnia-Herzegovina was once one of six autonomous "republics" in a multi-ethnic federation called the Federal People's Republic of Yugoslavia, hereafter referred to as the former (or "old") Yugoslavia. Ruled for decades by the Communist regime of Josef Broz Tito, the federation's different ethnic groups were compelled to both live and work together, gradually overlapping their communities; many Yugoslavs even intermarried. By the late 1980s Tito was dead, however, and the federation was starting to fray. In Kosovo, a province of Yugoslavia's Serbian republic, an ethnic Albanian majority enjoyed a degree of provincial autonomy until 1989, when the Serbian republic's leader, Slobodan Milosevic, ordered every ethnic Albanian disenfranchised from every powerful institution in Kosovo, including from the provincial government, the police, the mass media, and the educational system. The Serbian community, only 10 percent of Kosovo's population, ruled thereafter as a privileged minority. That ethnic chauvinism signaled an end to Tito's ideal of multi-ethnic tolerance.

Within two years the old Yugoslav republics of Slovenia, Croatia, and Macedonia each declared their independence. In April 1992, an elected Bosnian government met in the Bosnian capital of Sarajevo and declared the formal independence of Bosnia-Herzegovina as well. Soon thereafter, however, violent disagreements emerged between Bosnia's three main groups, ethnic Serbs, ethnic Croats, and "ethnic Muslims," the third so labeled by the officially atheist regime of Communist Yugoslavia to recognize that group's religious roots without legitimizing the religion. Most Bosnian-Muslims were secular and, racially, identical to both the Bosnian-Serbs, who were mostly East Orthodox Christians, and to the Bosnian-Croats, who were mostly Catholic Christians. Across all three groups, most Bosnians did not want to see their homeland and their own mixed neighborhoods torn apart by bloodshed and ethnic conflict.

Nevertheless, many Bosnian-Serbs did want to unite large parts of Bosnia-Herzegovina with the remnants of the Yugoslav federation, now dominated by Serbia, whereas many Bosnian-Croats wanted to unite large portions of Bosnia with the newly independent Croatia. Some racially opportunistic leaders fueled their desires with hateful ethnic-centered propaganda, and with increasingly gruesome violence.

The result was the Bosnian War, a war that was actually three simultaneous wars: one between Bosnian-Muslims and Bosnian-Serbs, the latter supported militarily by Serbia; another between Bosnian-Muslims and Bosnian-Croats, the latter supported by Croatia; and a third between Bosnian-Serbs and Bosnian-Croats. For almost four years, Bosnia-Herzegovina's mixed communities were forcibly divided by ethnic-prejudiced units and marauding bands using mass eviction, mass rape, and mass murder as their tactics. These genocidal campaigns were self-labeled with the chilling euphemism of *ethnic cleansing*. Most at risk were the Muslims.

The Bosnian War was not caused by historical feuds or by ethnic rivalry, although both were manipulated as excuses. It was caused by the ambitions of a powerful few. "The duplicities of the war in Bosnia-Herzegovina," wrote David Owen, a frustrated peace negotiator at the time, "have never been better illustrated than by a conversation between a Muslim commander and his Serb counterpart, picked up by intercept radios during the Muslim-Croat war." Owen continued:

First they bargained over the price, in Deutschmarks, of Serb shells which the Muslims wanted to buy from the Serbs to fire on the Croats in Mostar. After a price was agreed and routes for the supply in lorries arranged, the Muslim commander was heard to come back and ask if the Serbs could, for a little extra money, fire the shells if they were given the cross-bearings [i.e., the target coordinates]. After a brief haggle on the number of extra Deutschmarks this would involve, the Serbs duly fired on the Croats, paid for by the Muslims.

When [my fellow negotiator Thorvald] Stoltenberg and I told President Milosevic about this on 12 November 1993, he was very angry and asked [the Bosnian-Serb leader, Radovan] Karadzic in our presence whether this had happened. Karadzic confirmed that it had, but said orders had been issued that it must not happen again.[16]

There were instances when Bosnian-Muslim forces, largely run by corrupt commanders profiting from Sarajevo's wartime black market, deliberately fired upon Sarajevo's airport to temporarily close it to any incoming humanitarian aid flights supplying the city's Muslim civilians—to thereby worsen the city's food shortages, driving up prices on the black market.[17]

In 1995, Bosnian-Serb forces attacked Srebrenica, a city declared by the United Nations Security Council to be a "safe haven"—an official sanctuary for civilian refugees fleeing the war. Srebrenica was protected, albeit more with symbolism than weaponry, by a small group of UN soldiers whose presence, it was hoped, would deter attack. And for many months their presence did. But for years as the Bosnian War dragged on, the general credibility of the UN's forces had diminished into a general contempt. The problem, many analysts believe, was that the UN's forces wearing their renown blue helmets with UN insignia were not really owned by the UN Organization; they were actually national military contingents on loan to the Organization from the UN's member-states, national contingents that could be ordered by their respective contributors to avoid any serious risks in Bosnia—which they did. After witnessing this timid behavior for years, the Bosnian-Serb leadership concluded that Srebrenica could be seized with little or no retaliation by the United Nations.

So they attacked. Srebrenica's symbolic UN guardians radioed for troop reinforcements, for air strikes, for *anything* to help stop this illegal attack upon a UN-declared safe haven. But too little was done, and the Bosnian-Serbs captured Srebrenica. Almost immediately the victors expelled the city's relatively few UN soldiers—along with some 30,000 Muslim women and children. Many of the women were packed onto trucks and sent into Muslim territory. Others fled on foot. Some were raped. Some were killed. In a civil war known for its mass evictions, especially of Muslims, this was the largest yet.

But the worst fate befell some 7,000 Muslim men and adolescent boys—mass executed, the largest massacre on European soil recorded since the Second World War. At one particular mass grave, excavators and forensic experts deduced that the victims, all civilian males, had been lined up in the forest, shot through their skulls, and tumbled in. It was but one of several mass graves created near Srebrenica, later fingered by survivors or revealed on aerial photographs as discolored topsoil.

At least 100,000 people died in the Bosnian War. Investigators from the UN's International Criminal Tribunal for the former Yugoslavia, established during the war to prosecute Balkan war criminals, reported that 12,000 inhabitants of Sarajevo, mostly civilians, were killed by snipers or artillery fire during the capital's long siege. About 1,600 were children.

And the decade of Balkan "ethnic cleansing" was not yet over.

Genocide in Rwanda

Rwanda is a small central African country with fewer than 8 million people. Two ethnic groups (sometimes mistakenly called "tribes") predominate: the Hutu, the great majority, and the Tutsi, a minority. Historically the Hutu have been farmers, whereas the Tutsi were herdsmen. Since cattle has traditionally represented considerable wealth in central Africa, this distinction made the Tutsi the local economic elite. A stereotype holds that the average Hutu is short and stocky, whereas the average Tutsi is tall and thin. Through intermarriage and other factors, however, the two groups have become more physically alike than different. Some historians and ethnographers even assert that the Hutu and Tutsi are not really socioeconomic classes, not ethnic groups. Even many Rwandans have difficulty visually identifying their fellows as either Hutu or Tutsi.

In the nineteenth and early twentieth centuries, when Rwanda was a *de facto* colony ruled by Belgium, the stereotype of the tall slender Tutsi made him seem more "European" in the eyes of many racist-minded Belgian administrators, that is, more physically like the Belgians themselves. Consequently, the Belgians institutionalized the supremacy of the Tutsi minority over the Hutu majority, a societal division they further entrenched with individual identification cards, classifying each native cardholder as either "Hutu" or "Tutsi." If a cardholder's ethnicity was visually indiscernible, the ethnic designation marked was almost arbitrarily. Indeed, in the 1930s it was arbitrary, at least racially, because in those years Belgian census takers defined a "Tutsi" as anyone who owned nine or more cows.

The colonial legacy of the ethnic-stamped identification card should have been abandoned after Rwanda became independent in 1962. The card system was instead retained, however, because it enabled various Rwandan leaders to exploit the bigoted lie that some meaningful biological difference exists between Hutus and Tutsis. In later years, both in Rwanda and in neighboring Burundi, there were occasions when a Hutu regime massacred Tutsis or a Tutsi regime massacred Hutus.

Such a danger continued to exist in the early 1990s when Rwanda was ruled by a Hutu regime at war with a Tutsi guerrilla army. After a cease-fire was arranged in 1993, a small UN peacekeeping force was deployed to monitor it. But the peacekeepers soon uncovered clues of a massive anti-Tutsi slaughter being prepared: quasi-official radio broadcasts spouting hateful anti-Tutsi propaganda, growing stockpiles of machetes beyond any genuine need to clear the jungle, and reports of training camps where Hutu militiamen were being taught how to massacre Tutsi civilians. The peacekeepers' worried commander urged his UN superiors in New York to give his small force a new international mandate to stop these genocidal preparations. For various reasons, his request was refused.

On April 6, 1994, Rwanda's Hutu president died in a suspicious airplane crash. A bloody military takeover immediately ensued, during which many Hutu political moderates were murdered by Hutu political extremists. *Then the entire Tutsi minority was targeted.* Soldiers from Rwanda's Presidential Guard established roadblocks throughout the capital to inspect citizens' identification cards; those whose cards identified them as "Tutsi" were taken aside and slain. Armed gangs of Hutu men and boys swept through the city, and eventually throughout the countryside, encouraged by the new regime to kill every Tutsi they could find.

Nearly 800,000 people were murdered, most of them hacked to death with machetes. Male genitals were cut off. Female breasts were lacerated. Not even infants were spared. So many corpses were dumped into the Kagera River that, downstream in Lake Victoria, some 40,000 were eventually fished out.

The genocide raged for more than three months—and the international news media reported on it in ghastly detail almost every day. Television audiences worldwide were shocked, and demanded action. Yet the reaction of Western governments, expressed through the UN Security Council, was slow and timid. Many of the UN troops already in Rwanda wanted to stop the killings, forcibly if necessary, but their contributing governments inhibited them. Belgium's government even withdrew its UN contingent after ten Belgian peacekeepers were hacked to death. Despite the world's popular desire to see the genocide stopped, most Western governments did not trust that that popular enthusiasm would last if their own national soldiers started to get killed in Rwanda. And so, on June 6, 1994, on the fiftieth anniversary commemoration of the Western Allies' D-Day landings in Normandy against the Third Reich, those same Allied countries allowed another genocide to continue unhindered, five decades after the *Shoah*.

What ultimately stopped the Rwandan genocide was not the UN but the country's advancing Tutsi guerrillas, forcing the Hutu regime to flee in July. But in that regime's retreat into Zaire and Tanzania, it pulled along almost 2 million Hutu refugees. More than half of them ended their journey in a tiny Zairian border town named Goma. Soon tens of thousands were afflicted with cholera. Starvation threatened to kill even more. What had started months earlier as an ominous yet preventable killing spree in Rwanda had evolved into a genocide, and now a refugee nightmare. International relief agencies were overwhelmed. Foreign television audiences were incensed. Western governments, pressed by their voters, sent emergency aid worth hundreds of millions of dollars. They also sent troops: military specialists to manage an enormous humanitarian relief operation. It was a noble gesture. It was also very late.

Meanwhile, the deposed regime of the Hutu extremists, calling itself a "government-in-exile," imposed its rule on the overcrowded refugee camps, using threats, food deprivation, and beatings to keep any refugees from returning to Rwanda. If a sizeable UN force had been sent into those camps, the perpetrators of the recent genocide could have been physically separated from the refugees. But no member of the United Nations was willing to contribute enough troops to face the risks involved. Therefore, through neglect, some 2 million Rwandan refugees became permanent wards of the international aid community, along with their so-called rulers in exile. The frustrating absurdity of it all became a daily dilemma for the humanitarian relief agencies involved. One aid worker from CARE explained:

How do you justify feeding killers? You can't, of course, but that's basically what we've been doing for the past two years. And the flip side is this: *How do you justify letting innocent people starve, or go without medical help, just because you cannot easily distinguish between villain and victim?* It's the kind of question that leaves you sitting up nights, wondering what the hell you're doing with your life.

But 'come dawn, there you are, looking in the eye of human need. So you go out there, do what you can, and hope that by the end of the day you've done more good than harm. The world is what it is. It is complicated. It is shaded in grays. If you do more good than harm, you've probably done the best job you can.[18]

The collective misery of the refugee camps and their massive consumption of international aid all lasted for two years. It could have lasted even longer, but in 1996, troops from Rwanda, now ruled by Tutsis, attacked the camps in Zaire and dispersed the refugees' tormentors. Most of the refugees returned to Rwanda, although 100,000 of them fled into the Zairian jungle, their fate uncertain.

Their plight, globally televised, attracted the sympathy of Canada's Prime Minister Jean Chretien. An aide of his recalled that Chretien "was extremely concerned, frustrated with the foot-dragging and slow-motion diplomacy at the UN." Even today, the UN Organization typically needs at least three months to arrange, assemble, and organize any new UN peacekeeping force. Chretien refused to wait that long, so he personally telephoned the leaders of sixteen countries, including of South Africa, Britain, France, Germany, Chile, Senegal, Brazil, Argentina, and the United States—warning his counterparts that time was precious. *For a new UN peacekeeping force,* he asked each one, *how many troops and equipment can your country contribute?* It was a remarkable spectacle: a Canadian prime minister personally performing a task normally done by lower-level bureaucrats and functionaries. On his desk, recalled his aide, Chretien "had all these numbers promised by other countries scrawled on paper scraps." But Chretien had to make the arrangements himself because so little had been done to improve the UN's responsiveness after the Rwandan genocide.[19]

Later, in early 1997, guerrillas aided by Tutsi-ruled Rwanda overthrew the longtime regime of Zaire's dictator, Mobutu Sese Seko. Laurent-Desire Kabila, a Marxist guerrilla and a protégé of Che Guevera, took power and immediately renamed Zaire the "Democratic Republic of the Congo." Kabila was hardly an improvement over Mobutu. His Rwandan backers were soon disenchanted and, within a year, his regime was fighting ethnic Tutsi rebels actively supported by Rwanda, Burundi, and Uganda. Kabila enlisted the help of ex-militiamen from Rwanda's deposed Hutu regime; within a few months they butchered some 20,000 Congolese Tutsi civilians. Kabila also got support from the southern African countries of Angola, Namibia, and Zimbabwe. The sub-Saharan countries of Sudan and Chad also became involved. By 1998, the legacy of a genocide four years earlier in tiny Rwanda had spread to involve some of Africa's largest countries, especially the Congo, itself the size of Western Europe.

Whenever the international community ignores an obvious genocide, hoping that it will fizzle out without spreading its consequences across any international borders or against any foreign interests, those consequences are, instead, more likely to become inconceivably larger than was first supposed. This is because genocide incites fear and hatred on a monstrously grand scale. Such emotions do not subside easily and they do not respect international borders—but they do encourage the violence of the past to shape the future. This happened in central Africa. It also happened in the former Yugoslavia.

War Over Kosovo

After Slobodan Milosevic crushed the political autonomy of Serbia's Kosovo province, leaving its mostly ethnic Albanian inhabitants in a Serbian-dominated police state, popular resistance began in the form of nonviolent action. It eventually became guerrilla warfare. The latter sparked an especially zealous reaction in 1998: over a period of seven months, Serbian special police and military forces killed some 2,000 Kosovar-Albanians and forced nearly 270,000 others to flee. Entire towns were emptied, sometimes using artillery fire. Fifty thousand of the new refugees fled into the forests—where they stayed, exposed to the weather in whatever clothes they wore when they fled. Globally, there were calls for a humanitarian intervention, even demands that NATO, the West's primary military alliance, punish the offending Serb forces with air strikes. But Russia, a centuries-old ally of the Serbs and deeply suspicious of NATO, vocally opposed this. For this reason and others, seven months passed before Western governments finally set a deadline, over Russian objections, of mid-October for Milosevic to either pull his forces out of Kosovo or else face air strikes from NATO. Milosevic declared he was willing to negotiate.

For nine tense days he bantered with U.S. special envoy Richard Holbrooke. The resulting deal called for a separate Kosovar parliament, judiciary, and police force—in essence, autonomy. It also called for the new presence of an unarmed 2,000-person *Kosovo Verification Mission* from the Organization of Security and Cooperation in Europe (OSCE), aided by NATO reconnaissance aircraft. Even Holbrooke had concerns about this part of the deal. "The OSCE has never had more than a few hundred people in a mission; this is 2,000 or more," he explained in a television interview. "I'm worried that the international community will be too slow and leisurely in getting them there, and that they'll take six months to get there when we need them in six days or, at most, six weeks."[20]

His worries proved warranted. By mid-October the OSCE had deployed only a few hundred verifiers. Months later the figure was still only 800. Yet even if 2,000 verifiers could have been deployed immediately, all of them fully trained (somehow), there was no certainty that 2,000 would have been enough— and they were all unarmed.

On January 16, 1999, near the Kosovar town of Racak, forty-five ethnic Albanians were found murdered, including women and children, their bodies badly mutilated. The American head of the OSCE verifiers, William Walker, immediately blamed the Serbian security forces. Milosevic accused Walker of not being neutral and demanded that autopsies be performed. Autopsies were performed and the coroners blamed the Serbian security forces.

Milosevic's credibility in the West, never very high, was now gone. At a hastily arranged peace conference in Rambouillet, France, the West told his representatives to sign an accord giving a new NATO force—in effect, a foreign occupation force—both entry into Kosovo and sweeping powers of authority throughout Yugoslavia to protect both Kosovo and the NATO force itself. In lip-service to Yugoslavia's sovereignty, the accord would have also permitted Milosevic to station a token border force in Kosovo, and it postponed formal independence for Kosovo for at least three years, pending a referendum there.

Milosevic, however, doubtless aware of how long the UN would need to create a new (and typically very weak) peacekeeping force for Kosovo, replied that the UN, not NATO, must be the international organization to send foreign forces into Kosovo—and that those forces be unarmed. No, Western governments told him, only NATO was militarily capable of safeguarding Kosovo both internally and externally. Unless his regime signed the new Rambouillet accord, they warned, NATO's warplanes would bomb Yugoslavia. Milosevic, believing that the Russian government would support him, at least tacitly, refused.

In doing so, Milosevic exploited a Serbian national identity that viewed any forceful defiance of foreigners, even if clearly destined to fail, as necessary to uphold Serbia's national honor—especially to keep Kosovo, the medieval birthplace of Serbian nationalism, a land that the Serbian Orthodox Church considered to be holy.

The OSCE verifiers, now feeling endangered, departed. Soon thereafter, on March 24, 1999, NATO launched Operation *Allied Force*, expecting Milosevic to capitulate after a few days of bombing. But through his nationalistic appeals, he tightened his political grip—and unleashed a genocidal expulsion campaign against the Kosovar-Albanians. Codenamed Operation *Horseshoe* and secretly planned well in advance, its magnitude and brutality were shocking. With a viciousness honed in the Bosnian War, Serbian paramilitary gangs stormed into selected houses to murder the unsuspecting Albanian families within. The gangs massacred large groups of unarmed Albanian men and boys, raped Albanian women, murdered Albanian children and infants, and left the victims' corpses to burn up in the houses and mosques they torched, or to rot in mass graves and in village wells, contaminating the water. Within weeks perhaps as many 10,000 Kosovar-Albanian civilians were murdered, mostly by these paramilitary gangs. Meanwhile, some 850,000 Kosovar-Albanians—almost half the population—were forced out into Albania and Macedonia. Wherever the Yugoslav Army in Kosovo surrounded a town, village, or city neighborhood, Serbian special police abruptly evicted its ethnic Albanian inhabitants at gunpoint, brutalized them, and burned down their homes. At the border, Yugoslav police stripped the outgoing refugees of their identification and other legal documents, even removing the license plates from their cars and farm tractors, rendering the refugees officially stateless. Across the border they then crowded into hasty refugee camps or into the private homes of helpful strangers. Many families were separated, including children from their parents.

Various outsiders blamed NATO's bombing campaign for encouraging, or at least allowing, these mass expulsions from Kosovo. Most Kosovar-Albanians supported the bombing campaign, but it infuriated the Russians and other Slavic nations and even the Chinese. But NATO, having staked its political and military credibility upon the operation, refused to quit. At the same time, fearful of losing Western popular support if too many NATO personnel died for the sake of Kosovo, several Western leaders promised their voters never to let NATO resort to using ground troops. NATO's pilots were ordered to maintain a relatively safe altitude of at least 15,000 feet, even though from that height identifying and hitting particular ground targets, such as Serbian paramilitary gangs, was nearly impossible. So to improve the odds of hitting something, NATO's warplanes sometimes dropped cluster bombs: clusters of small mines called bomblets, each the size of a soft drink can. Anyone who disturbed one—including curious children—either by touching it or by simply walking too close to it, risked being maimed or killed by a sudden explosion of 2,000 steel fragments. Parts of Kosovo were saturated with these indiscriminately deadly devices. NATO, in addition to hitting Yugoslav military and special police installations (sometimes repeatedly, to emphasize the West's disgust), also hit military-related civilian facilities, including municipal electric power plants, mass media broadcasting stations, civilian factories, bridges far from Kosovo, and even some real estate holdings of Milosevic and his wealthiest supporters. The bombing rained down for two months.

On May 27, 1999, the UN's International Criminal Tribunal for the former Yugoslavia indicted Slobodan Milosevic for crimes against humanity—the first sitting head of state to be so indicted. Sometime thereafter the Russians, trying to negotiate a cease-fire, warned Milosevic that they would not support him forever. They may also have warned him that NATO, despite the denials of Western leaders, appeared to be preparing to invade Yugoslavia. Milosevic's own forces reported to him that ethnic Albanian guerrillas were learning how to lure Yugoslav forces out of their protective bomb shelters to where NATO's warplanes could destroy them more easily. Until then, most Yugoslav forces in Kosovo had evaded NATO's attacks.

Milosevic apparently decided to cut his losses. On June 3, he agreed to withdraw his forces from Kosovo and to let the province be governed as a United Nations-administered, NATO-guarded protectorate, bowing to terms little different from those rejected at Rambouillet three months earlier. But whereas before the war most Kosovar-Albanians might have tolerated living with their Kosovar-Serb neighbors, after the war many of them were filled with grief, bitterness, and a vengeful desire to see most Kosovar-Serbs expelled forever. The new NATO-run Kosovo Force (KFOR), in close cooperation with a Russian brigade, tried to protect the now imperiled Kosovar-Serb community, but KFOR's successes were overshadowed by its failures. Within two months more than 200 Kosovar-Serb civilians were murdered in scattered incidents of revenge and terror, causing nearly the entire community of 200,000 to flee their immediate homes. Some fled to Kosovo's Serbian-dominated north, others into Serbia proper. This reverse "ethnic cleansing" of Kosovo demonstrates how elusive reconciliation can be—and how dangerous a region can become—when a genocide is not quelled early on, for otherwise most of the local population may become hatefully intolerant.

WHY SHOULD WE CARE?

Why should we care about quarrels in faraway countries between peoples of whom we know nothing? Some variant of this question, a paraphrase of Neville Chamberlain, seems to be asked whenever the most basic rights of foreigners are discussed in the abstract. Yet watch how passionately the public demands a response when television screens are filled with images of vivid suffering.

When a few obscure killings—albeit terrible killings, but nonetheless obscure—were reported from places called Sarajevo and Srebrenica in the tiny country of Bosnia-Herzegovina, active concern was stirred as far away as New York, Moscow, Tehran, Kuala Lumpur, Paris, Washington, London, Berlin, as well as in nearby Tirana, Athens, and Ankara. When scenes of mutilated, putrid corpses were televised literally floating out of Rwanda on rivers of blood-colored water, concern was stirred from Pretoria to Paris, and from Nairobi to New York. The same has happened with regard to Kosovo, East Timor, and Iraqi Kurdistan. If indifference was ever a reasonable response to genocide, such a policy may no longer be viable in the Information Age. For despite the occasional dampening effect of what is sometimes called "compassion fatigue," television audiences can be outraged at almost any time—triggered, however unexpectedly, by the vivid brutality of any genocidal violence shown on the screen.

If morality alone is not a sufficient reason to oppose the crime, there are also plenty of coldly objective reasons. In 1995, a sample year, the great majority of the world's refugees were people who had crossed an international border to flee a genocide. Estimates range from 14 million to 23 million displaced. Fourteen million refugees is equivalent to the combined populations of New York City, Los Angeles, Chicago and Boston. A displacement of 23 million people would empty one of the world's most enormous metropolises, such as Mexico City, Shanghai, or Moscow—and *in addition* would empty the combined cities of Philadelphia, Houston, Detroit, San Francisco, Baltimore, Seattle, Denver, Atlanta, and Miami. It would empty the combined countries of Sweden, Norway, Denmark, and Finland.[21]

And those were only the world's official refugees. Genocide was likewise the main cause for as many as 27 million other people to flee their homes, though not yet their countries, into a category known as "internally displaced persons" —domestic refugees—a burden of care as expensive for humanitarian relief organizations as the official refugees. A movement of 27 million people would displace about 90 percent of the population of California, or 90 percent of the combined populations of Pennsylvania and New York State. It would displace almost the entire population of Canada, or the combined populations of Austria, Switzerland, and the Czech Republic.[22]

Such global multitudes of homeless and often stateless people have repeatedly drained the resources of the world's emergency aid services. After the Rwandan genocide, its resulting refugee crisis involving Zaire and Tanzania consumed an estimated $2 billion in only its *first two weeks*—about $142 million per day, almost $6 million every hour—for one avoidable crisis. That refugee crisis lasted for *years,* and it was not the only one.

Yet genocide's most disruptive consequences may not be its refugees, for every major genocidal crisis also shakes the international order. No one in 1994 expected that, within two years, mass killings in tiny Rwanda would plunge the enormity of Zaire/Congo into a civil war drawing in countries from almost half of Africa—but that is what happened. In Africa, and in the Balkans, genocide has fueled cross-border guerrilla warfare, massive black market trafficking, and powerful organized crime. Its impact is felt not only across continents but across decades. The legacy of the Holocaust, for example, goes far beyond the scandals of Nazi-era Swiss banks that defrauded their Jewish depositors, though that legacy, too, now haunts Switzerland. Yet far more dangerous is every genocide's legacy of group-oriented fear, hatred, and bitterness. In World War II more than half-a-million Serbs were butchered by Nazi-supported Croats and some Muslims. Decades later, the survivors of Milosevic's wars have only to glance up from re-reading their World War II history books and look at their now-divided ethnic neighborhoods to see a connection between one genocide and another. "Who still talks nowadays about the massacres of the Armenians?" asked Hitler in 1939. The answer is that today's Armenians still talk about it, as Jews still talk about the Holocaust and as Muslims still talk about "ethnic cleansing." Almost every religious and ethnic group on the planet can point to some nightmare time when its members were victimized. Those memories fuel fear, and fear can manipulate yesterday's events into tomorrow's inflammatory propaganda.

For genocide is the ultimate political mobilizer, inciting entire populations of ordinary people with little knowledge of politics or democratic ideals, instead energizing them with fear and resentment, group hatred, zealous nationalism, an ideology of intolerance, brutality and ultimately mass murder. And until those people realize that they are being manipulated, they typically pass along their vices unto the next generation—and the next, and the next—in the form of a volatile group identity. The Rwandan genocide orphaned more than 100,000 children, all of them traumatized and grief-stricken. Four years later some 65,000 Rwandan families were being headed by orphaned children, some as young as twelve years old. Can any Western country be so certain that Africa will remain so utterly unimportant over the next several decades that the West can, at present, willfully ignore how genocide shapes Africa's future adults?

Scholars and journalists, wondering what to call our era of global politics influenced by local concerns, have searched for a more descriptive label than simply the *post*-Cold War era. Somehow they have not noticed, or do not want to use, a very descriptive label already in popular usage: the Information Age. While this label is admittedly more technological than political, it reflects a major political change. The Information Age did not supplant the Cold War by coincidence: Information technologies helped to end the Cold War by exposing Communism's weaknesses in ways that were pervasive, unprecedented, and eventually uncontrollable. If knowledge is indeed power, the Information Age has empowered more individuals than ever before. And without any Cold War issues to distract the public's attention, the Information Age now publicizes more humanitarian emergencies than ever before.

Television coverage has made the crime of genocide appear to be more commonplace than it is. In comparison to earlier decades of the twentieth century, the 1990s actually experienced less genocide, not more. The crime is now being discouraged to some extent by the increasingly global acceptance of democratic principles such as free trade, an independent judiciary, and free elections. Even regimes that pay only lip-service to these principles must nonetheless face the prying questions and criticisms of foreign reporters, potential foreign investors, and the news media-informed foreign consumers of their exports. This is a major ideological shift away from the isolationism and secrecy characteristic of Stalin's Soviet Union and Mao's China. The world's genocidal trends can go downward—but only when enough people protective and supportive of human rights get involved.

More than a crime against any particular people, genocide is the ultimate crime against humanity because it violates the rights of the individual *and* of the group *and* of all humankind, simultaneously. Every signatory of the Genocide Convention, including the United States, is obligated to oppose this crime wherever it rages, even in countries that have not signed the Convention. Not even the Universal Declaration on Human Rights is so legally binding upon its signatories, a fact that makes the Genocide Convention arguably the most important human rights treaty in international law today. Instead of trying to ignore a brewing genocidal crisis until its consequences become too monstrous to ignore—an expense not even a superpower can pay repeatedly—the world's democratic powers need to prevent this crime's most murderous forms by acting to quell each genocidal crisis relatively early. What can be done in practical terms is the focus of this book.

NOTES

1. The 1984 motion picture *The Killing Fields* was based upon the memoirs of Sidney Schanberg, a *New York Times* reporter whose Cambodian interpreter, Dith Pran, was unable to leave Cambodia before the Khmer Rouge seized power.

2. Raphael Lemkin, "Genocide as a Crime under International Law," *The American Journal of International Law* (January 15, 1948), pp. 145-151. Also, Raphael Lemkin, "Genocide," *The American Scholar* (April 1946), pp. 227-230.

3. Raphael Lemkin, *Axis Rule in Occupied Europe: Laws of Occupation, Analysis of Government, Proposals for Redress* (Washington, DC: Carnegie Endowment for International Peace, 1944), p. 85.

4. Ibid., p. 79.

5. This qualification is also established in U.S. law. See U.S. Code, Chapter 50A, Section 1093(8).

6. R. J. Rummel, "1,883,000 Murdered: Turkey's Genocidal Purges," *Death by Government* (New Brunswick, NJ: Transaction Publishers, 1994), pp. 209-239.

7. Morgenthau and Elkus quotes published in *Fact Sheet: Armenian Genocide*, Knights of Vartan Armenian Research Center, University of Michigan-Dearborn, on website www.umd.umich.edu/dept/armenian/facts/genocide.html.

8. Ataturk quote published in the *Los Angeles Examiner* (August 1, 1926), and in *Quotes about the Armenian Genocide*, website www.cilicia.com/armo10a.html.

9. Jon Bridgman and Leslie J. Worley, "Genocide of the Hereros," in Samuel Totten, William S. Parsons and Israel W. Charny (editors), *Century of Genocide: Eyewitness Accounts and Critical Views* (New York & London: Garland Publishers Inc., 1997), pp. 3-40.

10. Quoted in Martin S. Bergmann and Milton E. Jucovy (editors), *Generations of the Holocaust* (New York: Basic Books, Inc., 1982), p. 54.

11. Figures based on those found in Rummel and in Zbigniew Brzezinski, *Out of Control: Global Turmoil on the Eve of the 21st Century* (New York: Collier Books, 1993), pp. 7-18.

12. Robert Conquest, *The Great Terror: Stalin's Purge of the Thirties* (New York: Macmillan Company, revised 1973), p. 713.

13. Brzezinski, *loc. cit.*

14. Rummel, pp. 1-27.

15. Ibid.

16. David Owen, *Balkan Odyssey* (New York: Harcourt Brace, 1995), p. 350.

17. Charles G. Boyd, "Making Peace with the Guilty," *Foreign Affairs* (September-October 1995), pp. 22-38.

18. Quoted in Colin Nickerson, "Relief workers shoulder a world of conflict," *Boston Sunday Globe* (July 27, 1997), pp. A-1 and A-24 to A-26.

19. Quoted in Elizabeth Neuffer, "Refugees flow into Rwanda," *Boston Sunday Globe* (November 17, 1996), pp. A-1 and A-30.

20. See "Holbrooke: Emergency in Kosovo May be Over, Not Crisis," *CNN Early Edition* (aired October 14, 1998), and "Crisis in Kosovo: Details Remain to be Settled in Holbrooke-Milosevic Agreement," *CNN Newsday* (aired October 14, 1998).

21. The UN High Commissioner for Refugees, *The State of the World's Refugees 1995* (New York: Oxford University Press, 1995). Population estimates, c. 1995: New York City (7.3 million), Los Angeles (3.5 million), Chicago (2.7 million), Boston (580,000), Mexico City (15 million), Shanghai (13.5 million), Moscow (8.8 million), Philadelphia (1.6 million), Houston (1.6 million), Detroit (1 million), San Francisco (750,000), Baltimore (730,000), Seattle (520,000), Denver (460,000), Atlanta (400,000), Miami (360,000), Sweden (8.8 million), Norway (4.3 million), Denmark (5.2 million), Finland (5.1 million). Base estimates from Brian Hunter (editor), *The Statesman's Year-Book 1996-1997* (New York: St. Martin's Press, 1996).

22. Population estimates, c. 1995: California (29.7 million), Pennsylvania (11.8 million), New York State (18 million). Canada (27.4 million), South Africa (40 million), Switzerland (7 million), Austria (8 million), the Czech Republic (10.4 million).

2

The Faith Behind Genocide

The predisposition to religious belief is the most complex and powerful force in the human mind and, in all probability, an ineradicable part of human nature. It is one of the universals of social behavior, taking recognizable form in every society from hunter-gatherer bands to Socialist republics.

— Edward O. Wilson
Harvard University sociobiologist, 1992

There is no one without a religious need, a need to have a frame of orientation and an object of devotion. . . . [Man] may be aware of his system as being a religious one, different from those of the secular realm, or he may think that he has no religion and interpret his devotion to certain allegedly secular aims like power, money or success as nothing but his concern for the practical and expedient. . . . If we want to understand how systems like Fascism and Stalinism can possess millions of people, ready to sacrifice their integrity and reason to the principle "my country, right or wrong," we are forced to consider the . . . religious quality of their orientation.

— Erich Fromm, *Psychoanalysis and Religion*, 1950

In the jungles of Malaysia there live about 25,000 people collectively known the Orang Asli, more commonly called the Senoi. They live in various tribes, among them the Semai and the Temiar. Their lives can be difficult. They have few material possessions, their homes being little more than grass huts. They subsist on fish, fruit, and animal game, in a jungle whose numerous dangers include wild tigers. Tropical diseases have long been so deadly that a Temiar custom has developed wherein infants are not named until, and unless, they survive to two years of age. Vicious raids by slave traders killed Senoi adults and abducted Senoi children well into the twentieth century. The Senoi have also experienced British colonial administrators, brutal Japanese invaders, ethnic Chinese Communist guerrillas, and condescending Malaysian bureaucrats.

The Senoi have known violence.

Yet the Senoi are remarkably peaceful. As tribes and as individuals, they abhor violence. Many report that they never feel anger. Family quarrels are rare. Virtually nonexistent are any instances of murder, maiming, or hitting. Their children are as naughty and selfish as children anywhere, but Senoi children are never punished physically. They are simply given verbal guidance and, as they grow older, they learn by example to become cooperative, unselfish, self-reliant adults. Any exceptions in Senoi society are regarded as overgrown children and are treated with tolerant good humor.

Some anthropologists have described Senoi society as a living utopia. That description is probably an exaggeration, but it is a society virtually without violence, a society whose overwhelming majority are emotionally mature people who experience love and happiness to a degree many outsiders would envy. But what is perhaps most extraordinary about Senoi society is that its social harmony is not unique. Throughout the world there are several "primitive" societies that are nonviolent—remarkably so in comparison to the outside world.

In the 1990s, in interviews with psychotherapists during the Bosnian War, a middle-aged victim, a Bosnian-Muslim, repeatedly referred to his attackers as "Chetniks"—a reference to Serbian partisans in World War II. The interviewers assumed that his attackers were strangers, thugs from afar. However, the man's wife was meanwhile telling her interviewers the couple was attacked by people whose dinner guests the couple had been only the week before. Another woman reported how Bosnian-Serbs had taken non-Serbian women and girls to her old grammar school every night to be raped. There she saw her old science teacher involved. When she tried to look him straight in the eye, he looked away, but did not stop his sexual assaults. Yet another women testified that the physician who had delivered her son had, more recently, overseen the mass murder of five hundred Muslims in their town.[1]

Such horrific brutality, inflicted upon the innocent and even upon personal acquaintances, has appeared in countless places besides the Balkans. It is not limited to any particular race, religion, or occupation. It was so common in the twentieth century that many people assumed that it must be human nature. Yet anything that is truly "human nature" must be innate to all normal human beings, because in scientific terms that is what *nature* means. The Senoi are natural, normal human beings—and their peaceable behavior debunks the myth that mass murder, if indeed it is human nature, is unavoidable.

There is a theory that to kill one's fellow human beings is something instilled by one's culture and heritage, by one's life experiences, by one's *nurture*. Some cultures are more violent than others. This theory has its limits, however, because in the midst of every violent culture, indeed amid every war and genocide, there are people who are nonviolent, opposed to hatred and revenge, stubbornly adhering to universal love and tolerance. Some of them are called saints. Most are ordinary people.

Why, therefore, do some human beings—seemingly normal and ordinary perpetrate atrocities on a scale so vast and so ghastly that the acts dumbfound as much as horrify? There is no single agreed-upon answer, in part because this subject is loaded with emotional sensitivities and popular preconceptions. This chapter is unlikely to resolve the controversy, but by incorporating the most frequently mentioned variables—genetic biology and human instincts, the human psyche, cultural environment and history, fear, bigotry, greed, politics and propaganda—this chapter does offer a general explanation that the average person may relate to.

THE ROLES OF NATURE AND NURTURE

In the first half of the twentieth century there were natural scientists, such as many biologists, who believed that biology alone, i.e., *nature*, utterly dominated human behavior, almost to the exclusion of any individual free will. Disputing them were the social scientists, including many behavioral psychologists, who believed that human behavior is largely the result of cultural training and social norms, i.e., *nurture*. And to some extent they, too, minimized the role of individual free will. The extremes of these two schools of thought fueled the twentieth century's two most genocidal ideologies: Nazism, which advocated nature in the form of racism, and Marxist-Leninist Communism, which advocated nurture in the form of coercion.

Most scientists now believe that human behavior is neither all dictated by nature nor all the reflex of some brainwashing nurture, as though every person is but a "blank slate" on which any personality can be written by one's environment. The prevailing theory today is that human behavior flows from the interaction of nature and nurture, creating a multitude of possible choices largely resolved by each individual's free will.[*] This freedom of choice is important to note because if human beings do not have enough free will to choose whether or not they

---

[*] In 1998, Dr. Dean Hamer, a genetic scientist at the U.S. National Cancer Institute, published a book with writer Peter Copeland entitled *Living With Our Genes.* It explained in laymen's terms how much influence genes have and, of equal importance, the limits of that influence. Hamer and Copeland used this analogy:

> If identical twins, who share exactly the same genes, can turn out differently, that means that genes are not fixed instructions. More than a musical score, genes are like the musical instruments. Genes don't determine exactly what music is played—or how well—but they do determine the range of what is possible.
>
> All the research shows that anger and hostility—and their visible outcomes, such as crime and violence—are caused neither solely by the environment nor by biology. . . . The mix is what's deadly: the combination of genes and environment, temperament and character. . . . In no other domain of human behavior are nature and nurture so thoroughly intertwined.

Dean Hamer and Peter Copeland, *Living With Our Genes* (New York: Doubleday, 1998), pp. 12 and 92.

ss murder—because either "nature" or "nurture" supposedly
ve would have no right to hold any perpetrators accountable
d it *is* a crime, both legally and innately.

ry that Heinrich Himmler, chief of the Nazi SS, nearly fainted
. mass shooting of prisoners. Himmler did admit, indeed on
s, that he hated the bloodiness of his job.[2] Likewise Adolf
Eichm...   SS bureaucrat who coordinated the murder of millions of Jews, confessed to his colleagues that "I simply cannot look at any suffering without trembling myself."[3] And among the ordinary executioners of the Final Solution, pangs of guilt also took a psychological toll. One SS general in charge of an *Einsatzgruppen*, an SS execution squad, urged his boss Heinrich Himmler to "Look at the eyes of the men of this command, how deeply shaken they are. These men are finished for the rest of their lives." For after shooting so many Jews, many of those SS men were tormented by nightmares. They had tried to drown their consciences in alcohol, repeatedly, but always with only a fleeting success.[4] Rather than face their victims' eyes and faces, they preferred to shoot their victims from behind. Even from behind, however, a Jew "dehumanized" by Nazi propaganda still looks like a human individual. So in their nightmares, instead of being haunted by murdered eyes and faces, the SS men were haunted by scores of murdered human necks, each neck the memory of an actual victim.[5] Their feelings of guilt caused body ailments so severe that many of the killers were hospitalized, including a few senior officers.[6] Himmler's own rumored queasiness led many SS men to complain resentfully, "He demands of us deeds the very sight of which makes him faint, break down, cry." [7]

To continue mass murdering Jews, but from a more emotionally tolerable distance, the SS eventually built the notorious gas chambers in Auschwitz and other concentration camps. And they forced condemned prisoners to do many of the most gruesome tasks.

No matter how much those SS men tried to rationalize and glorify what they were doing, they knew instinctively that their mass killings were wrong. At the same time, the notion that the Nazi regime threatened to kill them unless they slaughtered Jews is a myth. SS men could individually refuse to kill Jews without being officially rebuked. There were even highly publicized SS decrees authorizing such refusals, a fact pointed to by prosecutors in the later trials of Nazi war criminals. And a small few did refuse. Unfortunately, most SS men, despite their feelings of guilt and despite the alternative available, nevertheless chose to continue killing Jews, including women and children.

THE POWER OF CONDITIONING

Numerous research studies since World War II have confirmed what those SS men discovered in themselves: Most human beings have an innate resistance to killing other people. In 1995 this phenomenon was well explored in a book aptly entitled *On Killing: The Psychological Cost of Learning to Kill in War and Society*. "There can be no doubt," wrote its author, David A. Grossman, a career military officer and a teacher of psychology at the U.S. Military Academy at West Point, "that this resistance to killing one's fellow man is there and that it exists as a result of a powerful combination of instinctive, rational, environmental, hereditary, cultural, and social factors. It is there, it is strong, and it gives us cause to believe that there may just be hope for mankind after all." [8] He warned, however, that if and when a person is subjected to some particular conditioning and circumstances, "it appears that almost anyone can and will kill." [9]

In the 1950s a gruesome war was fought between Communist guerrillas and a British colonial government. Among the British allies were some tribesmen, inhabitants of the jungle known as simple hunters and fishermen. The British had recruited them with some reluctance, doubting that such nice peaceful chaps could be turned into effective soldiers. Yet those nice peaceful chaps became some of the most effective soldiers of the war. Even the elite commandos of Britain's Special Air Service (SAS) were amazed and humbled by the speed and effectiveness of their allies' jungle patrols. In combat, the tribesmen proved as fierce as anyone.

They were the Semai and Temiar tribesmen of the Senoi. With particular conditioning and circumstances—in the Senoi case, military training, in a war to protect their families—even the most peaceful of peoples will kill. Grossman explained:

When people become angry, or frightened, they stop thinking with their forebrain (the mind of a human being) and start thinking with their midbrain (which is indistinguishable from the mind of an animal). . . . The only thing that has any hope of influencing the midbrain is also the only thing that influences a dog: classical and operant conditioning. That is what is used when training firemen and airline pilots to react to emergency situations: precise replication of the stimulus that they will face (in a flame house or a flight simulator) and then extensive shaping of the desired response to that stimulus. . . . We do not *tell* schoolchildren what they should do in case of a fire, we *condition* them; and when they are frightened, they do the right thing.

Every aspect of killing on the battlefield is rehearsed, visualized, and conditioned. On special occasions even more realistic and complex targets are used. Balloon-filled uniforms moving across the kill zone (pop the balloon and the target drops to the ground), red-paint-filled milk jugs, and many other ingenious devices are used. These make the training more interesting, the conditioned stimuli more realistic, and the conditioned response more assured under a variety of different circumstances. Snipers use such techniques extensively. In Vietnam it took an average of 50,000 rounds of ammunition to kill one enemy soldier. But the U.S. Army and USMC snipers in Vietnam expended only 1.39 rounds per kill.[10]

Prior to the Rwandan genocide in 1994, many of the would-be killers attended secret training camps where they learned how to massacre people. Elsewhere in the 1990s, in places such as Bosnia, Kosovo, and East Timor, there was some evidence that at least a few of the perpetrators resorted to using mind-altering drugs to weaken their inhibitions. The earlier conditioning methods of the Nazi SS were not so sophisticated, but still there was some conditioning, including of women. The female SS guards at the Ravensbruck concentration camp—as cruel as their male colleagues—became cruel by watching and learning from their peers. Of those female guards, each known as an *Aufseherin,* one ex-inmate later wrote:

The beginners usually appeared frightened upon first contact with the camp, and it took some time to attain the level of cruelty and debauchery of their seniors. Some of us made a rather grim little game of measuring the time it took for a new *Aufseherin* to win her stripes. One little *Aufsehrin*, 20 years old, who was at first so ignorant of proper camp "manners" that she said "excuse me" when walking in front of a prisoner, needed exactly four days to adopt the requisite manner, although it was totally new for her. As for the others, a week or two, a month at the most, was an average orientation period.[11]

ROOTS OF SADISM

In every genocide a few perpetrators of cruelty—not all, but a few—inflict their heinous acts with a lustful enthusiasm, deriving a satisfaction apparently akin to a sexual orgasm. Is such sadistic enthusiasm an instinct? A *sociopath* is, by definition, a person who lacks any innate resistance to being violent; he does not feel empathy for his victims because he physically cannot. But among human beings only a tiny percentage, perhaps 3 percent or less, are true sociopaths. Most are not easily turned into obedient soldiers because, by nature, sociopaths rebel against authority. The SS employed a few of them, but the prime trait the SS searched for in its potential recruits was obedience.[12] Most sadists are not born as sadists. They become sadists.

The word *instinct,* warns a contemporary dictionary of psychology, is "a term with a tortured history indeed. . . . In actual use, the manner of application of the term has differed dramatically from theory to theory."[13] If the term is applied to every possible human behavior, including to behaviors few people ever display, then sadism can be labeled an "instinct"—and sadists can claim they are not responsible for their actions.

A much more scientific definition, however, defines *instinct* as a largely involuntary reflex with the ultimate purpose of safeguarding one's genes. Biologically, every human being is influenced by genes, which are tiny bits of information encoded in a chemical called deoxyribonucleic acid, or DNA. The desire to eat, sleep and be sexual are, at base, instincts to safeguard one's genes. To safeguard the lives of one's children is, at base, an instinct, because one's children pass along one's genes. The more intelligent the species, the more flexible its instincts are. Human instincts are so flexible that we can actually repress our instincts, sometimes remarkably so. A person on a hunger strike can willfully starve herself to death. A person devoted to celibacy can avoid sexual activity for a lifetime. And there are a few parents who murder their own children, unfortunately.

There is a human instinct called *aggression*, but it does not include all forms of aggressive behavior; indeed, murdering one's biological children is arguably contrary to one's aggressive instinct because that prevents one's genes from surviving. For unlike our instincts of hunger, sleepiness, and sexual arousal, our aggressive instinct is not a driving obsession needing to be satisfied like a drug addiction. It is, rather, a self-defense mechanism, triggered impulsively in a terrifying moment of kill or be killed, or at least of harm or be harmed. Intense fear, not rage or pleasure, is the trigger—reacting to an immediate peril.

If a person is not faced with that immediate peril, any violence he inflicts is not something involuntary: It is something deliberate. By inflicting his violence he may feel some bodily sensations, such as an exciting rush of adrenaline, but those sensations are not his aggressive instinct. They are his body's metabolism physically supporting the active behavior he has deliberately chosen, just as it would support some different active behavior that is nonviolent. Those exciting sensations, including sensations of power, can feel so thrilling as to be potentially addictive. To rekindle them over and over again, as he becomes bored by his last experience, he may inflict harsher and harsher acts of violence, ultimately becoming a sadist. He may self-rationalize this behavior by calling it his aggressive instinct, but the problem is really rooted in his psyche.

Our innate resistance to killing people was formed in our species' distant past. To understand why the human species developed this inhibition, and why it has not prevented the genocidal violence of the past few thousands of years of human history, we need to consider how much has changed between the way our prehistoric ancestors lived and the way our more recent ancestors have lived.

PREHISTORY AND CIVILIZATION

Human civilization is not entirely natural. Basic human society is natural in that human beings are social beings, but what we call *civilization*—with its towns, cities, farms, and numerous other technologies—is not the natural environment our early ancestors evolved in, and whose evolutionary legacy is literally our anatomy.

Most anthropologists date the beginning of human civilization to about 10,000 years ago, when our ancestors first invented farming. Ten thousand years may sound like a long time, for it includes every moment in human history since long before the founding of ancient Egypt, up through and including the moment you are now reading this. But in terms of natural evolution, it accounts for less than 1 percent of the approximately 4 million years that humanoids, including our distant ancestors, spent gradually evolving. Our own humanoid subspecies, the "human race" or *Homo sapiens,* has been around for at least 100,000 years.

Natural evolution is an extraordinarily slow, almost imperceptible process, occurring over the life cycles of thousands of generations, as each one passes along into their children, via their genes, whatever body traits may best help their children survive in their physical environment. This process is sometimes called *survival of the fittest,* but this does not mean that any single individual's fitness makes any difference to the species as a whole. The process of natural evolution is so slow that to change the entire human species in any appreciable way takes the process at least a few tens of thousands of years—far longer than civilization's mere ten millennia alone.

This means is that every human being alive today, everywhere on the globe, has virtually the same genetic code, the same DNA, as every person who has ever lived since prehistoric times, because we all have those eons of evolution in common. The racial differences between humans are almost entirely outward, reflecting our ancestors' gradual adaptation over many generations to different regional climates. Despite these racial differences, there is no particular racial group or ethnicity that is more likely, or less likely, to commit genocide because of some supposedly unique genes.

Before civilization, during that earlier 99 percent of our species' existence, our ancestors lived in what we now call *hunter-gatherer societies,* so named because for food the males hunted animals while the females gathered fruits and vegetables. Since a healthy diet for humans requires the combined nutrients found in both meat and edible vegetation, those early hunters and gatherers— those early males and females, both needing to procreate—also needed each other to survive. And since farming had not been invented yet, our ancestors had to constantly migrate in search of new hunting grounds and for unpicked vegetation. Starvation was a constant danger, along with a myriad of others, dangers so common that any person who lived to be twenty years old was lucky. To live until thirty years was almost impossible.

Faced with that very tenuous way of life, the emotional priorities of the average person were *family, tribe, self*—with *family* and *tribe* often being the same. Selfless cooperation was essential because no one could survive without help. And that mutual care, compelled by necessity, had the added benefit of providing everyone with a tremendous amount of loving emotional support.

The invention of farming began to change all that. Farming required that our ancestors build permanent homes from where they could tend their farms and their newly domesticated animals. In return, their farms provided them with enough food to last beyond their next meal, indeed for months or even years. They could stop migrating and, with more food available, some of them could even start pursuing nonfarming occupations. They could now produce things, eventually becoming craftsmen and artisans.

The invention of farming—and hence of civilization—changed our species' social environment so profoundly, and, by the relative standards of natural evolution, so abruptly, that its full magnitude may be difficult to grasp. In less than the minimal time needed by natural evolution to adapt a species to fit the challenges of its environment, civilization has dramatically changed our species' entire way of life. We now face an artificial environment, with countless major challenges, and natural evolution has not had enough time to prepare us.

Civilization is not problem-free. Our ancestors faced starvation if their farms failed—and when their farms did fail there was a tempting solution: conquer someone else's land and food supplies. In contemporary anthropology there is a theory that this was when human beings first became warlike, when men ceased to be exclusively hunters and, instead, also became soldiers.[14] In the words of Richard Leakey, the renowned paleoanthropologist:

I believe that warfare is rooted in the need for territorial possession once populations became agricultural [about 10,000 years ago] and necessarily sedentary. Violence then became almost an obsession, once populations started to grow and to develop the ability to organize large military forces. I do not believe that violence is an innate characteristic of humankind, merely an unfortunate adaptation to certain circumstances.

As always in science, the absence of evidence is not evidence of absence. But I take it to be a very reasonable inference. Not reasonable, in my opinion, is [the] assertion that because humans have been genocidal in recent times, they must have been so earlier.[15]

In fairness to this theory's critics, it is controversial.* Some anthropologists suspect that the humans of 30,000 years ago may have helped to extinguish the Neanderthals, a humanoid race similar to *Homo sapiens* but with a brain size (and therefore, perhaps, with an intelligence) about as developed as our own. Perhaps our ancestors saw the Neanderthals as dangerous rivals for food and territory, although no one knows for certain what happened to them. There are other possible explanations for their demise.

Once human civilization emerged, it had some unfortunate side-effects even in peaceful times. As economic trade grew so, too, did economic competition. Competition encouraged people to become more judgmental, basing their judgments about others (and about themselves) according to how well a person did something, or produced something, or represented something, with the subtle yet profound consequence that human respect, and eventually even love, became more and more conditional. By creating the first permanent settlements, farming created the phenomenon of the next-door neighbor. Earlier hunter-

---

* Since the human species is a primate species, some believers in the "genocide is an instinct" theory point to the violence of other primates. The basic genetic codes of *Homo sapiens* and, for example, chimpanzees, are over 98 percent identical. In other words, less than 2 percent of our species' DNA code makes us distinctly human instead of chimpanzees, or gorillas, or orangutans, or baboons, or some other nonhuman primate.

Chimpanzees have not yet developed their own civilization, but they do sometimes wage war for territory—deadly genocidal war, between rival chimpanzee tribes. Jane Goodall, the zoologist who first witnessed this chimpanzee phenomenon, described it as both shocking and fascinating. She also urged people to understand it in context. "Because violent and brutal behavior is vivid and attention-catching," she wrote, "it is easy to get the impression that chimpanzees are more aggressive than they really are. In fact, peaceful interactions are far more frequent than aggressive ones." The two warring chimpanzee tribes Goodall witnessed had lived as neighbors, peacefully and amicably, for at least ten years before relations between them started to deteriorate, a process that took a year before any physical fighting occurred. Throughout that year, groups of males from the two tribes increasingly taunted each other with hostile screams and grunts. The eventual war appeared to be about tribal group identities and tribal greed, not about any individual predisposition to violence.

Not all nonhuman primates are as violent as chimpanzees. Bonobos never wage war, and yet human share over 98 percent of our genetic code with them as well. Bonobos are the most promiscuous, erotic, unashamedly sexual primates anywhere, surpassing even humans. Whereas humans may say *Make love and not war*, bonobos actually do this. Their sexual behavior, so different from our own and likewise from that of chimpanzees, illustrates the risks of making sweeping assumptions about human instincts whenever we too readily equate our own behavior with that of other primates.

Jane Goodall, *Through a Window: My Thirty Years with the Chimpanzees of Gombe* (New York: Houghton Mifflin Company, 1991). Frans De Waal, *Bonobo: The Forgotten Ape* (Los Angeles: University of California Press, 1997).

gatherer societies had not included "neighbors"—people living separately within the same community—because in prehistoric times everyone had migrated with everyone else, knew everyone intimately, and had collectively shared what little each person could find. The physical distance created by separate homes with closed doors (or even without doors, but still separate) was accompanied by an emotional distancing between neighbors—and hence between human beings. Civilization has forced emotional intimacy to compete with judgmental envy and image.

THE DESPERATION OF THE HUMAN PSYCHE

How has civilization influenced the human psyche? Every individual is different, but when the average person is faced to a mirror and told to mentally set aside all of his accomplishments, achievements, appearance, and heritage, and then told to outwardly say to himself, reflected in that mirror, "I love you, *I love myself!*"—at such a moment many people cannot say this to themselves, not even to their reflection, not with a loving conviction free of doubt. Instead, their inner opinion of themselves are more akin to these words of *Hamlet* written by William Shakespeare:

I am myself indifferent honest, but yet I could accuse me of such things that it were better my mother had not borne me! I am very proud, revengeful, ambitious, with more offenses at my beck than I have thoughts to put them in, imagination to give them shape, or time to act them in! What should such fellows as I do, crawling between Earth and Heaven? [16]

People with self-hatred tend to hide it behind a well-crafted "self-identity" for others to see, so deeply that even their closest friends and family may not realize the extent of that self-hatred. And as these centuries-old words from Shakespeare suggest, people have been tormenting themselves with self-hatred for a very long time—probably since the beginning of civilization.

People burdened with this much fear, depression, and anxiety tend to define happiness in terms of accomplishing something or in enjoying material things. Theirs is the basic philosophy of Friedrich Nietzsche and Jean-Paul Sartre: *create meaning where there is none*. But people who feel a lasting inner peace, perhaps born of a spiritual transformation, tend to define happiness in terms of contentment and love. Theirs is the basic philosophy of Buddha and of the Jewish, Christian, and Sufi mystics. They can feel happy without having to always chase after some outward thing. People without that inner contentment tend to be mentally and emotionally vulnerable, dangerously at risk of becoming addicted to whatever they find most stimulating, be it physical or intellectual. In prehistoric times most people probably felt an inner contentment, because from birth until death they had the constant intimately loving support of their fellow group. Since the era of civilization, however, a large percentage of people have been denied that constant supportive love, many of them not even aware that their own lack of inner contentment and unconditional love is unnatural, because their artificial environment is unnatural. They may not express any apparent worries about the meaning of life, but this age-old question of meaning is essential. For if life feels dominated by constant trouble, sorrow, and suffering, why continue to endure life if it lacks any meaning to justify its constant pain?

One of the leading thinkers on this subject in the twentieth century was Erich Fromm, a psychoanalytic theorist. In Fromm's time the field of psychoanalysis, founded by Sigmund Freud, received as much criticism as popular interest, in part because the field was still relatively new. Nevertheless, psychoanalysis has revealed many insights into human behavior that people now consider almost common sense. Fromm's theories in particular have largely withstood criticism.

In 1956 Fromm published what has become one of his most popular books, *The Art of Loving*. More about emotional love than erotic love, his book emphasized the difference between selfishness, which is a conditional love, and true self-love, which is an unconditional love. Fromm explained:

If it is a virtue to love my neighbor as a human being, it must be a virtue—not a vice—to love myself, since I am a human being too. . . . The idea expressed in the Biblical *Love Thy Neighbor as Thyself* implies that respect for one's own integrity and uniqueness, love for and understanding of one's own self, cannot be separated from respect and love and understanding for another individual. The love for my own self is inseparably connected with the love for any other being.

Selfishness and self-love, far from being identical, are actually opposites. The selfish person does not love himself too much, but too little. In fact, he hates himself. This lack of fondness and care for himself leaves him empty and frustrated. He is necessarily unhappy and anxiously concerned to snatch from life the satisfactions which he blocks himself from attaining. He seems to care too much for himself, but actually he only makes an unsuccessful attempt to cover up and compensate for his failure to care for his real self.[17]

When faced with the materialistic demands of civilization, perhaps the most daunting inner challenge a person can face is to love oneself unconditionally. True love for oneself must be unconditional, because a conditional love is not a pure love. Conditional love is a "love" for (actually, an addiction to) a particular condition, such as for one's outer beauty or career success, but it is not love for the person who possesses that condition. To love someone "because" of some condition is actually a deception because that person is *not* loved—the condition is loved. Conditional self-love is nothing less than a mental bribe, extorted from oneself to oneself, used to pay off one's self-torment in exchange for one's accomplishments, self-appearance, or status. But it is not a lasting happiness because it is not a permanent contentment. It is only a passing amusement, a fleeting glee, all based upon a bribe. It is based upon material things outside of oneself. It is, in essence, a Faustian bargain.

We carry the genes of ancestors whose natural environment was so harsh, so devoid of material comfort, that our species evolved very powerful instincts of love and intimacy to help us survive together. Now we live amid the material comforts of civilization, but in deference to its accompanying pressures we have too often been forced to restrain our deepest compassionate instincts by treating unconditional love as naïve or improper. We may enjoy civilization's material benefits, but its materialistic demands are not altogether healthy. This is not a plea for us to live without civilization, but it is a warning that what we call "civilization" does not necessarily civilize us.

This emotional vulnerability can grip even nations. In 1941 Fromm published *Escape from Freedom*, a book wherein he asserted that public feelings of anxiety, alienation, and anger—feelings Fromm believed an impersonal, factory-centered society can encourage even in a democracy, as in Germany's pre-Nazi Weimar Republic—are perilously susceptible to political manipulation. Fromm himself was a personal eyewitness to this as a German-born secular Jew. He fled Nazi Germany in 1933 for the United States, where he later became a U.S. citizen. Fromm warned:

Looked at superficially, people appear to function well enough in economic and social life; yet it would be dangerous to overlook the deep-seated unhappiness behind that comforting veneer. If life loses its meaning because it is not lived, Man becomes desperate. People do not die quietly from physical starvation; they do not die quietly from psychic starvation either. If we look only at the economic needs as far as the "normal" person is concerned, if we do not see the unconscious suffering of the average automatized person, then we fail to see the danger that threatens our culture from its human basis: the readiness to accept any ideology and any leader, if only he promises excitement and offers a political structure and symbols which allegedly give meaning and order to an individual's life. The despair of the human automaton is fertile soil for the political purposes of Fascism.[18]

Previously, for thousands of years, people in search of meaning turned to religion. By the early twentieth century, however, the traditional religions, with their ancient dogmas and, in some cases, their organizations' hypocritical self-serving behavior, had disenchanted many, especially in Europe. Yet the human need for meaning remained. Fromm noted:

There is no one without a religious need, a need to have a frame of orientation and an object of devotion. . . . [Man] may be aware of his system as being a religious one, different from those of the secular realm, or he may think that he has no religion, and interpret his devotion to certain allegedly secular aims like power, money or success as nothing but his concern for the practical and expedient.

If we want to understand how systems like Fascism or Stalinism can possess millions of people, ready to sacrifice their integrity and reason to the principle "my country, right or wrong," we are forced to consider the . . . religious quality of their orientation.[19]

Likewise, an aspiring politician once said:

We do not judge merely by artistic or military standards, or even by purely scientific ones. We judge by the spiritual energy which a people is capable of putting forth. . . . Only a far-sighted people can act as a spur to history. The men called to lead a people to great and mighty achievements are its artists and strategists, philosophers and politicians, men thrown up by destiny and Providence.[20]

That aspiring politician was Adolf Hitler, in 1931, two years before he gained power in Germany through democratic elections, parliamentary maneuvers, and the tactics of hatred. "I intend to set up a 1,000-year Reich," he declared, "and anyone who supports me in this battle is a fellow-fighter for a unique spiritual—I would almost say divine—creation."[21]

GROUP IDENTITIES: A PREREQUISITE FOR GENOCIDE

In 1921, in a book he entitled *Group Psychology and the Analysis of the Ego,* Sigmund Freud introduced the psychoanalytic term of *identification.* A modern dictionary of psychology defines the term as "a mental operation whereby one attributes to oneself, either consciously or unconsciously, the characteristics of another person or group." An *identity* is defined as "a person's essential, continuous self; the internal, subjective concept of oneself as an individual." [22]

An *identity,* in other words, does not need a group to be an identity, but, through identification, an identity can manifest itself as part of a group. A group by itself is simply a numerical set, but a group identity has a collective personality: collective beliefs and passions deeply protective of its image, reputation, wealth, security, and power.

Group identities are not new. Ambitious leaders and astute observers have long recognized the powerful psychological draw that a group identity can exert: *This is my family, my tribe, my nation—not yours! You don't belong here!* Group identities find meaning in difference, defining themselves as much by what they are not (or what they say they are not) as by what they do represent (if only to themselves). Among human beings there are countless divisions, all superficial, that people have nonetheless used to demarcate group identities. The most common are race, ethnicity, nationality, culture, religion, economics, gender, sexual preference, and social class.

By proclaiming the ancient maxims of *Take care of your own* and *In unity there is strength,* a group identity can distort moral fundamentals, supplanting universal values such as compassion and forgiveness with more subjective interpretations of "justice" and "fairness" designed to accommodate that group's material interests and beliefs. Any compassion a group member shows towards someone representing a rival group identity is considered to be an act of betrayal against one's own people. Forgiveness becomes dependent upon conditions to be satisfied, without the moral realization that "conditional forgiveness" is a contradiction in terms.

Group identities diminish their members' individuality through conformity, and, through stereotyping, diminish the individuality of other people as well. Someone born of a Jewish parent may not practice Judaism, or even think of herself as a Jew—but according to a Nazi anti-Semite, that person is a Jew and thus a threat. Someone who wears eyeglasses may have barely enough education to work as a low-level clerk—but according to a Khmer Rouge Communist, that person is a bourgeois intellectual and thus a threat.[23] In this Social-Darwinian interpretation of reality, "groups" (group identities) either tolerate each other at some safe distance or they exploit, undermine, resist, and destroy each other. The group members may display an outward arrogance, but their underlying emotion is fear. The most fearful group identity does not try to live in close, integral cooperation with groups it views as its rivals; rather, it perceives itself as being destined for greatness, but only if it can avoid being destroyed by its enemies. It therefore seeks to defeat its rivals first, if necessary by eliminating them.

Joseph Goebbels, Nazi Germany's propaganda minister, once confessed to his diary that Europe's Jews were being exterminated by, as he put it, a "rather barbarous procedure whose details cannot be described." After penning this extraordinary admission, he scribbled: "One must not allow sentimentality to prevail in these matters. The Jews would destroy us if we did not ward them off. It is a life and death struggle between the Aryan race and the Jewish bacillus." [24]

I must do this because my group does it. I must believe what my group believes. Despite the narrow parameters of this reasoning, group identities are not confined to uneducated people. The bloodiest genocides of human history, especially in the twentieth century, were orchestrated by intellectuals. This is because what matters most to such people is not their intellect but their group identity, the embodiment of what they consider to be meaningful. Fromm described the phenomenon this way:

Man by origin is a herd animal. His actions are determined by an instinctive impulse to follow the leader and to have close contact with the other animals around him. Inasmuch as we are sheep, there is no greater threat to our existence than to lose this contact with the herd and be isolated. Right or wrong, true and false are determined by the herd. . . . A few individuals can stand this isolation and say the truth in spite of the danger of losing touch. They are the true heroes of the human race but for whom we should still be living in caves.[25]

Even in cultures that emphasize human individuality, the willingness of individuals to conform and obey can be enormous. To discover how enormous, Stanley Milgram, a research scientist at Yale University, in 1960 conducted a now-famous social experiment whose results have since been replicated many times in several countries. An ordinary person was told that to (supposedly) test the effects of punishment upon another person's memory, the first person (the actual test subject) must press a button, repeatedly, to inflict increasingly painful amounts of electric shocks on the second person—but only at the command of a supervisor, the "experimenter," a man wearing a white laboratory coat and carrying a clipboard. The electric shock device was marked with voltage levels ranging from 15 to 450 volts, along with verbal markings ranging from "Slight Shock" to "Danger: Severe Shock." The electric shocks were actually harmless, but they appeared to be increasingly painful because the "victim" was an actor feigning more and more agony, eventually crying out for the shocks to stop. And the test subject could stop the ordeal by simply not pressing the button whenever the supervisor (the obvious authority figure) ordered more shocks. Yet despite the apparent agony of the "victim"—and the very real anguish of the test subjects—65 percent of them, all of them ordinary people, continued to obey the "experimenter" by inflicting up to and including the maximum voltage possible, the supposed 450 volts, two steps higher than the "Danger: Severe Shock" marking. One of Milgram's researchers noted:

I observed a mature and initially poised businessman enter the laboratory smiling and confident. Within 20 minutes he was reduced to a twitching, stuttering wreck who was rapidly approaching a point of nervous collapse. He constantly pulled on his earlobe, and twisted his hands. At one point he pushed his fist into his forehead and muttered: "Oh God, let's stop it." And yet he continued to respond to every word of the experimenter, and obeyed to the end.

In this situation there may not have been a long-established group identity, but there was a group of people who believed that the "experimenter" was a legitimate authority, a scientist simply supervising an experiment, seeing and hearing the agony of the "victim" as clearly as the test subject and yet ordering more shocks. *The scientist must have a good reason,* assumed the test subjects, and so they continued to obey him despite their own personal anguish.[26]

CULTURAL INFLUENCES

In 1996 a professor at Harvard University named Daniel Jonah Goldhagen published a controversial book entitled *Hitler's Willing Executioners: Ordinary Germans and the Holocaust.* He asserted that the overwhelming majority of Germans who killed Jews in the Holocaust did so because those Germans were anti-Semitic—and had been anti-Semitic since before the Nazi era—influenced by a German culture that had long encouraged ideas that were racist, anti-Semitic, and ultranationalist, often intertwined. For reasons of bigotry and the stereotype-induced fears that accompany bigotry, Goldhagen asserted, ordinary Germans had killed Jews because they had wanted to kill Jews.

Goldhagen was not the first scholar to propose a culture-based theory of genocide, but he pushed his theory so strongly—and, his critics charged, without enough documentation to support his harsh language—that his book caused an academic and media stir. Critics said he too readily dismissed the influences of peer pressure, Nazi propaganda, and the fact that the Nazi regime, whatever its faults, was perceived by most Germans to be their legitimate government and therefore worthy of their obedience. Amid the controversy over Goldhagen's book, however, there was some agreement: Germany's pre-Nazi culture did indeed include some racist, anti-Semitic aspects that the Nazis could, and did, exploit. Though some ordinary Germans did resist the Nazis, if only by hiding a Jewish friend in some cases, their national culture contained enough bigotry to persuade many others that bigotry was acceptable, patriotic, even scientifically reasonable. Most of the perpetrators of the Holocaust were indeed ordinary Germans.[27]

However, any theory which suggests that a particular nation's culture can cause a genocide runs the risk of being misunderstood and misused to promote ethnic stereotypes and notions of collective guilt. Neither Goldhagen nor most historians have argued that the Final Solution was inalterably predetermined in Germany, somehow destined to erupt even if the Nazis had never come to power. "As I have written and said many times," Goldhagen declared, "my book owes nothing to the indefensible notion of collective guilt." Rather, "it champions the notion of Germans' individual responsibility for their actions and shows that many more ordinary Germans willingly took part in the genocide than has been maintained." [28] After his book was published amid considerable media coverage in the Federal Republic of Germany, Goldhagen wrote that "for Germans to confront this horrific part of their past is enormously unpleasant. That so many are willing to do so is yet another indication of how transformed the Germany of today is compared to 1933 or 1945. In this sense, Germany is the great cultural and political success story of the postwar period." [29]

Human cultures are not monolithic, nor unchanging, nor eternally focused upon some sinister goal to which different generations at different times all inevitably drift. But foreign cultures are easily stereotyped, and in the 1990s this tendency gave rise to various notions of a "clash of civilizations" between the Christian and Islamic civilizations, or between Western civilization and Asian Confucianism. Samuel Huntington, another Harvard professor, coined the phrase. In a book he entitled *The Clash of Civilizations and the Remaking of World Order,* published in 1996, he asserted that, when formulating a foreign policy, cultural differences should not be discounted, not even in today's era of so-called globalization. His was reasonable advice, but some of his slogan-style "quotable quotes" were easy to misinterpret if taken out of context. One typical example: "In the clash of civilizations, Europe and America will hang together or hang separately." The two sentences with which Huntington surrounded this provocative remark are no less important than the remark itself:

The futures of both peace and Civilization [in general] depend upon understanding and cooperation among the political, spiritual, and intellectual leaders of the world's major civilizations.

In the greater clash, the global "*real* clash" between Civilization and barbarism, the world's great civilizations, with their rich accomplishments in religion, art, literature, philosophy, science, technology, morality, and compassion, will also hang together or hang separately. [30]

Huntington also wrote:

Whatever the degree to which they divided humankind, the world's major religions— Western Christianity, Orthodoxy, Hinduism, Buddhism, Islam, Confucianism, Taoism, Judaism—also share key values in common. If humans are ever to develop a universal civilization, it will emerge gradually through the exploration and expansion of these commonalties. [31]

Universal values, including the Golden Rule and *Love Thy Neighbor,* are commonalties taught by virtually every spiritual religion. "There shall be no compulsion in religion," commands the Quran, the holy book of Islam, for God "made you into nations and tribes that you might get to know one another. The noblest of you in God's sight is the one who is most righteous." [32] When Confucius, the great Chinese philosopher, was asked by an ancient ruler if evil people should be killed for the good of everyone else, Confucius replied: "Sire, what need has a ruler to kill? Were you set on good, Sire, your people would do good." [33]

All human beings belong to the same species, with the same evolutionary legacy and having the same basic psychological needs, including moral and spiritual needs—and so we ought not be entirely surprised that universal values do exist, despite humankind's multiplicity of cultures. A major reason why so many of us are surprised is because, over the centuries, some ambitious people with some very worldly agendas have twisted religious teachings to suit their materialistic aims. But their intolerant views are not the only versions of those religions, an assumption outsiders too often make. Unfortunately, every major religion has its share of violent disciples. Yet even in the twentieth century, the bloodiest century yet recorded, the largest spiritual religions also produced great pacifist leaders, including Hinduism's Mohandas Gandhi, Islam's Abdul Ghaffar Khan, Christianity's Martin Luther King, and Buddhism's Tenzin Gyatso, the Fourteenth Dalai Lama of Tibet.

THE IMPORTANCE OF POLITICS

Any genocide worthy of the label does not erupt spontaneously. It requires planning, preparation, an organization, and a form of government whose human rights protections are inadequate. Bigotry and cultural chauvinism may form a genocide's emotional kindling, but these are incited and fueled by politics, exploiting an undercurrent of fear. The Rwandan genocide of 1994 was not exclusively anti-Tutsi. In addition to massacring more than 800,000 Tutsis, it murdered an estimated 50,000 Hutus, including Rwanda's politically moderate female prime minister—all because its perpetrators, the most politically extreme of Rwanda's Hutus, wanted absolute control over the country.

"When are you going to stop killing people?" a foreign visitor once asked Joseph Stalin, remarkably bluntly. "When it is no longer necessary," Stalin replied.[34] This supposed necessity to commit mass murder may sound like a pathetic excuse, but a perpetrator-regime's ideology, that is, its religion of sorts, may encourage such paranoid thinking. And the danger is worse if a conniving, all-powerful "high priest" can decide what that religion says. Adolf Hitler once confessed that if the Jews did not exist, "We would have to invent them. One needs a visible enemy, one in plain sight. The Jew is always within us, but it is simpler to fight him in bodily form than as an invisible evil."[35]

For scholars, the essence of Hitler's confession raises a small controversy. Does an aspiring dictator capable of ordering a genocide seek power for its own sake, so almost any group will suffice as his propaganda scapegoat? Or does that aspiring dictator hate that particular group so genuinely that he seeks power to destroy it? The answer may be a bit of both. Human obsessions, whether as bigotry or a lust for power, can be irrationally intertwined in the human psyche.

Propaganda is the manipulative voice of politics. Warren Zimmermann, the last U.S. ambassador accredited to the old Yugoslavia, explained in his memoirs how, in the 1990s, propaganda manipulated the Balkans:

Those who argue that "ancient Balkan hostilities" account for the violence that overtook and destroyed Yugoslavia ignore the power of television in the service of officially provoked racism. . . . People who think they're under ethnic threat tend to seek refuge in their ethnic group. Thus did the media's terror campaign establish ethnic solidarity on the basis of an enemy to be both hated and feared. Many people in the Balkans may be weak or even bigoted, but in Yugoslavia it's their leaders who have been criminal.[36]

THE LIMITS OF RATIONALITY

Leaders are powerless without followers. What attracts masses of people to a genocidal faith? Many defenders of science assert that until enough people become free-thinking individuals enlightened by scientific knowledge, instead of pawns enslaved to some religious dogma manipulated by others, the worst behavior of human beings will continue. While these defenders of science generally acknowledge that religion has promoted a considerable amount of good, they also note, correctly, the great plethora of cruelties too often sanctified by religion, including mass murder. Such cruelties contradict the universal values that virtually all religions share, but their justification can nonetheless be traced to what many organized religions rely upon for their very existence and acceptance: the concept of "revealed truth"—precepts of behavior demanded of religious believers by some great sage or divine authority. Science by contrast, assert its defenders, seeks truth through the objective testing of hypotheses, refining those hypotheses as more empirical data are collected and analyzed.

This critique of religion versus science is generally accurate as far as it goes, but only with the qualification that a dogma can become a religion without being called a religion. For as philosophers such as Karl Popper have warned, science may be perfect in theory but scientists in practice are not. Scientists are human beings, with prejudices, biases, and agendas like everybody else. The ideal of science is to overcome any bias by interpreting enough empirical data, gathered through objective experiments, to discover patterns that a hypothesis can then predict consistently. But the practical reality is that "science" cannot overcome the prejudice of a human scientist unless that scientist is emotionally willing to see, and likewise accept, any uncomfortable finding. The decisions that scientist makes in choosing which empirical data to collect, what methods to use for collecting that data, how to interpret that data, and how to fit that data into his personal hypothesis—those are all subjective decisions, no matter how objective the scientist tries to be. Over time, through the involvement of other scientists, the data may be checked, the tests verified, and the theory further developed and refined. But does that theory truly represent reality? A single scientist can be wrong. Many scientists can be wrong. Even the scientific community of an entire country can be wrong. It has happened before, many times.

The bloodiest wars and genocides of the twentieth century, the bloodiest century in human history, were waged for theories of science. A scientific theory can become a dogma; we usually call it an ideology. Marxism-Leninism and its theory of "scientific socialism" emerged from the social sciences of economics and sociology. Nazism laid claim to the natural sciences of biology and genetics. Fascism and its offspring, including the Baathist ideology of Saddam Hussein and the political aspects of Hitler's Nazism, arose from the academic disciplines of history, geography, linguistics, military science, and a favorite idea born of political science, nationalism. Nationalism began as the classical liberal idea that people who share the same language and culture should rule themselves. Fascism asserted that people with the same language and culture should rule themselves with a military efficiency—to enable the State to pursue imperialist ambitions.

These ideologies were not really created by science *per se*, but by human beings, and likewise believed by human beings, by people with spiritual needs even if they refused to openly admit they had any spiritual needs. They were attracted to these ideologies because they had made a spiritually related assumption that the only true reality is physical reality, material reality, a reality of natural laws and especially of *things*. They believed their mind-set was very scientific, but it was not, because it encouraged a belief in absolute certainty that genuine science cannot provide.

Bertrand Russell, perhaps the most eminent science-oriented philosopher of the twentieth century, gained notoriety for his harsh criticisms of traditional religion. When it came to his own beliefs about God, however, Russell—speaking scientifically—declared himself an agnostic, not an atheist, because he knew that genuine science cannot "prove" atheism, if only because it is not designed to. Limited literally by nature to exclusively material tests, science can neither prove nor disprove the existence of a nonmaterial reality. Science can test materialist phenomena to which some people ascribe spiritual meaning, such as the purported predictions of tarot cards, but pure spirituality is about love, contentment, devotion, and faith—not about materialism *per se*. To claim that science can provide absolute certainty about literally everything, both the nonmaterial and the material, is actually an arrogant abuse of science, usually done by people trying to cloak their opinions in its credibility.

Unfortunately, the inherent limits of science have not kept people from believing whatever they want about science. And if a person traps himself in an exclusively materialist mind-set, spiritually addicted to a material interpretation of literally everything because he believes materialism is the only thing he can be truly certain about, his beliefs can become very dogmatic—because his deepest spiritual needs are at stake. In such a mind-set the Universe can seem a very lonely, scary, uncaring place, with the inevitability of one's death always too terribly close. Such fears are especially acute among insecure adolescents and impressionable young adults, leaving them feeling alone, helpless, and individually worthless. The "scientific" ideologies of the twentieth century offered such people a feeling of religious meaning, a "church" in the form of a political party, as well as the group identity of their race, class, nationality, whatever. The idea that reality might be subjective, and thus to some degree uncertain, appeared to them to be so irrational (and deeply terrifying?) that they dismissed it as nonsense, as scientifically disproven, as politically subversive. They had convinced themselves that *SCIENCE IS CERTAIN!*—not realizing, or refusing to accept, that genuine science must always assume that there is no certainty, only educated guesses by imperfect human beings.

This is why wherever a scientific theory has become a regime's guiding ideology, its *de facto* religion, the pursuit of genuine science in that country has actually suffered. Nazi Germany treated nuclear physics with contempt, calling it a "Jewish science" not worthy of much Aryan study. In the Soviet Union the study of genetics was nearly destroyed by Trofim Lysenko, a pseudoscientist whose flawed theories about biology held forth only because he enjoyed the support of Joseph Stalin. In any totalitarian state the officially approved theory is not to be questioned, only accepted as a supposed fact. And since spiritual religions offer an alternative source of human meaning and purpose, the ruling regime usually tries to control both science and religion.

THE "RELIGION" OF NAZISM

To quench the spiritual thirst of Germany's masses, the Nazis deliberately gave their own ideology the accoutrements of a religion, complete with a new "chosen people" to carry forth the Nazi faith and even a Nazi afterlife, albeit a strangely impersonal one. It is no coincidence that the following Nazi "creed" mimics Christianity's Nicene Creed. Note its dominant emphasis on materialism, expressed as a national group identity:

I believe in the land of all the Germans, in a life of service to this land; I believe in the revelation of Divine creative power and the pure Blood shed in war and peace by the sons of the German national community, buried in the soil, thereby sanctified, risen and living in all for whom it is immolated. I believe in an eternal life on earth of this Blood that was poured out and rose again in all who have recognized the meaning of the sacrifices and are ready to submit to them. . . . Thus I believe in an eternal God, an eternal Germany, and an eternal life.[37]

Germany's history of anti-Semitism dates back to before Martin Luther, the medieval theologian whose own anti-Semitic writings were quoted approvingly by the Nazis. But while the Nazis shamelessly imitated what they liked about institutional Christianity, their own spiritual beliefs were utterly opposed to the Christian ideal. In 1941 Hitler's powerful deputy, Martin Bormann, issued a secret directive down to the Third Reich's district governors, declaring the Nazi leadership's attitude towards Christianity and science. Some excerpts:

National Socialism and Christianity are irreconcilable. Christian churches build on the uncertainty of human beings and attempt to preserve this fear in as wide segments of the population as possible, for only in this way can Christian churches keep their power. In opposition to this, National Socialism is based on scientific foundations.

When we National Socialists speak of a belief in God, we do not understand by God, like naïve Christians and their spiritual opportunists, a human-type being, who sits around somewhere in space. . . . The force of natural law [is what] we call the Almighty or God. The claim that this world force is concerned about the fate of every single being, of every smallest earth bacillus, or can be influenced by so-called prayers or other astonishing things, is based on a proper dose of naïvete.

In opposition to this, we National Socialists impose on ourselves the demand to live naturally as much as possible, i.e., biologically. The more accurately we recognize and observe the laws of nature and of life, the more we adhere to them, so much the more do we conform to the will of the Almighty. The more insight we have into the will of the Almighty, the greater will be our successes.[38]

It is psychologically revealing that this Nazi directive refers to "bacillus" as something so contemptuous that God has no concern for it: "Bacillus" was a label the Nazis also applied to Jews. Mass murdering ("exterminating") Jews was promoted by Nazi biology as a form of racial hygiene. And this idea, this mind-set, was not confined to the Nazi leadership and the SS; as Robert Jay Lifton detailed in his book *The Nazi Doctors: Medical Killing and the Psychology of Genocide,* it engulfed the entire medical and biological sciences community of Germany, one of the world's most technologically advanced countries.[39]

Erich Fromm, through a careful reading of Hitler's book *Mein Kampf,* easily guessed the object of devotion in Hitler's spirituality:

The power which impresses Hitler probably more than God, Providence, and Fate, is *Nature.* While it was the trend of the historical development of the last four hundred years to replace the domination over men by the domination over Nature, Hitler insists that one can and should rule over men but that one cannot rule over Nature. [He has even said] the history of Mankind probably did not start with the domestication of animals, but with the domination over inferior people. He ridicules the idea than Man could conquer Nature.[40]

Hitler was also a vegetarian—for humanitarian reasons. In a German culture known for its sausages and meaty cuisine, he berated people who ate meat in his presence; he called it "corpse eating." Hitler was so fond of animals that his regime conceived of and enacted some of the most humane animal treatment laws in the world. Remarkably humane even by today's standards, many of those laws are still enforced in the Federal Republic of Germany.

But the Nazis' spiritual yielding to Nature did not mean that the Nazis always left Nature undisturbed; quite the contrary. Hitler's plans to transform Berlin into an imposing megatropolis with overwhelming monuments and enormous buildings only hint at the changes he planned for the rest of Europe's landscape. While promoting a Nazified pagan mythology, in general the Nazis thought of Nature as the harsh reality of materialism, not as ecology or as "gentle" Mother Earth. They took unabashed pride in harnessing and expanding Germany's industrial might, and Hitler himself was fascinated by mechanical things such as automobiles, tanks, and warships. Hitler wanted to exploit the natural resources of Germany, and of everywhere else he could conquer, to build ever more and bigger *things.* Materialism emphasizes *things.*

Does Nature deserve to be so worshipped? If a giant meteor struck the Earth tomorrow and obliterated all life on the planet, that would be as natural as today's sunshine and lush forests. The material phenomena of Nature probably deserve to be respected; but respect alone, while prudent, is not worship. Infectious diseases are natural, but not even the Nazis assigned much spiritual value to them. What ought to matter most in any religion, pagan or otherwise, is not what material accoutrements it displays but what its spiritual essence teaches about universal values. Forgiveness is a universal value because most religions teach it and understand it in much the same way. To forgive means to release one's envy and hatred of someone by recognizing that forgiveness is more important than property, even the emotional property of a grudge. To a great extent universal values require this independence from material things. For because materialism is physical, it is conceptually inflexible, and therefore spiritually inflexible. Since Nazi spirituality was mixed with materialism, Nazi spirituality was enslaved to materialism. For how can the soil of Germany emotionally forgive anything? Soil is not emotional. Soil is not human. Only living beings can forgive—when they allow themselves to. Since the Nazis assigned a divine importance to soil, and to their own interpretation of racial biology, they refused to forgive almost any perceived affront to their nation.

THE "RELIGION" OF MARXISM-LENINISM

Many social scientists still treat Marxism as a scientific theory. Many also criticize how Communist regimes applied it, calling the practice deeply flawed and even not truly Marxist, but this criticism does not change the fact that the leading Communist revolutionaries of the twentieth century sincerely believed that Marxist theory was scientific, and certain. One Russian intellectual, living in exile in Paris, wrote that "Marx's historical materialism was the greatest achievement of scientific thought."

He was born Vladimir Ilyich Ulyanov. The world knows him by the name he adopted, Lenin. "Materialism has proved to be the only philosophy that is consistent," Lenin emphasized, "true to all the teachings of natural science and hostile to superstition, cant and so forth." So convinced was he of materialism, and so determined to protect his faith against any Marxist heretic, that in 1909, while still in exile, Lenin published a 300-page book he entitled *Materialism and Empirio-Criticism,* attacking almost every philosophy other than materialist Marxism. Years later, as the Soviet Union's first dictator, Lenin declared that his enemies had "exerted all their efforts to 'refute', undermine and defame materialism, and advocated various forms of philosophical idealism, which always, in one way or another, amounts to an advocacy or support of religion."[41]

Lenin never apparently realized that he, too, had established a religion of sorts, with its own superstitions and cant, with its own heretics and infidels (lots of them), a religion whose leading disciples later preserved Lenin's corpse as a pseudo-holy relic for Communist worshippers. Although the atrocities of his regime were later dwarfed by Stalin's, it was Lenin's regime that first erected the infamous GULAG prison system and, through deliberate famine and mass executions, murdered at least 6 million people. His words reprinted here were taken from a booklet entitled *On Marx and Engels* by V. I. Lenin, republished in 1975 by the People's Republic of China. At that year China was suffering through the Cultural Revolution ordered by China's first Communist patriarch, Mao Zedong. "The scientific world outlook of Marxism is an ideological weapon with which the Communists can overcome all enemies and difficulties," Mao declared. "History has given the proletariat the task of eliminating classes, and the Proletariat use dialectical materialism as the spiritual weapon for their struggle and as the philosophic basis of their viewpoints." [42]

As recently as 1999, with fewer and fewer genuine believers in China, its regime published a booklet to help rejuvenate the Marxist-Leninist faith, aptly entitled *Marx, Engels, Lenin, Stalin, Mao Zedong, Deng Xiaoping, and Jiang Zemin on Materialism and Atheism.*

Yet communistic societies are not inherently genocidal. Prehistoric hunter-gather societies were communistic, as were the earliest Christian communities and those of most other religions. Most monasteries today are still, by and large, communistic. So, too, are Israel's *kibbutz* communities, even though many are very secular in their beliefs and behavior. So what made Marxism-Leninism so different, so murderous? The reason is psychological maturity, or rather the lack of it.

Marxism-Leninism asserts that human priorities can be wholly reshaped by one's surrounding environment. While the ideology recognizes that people may dislike being forced to live in a selfless collectivist environment, at least at first, it asserts that, eventually, they will become habitually good. This transformation can even be speeded up, Marxist-Leninists believed, if every bad influence that might contaminate the average person is removed from society. And so, for the good of society, Marxist-Leninist regimes condemned ultimately tens of millions of people as "bad influences" and had them "removed"—either by killing them or by imprisoning them in "re-education" camps where they toiled as slaves between indoctrination sessions. Marxism-Leninism also emphasized the grand construction of things: monuments, factories, and other great showpieces of industrialization, all built with only scant ecological concern. Today the most obvious legacy of that materialist mind-set is the vast pollution which oozed unhindered throughout the Soviet Union, Eastern Europe, and elsewhere, all because material productivity was deemed to be all-important. What may not be so obvious today is that many of those Marxist-Leninist showpieces, especially those fashioned in Stalin's time including the Moscow subway, were built by slave labor.

In a society purposely devoid of money, at least not "money" in the capitalist sense, many Marxist-Leninists nonetheless became greedy. As revolutionaries they created mass movements, and through those movements they collected power. As social engineers they created new public hierarchies, and through those hierarchies they collected social status. As bureaucrats they created state-run monopolies, and through those monopolies they collected privileges. More and more, in their Communist group identity and in their individual behavior, they became the system they had created. They identified themselves with their fiefdoms, bureaucratic routines, and special privileges. And when the system gradually stagnated and eventually floundered, they could not properly reform it because they would have had to reform themselves. They would have had to release their addiction to material accomplishments and to things, to their group identity in and of the system, and face the personal consequences. Too few of them had nurtured any inner contentment, spiritually independent of things, to do this. In this spiritual-material trap, Marxist-Leninist Communism suffocated itself into collapse.

When human beings assume that material reality is the only reality, that their worth and meaning as human beings depend entirely upon what material things they can create and collect, invariably such people identify themselves with those things they have created and collected. And when those things are endangered, such people will desperately fight to preserve them, in some cases by resorting to genocide, because their things represent more than something physical. Their things represent their personal spiritual worth and meaning.

THE MATURITY OF THE SENOI

Senoi communities are also communistic. Each one is presided over by a headman and a council of elders, although their power is limited to mere verbal persuasion, mediation, and moral arguments. The council meets only irregularly because the community has few political needs; individual liberties, though unwritten, are widespread. If some quarrel or crime does require the council's attention, the usual practice is to gather everyone involved, and their kin, and openly air all the negative feelings until some resolution is found. In severe cases such meetings can last for days.

The Senoi do have group identities. Terms such as *father, mother, brother,* and *sister* are used to describe entire groups of relatives between whom mutual obligations exist, making Senoi communities almost literally extended families. The Senoi identify with their families so closely that if someone from one family physically harms anyone from another, that second family can extract retribution by harming *anyone* from the first family—and Senoi families are immense. Such broad codes of family honor have produced volumes of bloody history in other parts of the world, but Senoi families, instead of killing each other, preserve peace. For the Senoi are not enslaved to their group identities as families: Their psychological maturity permits them to discuss their grievances face to face, to honestly hear one another, to find a nonviolent solution, and ultimately to forgive.

In other societies the Senoi concept of marriage may also sound like a recipe for a societal breakdown. Formal "marriage" does not exist. When a Senoi couple lives together, they are considered "married"—but only as long as they live together. Some Senoi women have been "married" several times. Aside from some social prohibitions against rape and incest, there are few sexual taboos. Premarital sex is common and socially acceptable, and so, too, is martial infidelity. Yet jealousy is discouraged, and most Senoi are mature enough that this discouragement generally works. One happy consequence is that everyone raises everyone's children because there is no concept of illegitimacy. In this sense there are no orphans, no abandoned children, no children suffering alone in broken homes, and no dysfunctional families.

One intriguing Jungian theory holds that the Senoi developed their profound psychological maturity by practicing a form of dream therapy. In Senoi families almost every day, especially at mealtime, children and adults are encouraged to describe their dreams, which are then interpreted. Since dreams can reveal a person's innermost feelings, desires, anxieties, and embarrassments, at least in symbolic terms, the Senoi address these human concerns openly and lovingly, from childhood and throughout adulthood. Simply the mere discussion of these concerns in a lovingly supportive environment can be of immense psychological benefit.

Saddam Hussein, by contrast, experienced a childhood of physical abuse at the hands of his stepfather. Hitler, too, confessed having been beaten as a child by his father. Compare the social environment of the Senoi to what Hitler's Army chief of staff, General Heinz Guderian, observed about Hitler later in life:

He had no real friend. His oldest Party comrades were, it is true, disciples, but they could hardly be described as friends. So far as I could see there was nobody who was really close to him. There was nobody in whom he would really confide his deepest feelings. There was nobody with whom he could talk freely and openly. . . . His relationship with Eva Braun may be cited as a contradiction of what I have here written. I can only say that I knew nothing of this and that so far as I am aware I never once saw Eva Braun, though for months on end I was with Hitler and his entourage almost every day.[43]

RELIGIOUS FREEDOM AND SPIRITUAL WISDOM

Raphael Lemkin, the man who coined the word *genocide*, listed among the crime's variants what he called "moral" genocide:

In order to weaken the spiritual resistance of the national group, the [perpetrator] attempts to create an atmosphere of moral debasement within this group. According to this plan, the mental energy of the group should be concentrated upon base instincts and should be diverted from moral and national thinking. It is important for the realization of such a plan that the desire for cheap individual pleasure be substituted for the desire for collective feelings and ideals based upon a higher morality.

Therefore, the [Nazi] occupant made an effort in Poland to impose upon the Poles pornographic publications and movies. The consumption of alcohol was encouraged, for while food prices have soared, the Germans have kept down the price of alcohol, and the peasants are compelled by the authorities to take spirits in payment for agricultural produce. The curfew law, enforced very strictly against Poles, is relaxed if they can show the authorities a ticket to one of the gambling houses which the Germans have allowed to come into existence.[44]

This moral grievance of Lemkin's may seem a bit old-fashioned today, since most consumers now have access to pornography and alcoholic beverages by right. Genocide is supposed to denote the ultimate denial of human rights. But while Lemkin the legal professor may not have been as eloquent as Fromm the psychoanalyst, both men recognized the dangers of addiction, whether it be to pornography, alcohol, or to a materialist-oriented faith. For when addicted to materialism, the human intellect finds ways to ignore or pervert morality. Many perpetrators of genocide genuinely believe that their acts will produce a better society, a better world, even a better human being. At the root of their addiction is self-hatred and, at best, a cruelly conditional love. Fromm emphasized that, regardless of whether or not the great religions are truly supernatural, their core teachings contain spiritual wisdom for the joyous living of life. He wrote:

The command to *Love Thy Neighbor as Thyself* is, with only slight variations in its expression, the basic principle common to all humanistic religions. But it would indeed be difficult to understand why the great spiritual teachers of the human race have *demanded* of Man that he should love, if love were as easy an accomplishment as most people seem to feel. . . . In our marketing orientation people think they are not loved because they are not "attractive" enough, attractiveness being based on anything from looks, dress, intelligence, money, to social position and prestige. They do not know that the real problem is not the difficulty of being loved but the difficulty of loving. . . . Love is based on an attitude of affirmation and respect, and if this attitude does not also exist toward oneself, who is after all only another human being and another neighbor, it does not exist at all.[45]

For thousands of years, our wisest moral and spiritual sages have warned us against the dangers of worshipping materialism, even if we do not necessarily call it worship. They do not call upon us to renounce civilization, but to adhere to universal values to thereby avoid civilization's worst temptations. Religions and *de facto* religions too often become genocidal crusades when materialist agendas and mind-sets seduce their followers.

We cannot put every would-be perpetrator of genocide on a psychiatrist's couch in an effort to prevent the crime. What we can do is use our accumulating knowledge of genocide's causes to forecast where and when the crime may occur—and seek to prevent it. No less importantly, we can use our knowledge of genocide's causes to look into ourselves. What daily values, what faith, do we practice and why? Does what we practice prevent genocide, or permit it?

NOTES

1. Stevan Weine and Dori Laub, "Narrative Constructions of Historical Realities in Testimony with Bosnian Survivors of 'Ethnic Cleansing'," *Psychiatry* (August 1995), pp. 246-260.

2. Erich Goldhagen, "Albert Speer, Himmler, and the Secrecy of the Final Solution," *Midstream* (October 1971), pp. 43-50. The "Notes" section of this article is extremely detailed and as informative as the article itself.

3. Robert Edwin Herzstein, *The Nazis* (Alexandria, VA: Time-Life Books, 1980), p. 143.

4. Raul Hilberg, *The Destruction of the European Jews* (New York: Holmes and Meier Publishers, 1986), pp. 125-138.

5. John M. Steiner, *Treblinka* (New York: Simon & Schuster, 1967), p. 73.

6. Hilberg, *loc. cit.*

7. Goldhagen, *loc. cit.*

8. David A. Grossman, *On Killing: The Psychological Cost of Learning to Kill in War and Society* (New York: Little, Brown and Company, 1995; paperback edition, 1996), p. 39.

9. Ibid., p. 4.

10. Ibid., pp. xviii and 254.

11. G. Tillion, *Ravensbruck* (Garden City, NY: Anchor Books, 1975), p. 69.

12. Joel E. Dimsdale (editor), *Survivors, Victims, and Perpetrators: Essays on the Nazi Holocaust* (New York: Hemisphere Publishing Corporation, 1980), in particular: John M. Steiner, "The SS Yesterday and Today; A Sociopsychological View," pp. 405-443.

13. Arthur S. Reber, *The Penguin Dictionary of Psychology* (New York: Viking, 1985), pp. 360-361.

14. See Levinson and Ember, specifically the entry "Peace and Nonviolence" by Leslie E. Sponsel, pp. 908-912, and the entry "War" by Jonathan Haas, pp. 1357-1360.

15. Richard Leakey and Roger Lewin, *Origins Reconsidered: In Search of What Makes Us Human* (New York: Anchor Books, 1992), pp. 233-234.

16. William Shakespeare, *The Tragedy of Hamlet, Prince of Denmark*, Act III, Scene 1:122-129.

17. Erich Fromm, *The Art of Loving* (New York: Harper & Row, 1956), pp. 53 and 56.

18. Erich Fromm, *Escape from Freedom* (New York: Henry Holt & Company, 1941), p. 256.

19. Erich Fromm, *Psychoanalysis & Religion* (New York: Harper & Row, 1950), p. 47.

20. Edouard Calic (editor), *Secret Conversations with Hitler* (New York: The John Day Company, 1971), p. 68.

21. Ibid.

22. Arthur S. Reber, *The Penguin Dictionary of Psychology* (New York: Viking-Penguin, Inc., 1985).

23. For a psychological appraisal of group identities and genocidal behavior, see Neil Kressel, *Mass Hate: The Global Rise of Genocide and Terror* (New York: Plenum Press, 1996).

24. Joseph Goebbels, *Goebbels' Tagebucher 1942-1943* (Zurich: 1948), pp. 114-143.

25. Fromm, *Psychoanalysis & Religion,* pp. 58-59.

26. Stanley Milgram, "Behavioral Study of Obedience," *Journal of Abnormal and Social Psychology* (1963), Vol. 67, pp. 371-378. Also, Stanley Milgram, *Obedience to Authority: An Experimental View* (New York: Harper & Row, 1974).

27. Daniel Jonah Goldhagen, *Hitler's Willing Executioners: Ordinary Germans and the Holocaust* (New York: Alfred A. Knopf, 1996). Norman G. Finkelstein and Ruth Bettina Birn, *A Nation on Trial: The Goldhagen Thesis and Historical Truth* (New York: Henry Holt & Company, 1998). Robert R. Shandley (editor), *Unwilling Germans? The Goldhagen Debate* (Minneapolis: University of Minnesota Press, 1998). Christopher R. Browning, *Ordinary Men: Reserve Police Battalion 101 and the Final Solution in Poland* (New York: HarperCollins, 1992, 1998); the 1998 edition has a new afterword with Browning's reply to Goldhagen.

28. Daniel Jonah Goldhagen, "Germans vs. the Critics," *Foreign Affairs* (January-February 1997), p. 163.

29. Daniel Jonah Goldhagen, "Hitler's Willing Executioners" (Interview & Response), *Society* (January-February 1997), p. 37.

30. Samuel P. Huntington, *The Clash of Civilizations and the Remaking of World Order* (New York: Simon & Schuster, 1996), pp. 320-321.

31. Ibid.

32. Surahs 2:256 and 49:13. From the English interpretation by N. J. Dawood, *The Koran* (London: Penguin Books, 1990).

33. Sayings from *The Analects,* one of the core texts of Confucian philosophy.

34. This question was put to Joseph Stalin by Great Britain's Lady Nancy Astor. Quoted in Nicholas Bethell, *Russia Besieged* (Alexandria, VA: Time-Life Books, 1977), p. 34.

35. Quoted in Hermann Rauschning, *Gespreche mit Hitler (1939)* (Vienna, Austria: Europaverlag, 1973), p. 223.

36. Warren Zimmermann, *Origins of a Catastrophe* (New York: Times Books, 1996), pp. 120-121.

37. Quoted in John S. Conway, *The Nazi Persecution of the Churches: 1933-45* (New York: Basic Books, 1968), pp. 148-149.

38. Quoted in Conway, pp. 383-386 (Appendix 15).

39. Robert Jay Lifton, *The Nazi Doctors: Medical Killing and the Psychology of Genocide* (New York: Basic Books, 1986).

40. Fromm, *Escape from Freedom*, pp. 234-235.

41. V. I. Lenin, *On Marx and Engels* (Peking: Foreign Languages Press, 1975), pp. 7-8 and 64.

42. Mao Zedong, "Dialectical Materialism (Outline Lecture Script)" (1937), found in *Marx, Engels, Lenin, Stalin, Mao Zedong, Deng Xiaoping, and Jiang Zemin on Materialism and Atheism* (Beijing: Central Party Literature Publishing House, 1999).

43. Heinz Guderian, *Panzer Leader* (abridged) (New York: Ballantine Books, 1980), p. 370.

44. Raphael Lemkin, *Axis Rule in Occupied Europe: Laws of Occupation, Analysis of Government, Proposals for Redress* (Washington, DC: Carnegie Endowment for International Peace, 1944), pp. 89-90.

45. Fromm, *Psychoanalysis & Religion*, pp. 86-87.

3

War Crimes and Acts of Genocide:
Matters of International Law

Kill the [boys] and the luggage!—'tis expressly against the law of arms. . . .
'Tis certain there's not a boy left alive; and the cowardly rascals that ran from
the battle have done this slaughter. . .

— William Shakespeare, *King Henry V*, Act IV, Scene 7:1-8

The Genocide Convention is the world's first attempt to [legally] eliminate
planned destruction of human groups. . . . Similar to treaties for suppression
of piracy and slave traffic in that it defines an international crime and binds
signatory nations to apprehend and punish offenders, the Convention is
unlike them in that it provides some measure of United Nations enforcement
and contemplates future establishment of a world criminal court having
original jurisdiction over the offense.

— Raphael Lemkin, *The Yale Law Journal,* 1948

People who commit acts of genocide, or who justify acts of genocide committed
by others, sometimes claim that those acts are legitimate acts of war. But their
claims, if not outright lies, are excuses born of ignorance because acts of
genocide even in wartime violate a longstanding body of international law. This
chapter will review that body of international law and the premier international
organization at its core, the United Nations. For international law and the UN to
serve humanitarian purposes, the parameters of their jurisdiction, as well as their
practical limitations, both need to be understood.

Self-imposed prohibitions against what we now call *war crimes* date back to
ancient times. Christianity's John the Baptist preached at least two such moral
injunctions, specifically against looting and corruption. "Don't extort money,"
he told soldiers, "and don't accuse people falsely—be content with your wages."
(Luke 3:14) Other injunctions against war crimes exist in the legal traditions of

both Western and non-Western peoples, including in the Quran, the Islamic holy book that for centuries has had the force of law in various Muslim societies.

Armies in modern times have also prohibited war crimes through military regulations such as the Lieber Code, adopted by the United States Army during the American Civil War. Officially known as General Orders No. 100 and issued by President Abraham Lincoln in his capacity as Commander-in-Chief, this code of conduct consisted of 157 articles prepared by Francis Lieber, a German-American professor of law at Columbia University. The subsequent Geneva and Hague Conventions, the so-called laws of war, are based on articles first enacted in the Lieber Code.[1]

THE GENEVA AND HAGUE CONVENTIONS

The first international Geneva Convention, held in 1864, established the International Committee of the Red Cross (ICRC) to provide medical assistance to wounded soldiers in wartime regardless of their nationality. Today the ICRC, a coordinator of the world's various Red Cross and Red Crescent societies, still serves as a neutral intermediary as well as an advocate for the wartime needs of civilians and prisoners of war, urging all sides to adhere to the laws of war.

In 1899, after a preliminary convention at The Hague, many of the first international laws of war—legally binding upon the countries that signed them and still in effect today—were agreed upon at the Second Hague Convention. The articles were reaffirmed in 1907, seven years before the First World War, at the Fourth Hague Convention. Among their provisions are the following:

The armed forces of the belligerent parties may consist of combatants and non-combatants. In case of capture by the enemy, both have a right to be treated as prisoners of war. . . . They must be humanely treated. All their personal belongings, except arms, horses, and military papers, remain their property.

The attack or bombardment of towns, villages, habitations or buildings which are not defended, is prohibited. . . . In sieges and bombardments all necessary steps should be taken to spare as far as possible edifices devoted to religion, art, science, and charity, hospitals, and places where the sick and wounded are collected, provided they are not used at the same time for military purposes. . . . The pillage of a town or place, even when taken by assault, is prohibited.

Family honors and rights, individual lives and private property, as well as religious convictions and liberty, must be respected. Private property cannot be confiscated. . . . The property of the communes, that of religious, charitable and educational institutions, and those of arts and science, even when State property, shall be treated as private property. All seizure of and destruction, or intentional damage done to such institutions, to historical monuments, works of art or science, is prohibited, and should be made the subject of proceedings.[2]

Four of the most important Geneva Conventions took place in 1949, notably the *Geneva Convention Relative to the Protection of Civilian Persons in Time of War*. Part II of it covers "the whole of the populations of the countries in conflict, without any adverse distinction based, in particular, on race, nationality, religion or political opinion, and are intended to alleviate the suffering caused by war." Part II specifies:

The Parties to the conflict shall endeavor to conclude local agreements for the removal from besieged or encircled areas, of wounded, sick, infirm, and aged persons, children and maternity cases, and for the passage of ministers of all religions, medical personnel and medical equipment on their way to such areas.

Each High Contracting Party shall allow the free passage of all consignments of medical and hospital stores and objects necessary for religious worship intended only for civilians of another High Contracting Party, even if the latter is its adversary. It shall likewise permit the free passage of all consignments of essential foodstuffs, clothing and tonics intended for children under 15 years of age, expectant mothers and maternity cases.[3]

The Geneva Conventions of 1949 also include prohibitions against genocidal violence. Here the term *protected persons* refers to civilians as well as to military prisoners of war:

Protected persons are entitled, in all circumstances, to respect for their persons, their honor, their family rights, their religious convictions and practices, and their manners and customs. They shall at all times be humanely treated, and shall be protected especially against all acts of violence or threats thereof and against insults and public curiosity. Women shall be especially protected against any attack on their honor, in particular against rape, enforced prostitution, or any form of indecent assault.

The High Contracting Parties specifically agree that each of them is prohibited from taking any measure of such a character as to cause the physical suffering or extermination of protected persons in their hands. This prohibition applies not only to murder, torture, corporal punishment, mutilation and medical or scientific experiments not necessitated by the medical treatment of a protected person, but also to any other measures of brutality whether applied by civilians or military agents.[4]

The Geneva Conventions of 1949 apply to wars not only between countries but also within countries, that is, civil wars. If a country has signed any of the Conventions (and most countries have), that entire country, and not merely the particular government which penned the actual signature, is legally required to adhere forever. Thus, in a civil war, every warring side—both the government and the rebels—must fully adhere to whatever Geneva Conventions the country has signed, even if that side has not, itself, actually signed. War crimes cannot be permitted or excused away as an "internal affair" supposedly beyond the jurisdiction of international law:

In the case of armed conflict not of an international character occurring in the territory of one of the High Contracting Parties, each Party to the conflict shall be bound to apply, as a minimum, the following provisions:

Persons taking no active part in the hostilities, including members of armed forces who have laid down their arms and those placed *hors de combat* by sickness, wounds, detention, or any other cause, shall in all circumstances be treated humanely, without any adverse distinction founded on race, color, religion or faith, sex, birth or wealth, or any other similar criteria. To this end, the following acts are and shall remain prohibited at any time and in any place whatsoever with respect to the above-mentioned persons:

(a) Violence to life and person, in particular murder of all kinds, mutilation, cruel treatment and torture;

(b) Taking of hostages;

(c) Outrages upon personal dignity, in particular humiliating and degrading treatment;

(d) The passing of sentences and the carrying out of executions without previous judgment pronounced by a regularly constituted court, affording all the judicial guarantees which are recognized as indispensable by civilized peoples.[5]

Two protocols were added to the Geneva Conventions in 1977, including the following provisions:

The following acts are and shall remain prohibited at any time and in any place whatsoever, whether committed by civilian or military agents: murder; torture of all kinds; mutilation; outrages upon personal dignity; enforced prostitution and any form of indecent assault; the taking of hostages; collective punishments; and threats to commit any of the foregoing acts.

The civilian population as such, as well as individual civilians, shall not be the object of attack. Acts or threats of violence, the primary purpose of which is to spread terror among the civilian population, are prohibited.... Indiscriminate attacks are prohibited.... Attacks against the civilian population or civilians by way of reprisals are prohibited.... It is prohibited to commit any acts of hostility directed against the historic monuments, works of art or places of worship which constitute the cultural or spiritual heritage of peoples.... Starvation of civilians as a method of warfare is prohibited.

The civilian population and aid societies . . . shall be permitted, even on their own initiative, to collect and care for the wounded, sick and shipwrecked, even in invaded or occupied areas. No one shall be harmed, prosecuted, convicted or punished for such humanitarian acts.

The Parties to the conflict . . . shall allow and facilitate rapid and unimpeded passage of all relief consignments . . . even if such assistance is destined for the civilian population of the adverse Party. The Parties to the conflict shall have the right to prescribe the technical arrangements, including search, under which such passage is permitted, [but they] shall in no way whatsoever divert relief consignments from the purpose for which they are intended nor delay their forwarding, except in cases of urgent necessity in the interest of the civilian population concerned.[6]

The Geneva and Hague Conventions were not devised to justify foreign, armed humanitarian interventions to enforce them. Governments are supposed to improve their own wartime behavior through the self-incentive of national honor and global reputation. Yet these Conventions can be used to help build a legal case to at least pressure the warring parties to refrain from committing acts of genocide.

OTHER SUPPLEMENTARY CONVENTIONS

To further build a legal case against an offender, the following are but a few of several other international humanitarian agreements in legal force today, with excerpts from each text:

The Convention for the Protection of Cultural Property in the Event of Armed Conflict (1956):

The High Contracting Parties undertake to respect cultural property . . . by refraining from any use of the property and its immediate surroundings . . . for purposes which are likely to expose it to destruction or damage in the event of armed conflict; and by refraining from any act of hostility directed against such property [including] monuments of architecture, art or history, whether religious or secular, archeological sites, works of art, manuscripts, books and other objects of artistic, historical or archaeological interest.[7]

The International Convention on the Elimination of All Forms of Racial Discrimination (1965):

States-Parties condemn all propaganda and all organizations which are based on ideas or theories of superiority of one race or group of persons of one color or ethnic origin, or which attempt to justify or promote racial hatred and discrimination in any form, and undertake to adopt immediate and positive measures designed to eradicate all incitement to, or acts of, such discrimination . . . with due regard to the principles embodied in the Universal Declaration of Human Rights . . .[8]

The International Covenant on Civil and Political Rights (1966):

All peoples have the right of self-determination. By virtue of that right, they [must be allowed to] freely determine their political status and freely pursue their economic, social and cultural development . . . without distinction of any kind, such as race, color, sex, language, religion, political or other opinion, national or social origin, property, birth or other status . . . When deprivation of life constitutes the crime of *genocide*, it is understood that nothing in this article shall authorize any State-Party . . . to derogate in any way from any obligation assumed under the provisions of the Convention on the Prevention and Punishment of the Crime of Genocide.[9]

The Convention against Torture and Other Cruel, Inhuman or Degrading Treatment or Punishment (1987):

The term *torture* means any act by which severe pain or suffering, whether physical or mental, is intentionally inflicted on a person for such purposes as obtaining from him, or a third person, information or a confession, punishing him for an act he or a third person has committed, or is suspected of having committed, or intimidating or coercing him or a third person, or for any reason based on discrimination of any kind. . . . No exceptional circumstances whatsoever, whether a state of war or a threat of war, internal political instability, or any other public emergency, may be invoked as a justification of torture.[10]

The Convention on the Rights of the Child (1989):

States-Parties recognize that every child has the inherent right to life. . . . No child shall be subjected to torture or other cruel, inhuman or degrading treatment or punishment. Neither capital punishment nor life imprisonment without possibility of release shall be imposed for offenses by persons below 18 years of age. . . . [States-Parties] shall respect and ensure the rights set forth in this Convention to each child within their jurisdiction without discrimination of any kind, irrespective of the child's or his or her parent's or legal guardian's race, color, sex, language, religion, political or other opinion, national, ethnic or social origin, disability, birth or other status.[11]

THE CONVENTION ON THE PREVENTION AND PUNISHMENT OF THE CRIME OF GENOCIDE

The Geneva and Hague Conventions, being laws for wartime, prohibit acts of genocide in wartime only. By contrast, the Convention on the Prevention and Punishment of the Crime of Genocide, first signed in 1948 and in effect since 1951, prohibits acts of genocide at all times, anywhere, even in countries that have not signed the Convention. Article 2 states:

In the present Convention, *genocide* means any of the following acts committed with intent to destroy, in whole or in part, a national, ethnical, racial or religious group, as such:

(a) Killing members of the group;

(b) Causing serious bodily or mental harm to members of the group;

(c) Deliberately inflicting on the group, conditions of life calculated to bring about its physical destruction in whole or in part;

(d) Imposing measures intended to prevent births within the group;

(e) Forcibly transferring children of the group to another group.

Moreover, Article 3 states:

The following acts shall be punishable: (a) Genocide; (b) Conspiracy to commit genocide; (c) Direct and public incitement to commit genocide; (d) Attempt to commit genocide; (e) Complicity in genocide.

The Genocide Convention makes these acts international criminal offenses, similar to piracy and likewise punishable by the legal courts of any signatory, regardless of the legal defendant's nationality. The coverage of the Genocide Convention is universal in that it requires every signatory to take action against genocide anywhere on the globe. But the Convention is not universal with regard to what specific form that action is to take: that is a national decision belonging to each signatory's government. The Convention does, however, offer a preference of sorts. According to Article 8:

Any Contracting Party may call upon the competent organs of the United Nations to take such action under the Charter of the United Nations as they consider appropriate for the prevention and suppression of acts of genocide, or any of the other acts enumerated in Article 3.

THE UNITED NATIONS ORGANIZATION

Winston Churchill once said the United Nations was never meant to create Heaven on Earth, only to save it from Hell. Perhaps the UN does not deserve even that much credit, but it has benefited the world at large, including the United States, more than its battered reputation might suggest. Loved or hated, the United Nations is a legitimate institution and the world's premier international organization. Most of the world's most important international organizations, from the International Monetary Fund (IMF) to the NATO alliance, are dominated by the United States. And the UN, despite some fearful American stereotypes to the contrary, is arguably the most U.S.-dominated international organization of all.

Although official delegates to the UN are sometimes called "ambassadors" by the news media, the correct title is *Permanent Representative* because the United Nations is neither a country nor a world government. It is a gathering of governments, approximately two hundred of them, many of them elected, others dictatorial, all of them very protective of their own sovereignty. Article 2 of the United Nations Charter, written in 1945, requires that the UN Organization respect each country's sovereignty:

Nothing contained in the present Charter shall authorize the United Nations to intervene in matters which are essentially within the domestic jurisdiction of any state or shall require the Members to submit such matters to settlement under the present Charter; but this principle shall not prejudice the application of enforcement measures under Chapter VII.

The last clause, permitting the application of enforcement measures, refers to international actions to oppose wars of illegal aggression by one country against another, such as by North Korea against South Korea in 1950-1953 or by Iraq against Kuwait in 1990-1991.

No member-government is forced to belong to the UN; any member can withdraw at any time. The only country ever to have left the UN is Indonesia, in 1965, only to rejoin less than two years later. Even Israel, historically one of the UN's most unpopular members and long distrustful of the UN, nevertheless has always remained a UN member. The modern state of Israel owes its legal birth in 1947 to early efforts by the UN to create the country in the aftermath of the Holocaust.

The best known organs of the United Nations are its Security Council, the General Assembly, and thirdly the Secretary-General and his Secretariat staff.

The Security Council

The UN Security Council consists of five permanent member-countries (the "Permanent Five" or P-5) and ten nonpermanent member-countries that rotate for two-year terms in proportional geographic distribution.

During World War II, before the UN Organization existed, the Allies had sometimes referred to themselves as the *United Nations*. In 1945 U.S. President Franklin Roosevelt suggested that this same term become the name of the new organization he proposed to replace the failed League of Nations. Both British Prime Minister Winston Churchill and Soviet leader Joseph Stalin agreed, and together they and their staffs negotiated the UN's conceptual framework. Today the involvement of Stalin would likely appall most people, but his involvement, as well as Churchill's, ultimately benefited the United States in ways few people realized in 1945.

Stalin and Churchill were both determined to protect their respective empires as best they could. Partly as a result of their determination, the Security Council is the UN's most powerful organ, more powerful than the much larger General Assembly and far more powerful than the Secretary-General and his staff. Articles 24 and 25 of the UN Charter explicitly declare:

In order to ensure prompt and effective action by the United Nations, its Members confer on the Security Council primary responsibility for the maintenance of international peace and security, and agree that in carrying out its duties under this responsibility the Security Council acts on their behalf.

The Members of the United Nations agree to accept and carry out the decisions of the Security Council in accordance with the present Charter.

In today's era of fervent nationalism and ethnic identity, the full meaning of these two articles is quite extraordinary. While every UN member retains its sovereignty as a country, the UN Charter requires each member *as a condition for membership* to obey the decisions of the Security Council—a council of foreign governments, including that of the world's strongest country, the United States. Before 1945 no international body as legally powerful had ever existed, and in today's nationalistic world it seems very unlikely that anything as legally powerful could ever be created again. From this perspective of international law, the UN Security Council is unique and probably irreplaceable.

To prevent the Council from becoming ruled by a "tyranny of the majority," each permanent member has the power to veto (cancel) the Council's majority vote on any issue. Interestingly, the word *veto* is not stated in the UN Charter; someone could read through Article 27 and almost miss this potent privilege of the select few:

Decisions of the Security Council on all [non-procedural] matters shall be made by an affirmative vote of nine members, including the concurring votes of the permanent members. . .

This power to veto the majority has long been criticized as undemocratic, but without it each the Council's permanent members would likely have abandoned the UN at one time or another. Until the late 1960s, for example, the Security Council was a very unfriendly place for Communist powers, which is why the Soviet Union cast its veto over one hundred times, far exceeding the other permanent members. And despite decades of Soviet pleading, the Security Council refused to even seat China's Communist government until 1971, long after Soviet-Chinese relations had soured; until then, the Council's permanent "China" seat was occupied by the pro-American Nationalist Chinese government on Taiwan. Britain and France both cast vetoes for the first time in 1956, in political opposition to the United States, during a crisis involving British and French troops seizing the Suez Canal in Egypt. The United States has often cast its veto as well. As a result, no UN Security Council resolution has ever passed without U.S. approval—none.

The General Assembly

Unfavorable American stereotypes about the UN mostly stem from the 1970s, when the General Assembly was noisy with anti-American rhetoric, frequently from Marxist-Leninist regimes. Fortunately for the United States, the UN Charter grants the General Assembly very little substantive power. The

Assembly was conceived to be, and is, the international equivalent of a debating society. Its vote tallies are largely symbolic. Although it does have the power to approve the UN's budget, neither the General Assembly nor the UN as a whole can actually collect the funds except through the international equivalent of begging and pleading.

The General Assembly can assert itself more during an international crisis by invoking what is called the "Uniting for Peace" resolution. Originally proposed and sponsored by the United States in 1950, the "Uniting for Peace" resolution arose from American fears that future Soviet vetoes in the Security Council might paralyze the Council altogether. In such situations, asserted then-U.S. Secretary of State Dean Acheson, the UN Charter justified the emergency involvement of the General Assembly. Acheson argued:

Article 1 ascribed to the United Nations as a whole and to its members the purpose of maintaining peace and opposing aggression. The Security Council was the principle instrument for carrying out this purpose, but if it should be paralyzed by a veto the duty remained, and powers given by Articles 10, 11, and 14 gave the General Assembly responsibility and authority in maintaining international peace.[12]

The "Uniting for Peace" resolution can be activated by a simple majority vote of the General Assembly or by a nine-member majority on the Security Council. The General Assembly can then convene an emergency special session within twenty-four hours and, in the original version of the resolution, establish a special committee to develop international options to respond, as well as field an international "peace patrol" to provide immediate and independent observation at the location of the crisis.

Some UN critics fear that any international body that contains most of the world's governments, including its most odious, could endanger the world's democracies with even the limited powers of the "Uniting for Peace" resolution; therefore, they contend, the General Assembly should not be trusted under any circumstances. But the UN Charter constricts such a danger. Article 18 requires that "decisions of the General Assembly on important questions shall be made by a two-thirds majority of the Members present and voting. These questions shall include recommendations with respect to the maintenance of international peace and security. . ." Since the Charter requires at least a two-thirds majority vote on these issues, any abuse of the "Uniting for Peace" resolution can be blocked by slightly little more than one-third of the Assembly's members.

That one-third voting threshold can be easily reached, and could be even in the notoriously anti-American 1970s. In the year 2000 the UN consisted of 189 countries. Of them, fifty (about 26 percent) were European countries and/or republics of the former Soviet Union, the majority being members either of NATO or of NATO's Partnership for Peace program.[13] Meanwhile, the Western hemisphere had thirty-five countries, including the United States, Canada, the Latin American republics, and the island-states of the Caribbean, totaling almost 19 percent of the General Assembly's membership.[14] With the exception of Cuba, all the Western hemisphere countries have governments generally friendly to the United States, many being U.S. allies via the Rio Treaty, while Canada is a member of NATO. By counting only its friends and allies in Europe and the Western hemisphere, the United States leads a voting bloc exceeding one-third of the General Assembly's members—more than enough, if necessary, to block a two-thirds majority decision.

Furthermore, of thirty-six countries in East Asia and the Pacific—19 percent of the General Assembly—many are also U.S. allies, including Australia, Japan, and South Korea.[15] Most experts count about seventeen countries as comprising the Middle East—about 9 percent of the General Assembly—and while these include a few anti-American pariah states, such as Iraq, most are U.S. allies, including Israel, Egypt, Turkey, Jordan, Kuwait, and Saudi Arabia.[16] Africa, not counting Mideast countries such as Libya and Egypt, is sometimes portrayed as a single voting bloc of about fifty countries. Yet even fifty voters in the General Assembly comprise less than one-third of the Assembly's total, and Africa is not a monolith.[17] Some African countries are friendly to the United States, such as Morocco and majority-ruled South Africa, while others are French allies (and pro-West) such as Djibouti and Gabon. There are no longer any Soviet client states in Africa, the USSR having collapsed and the once pro-Soviet states of Angola, Ethiopia, and Mozambique having changed themselves.

The United States cannot command two-thirds of the General Assembly's voters on literally every issue all of the time. Nor can any country. But the United States does have enough influence to win, or at least block, any proposed General Assembly resolution directly affecting U.S. national security. Whenever the United States has been outvoted in the General Assembly, the resolution was always a nonbinding declaration. A survey of post-Cold War voting patterns reveals that the old East-West split, when most East European countries voted against the United States, has, in general, been replaced by a North-South split between the world's rich and poor countries. However, when the issue concerns basic human rights, such as condemnations of genocidal violence, even that North-South split becomes less apparent. Majorities in the General Assembly have consistently voted to condemn genocidal violence, be it warfare in Bosnia-Herzegovina, civil war in the Sudan, or abuses of human rights in Iraq.[18] If the Security Council is paralyzed by a veto, the General Assembly has the power to approve a humanitarian intervention under the U.S.-sponsored "Uniting for Peace" resolution and can probably be trusted to do so.

The Secretary-General

When Roosevelt, Churchill, and Stalin devised the UN's basic structure, they were careful not to create a "world president" even though they needed someone to manage the Organization's day-to-day administration. So they devised the job of Secretary-General, a position not co-equal with the Security Council and General Assembly but rather subordinate to both. Aside from heading his staff, known as the Secretariat, he has only one power granted to him by the Charter, specified in Article 99: "The Secretary-General may bring to the attention of the Security Council any matter which, in his opinion, may threaten the maintenance of international peace and security." In essence, the Secretary-General has the power to express his opinion, nothing more. Article 97, which describes the

Secretary-General as the UN Organization's chief administrative officer (not its chief executive officer, because there is no such position), requires that he be "appointed" (elected) by the General Assembly "upon the recommendation of the Security Council." Since having the approval of the Security Council is necessary to get the job, this means he needs the approval of the United States.

An incident in 1996 revealed how true this is. Late that year the Secretary-General at that time, Dr. Boutros Boutros-Ghali of Egypt, wanted to be reelected to another five-year term. He was very popular in the General Assembly and with the Security Council—except with the United States, which saw him as too arrogant. He had once promised he would not to seek a second term. What emerged was a major confrontation between the United States versus almost everyone else in the entire UN Organization, including most of the General Assembly, most of the Security Council, and even the Secretary-General himself. Yet, with remarkably little effort, the United States won. Boutros-Ghali soon retired, replaced as Secretary-General by Ghana's Kofi Annan, known for his American-based education and for recently heading the UN's Department of Peacekeeping Operations.

While many American critics fear that the UN Organization could somehow dominate the United States, the forced retirement of Boutros-Ghali shows that the truth is much closer to the reverse.

Bureaucracy and Cost

Other American complaints about the UN typically criticize its bureaucracy and cost. Such complaints were more justified in the 1970s and early 1980s. Since then, however, due to U.S. influence, the Organization has greatly reduced its cost. Throughout the 1990s the UN's bureaucracy actually shrank. From a high of over 12,000 employees in 1985, the Secretariat by 1998 was down to 9,000. Incidentally, Secretariat employees do not have diplomatic immunity; about one-third of their salaries are deducted for U.S. taxes. And although the Secretariat is broadly international, U.S. citizens hold more of its jobs than the citizens of any other UN member-country. The Secretariat's Under Secretary-General for Administration and Management is a U.S. citizen, and under his supervision the Secretariat had an annual zero-growth budget of $1.3 billion in both 1996 and 1997, a savings of over $250 million gained through higher efficiency and the elimination of some 1,000 staff jobs. In 1998 and 1999 the Secretariat's budget fell to approximately $1.24 billion per year.[19]

New York City, where the United Nations is headquartered, has a municipal government that dwarfs the size of the entire UN Organization. While the UN's Secretariat has an annual budget of less than $1.3 billion, the annual budget of New York City's government is about $32 billion—*nearly twenty-five times higher*. Whereas the Secretariat has about 9,000 employees, New York City's fire department alone has nearly 15,500. The Secretariat figure does not include the number of soldiers serving in UN peacekeeping operations worldwide, a number that fluctuates. In 1996 that number was about 23,600, while in that same year the New York Police Department employed nearly 44,300 personnel.

New York City frequently has more policemen patrolling its streets than the entire world has UN peacekeepers deployed around the globe.[20]

The UN bureaucracy is not a monolith; it consists of twenty-eight agencies along with the Secretariat. The amount of legal authority the Secretary-General has over each agency varies considerably; he cannot, for example, give orders to the UN High Commissioner for Refugees (UNHCR), whose agency is funded independently through voluntary contributions. Many UN agencies are headed by U.S. citizens, all of whom are, in effect, appointed by the President of the United States. In 1997 U.S. citizens headed the UN Children's Fund (UNICEF), the UN Development Program (UNDP), the World Food Program (WFP), and the Universal Postal Union. Not including UN peacekeepers abroad, some 53,300 people work in the UN system. That figure is, again, dwarfed by the government of New York City, which has more than 232,500 employees.[21]

For years the UN Organization has been deeply in debt. As recently as 1999, member-countries owed it a total of $2.3 billion, including $1.6 billion for peacekeeping operations. The worst debtor by far was the United States, which owed more than $1 billion. Each member's share is determined by its share of the world economy and by its ability to pay. Almost three-quarters of the UN's regular budget is provided by seven countries: the United States (25%), Japan (15.7%), Germany (9.1%), France (6.4%), Britain (5.3%), Italy (5.2%), and Russia (4.3%). But if a member refuses to pay, there is almost nothing the UN can do except beg and complain. The UN Charter warns that a consistent debtor can be denied its vote in the General Assembly, but that provision has never been enforced effectively and, in any event, it does not apply to votes in the Security Council, which are much more valuable. By law the UN Organization cannot borrow money from commercial institutions such as banks, and so for years the UN was forced to draw money from its own separate peacekeeping accounts to pay its other bills. Consequently, the UN has failed to reimburse more than seventy countries a total of $800 million for the use of their troops and equipment for peacekeeping operations.[22]

It was in 1988 that President Ronald Reagan first urged the U.S. Congress to start paying off America's UN debt, for in that year the UN bureaucracy stopped growing, thus fulfilling a key U.S. demand for further funding. Later Presidents George Bush, Sr., and Bill Clinton reiterated Reagan's desire. But the Congress —Democrat-controlled and later Republican-controlled—failed to pay up. Not until 2000, after lengthy Congressional negotiations and after seven past U.S. Secretaries of State—Henry Kissinger, Cyrus Vance, Alexander Haig, George Shultz, James Baker, Lawrence Eagleburger, and Warren Christopher—urged Congress to do so, did the United States finally start. In a published letter the former secretaries warned: "We are deeply concerned that our great nation is squandering its moral authority. It is simply unacceptable that the richest nation on earth is also the biggest debtor to the United Nations. . . . *Great nations pay their bills.*"[23]

Imperfect but Irreplaceable

Some radical American opponents of the UN believe in conspiracy theories involving mysterious black helicopters, the vanguard of a supposed UN army secretly waiting to conquer the United States at some apocalyptic moment. Better informed Americans dismiss such theories as absurd, but from the same ignorance that fuels such theories come more respectable calls for the United States to leave the UN Organization. The United States needs the UN, however, to help address American humanitarian concerns worldwide in ways that may otherwise distract the United States from fulfilling its own, arguably more important national security needs. The UN is not a burden upon America; the UN lightens America's burden.

Only the United Nations has the status of the world's premier international organization, representing almost every country. Only the United Nations has the General Assembly, a symbolic jury of one's peers of the world's governments. Only the United Nations has the Security Council, the only international body with the global legal right to compel countries to adhere to international humanitarian treaties and customs, by force if necessary. The Security Council did not seize this right: It is granted this right by every UN member, as a precondition for UN membership. Moreover, by signing the UN Charter, every member has obligated itself to adhere to the most basic norms of civilized conduct, which means that only through outright hypocrisy can a government commit a crime as grievous as genocide. It is for this reason that the average perpetrator-regime, when it does commit gross violations of human rights, instructs its own official defenders to say things like, "Your information is incorrect"—not, "It's none of your business because we will do whatever we want in our own country."

JUDICIAL ACTION

The Genocide Convention requires every signatory, if its national legal code does not already define acts of genocide as criminal offenses, punishable by its national courts, to enact the appropriate "enabling legislation." The "enabling legislation" of the United States is Chapter 50A, Sections 1091 to 1093, of the U.S. Code.

Another option are international courts of law. The Genocide Convention's Article 6 states:

Persons charged with genocide . . . shall be tried by a competent tribunal of the State in the territory of which the act was committed, *or by such international penal tribunal as may have jurisdiction with respect to those Contracting Parties which have accepted its jurisdiction.* [Emphasis added]

The Genocide Convention was written in 1948. An earlier legal precedent for international tribunals, though not without controversy, were the Nuremberg war crimes trials of 1945-1946, conducted in the German city of Nuremberg against senior Nazi officials after World War II. Similar trials were conducted in Tokyo against Japanese war criminals. The idea of tribunals originated in the

United States whereas other Allied Powers, such as the Soviet Union, favored a summary execution of Axis officials. To counter criticism that postwar tribunals impose an unfair "victor's justice" upon the defendants *ex post facto*, the Allies' International Military Tribunal asserted that the acts it prosecuted had been regarded as criminal since before World War II. Its indictment against the Nazis involved four counts:

1. "Crimes against Peace"—the waging of international wars of aggression in violation of international treaties and agreements;
2. "War Crimes"—violations of the laws of war, as specified in the Geneva and Hague Conventions;
3. "Crimes against Humanity"—the mass extermination of peoples and other acts of genocide; and
4. "A common plan or conspiracy to commit" the acts listed in the other three counts.

In later years other Nazi war criminals were tried by the national courts of the Federal Republic of Germany and by other countries. In 1960, Israeli agents entered Argentina and seized one of the most notorious, Adolf Eichmann, and smuggled him to Israel. Eichmann was tried by an Israeli court in 1961 and executed by hanging in 1962.

Not until the 1990s, however, after the Cold War, did major efforts resume to establish truly international courts empowered to try individuals for war crimes and acts of genocide. The UN Security Council, frustrated at trying to stop the atrocities of the Bosnian War, established the International Criminal Tribunal for the former Yugoslavia (ICTY) on May 25, 1993. Unofficially called the "international war crimes tribunal" and headquartered in The Hague, a city in the Netherlands, the ICTY was authorized to investigate war crimes throughout the old Yugoslavia, indict suspected perpetrators, issue worldwide warrants for their arrest and, if they could be brought to The Hague for trial, try them, and, if convicted, sentence and jail them. But the ICTY began short-staffed and poorly funded and, because the Bosnian War remained grisly, it did not seem to deter many war crimes. When the ICTY did indict some Balkan politicians and generals, calling them suspected war criminals, it complicated the peacemaking efforts of Western diplomats who had to negotiate with those same people to end the Bosnian War.

The ICTY gained more respect as a result of the Kosovo War of 1999. When the tribunal's investigators sought help uncovering evidence of atrocities, the Kosovar-Albanian population responded eagerly, as did Western human rights groups and Western governments, several of whom sent forensic experts to help investigate the mass graves. Furthermore, the first sitting head of state ever indicted for war crimes, Yugoslav President Slobodan Milosevic, was indicted by the ICTY. When asked about the diplomatic complications that that indictment caused, the ICTY's chief prosecutor, Louise Arbour, replied:

My position is very simple: there can be no durable peace without justice. Some politicians are complaining about the timing, but that is not our business. The Security Council gave us a mandate which could be summarized as follows: *If you have evidence, then act.* It is not for us to get used to the politicians. It is for the politicians to get used to the idea that, from now on, a tribunal exists.[24]

If the ICTY was born of frustration, the International Criminal Tribunal for Rwanda (ICTR) was born of feelings of guilt after the UN failed to thwart the Rwandan genocide in 1994. Headquartered in Arusha, Tanzania, the ICTR was officially established on November 8, 1994, and began operating in late 1995. Its relationship with Rwanda has been strained. It produced relatively few indictments and trials, and its competence has been severely questioned. It did convict a former mayor, Jean-Paul Akayesu, of genocide charges in 1998—an important achievement, since genocide charges are more difficult to prove than even murder or war crimes charges. But in late 1999 the ICTR's own Appeals Court ordered the release of another genocide suspect, Jean-Bosco Barayagwiza, because the tribunal had failed to follow its own procedural rules and give him a speedy trial. The release order infuriated the Rwandan government, and the ICTR's embarrassed prosecutors quickly found other legal reasons to keep Barayagwiza in pretrial detention.

Meanwhile, some 120,000 other genocide suspects were languishing in Rwanda's prisons awaiting their own trials, a caseload for which Rwanda had only 200 judges, 130 prosecutors, and 160 investigators, spread among a mere twelve courts. If each court tried one case per day, the entire caseload would take nearly thirty years to finish. Most of the crimes' key witnesses were dead, while few survivors could credibly identify which suspect had committed which act. So at first Rwanda's legal system encouraged suspects to confess (and to testify against each other) in exchange for shorter prison terms. Perpetrators whose acts were considered so gruesome as to warrant capital punishment were classified as Category 1; all other killers were Category 2. The distinction was exemplified in the following answer to this question: Which is legally worse, to bury one victim alive or to kill ten victims with a machete? A Rwandan official replied:

With a machete, you can do it with one hack. To bury somebody alive, it takes him a long time to die. Sometimes they didn't bury him completely; they left him there alive, and came back in a couple of days with a stick to finish. Others killed pregnant women and cut the babies out of their wombs. That is a cruel way to kill. Category 1.[25]

Statistically, unless a Category 2 suspect confessed before he was tried, he faced seven to eleven years in prison awaiting his trial. If he confessed once his trial began, his sentence was to be twelve to fifteen years. If he refused to confess but was ultimately convicted, his sentence was to be life in prison.

In 1998, twenty-two of the leading perpetrators of the Rwandan genocide—all Category 1 offenders—were publicly shot on a single day. As thousands of spectators cheered wildly, four of the condemned (three men and a woman) were hooded and tied to poles embedded in a Kigali soccer field; they stood bound for twenty minutes as the vast surrounding crowd jeered them and grew impatient. Suddenly a few masked policemen drove up. Each chose a prisoner, aimed close to the chest, and then all of them fired several times. Then they switched places and fired again. Finally a police captain fired his pistol twice into each hooded head. The executions were carried out despite appeals for clemency, or at least for less sensationalism, from the Pope, the European Union, the United States, and several human rights organizations. The trials had lasted, on average, only four hours—some without the presence of a defense attorney.

Does the public spectacle of an execution make a society less vulnerable to genocide? Or does that spectacle only add kindling to the hatred that helps cause genocide? Even an execution away from public view is not necessarily a deterrent. If a genocide's perpetrators believe they must kill or be killed, the legality of capital punishment might actually be part of the problem.

In 1997, Cambodia's Pol Pot was put on "trial" for the genocide inflicted by his Communist Khmer Rouge followers in 1975-1979. They had later fled into the jungle and waged a guerrilla war, indiscriminately sowing the countryside with landmines. Eventually most of the Khmer Rouge either died or deserted, and the rest deposed Pol Pot as their leader. They videotaped him in July 1997, enduring a show trial staged against him. "We've all undergone tough lives, full of massacres!" one accuser screamed at him (and into a convenient microphone), adding, "Hundreds of thousands of people were killed and injured! *Why?!!*" The 69-year-old Pol Pot, clearly frail and dejected, said nothing. A young crowd then shouted in perfect unison, "Crush, crush, crush the Pol Pot clique!" as they waved their fists in equal unison. The Khmer Rouge then "sentenced" Pol Pot to life imprisonment, presumably to be spent in the same jungle camp where his guerrilla "jailers" were also prisoners of a sort—surrounded by a Cambodian nation that despised them all. In April 1998, as the U.S. government and others prepared to capture Pol Pot to stand trial before an international tribunal, the Khmer Rouge announced that he had died of a heart attack. A videotape was shown of his lifeless body and of its cremation. No autopsy had been performed. Suspicions abounded that Pol Pot had either committed suicide or was murdered by his once loyal Khmer Rouge.

Although Pol Pot suffered the same fate his regime had inflicted upon so many others—a show trial, and then death—the penalty he actually paid, in comparison to his crimes, was arguably too lenient. When Jean Kambauda, Rwanda's exiled ex-prime minister, pleaded guilty to charges brought by the ICTR in 1998, the international tribunal imposed the highest penalty available to it: life imprisonment. Can any legal penalty for the crime of genocide truly fit the crime? Millions of Adolf Eichmann's victims were murdered by prolonged torture, starvation, medical experiments, gassed while pressed together naked, or literally worked to death. After these crimes no form of punishment could "rehabilitate" Eichmann—but the Israeli judges who sentenced him could not bring themselves to order his death by any of these inhuman methods. Instead, they explained Eichmann's sentence to him as follows:

You admitted that the crime committed against the Jewish people during the war was the greatest crime in recorded history, and you admitted your role in it. . . . You told your story in terms of a hard-luck story, and knowing the circumstances we are, up to a point, willing to grant you that under more favorable circumstances it is highly unlikely that you would ever have come before us or before any other criminal court.

There still remains the fact that you have carried out, and therefore actively supported, a policy of mass murder. . . . And just as you supported and carried out a policy of not wanting to share the Earth with the Jewish people and the people of a number of other nations—as though you and your superiors had any right to determine who should and who should not inhabit the world—we find that no one, that is, no member of the human race, can be expected to want to share the Earth with you. This is the reason, and the only reason, you must hang.[26]

Eichmann was executed away from public view.

National courts such as Israel's may continue to wrestle with the question of whether or not capital punishment befits the crime of genocide. At the level of international courts, however, the question is almost mute. At an international conference in Rome in July 1999, governments voted overwhelmingly in favor of creating an International Criminal Court (ICC), a permanent international tribunal, to try individuals for war crimes and crimes against humanity. Life imprisonment, not death, is the highest penalty the ICC is empowered to impose.

Not to be confused with the International Court of Justice, which arbitrates disputes between states but cannot try individuals, the International Criminal Court will take legal effect after sixty countries ratify the Rome Treaty, also known as the Rome Statute. Critics call the ICC a threat to national sovereignty, and even its supporters acknowledge that the treaty is complicated. In deference to national sovereignty, the treaty prohibits the ICC from acting unless several prerequisites are met. The ICC cannot investigate a case unless ordered to by the UN Security Council or unless at least one of the countries involved (either its nationals or the country where the crime was committed) is a party to the Rome Treaty. Moreover, the ICC can prosecute only the crimes within its legal jurisdiction, such as crimes against humanity, a prerequisite that binds the Court to a very high standard. Even crimes as egregious as "rape, sexual slavery, enforced prostitution, forced pregnancy, enforced sterilization, or any other form of sexual violence of comparable gravity" are not considered crimes against humanity, no matter how widespread, unless those crimes are "committed as part of a widespread or systematic attack directed against any civilian population . . . *pursuant to, or in furtherance of, a State or organizational policy."* This standard, especially the clause in italics, compels the ICC's prosecutor to present a daunting amount of persuasive evidence.

Even then, the ICC cannot take the case if a national judicial system has jurisdiction. The ICC is not supposed to replace national courts; rather, it is an alternative court when national courts cannot act. A panel of international judges must first determine that the relevant country's national judicial system is "unwilling or unable genuinely" to investigate and prosecute the case. To be "unwilling" does not mean that a prosecution must result; the national obligation is only to investigate, not necessarily to prosecute, and if that investigative obligation is fulfilled, the ICC is barred from acting. For a national judicial system to be considered "unable genuinely" of functioning means that it must have experienced "a total or substantial collapse"—as when a country's legal institutions disintegrate into anarchy, as Somalia's did in the 1990s. The term *unable genuinely* does not apply to any country with an established, functioning, independent national judicial system.

Even then, even after the ICC has asserted its jurisdiction over a case and is prepared to act, the UN Security Council can order the ICC to defer its proceedings—no investigation, no prosecution—for a renewable twelve-month period, with no limit on the number of renewals the Council can order. But such a deferral cannot be ordered by any single Council member acting alone; the deferral must be ordered by a majority vote of the Security Council without a veto.

American critics of the ICC fear that if the ICC ever becomes overzealous and anti-American, it might try to indict and prosecute U.S. military personnel for war crimes (though only if the ICC's panel of international judges also declares the U.S. judicial system "unwilling" to act). The likelihood of this scenario is remote, but it nevertheless exists. In late 1999 the ICTY was pressed to consider numerous accusations that NATO had committed war crimes in the Kosovo War. Although the tribunal's chief prosecutor decided the accusations did not merit legal action, the alternative possibility fed the worst fears of the ICC's critics in the United States.

Among those fears is how the indicted suspects might be apprehended. The Rome Treaty does not specify how, but when Raphael Lemkin contemplated such a court back in 1948, he warned: "Successful foundation of world criminal jurisdiction must ultimately look to the creation of a world police force which could force removal of accused persons from national to international control." [27] The idea of a world police force is, to its contemporary critics, terrifying—although in Lemkin's time the idea was not generally associated with a UN-run police agency. During the Second World War, INTERPOL, an international organization through which national police agencies exchange information, was taken over for a time by the Nazi Gestapo; no one in 1948 wanted to see another international version of the Gestapo. In Lemkin's time the idea of a "world police force" usually referred to the Great Powers using their national armed forces in a collective way to preserve international peace and security. What has since changed is that the world's national police agencies now work more closely together. Moreover, in some places, such as Kosovo, a local UN police force even apprehend suspected war criminals.

In October 1998, during a trip to London for medical treatment, Chile's retired dictator General Augusto Pinochet was arrested by British authorities in response to an extradition warrant issued by Baltasar Garzon, a Spanish judge, for "crimes of genocide and terrorism" committed against Spanish citizens during Pinochet's regime. Only a few of the more than 3,000 people who were shot or "disappeared" in Chile during that time were Spaniards, a fact which made the Spanish charge of outright genocide somewhat surprising. Even more surprising is that Pinochet was arrested in a third country, the United Kingdom, as an 82-year-old former head of state who was also a current, though unelected, member of the Chilean Senate. The episode caused U.S. Senator Jesse Helms, the Republican chairman of the Senate Foreign Relations Committee, to publish a *Washington Post* editorial in response. "If dictators cannot be offered amnesty or safety in exile, they will never hand power to democratic movements," Helms asserted. "The incentive will be for greater repression, not less. This is the world crusaders for an International Criminal Court are unwittingly creating." [28]

A year later Fidel Castro cancelled at least two trips out of Cuba, apparently fearing he could be arrested on U.S. criminal charges, including for war crimes committed by his regime's Cuban military advisors in Angola and Vietnam. Human rights groups tried to have arrested Iraq's Izzat Ibrahim al-Duri, a notorious crony of Saddam Hussein, while he underwent medical treatment in Austria. He fled back to Baghdad. Likewise Mengistu Haile Mariam, the ex-dictator of Ethiopia, faced an arrest threat in South Africa while receiving medical treatment there, causing him to return to safer exile in Zimbabwe. Not even at international conferences were suspects immune from arrest warrants. General Momir Talic, chief of staff of the postwar Bosnian-Serb army, was arrested in Vienna while attending an OSCE-sponsored symposium on European security. The ICTY, having heard Talic would attend, had notified the Austrian police that Talic had been secretly indicted for war crimes.

Now more than ever, perpetrators of state-sanctioned crimes must be wary of where they travel. But Helms had a point: If dictators have nowhere safe to go, why should they relinquish power? When the government of Zimbabwe was criticized for harboring Mengistu, it countered that the U.S. government had arranged for Mengistu's safe exile there to ease him out of power in Ethiopia in 1991. Nor are people like Mengistu the only ones worried about foreign arrest warrants. Margaret Thatcher, Britain's former prime minister, has reportedly had to consider which countries might arrest her if she visits.

Apprehending suspects when they travel abroad is not the same as seizing them where they live, as happened to Adolf Eichmann. The Israelis' seizure of Eichmann made the practice look easy, but it is not—as demonstrated by the Israelis' own failure to capture Josef Mengele, the infamous Nazi doctor who died in hiding in Brazil. In Somalia in 1993 a deadly ambush of a few UN soldiers led the United Nations (with U.S. concurrence) to try to seize the guilty Somali clan leader, General Farah Mohammed Aideed. He alluded capture as hundreds of Somali civilians died in gunbattles with UN-affiliated U.S. troops.

After the Bosnian War ended in 1995, NATO-led troops of the Dayton accords' Implementation Force (IFOR) and its follow-on Stabilization Force (SFOR) were supposed to seize suspected war criminals indicted by the ICTY, including the Bosnian-Serb leader, Radovan Karadzic, and his close subordinate, General Ratko Mladic. But IFOR was hesitant, despite its intimidating military strength, and likewise SFOR did not actively begin apprehending suspects until mid-1997. IFOR and SFOR worried that, by arresting Bosnian-Serbs, this might make their troops so hated by the Bosnian-Serb populace that they might fall victim to mass harassment and terrorism. Indeed, when SFOR did begin seizing suspects—individuals far less known than the locally popular Karadzic and Mladic—some SFOR troops were harassed, a few even physically harmed. But the seizures continued, especially in SFOR's British-patrolled sector. Later in 1999, in the ethnic Albanian and Serbian communities of Kosovo, KFOR and the local UN police arrested many suspects amid a much more supportive population—but only when the suspects belonged to the other ethnic group.

Many human rights groups assert that unless a society has a "culture of justice" upheld by an egalitarian rule of law, a "culture of impunity" may prevail, wherein the armed can brutalize the unarmed. They note that, in Western-type constitutional democracies, the classical philosophy of law and accountability found has worked relatively well. Raphael Lemkin spent his life promoting it. But whereas the international tribunals in Nuremberg, Tokyo, The Hague, and Arusha may have deterred some acts of genocide, an abundance of grisly history grimly illustrates what genocidal acts those tribunals also failed to deter. The ICTY's indictment of Slobodan Milosevic during the Kosovo War may have rendered him less excusable to support, embarrassing his Russian supporters in particular, but the ICTY's existence did not deter his regime from perpetrating war crimes in the first place. To internationally prosecute a few offenders may produce some practical benefits, but until those benefits are seen to outweigh the potentially immediate results of conditional amnesties or places of exile for tyrants, international tribunals may have as many critics as proponents.

A prudent compromise, therefore, could be a truth commission. While not applicable to every situation, a truth commission investigates and publicizes atrocities of the recent past, sometimes for the first time. Truth commissions in South Africa and Argentina did much to heal the societal wounds left by racial apartheid and the genocidal "Dirty War." The head of South Africa's Truth and Reconciliation Commission was the Archbishop Desmond Tutu, a Nobel Peace Prize laureate. Tutu explained the truth commission's underlying philosophy:

We seek to do justice without perpetuating the hatred aroused. We think of this as *restorative* justice. We recognize that the past can't be remade through punishment; instead, since we know that memories will persist for a long time, we aim to acknowledge those memories. . . . Restorative justice is different from *retributive* justice. Retributive justice will adjudicate guilt—then the case is closed. But restorative justice is about the profound inability of retributive justice to effect permanent closure on great human atrocities. To get justice, we must strive to undo the top-dog/underdog reversals that make human horror endure. There is no point exacting vengeance now, knowing that it will be the cause for future vengeance by the offspring of those we punish.[29]

To obtain much of its grisly information, the South African commission offered a potential amnesty to any perpetrator who made a detailed confession before the commission. No guarantees were offered, though many amnesties were granted. The confessions, widely publicized, shocked the public, including Tutu himself. Nevertheless, he explained, "I've been inspired that there also is the other side, the side of the magnanimity of people who are ready to reach out to make change and to forgive. So I have two lasting impressions: the horror of what we are able to do to each other, and almost exhilaration at the nobility of the human spirit that so many victims demonstrate."[30]

In the mid-1990s the ICTY acted as a sort of truth commission by widely publicizing the atrocities of the Bosnian War. The tribunal's proceedings were televised as investigators and prosecuting attorneys told the tribunal (and a global television audience) what war crimes had been committed in Bosnia, such as the Srebrenica massacre. One of the prime reasons the Israeli government publicized the trial of Adolf Eichmann—it was held in a large auditorium and televised globally—is because in 1961 the basic facts of the Holocaust were not as commonly known as they are today, in part because most of the survivors were still too traumatized to talk about their experiences. The world's sudden attention upon the dark notoriety of Eichmann, as well as his daring capture by Israeli agents, provided the Israeli government with an opportunity to expose the Holocaust as never before. Not even the Nuremberg trials, held fifteen years earlier, had focused so exclusively upon the Holocaust.

Whether or not a truth commission can help reconcile a postgenocide society may well depend upon how recent the genocide was, how long its killings went on, how many and exactly how its victims were killed, and how many survivors remain to testify. More importantly, unless enough people in that torn society want to be reconciled, victims and victimizers alike, there is little which a truth commission alone can do to help the healing process. A truth commission can try to encourage some psychological changes, but real reconciliation may well require sweeping political and economic changes throughout the society as a whole.[31]

NOTES

1. Dieter Fleck (editor), *The Handbook of Humanitarian Law in Armed Conflicts* (New York: Oxford University Press, 1995). Also see the website of the International Red Cross: www.icrc.org

2. Excerpts from Articles 3, 25, 27, 28, 46, 50, and 56 of the Annex to Hague Convention No. II ("Regulations Respecting the Laws and Customs of War on Land"), signed July 29, 1899.

3. Excerpts from Articles 17 and 23 of the Geneva Convention Relative to the Protection of Civilian Persons in Time of War, signed on August 12, 1949.

4. Excerpts from Articles 27, 32, and 33 of the Geneva Convention Relative to the Protection of Civilian Persons in Time of War, opened for signature on August 12, 1949.

5. Article 3 of the Geneva Convention Relative to the Protection of Civilian Persons in Time of War, opened for signature on August 12, 1949. The same provisions are repeated in Article 3 of the Geneva Convention for the Amelioration of the Condition of the Wounded and Sick in Armed Forces in the Field, opened for signature on August 12, 1949.

6. Excerpts from Articles 17, 51, 53, 54, and 70 of Protocol I, Additional to the Geneva Conventions of August 12, 1949, Relating to the Protection of Victims of International Armed Conflicts; opened for signature on June 8, 1977 and came into legal force on December 7, 1978.

7. Excerpts from Articles 1 and 4 of the Convention for the Protection of Cultural Property in the Event of Armed Conflict; signed on May 14, 1954 and came into legal force on August 7, 1956.

8. Excerpts from Article 4 of the International Convention on the Elimination of All Forms of Racial Discrimination; opened for signature on December 21, 1965 and came into legal force on January 4, 1969.

9. Excerpts from Articles 1, 2, and 6 of the International Covenant on Civil and

Political Rights; opened for signature on December 16, 1966 and came into legal force on March 23, 1976.

10. Excerpts from Articles 1 and 2 of the Convention against Torture and Other Cruel, Inhuman or Degrading Treatment or Punishment; adopted by the UN General Assembly in December 1984 and came into legal force on June 26, 1987.

11. Excerpts from Articles 2, 6 and 37 of the Convention on the Rights of the Child; adopted by the UN General Assembly on November 20, 1989.

12. Dean Acheson, *Present at the Creation: My Years in the State Department* (New York: W. W. Norton & Company, 1969), p. 450.

13. Those European countries and former Soviet republics are: Albania, Andorra, Armenia, Austria, Azerbaijan, Belarus, Belgium, Bosnia-Herzegovina, Bulgaria, Croatia, Cyprus, the Czech Republic, Denmark, Estonia, Finland, France, Georgia, Germany, Greece, Hungary, Iceland, Ireland, Italy, Kazakhstan, the Kyrgyz Republic, Latvia, Liechtenstein, Lithuania, Luxembourg, Macedonia, Malta, Moldova, Monaco, the Netherlands (Holland), Norway, Poland, Portugal, Romania, the Russian Federation, San Marino, Slovakia, Slovenia, Spain, Sweden, Tajikistan, Turkmenistan, Ukraine, the United Kingdom, Uzbekistan, and the "new" Federal Republic of Yugoslavia. Switzerland and the Holy See (the Vatican) are not members of the United Nations, but both have a non-voting observer status.

14. The countries of Latin America are: Argentina, Belize, Bolivia, Brazil, Chile, Colombia, Costa Rica, Cuba, Ecuador, El Salvador, Guatemala, Guyana, Honduras, Mexico, Nicaragua, Panama, Peru, Suriname, Uruguay, and Venezuela. The Caribbean countries are: Antigua and Barbuda, the Bahamas, Barbados, Cuba, Dominica, the Dominican Republic, Grenada, Haiti, Jamaica, Saint Kitts and Nevis, Saint Lucia, Saint Vincent and the Grenadines, and Trinidad and Tobago.

15. The countries of East Asia and the Pacific are: Australia, Bangladesh, Bhutan, Brunei Darussalam, Cambodia, the People's Republic of China, Fiji, India, Indonesia, Japan, Kiribati, North Korea, South Korea, Laos, Malaysia, Maldives, the Marshall Islands, Micronesia, Mongolia, Myanmar (Burma), Nauru, Nepal, New Zealand, Pakistan, Palau, Papua New Guinea, the Philippines, Samoa, Singapore, the Solomon Islands, Sri Lanka, Thailand, Tonga, Tuvalu, Vanuatu, and Vietnam.

16. Afghanistan, Bahrain, Egypt, Iran, Iraq, Israel, Jordan, Kuwait, Lebanon, Libya, Oman, Qatar, Saudi Arabia, Syria, Turkey, the United Arab Emirates (UAE), and Yemen.

17. Algeria, Angola, Benin, Burkina Faso, Burundi, Cameroon, Cape Verde, the Central African Republic, Chad, Comoros, Congo, Republic of (capital at Brazzaville), Congo, Democratic Republic of (capital at Kinshasa; formerly the country of Zaire), Cote d'Ivoire (Ivory Coast), Djibouti, Equatorial Guinea, Eritrea, Ethiopia, Gabon, Gambia, Ghana, Guinea, Guinea-Bissau, Kenya, Lesotho, Liberia, Madagascar, Malaysia, Mali, Mauritania, Mauritius, Morocco, Mozambique, Namibia, Niger, Nigeria, Rwanda, Sao Tome and Principe, Senegal, Seychelles, Sierra Leone, Somalia, South Africa, Sudan, Swaziland, Tanzania, Togo, Tunisia, Uganda, Zambia, and Zimbabwe.

18. Soo Yeon Kim and Bruce Russett, "The new politics of voting alignments in the United Nations General Assembly," *International Organization* (Autumn 1996), Vol. 50, No. 4, pp. 629-652.

19. UN figures were taken from *Setting the Record Straight: Facts about the United Nations* (New York: UN Department of Public Information, August 1997).

20. New York City government employment figures taken from Mayor Rudolph W. Giuliani (and edited by E.C. Robbins), *The Green Book 1996-97: Official Directory of the City of New York* (New York: City Publishing Center, 1997), pp. 600-601.

21. All figures from *Setting the Record Straight.*

22. Ibid.

23. "Former U.S. Secretaries of State Urge Congress to Pay U.S. Debt to United Nations," PR Newswire (March 18, 1999)

24. Jean-Jacques Frank, "Louise Arbour: 'I Am Not Bluffing'," *Brussels Le Soir* (May 28, 1999), p. 8. In French.

25. Alan Zarembo, "Judgement Day: In Rwanda, 92,392 genocide suspects await trial," *Harper's* (April 1997), pp. 68-74.

26. Quoted in Hannah Arendt, *Eichmann in Jerusalem: A Report on the Banality of Evil* (New York: Viking Press, 1963-64), pp. 277-279.

27. Raphael Lemkin (unsigned), "Genocide: A Commentary on the Convention," *The Yale Law Review*, Vol. 58:1142 (1949), p. 1150.

28. Jesse Helms, "And After Pinochet?" *Washington Post* (December 10, 1998), p. A-31.

29. Colin Greer, "Without Memory, There Is No Healing. Without Forgiveness, There Is No Future" (An Interview with Bishop Desmond Tutu), *Parade Magazine* (January 11, 1998). pp. 4-6.

30. Ibid.

31. Michael Ignatieff, Z.C.A. Luyendijk, and James Brittain, "How can past sins by absolved? Truth commissions can find out the truth but they cannot change the military apparatus or society," *Index on Censorship* (Sept/Oct 1996); reprinted in *World Press Review* (February 1997), p. 6-8.

4

Forecasting and Detection of Genocide

The capacity to anticipate and analyze possible conflicts is a prerequisite for prudent decision-making and effective action. Indicators of imminent violence include widespread human rights abuses, increasingly brutal political oppression, inflammatory use of the media, the accumulation of arms, and sometimes a rash of organized killings. This was certainly true of the violence in Rwanda and Bosnia in the first half of the 1990s.

— Report of the Carnegie Commission on Preventing Deadly Conflict, 1997

There was no question of a lack of early warning; there always is in situations such as these, whether in the form of journalist, human rights, or relief agency reports.

— Edward Girardet, a veteran journalist recalling the genocide in Rwanda

In December 1998, in the fiftieth anniversary year of the Genocide Convention, U.S. President Bill Clinton announced his administration's intention to create a Genocide Early Warning System (GEWS) that would use secret and nonsecret reports to forecast and detect places of possible genocide. It was not a new idea. In 1977, two Israeli social scientists, Israel Charny and Chanan Rapaport, had proposed such an idea wherein a central information center could receive, categorize, and investigate reports of trouble. After a careful analysis of the data, the center could then warn of particular dangers in particular countries.[1] In 1985 a similar proposal was made in a United Nations study. Concerned with how to better enforce the Genocide Convention, that UN study said:

In cases where evidence appears of an impending genocidal conflict—mounting repression, increasing polarization, or the first indications of an unexpected case—an effective early warning system could help save several thousands of lives. This requires an efficient coordinating network, maintained in a state of permanent readiness, which could possibly also watch for early indications of mass famine and exoduses of refugees in conjunction with bodies such as the Office of the United Nations Disaster Relief Coordinator and the International Committee of the Red Cross. . . . Intelligent anticipation of potential cases could be based on a databank of continuously updated information which might enable remedial, deterrent, or averting measures to be planned ahead.[2]

The GEWS project initiated by Clinton did not have much time to warn of the trouble then-brewing in Kosovo, but the later Kosovo War of 1999 can be seen as a lesson more than a failure. The lesson is this: having three or four months of early warning, while better than no warning at all, is not much time to prevent a genocide. For instance, to arrange a multinational peacekeeping force typically takes the UN at least three months of planning and preparation—and that is after the Security Council has debated the issue and agreed to act. Ideally, therefore, a genocide early warning system should forecast a genocide, or at least genocidal trouble, several months or even years in advance. Since the forecast needs only to be credible, not a prophecy, this is not too ambitious a timetable. If it encourages preventive action, the forecast succeeds by not coming true.

SOURCES OF INFORMATION

The Cold War encouraged the development of some remarkable forms of intelligence collection, most famously overhead "spy" satellites. But whereas overhead photography might reveal a mass grave, and a radio intercept might reveal an incriminating conversation, these are neither timely nor reliable means of detecting a genocide. Moreover, the budgets of secret intelligence agencies have their limits, limits that necessitate prioritizing. Most governments prefer to give a higher priority to their own national security needs, narrowly defined, than to searching for a foreign genocide beyond their borders.

Fortunately, there is an inexpensive alternative to secret sources.

In the early 1980s the U.S. Central Intelligence Agency (CIA) was directed by William Casey, an eccentric, well-read man who during World War II had worked for the CIA's predecessor, the Office of Strategic Services (OSS). Casey's CIA deputy was Robert Gates, a future CIA director himself. In Gates' later memoirs, he wrote admiringly of Casey's detailed knowledge of current events, statistics, and facts—impressive even for a man who headed the CIA. "Bill Casey was one of the smartest people I have ever known and certainly the most intellectually lively," Gates wrote. "He subscribed to newsletters and information sheets that I sometimes thought couldn't have more than five readers in the world, and then he would ask if I had seen one or another item in them. . . . Too often at CIA, people would dismiss an unconventional view or criticism because of the source or because one or another element of a presentation was flawed or mistaken. Casey, more than anyone I ever knew, was able to separate the few grains of wheat from a pile of intellectual chaff and make a conversation or something he read worth his while." [3]

Among intelligence professionals, what Casey read is called *unclassified information*; the more technical term for it is *open source reporting*. The best information that he gleaned from it—the "wheat" from the "chaff" in Gates' words—is called *open source intelligence* (OSINT). Although in Casey's day the Information Age was only just beginning, even in his day there was enough valuable information available that Casey believed that it complemented, and sometimes even surpassed, what the CIA could provide him from its secret sources.

Since then the Information Age has become an information flood, although most of its data is either irrelevant, inaccurate, or in some other way not helpful. Who reads literally every article, advertisement, and want ad in the average daily newspaper? Only a portion of that newspaper pertains to any particular subject, and only a fraction of that portion may actually be helpful. And a newspaper is designed to be convenient; not all open source reporting is. An Internet search of the word *genocide* is likely to pull up a cornucopia of unhelpful references, including hard-rock music bands and computer network games all named "Genocide" as well as websites about the Holocaust, the Cambodian "killing fields," and the Armenian massacres. To find any usable OSINT amid all the open source reporting available requires a trained analyst who knows where to look and what to look for. The untrained novice will typically gather everything even remotely related to the subject and become overwhelmed by a mass of data that may appear relevant but which, in fact, obscures what is really needed. The collection effort must be focused and selective.

Hate Literature and Propaganda

The first publicly available indication of a group's genocidal intentions can be its own ideological or religious literature. That of Nazism, Marxism-Leninism, Arab Baathism, Rwandan "Hutu Power," and Serbian ultranationalism appeared years before the genocides those ideologies spawned, indeed years before their followers achieved political power. Even a cursory review of such literature can reveal some ominous ideas. In the case of Hitler's (notoriously boring) book *Mein Kampf* ("My Struggle"), even an analyst without the patience to read through every page can still see that almost every chapter expresses hatred, tyrannical notions, and anti-Semitism.

But the hate literature of a contemporary foreign group, especially a small one, can be difficult to obtain and may not be available in English or any European language. And since there are a very large number of hate groups worldwide, only a fraction of whom will ever become a major political menace, the analyst must be selective, investigating particular hate groups only when each becomes large enough, or at least vocal enough, to warrant attention.

In some cases this may not happen until that group has already achieved power, unfortunately. Thereafter, though, even the most secretive of genocidal regimes must spout propaganda to promote its agenda. Its propaganda might be mixed with talk of peace, as the Nazis' initially was, or attempts might be made to channel it towards a particular audience, as in Rwanda in the early 1990s, when hateful anti-Tutsi radio broadcasts were aired in the country's indigenous language while more conciliatory messages, to deceive foreign listeners, were broadcast in French. Nevertheless, a core of hateful propaganda exists, it is publicly available, and it can become an important clue in forecasting a genocide. It might even declare a regime's genocidal intentions outright; at the very least, it can reveal what groups the regime despises.

The News Media

Most contemporary genocides are detected early by the international news media, although the coverage can be sparse. One might expect that a genocidal regime would not tolerate any press freedom, and this is true in some countries such as Saddam Hussein's Iraq. Yet even totalitarian countries have hosted the presence of foreign correspondents, including Nazi Germany, the Soviet Union, Khomeini's Iran, and even Hussein's Iraq. Many foreign correspondents live in the country they cover, usually in its capital. Moreover, in countries where even a little press freedom is permitted, some of the best reporters available are native journalists. They know how to operate in their own country, they watch its social and political trends, and for the sake of their own professional ethics they are often willing to investigate politically sensitive stories, despite threats of harassment or censorship. Even as Slobodan Milosevic's Yugoslavia kept Serbian television under state control and promoted newspapers that spouted the party line, the regime allowed independent newspapers and even radio stations a surprisingly high degree of press freedom. Articles by independent newspapers and journalists, if interesting, are sometimes cited, summarized or even reprinted verbatim by international newswire services, such as The Associated Press, Reuters, and Agence France-Presse.

Also available are television news organizations, among them Cable News Network (CNN). In general, however, television news tends not to be very timely for genocide-detection purposes. For a story to be considered "worthy" of television coverage, television producers must make the story photogenic, summarize it in brief sound bites, have no other story more "news worthy" to broadcast in its place, and hope the viewing audience finds the story interesting, for otherwise they may not broadcast such a story again. By the time these broadcast requirements are fulfilled by a genocide-related story, such as a massacre, the larger crisis underlying that massacre is usually already days, weeks, or even months old.

Television is, at base, an entertainment medium, subject to the pressures of commercial marketing. More informational scope and depth can be found in the world's major newspapers, but they, too, face these marketing pressures. Edward Girardet, editor of the journal *Crosslines Global Report* and a co-founder of Media Action International, elaborates:

In Rwanda, although a small group of foreign correspondents from newspapers ranging from *Le Monde* to *The New York Times* reported events leading up to the massacres in early 1994, it took the concept of genocide—the deliberate destruction of human life based on ethnic, racial, or religious discrimination—to convince most editors finally to cover the story. There was no question of a lack of early warning; there always is in situations such as these, whether in the form of journalist, human rights, or relief agency reports. The policymakers failed to take heed and the editors (notably in television) refused to budge until various circumstances, including a host of reporters on their way back from the elections in South Africa, decided that they had a salable "humanitarian" story.[4]

Journalists, whether native or foreign, tend to put into their reports only a fraction of what they really know or at least suspect, even when not subject to censorship. A genocide early warning system should therefore seek them out to interview them, not merely read their reports in print. Their answers then need to be compared, both to others' answers and to other pieces of information, to assess their accuracy and credibility.

Non-Governmental Organizations

A non-governmental organization (NGO) is a private, generally not-for-profit group devoted to improving human welfare through charitable assistance, economic development, or political reform. Perhaps the most famous is the International Committee of the Red Cross (ICRC), which provides humanitarian assistance to victims of conflict and encourages the warring sides to adhere to the international laws of war, particularly the Geneva Conventions. To stay ready to respond to a crisis on short notice almost anywhere in the world, the ICRC has representatives all over the globe, supplying its Geneva headquarters with assessments of ongoing crises and early warning data about places to which the ICRC may soon render assistance. Other major relief-aid NGOs, such as CARE and *Medecins Sans Frontieres* ("Doctors Without Borders"), have contacts of their own and, in the countries where they have a presence, know the situation because they work within it. They are often eager to share their concerns about the dangerous trends they see.

Even more eager to share their concerns are NGOs that monitor human rights. Some, such as Human Rights Watch and Amnesty International, are global in their coverage, monitoring every country to uncover at least the most severe of human rights abuses. Other NGOs are more specialized. Physicians for Human Rights (PHR) uses medical science, including forensics, to investigate atrocities. Freedom House is known for its ratings of political liberty per country. Some NGOs cover entire regions, such as *Derechos* for Latin America. Quite a few NGOs, such as Human Rights in China (HRIC), are country-specific.

Almost anyone anywhere can call himself a human rights NGO; there are no formal requirements for objectivity, nor even for accuracy. For this reason the largest NGOs, having developed a reputation for reliable documentation, tend to be the most credible. But a small NGO is not necessarily an amateur NGO; several are especially competent and knowledgeable, and on occasion consulted by the larger NGOs. A few small NGOS, including the PIOOM Foundation and International Alert, have combined their efforts to form a genocide-related early warning organization of their own, the Forum for Early Warning and Early Response (FEWER).

Religious Groups

Religious groups are usually among the first people to learn of a religious persecution, especially against their own faith. Religious groups are not generally called NGOs, but the difference between them is negligible if not nonexistent. One anti-slavery NGO is even named Christian Solidarity International (CSI). Tibetan Buddhist groups have long monitored events in Chinese-occupied Tibet, while the Baha'i International organization watches the situation of the Baha'i faithful in Iran and elsewhere. Jewish groups are concerned about anti-Semitism anywhere in the world. The Roman Catholic Church has a network of churches and Catholic groups that is global, present in almost every country.

International Organizations

International organizations, most notably within the United Nations system, offer further possible sources for genocide early warning. UN agencies have employees all over the world, including its most volatile places. In this regard the employees of the UN High Commissioner for Refugees (UNHCR) and the World Food Program (WFP) are especially active. Many of their activities are coordinated via the Secretariat's Office for the Coordination of Humanitarian Affairs (OCHA). Like the International Red Cross, these UN entities monitor international crises, often with employees either there or nearby, to remain ready to respond on short notice.

The United Nations also has entities and officials specifically responsible for the investigation and promotion of human rights issues, most notably the Office of the UN High Commissioner for Human Rights (OHCHR). A few human rights officials report directly to the UN Secretary-General; there is, for example, a "Representative of the Secretary-General on Internally Displaced Persons" and a "Special Representative of the Secretary-General for Children and Armed Conflict."

A *special rapporteur* is an issue-specific investigator, typically a university professor on loan to the UN for a period of weeks, months, or years. He or she visits the relevant country, or countries, to talk with government and opposition leaders, local UN personnel, NGOs, the news media, and others with pertinent information. A report is then produced that can be very informative. A few countries with especially notorious regimes have a special rapporteur specifically assigned; there is a Special Rapporteur on Human Rights in Iraq, for example. Others monitor genocide-related issues in several countries. There is a Special Rapporteur on Religious Intolerance; a Special Rapporteur on Contemporary Forms of Racism, Racial Discrimination, Xenophobia and Related Intolerance; a Special Rapporteur on Extrajudicial, Summary or Arbitrary Executions; a Special Rapporteur on Torture; a Special Rapporteur on Violence against Women; a Special Rapporteur on the Sale of Children, Child Prostitution and Child Pornography; as well as a Special Rapporteur on the Independence of Judges and Lawyers. Most of their reports are publicly available.

Many human rights treaties, such as the International Covenant on Civil and Political Rights, require that their signature-countries (actually, those countries' governments) submit an annual report to a UN panel on how well that country is complying. That government's report may consist of nothing but propaganda, but it is a piece of open source reporting, and the reaction of the receiving panel can be quite revealing as well. In 1999 the regime of the Democratic Republic of the Congo (DRC) submitted a self-report required by the Convention on the Elimination of All Forms of Racial Discrimination. The reaction of the receiving panel was as blunt as most diplomats permit themselves to be: "The Committee on the Elimination of Racial Discrimination . . . expressed deep concern about the persistence, in flagrant violation of the Convention, of ethnic conflicts [in the DRC] which were in general inspired by a policy of ethnic cleansing and might constitute acts of genocide." [5]

Confirming that a genocidal threat does indeed exist can be one of the most important services provided by the UN and other international organizations. Although many different unofficial sources, from NGOs to knowledgeable individuals, can warn of a genocide, their reports need to be verified and perhaps elaborated upon by trained investigators having international legitimacy and credibility. A special fact-finding team of about a dozen or so investigators per case is probably sufficient. Ideally they should be protected by diplomatic immunity, *de facto* if not *de jure,* as well as legally empowered by a legitimate international mandate. On occasion the UN High Commissioner for Human Rights has, herself, led fact-finding missions.

Academia

Academia consists of independent research institutes as well as universities. Throughout academia there are professors, graduate students, university fellows, and others who specialize in knowing a particular foreign country. They speak its language, have personal friends and contacts there, and monitor its current events. Quite a few of them read and indeed analyze the propaganda and related literature of its regime and of other important groups. If asked, many of these individuals are quite willing to relate their impressions and concerns about human rights.

Since genocide is a problem that can be studied from several different intellectual perspectives, several academic disciplines can be consulted aside from the obvious ones, such as political science. At Harvard University, for example, the Harvard School of Public Health is very concerned about the problem of genocide and has done some insightful research. Anthropologists are also concerned; the American Anthropological Association even has a Committee for Human Rights, responsible for studying and promoting action against "ethnic cleansing" and other human rights abuses. Sociologists, law professors, criminologists, and even theologians have studied the problem of genocide. Their insights are as worthy of review as those of political scientists and Holocaust scholars.

There are also academic institutes devoted solely to the study of genocide. A comprehensive *Encyclopedia of Genocide* has been produced by the Institute on the Holocaust and Genocide, located in Jerusalem. The Institute for the Study of Genocide (ISG), based in the John Jay College of Criminal Justice at the City

University of New York, has been a pioneer in the field of genocide studies. So, too, has the Montreal Institute for Genocide and Human Rights Studies (MIGS), based in the Departments of History and Sociology at Concordia University in Montreal.[6] There are numerous other centers and institutes, and likewise many genocide scholars. There is even an Association of Genocide Scholars (AGS), many of whom seek to develop predictive theories to forecast the crime.

NOTIONS VERSUS FACTS

Notions are subjective perceptions and opinions of what seems true without necessarily being true. In a field as emotionally sensitive as genocide studies, including Holocaust studies, there are a great many opinions, and consequently quite a few notions of what causes genocide and what to watch for. Many of these notions seem to reflect the inner good wishes of the people who believe them—such as the wish to alleviate global poverty, or to provide people with humane forms of birth control—but these notions are not necessarily based on an objective analysis of the relevant facts.

For example, the notion that economic upheaval can cause a genocide is based, at least in part, on the idea that if Germany's Weimar Republic had not suffered through hyperinflation and then the Great Depression, leaving enough Germans desperate enough to seek a radical change in their lives, the Nazis might never have been elected to power. This notion, when used for forecasting, is very amenable to trend-oriented statistical measurements and is therefore potentially predictive. But the relationship between economics and genocide is not always straightforward. Propaganda can exploit economic resentments, especially during an election campaign, but severe economic troubles do not necessarily cause mass murder; indeed, they rarely do, for otherwise genocides would be as frequent as business cycles. Even during the Great Depression in Weimar Germany, the rising Nazi Party won only 38 percent of the vote in its last free election. Not a majority, only a plurality, though it permitted Hitler to politically maneuver himself to become Germany's next chancellor. Hitler achieved power as much through luck and political tactics as he did through economics.

That said, at least some relationship does seem to exist between economics and genocide. The Nazi regime, and likewise many Marxist-Leninist regimes, did avidly confiscate the property of the groups they persecuted and, as a result, amassed immense amounts of wealth. But did those regimes plunder their victims—and then murder them—solely because the overall economy was in trouble? Or were there other reasons as well? Though the Nazi regime did abolish Jewish legal rights soon after Hitler achieved power in 1933, it was not until early 1942 that the Final Solution officially began, when the Third Reich was economically thriving because it ruled most of Europe. Earlier, in the mid-1920s and 1930s, the Soviet Union experienced several years of substantial economic growth—and yet that was when Stalin's regime inflicted one of the largest campaigns of human destruction in history: the deadly collectivization, and often starvation, of the Soviet Union's peasantry, followed by the Great

Purges. Many genocidal regimes have preferred to impoverish their countries rather than stop a genocide that, in cold economic terms, is no longer profitable.

Overpopulation is another notion commonly presumed to cause genocide, via an intense competition for limited space and resources. In propaganda, at least, it has certainly been used as an excuse for genocide: Hitler asserted that the German nation needed more *lebensraum* ("living space"), and so he started World War II. Any contemporary leader who calls for the equivalent of more *lebensraum* ought to be watched with concern. But analysts should be careful about attributing any particular genocide, such as Rwanda's in 1994, to a cause as simplistic as "overpopulation." Overpopulation alone does not explain every genocide.

In 1925 the Soviet Union was the world's largest contiguous country, a landmass spread over eleven time zones, with a population recently decreased by several millions due to the massive casualties and emigration caused by the First World War, the subsequent Russian Civil War, and by the first years of Communist rule. Finding a vacant apartment may have been an urban problem in a few Soviet cities, but by 1925 the overall Soviet economy was recovering well and overpopulation was not a countrywide problem. Yet it was in 1925 that Stalin initiated mass collectivization. Nor does overpopulation explain why Stalin later purged the Soviet Communist Party and Red Army.

One might assume that overpopulation would cause genocide for the same reason that overcrowded cities often have high rates of crime. With the possible exception of a race riot, however, most city crimes are not acts of genocide. Genocide is the attempted mass murder of an entire group (or group identity) based on some ethnic, religious, or political criteria—a group publicly targeted to be a scapegoat. Such a group is not a collection of utterly random victims, mugged by random muggers, as though any victim will suffice, regardless of one's ethnic or religious background. While an analysis of demographic trends may reveal something for genocide forecasting, those demographic trends must not become the forecast itself.

The core of the forecasting effort needs to be the identification of group identities and how they are being politically manipulated, because group identities and politics ("identity politics") define what a genocide truly is: the intentional destruction of a *particular* group, not an incidental group. The Final Solution was perpetrated by Nazis against Jews, not by anyone against anyone else. That may sound obvious, but only because the Holocaust is so well known today. A future genocide in Africa, Asia, or even Europe may not be so well known, not at first, at least not by outsiders, and that ignorance can encourage outsiders to assume that the killings must be due to some simplistic notion like "overpopulation."

OCCUPATIONAL STEREOTYPES

Another common notion about genocide is that some occupations are more conformist, more violent, and hence more potentially genocidal than others. This notion, though some evidence does support it, can nevertheless lead to some counterproductive stereotyping unless the analyst (or, indeed, anyone) is willing to consider possibilities that contradict the apparent norm, being neither cynical nor naïve, but simply skeptical. As an example, military and police institutions have a conformist, sometimes violent "culture." In countries where severe abuses of human rights have occurred, these institutions are frequently culpable, and for reason they should be watched in every country. However, the stereotype that almost anyone who pursues a military or police career has a violent nature likely to perpetrate human rights abuses—especially in comparison to the apparently more civilized fields of art, music, philosophy, literature, medicine, law, or academia—is simply false.

It might come as a surprise to learn the original occupations of people who later orchestrated the worst genocides of the twentieth century. Adolf Hitler began as an aspiring artist. Joseph Goebbels, his propaganda minister, wanted to be a journalist and novelist. Heinrich Himmler, the notorious chief of the SS, began as a part-time chicken farmer. Reinhard Heydrich, Himmler's deputy, entered the SS as a disgraced naval lieutenant, expelled for seducing a shipyard owner's daughter and refusing to marry her. Adolf Eichmann, Heydrich's deputy, began as a traveling salesman for an oil company. Martin Bormann, Hitler's infamous deputy, was once a farm hand. Joseph Mengele, the man who performed gruesome medical experiments upon human prisoners in Auschwitz, was a genuine physician who had earned his medical degree while also earning a degree in philosophy. Slave labor was exploited in the Nazi ministries of both Robert Ley, an ex-chemist and trade unionist, and Albert Speer, an architect. Alfred Rosenberg, the Nazi "philosopher" of the Party's anti-Semitic ideology, likewise had an architect's degree. Hans Frank, the Nazi overlord of Poland, began as a lawyer.

Some Nazi leaders had military experience, others did not. Herman Goering distinguished himself in World War I as a fighter pilot. Adolf Hitler, literally in the trenches at that time, earned one of Germany's highest medals—the Iron Cross, First Class—but in rank Hitler rose only as high as corporal. Of the original Nazi leaders, only the very old General Erich Ludendorff, retired after World War I, had had a professional military career—and by the 1930s he was so mentally unbalanced that Hitler wanted almost nothing to do with him. Ludendorff died in 1937. Many German war veterans, unemployed after World War I, were attracted to the ultranationalist, pro-labor rhetoric of the Nazi movement. But within the German Army itself, particularly among its generals, there was a general suspicion of the Nazis and their anti-elitist tone. Many German officers did not support Hitler until he decimated the leadership of the Nazis' brown-shirted thug force, the SA, considered an unruly rival to the Army.

Of the Marxist-Leninists, Vladimir Lenin began as a lawyer, Joseph Stalin studied for the priesthood at an East Orthodox Christian seminary, Genrikh Yagoda (who headed Stalin's secret police) began as a pharmacist, Nikolai Yezhov (who replaced Yagoda) labored as a semi-literate factory worker, Lavrenti Beria (who replaced Yezhov) studied industrial engineering, Mao Zedong studied the Chinese classics, and Pol Pot studied carpentry and later radio electronics. Some were born to middle-class backgrounds, others were the sons of peasant farmers. Some had military experience; others, notably Lenin, did not. What all of them did have in common was, not the military, but their passionate activism in student politics. All of them became Marxists while they were still young adults.

Radovan Karadzic began as a practicing psychiatrist; during the Bosnian War, he was indicted as the Bosnian-Serb leader responsible for ordering acts of genocidal "ethnic cleansing." In Rwanda, prior to its genocide in 1994, many ethnic Hutu professors promoted a socioracial theory that was considered, at least in Rwanda, to be academically respectable—a theory that called for Hutu supremacy and a hatred for all ethnic Tutsi.[7]

Technicians, architects, engineers, businessmen, bureaucrats, academicians, physicians, scientists, media consultants, writers, railway employees, common laborers, soldiers and police—all these occupations were needed to perpetrate the Holocaust, as well as other genocides. In any genocide the involvement of soldiers and policemen should not be ignored, but neither should their roles be exaggerated. Political directives and hateful propaganda play decisive roles, roles that are not necessarily performed by soldiers and policemen.

The stereotype that literally everyone in uniform automatically approves of the cruelest policies of their government can blind one to opportunities to sow and exploit dissent within a genocidal regime. Many people wanted to depose Hitler, but the group that came closest to succeeding were anti-Nazi conspirators within Germany's own traditional armed forces. Among the supporters of those conspirators was Hitler's own chief of military intelligence, Admiral Wilhelm Canaris, chief of the *Abwehr*. More recently, in Myanmar in the 1990s, the Burmese democracy movement led by Aung San Suu Kyi, herself the daughter of a general, included several retired generals as her closest colleagues—all of them opposed to Myanmar's military dictatorship. And in Serbia in 2000, the popular uprising that deposed Slobodan Milosevic was secretly spearheaded by current and former members of elite military and police units. Said one such member at that time, "In the special forces, mostly the chiefs are for Milosevic. The 72nd brigade was guarding Milosevic all the time. It's still responsible for his security—and within that guard about 70 percent do not support him." [8]

In some countries, simply because the national leader wears a military-type uniform does not necessarily mean that he has a military background. Saddam Hussein of Iraq liked to wear military uniforms, portraying himself as a great military leader of the Arab world, but he never spent a day in genuine military service. In the 1980s, during the Iran-Iraq War, if an Iraqi general became extremely successful at winning victories on the battlefield, Hussein, rather than be pleased that he had a winning general under his command, treated that general as a potential political rival and had him executed. Hussein refused to let anyone other than himself win the war. Consequently, the war dragged on for eight bloody years.

A few decades ago, Harvard professor Samuel Huntington published what has become an influential book on the subject of military attitudes in the modern era, *The Soldier and the State*. After studying the military profession, he concluded:

The military man tends to see himself as the perennial victim of civilian warmongering. It is the people and the politicians, public opinion and governments, who start wars. It is the military who have to fight them. Civilian philosophers, publicists, academicians, not soldiers, have been the romanticizers and glorifiers of war. For the professional military man, familiar with war, this type of mentality has little appeal.[9]

No less an authority than Hitler himself has substantiated this conclusion. More than once, Hitler complained, his German General Staff had "opposed rearmament, the occupation of the Rhineland, the invasion of Austria, the occupation of Czechoslovakia, and finally even the invasion of Poland. The General Staff advised me not to make war on Russia. It is I who always have first to urge [it] on." [10]

Most national military institutions have long distinguished histories with very proud traditions, usually much older than the current regime in power. Having a proud heritage has not kept military institutions out of politics, but in even totalitarian societies it has given those institutions a relative independence, especially when a narrowly military concern is at stake. After some of Iran's Army units were used to suppress a local uprising in 1995, a few courageous Iranian generals sent an extraordinary letter of complaint to Iran's ruling mullahs. "The role of a country's armed forces," the generals' letter declared, "is to defend its borders and to repel foreign enemies from its soil, not to control the internal situation or to strengthen one political faction against another." [11]

This relative independence of the military as a self-perceived guardian of the nation, though not necessarily of the State, is a major reason why dictators such as Stalin and Hussein have inflicted genocide against even their own soldiers. Stalin's Great Purges murdered or imprisoned approximately half of the entire Soviet officer corps: some 30,000 professional military officers, including most of the USSR's best generals and admirals. (They were sorely missed when Nazi Germany invaded the USSR in 1941.) Such dictators, needing a force they can more readily trust, have also been known to create their own personalized militaries: the NKVD/KGB troops of the USSR, the Republican Guard of Iraq, the *Waffen-SS* of Nazi Germany, the paramilitary units of Milosevic's Serbia—with names like the White Eagles, the Gray Wolves, and the Serbian Volunteer Guard ("Arkan's Tigers"). Treated as an elite rival to the traditional military, the very existence of this alternative force, along with its special privileges and elite mystique, all depend upon the future survival of the regime—a fact that its members are well aware of, energizing their dedication.

Having an alternative force can create perils of its own, however. When the guards doubt the benefits of their leader's continued rule, they may dispose of that leader they are supposed to protect. Such a betrayal may have occurred in 1994, when the Rwandan Army's Presidential Guard refused to permit any investigation into a suspicious airplane crash that killed Rwanda's president, returning from a Hutu-Tutsi peace conference. The Presidential Guard, more politically extremist than militarily proficient, then initiated the genocide of that year. But while Rwanda's Regular Army and its irregular *Interahamwe* militia also participated in that genocide, not every member actively did so. Many, courageously, did not.

The stereotype of the utterly obedient military automaton is only that—a stereotype. No military or police organization has ever succeeded in turning human beings into true automatons. Strict obedience is always, at its core, an individual choice.

INDICATORS OF GENOCIDE

Some forecasting models have been developed by the scholars who study genocide as a phenomenon. By comparing and contrasting different genocides to obtain empirical data, they have uncovered what they call *indicators*, which are events or preconditions in a society. Each active indicator marks another step toward a genocide.

The models tend to be very elaborate, but their underlying premises are easily summarized. A society at risk of experiencing a genocide has few if any checks and balances restraining its regime; in other words, dictatorships have much more capacity for genocide than do constitutional democracies. The risk is even higher if the society is psychologically and sociologically stratified into potentially rival group identities. The risk is higher still if at least one of those group identities practices morality in ways that deny the dignity of their perceived enemies, such as with mass contempt or hatred. This usually reflects a quasi-religious ideology such as Nazism or Marxism-Leninism.

History is also indicative. If, in the past thirty years, genocidal acts were committed in that society and were socially rewarded (i.e., the perpetrators were punished lightly, if at all), then a definite danger exists that those acts will be repeated. Indeed, those acts may be gruesomely exceeded if, in the past four years, that society's government has either broken down or, instead, has entrenched its power by violating human rights on a large scale. Outwardly, the last noticeable indication before an organized genocide begins could be the start of a war, a rebellion, or a very intense propaganda campaign that portrays a particular group (a group identity) as a demonic enemy and public scapegoat.

Trying to guess the specific day a genocide may begin can be extremely difficult, but for even this goal there are some forecasting models. Barbara Harff, a political science professor at the U.S. Naval Academy, is the scholar who coined the term *politicide* to describe purely political mass murders. Collaborating with her husband, Ted Robert Gurr, head of the genocide-related Minorities at Risk Project at the University of Maryland, Harff has studied what are called *processual models*. In 1998, she wrote:

At the most basic, processual models are based on the assumption that all conflicts proceed through stages of development, similar to life cycles, [although] this process is obviously not inevitable. . . . Triggers are the equivalent of a match thrown onto a combustible pile, whereas accelerators are the gasoline poured on the pile making it combustible.

Certain events cluster prior to the outbreak of geno/politicide and . . . some events influence either crisis escalation or de-escalation. . . . In Rwanda, a last international mediating effort led to a brief lull in violence, only to explode (10 days later) into genocide. . . . In Bosnia, verbal international criticism of Serbs encouraged their defiance and led to increases in aggressive posturing by Bosnian-Muslims, then to violent clashes with Serbs and a spiraling of violence.

The results suggest an important policy lesson. In [each] case, low-key international support for targeted groups increased the violence used by perpetrators. Evenhanded mediation or forceful intervention are credible alternative strategies. However, well-intentioned international meddling not backed up by credible tactics and strategies is potentially deadly to the targeted groups.[12]

Even without forecasting models, the day when a genocide will likely begin can sometimes be guessed. This is possible when the date of an obviously related event is publicly scheduled. In the case of East Timor, a UN-supervised referendum on independence from Indonesia was scheduled for August 30, 1999. As the referendum day approached, pro-Indonesian militias supported by elements in the Indonesian Army increasingly brutalized many Timorese to frighten them from voting. It was easy to predict that the coming referendum could be followed by even worse violence, especially if most Timorese voted for independence. And that prediction turned out to be true.

ASSESSING THE PERPETRATOR'S COMMITMENT

Once a place at risk of experiencing a genocide is identified, along with its relevant group identities, the next step toward crafting a preventive response is to assess the dedication of that genocide's would-be perpetrators, especially its leaders.

A regime willing to commit genocide is not a typical dictatorship. A typical dictatorship has relatively few domestic opponents and, so long as it retains its authoritarian powers, can even tolerate a few opponents. If it yields on occasion to some international pressure to improve its treatment of human rights, it does so because that "sacrifice" (respecting a few human rights) is not perceived to be politically unbearable. But a genocidal regime perceives that entire ethnic or religious groups are its opponents. In its generally paranoid mind-set, the risks associated with even a little compromise (in the regime's view, self-capitulation) are severe. Such a regime may even believe that its genocidal policies are in its country's vital national interest.

How any government calculates a so-called vital national interest tends to involve three factors: *ideology, survival of the government,* and *national honor. Ideology* is the belief system of the government, a worldview of perceived group identities in some sort of rivalry. This factor is sometimes referred to as the country's "political culture" or its "values system." The driving ideology may be constitutional democracy, Nazism, Marxism-Leninism, Baathism, whatever. *Survival of the government* refers to the actual leadership in power, such as an elected administration within a representative democracy, a factor separate from the constitutional (i.e., the ideological) framework through which it rules. Finally, *national honor* is self-pride, a factor partly cultural, partly political, and partly psychological.[13]

Sometimes these three factors coincide. If an elected government is about to be overthrown by an invading foreign army, it may choose to resist despite the odds against it because it deems all three factors to be endangered. Yet these factors can also diverge. A regime may choose to sacrifice itself, its ideology, or the national honor, all according to how the regime ranks their relative importance. Hitler valued his Nazi ideology more than Germany's survival as a nation; as the Allies' armies closed in, he even wanted the last life-sustaining remnants of the German nation needlessly destroyed, including its food stocks, fuel, and basic infrastructure.[14] By contrast, the Communist regime of China seems to value its survival in power more than its own Marxist-Leninist-Maoist ideology. Some would argue that the United States, during the Cold War, sometimes valued its national honor more than its democratic ideology, on occasion even more than a ruling administration's (i.e., a government's) political survival. In 1968 U.S. President Lyndon Johnson renounced any bid for his reelection as a consequence of his administration's war policies in Vietnam; he thereby sacrificed any possible continuation of his own government.

The factor the regime holds most dear can vary. If the regime is driven by its ideology, it may want to "purify" (socially re-engineer) its country through mass murder; hence the terms *purge* and *extermination*. Such a regime might be willing to delay its murderous policies if offered an alternative that satisfies its ideology, such as *ethnic cleansing*—the mass expulsion of its perceived enemies. If the regime favors its own survival over everything else, it might be willing to co-opt rather than mass murder its perceived enemies, although the chances of this are slim if the regime has already decided to kill them. If national honor is deemed to be most important, the regime may interpret any resistance to its rule, real or imagined, as uncompromisingly intolerable. Such are the effects of political paranoia.

The Example of Tibet and China

The factor which drives a genocidal regime can also change over time. This appears to have happened to the Chinese regime ruling Tibet. The formerly sovereign country of Tibet was annexed by the People's Republic of China in 1959, nine years after Communist Chinese forces invaded the country. The Dalai Lama, the spiritual leader of Tibetan Buddhism, is also the exiled political leader of Tibet. Although the Communist Chinese regime kept the Dalai Lama nominally in power during its first nine years of Tibetan occupation, he fled after he could no longer influence the regime to moderate its brutal occupation policies. Later, in 1989, the Dalai Lama was awarded the Nobel Peace Prize for his nonviolent campaign on behalf of Tibet and Tibetans. "As a result of the Chinese invasion and the ensuing occupation," he wrote in 1994, "over 1 million Tibetans have died of unnatural causes and over 6,000 of our monasteries, the learning centers and repositories of our culture, have been destroyed."[15] Tibet has suffered a gradual genocide.

The man who ordered China's conquest of Tibet was Mao Zedong. To Mao, spreading his *ideology* was a vital national interest. Ever since his death in 1976, however, his ideology has ceased to be very important in China. Instead, the regime has emphasized a materialist conception of Chinese nationalism and, consequently, its policies toward Tibet are tied to that perception of Chinese *national honor*. Recognizing that tie, the exiled Dalai Lama has long tried to accommodate it. He declares:

It has always been my belief that the only way to achieve a lasting solution to the Tibetan-Chinese conflict is through earnest, substantive negotiations. While it is the overwhelming desire of the Tibetan people to regain their national independence, I have over the years repeatedly and publicly stated that I am willing to enter into negotiations and work from an agenda that does not include independence.

My concern is the welfare of the . . . Tibetans living in Tibet and the protection of their rights, freedoms and distinct culture.[16]

Note the last sentence, especially its second half: the potentially democratic goals it implies could be what terrifies the Chinese regime most. For if the regime were to permit a few democratic reforms in Tibet, that could encourage the general population throughout China to demand the same, if not more, eventually endangering the *survival of the government*. Unable to admit this publicly, however, the Chinese regime has long equated any discussion of democratic reform in Tibet as "separatist" and therefore forbidden. Over the decades the factor that dominates the regime's gradual genocide of Tibet may have changed from one, to another, to another.

THE IMPORTANCE OF
A GENOCIDE EARLY WARNING CENTER

An *early warning center* is an entity specifically devoted to forecasting places of potential trouble and issuing alerts accordingly. It is different from a *watch center* which, while also responsible for issuing alerts, only monitors ongoing events. It is also different from a system of early warning, a system which may be spread among several departments or even agencies. A criticism sometimes raised against early warning centers is that, historically, having enough early warning has rarely been a serious problem. The warnings were usually there, specified in secret reports by the relevant agencies, but those warnings were ignored. Early warnings do not always produce early action.

There is a difference between having some early warnings versus having an early warning center, however. Key decision makers and their staffs typically have very busy schedules as a multitude of people, meetings, events, and reports vie for their daily attention—with little hint of which potential crisis somewhere deserves their attention at the expense of more immediate issues. But an early warning center can help identify and urgently emphasize which situations they should watch and heed. With its special sources and unique analytical methods, an early warning center has few if any bureaucratic peers. This privileged status renders its warnings very difficult to dispute—or ignore.

Being able to emphasize such warnings, repeatedly, at the highest levels instead of through intermediaries, is a lesson an independent, UN-sanctioned commission of inquiry underscored after reviewing the UN's abysmal response to the Rwandan genocide in 1994. In its highly critical report, issued in December 1999, it noted:

At [UN] Headquarters there was not sufficient focus or institutional resources for early warning and risk analysis. Much could have been gained by a more active preventive policy aimed at identifying the risks for conflict or tension, including through an institutionalized cooperation with academics, NGOs and better coordination within different parts of the United Nations system dealing with Rwanda.

The commission of inquiry also noted that, almost a year before the genocide erupted in earnest, the UN had

published a report which gave an ominously serious picture of the human rights situation in Rwanda. The report described the visit to Rwanda by the Special Rapporteur . . . on extrajudicial, summary or arbitrary executions, Mr. Waly Bacre Ndiaye, from 8 to 17 April 1993. Ndiaye determined that massacres and a plethora of other serious human rights violations were taking place in Rwanda. The targeting of the Tutsi population led Ndiaye to discuss whether the term *genocide* might be applicable. He stated that he could not pass judgment at that stage, but, citing the Genocide Convention, went on to say that the cases of intercommunal violence brought to his attention indicated "very clearly that the victims of the attacks, Tutsis in the overwhelming majority of cases, have been targeted solely because of their membership in a certain ethnic group and for no other objective reason." Although Ndiaye—in addition to pointing out the serious risk of genocide in Rwanda—recommended a series of steps to prevent further massacres and other abuses, his report seems to have been largely ignored by the key actors within the United Nations system.[17]

The warnings did not end there. Three months before the main genocide, Canadian Major General Romeo Dallaire, the force commander of a small UN peacekeeping force in Rwanda called UNAMIR, received some information he deemed to be so dire, and yet so credible, that he faxed it back to his superiors in New York. Some excerpts from that fax:

January 11, 1994 — *Most Immediate*
Subject: Request for Protection for Informant

Force Commander [was] put in contact with informant by very, very important government politician. Informant is a top-level trainer in the cadre of the *Interahamwe*-armed militia. . . . He informed us he was in charge of last Saturday's demonstrations, whose aims were to target deputies of opposition parties coming to ceremonies and Belgian soldiers [in UNAMIR]. They hoped to . . . provoke a civil war. Deputies were to be assassinated upon entry or exit from [Rwanda's] Parliament. Belgian troops were to be provoked and, if Belgian soldiers resorted to force, a number of them were to be killed and thus guarantee Belgian [contingent's] withdrawal from Rwanda. . . . He believes [Rwanda's] President does not have full control over all elements of his old party/faction. . .

[The informer, a Hutu, was also] ordered to register all Tutsis in Kigali [the Rwandan capital]. He suspects it is for their extermination. Example he gave was that, in 20 minutes, his personnel could kill up to 1,000 Tutsis. . . . [The informer provided us with this information because] he disagrees with anti-Tutsi extermination.[18]

Dallaire ended this fax with a personal plea for action: "*Peux ce que veux. Allons-y*," he scribbled. ("Where there's a will, there's a way. Let's go.")

Unfortunately, the UN Headquarters at that time did not have a genocide early warning center. Consequently, Dallaire's fax became one of but many reports received daily from UN peacekeeping forces scattered all over the world. The UN Secretary-General at that time, Boutros Boutros-Ghali, later explained: "Such situations and alarming reports from the field, though considered with the utmost seriousness by United Nations officials, are not uncommon within the context of peacekeeping operations." [19] Dallaire's fax was not ignored, but it did not spark the reaction he had hoped for, either. Instead, his immediate superiors in New York ordered him to share his information with the Kigali-based embassies of Belgium, France, and the United States, as well as with Rwanda's Hutu president—to urge *him* to take action. Aside from sharing his information, however, Dallaire was ordered to keep the activities of his small UN force within the narrow limits of its official peacekeeping mandate. When Dallaire tried to get that mandate changed, to fit Rwanda's rapidly deteriorating situation, his request was refused. The Security Council was not very interested, although neither was it shown Dallaire's fax. Some senior officials in the UN Secretariat later testified that they, too, were not shown Dallaire's fax when it first arrived. Such are the mistakes of busy bureaucracies.

If a genocide early warning center had existed in the UN, that center could have noticed Dallaire's fax and treated it as but the latest piece in a growing mosaic of ominous clues and worrisome reports. Very soon, if not immediately, that center could have alerted the highest officials of the Secretariat and, more importantly, the Security Council as well. It could have presented more than a single fax, but indeed its entire analytical assessment and its evidence—all of which, when presented together, would have been extremely difficult to ignore. And to ensure that its warnings were fully understood, the center's staff members could have had face to face contact with the people they informed, if necessary on a daily basis.

WHAT IS TO BE DONE?

If a genocide early warning center does not, by itself, spur timely action, its activities may nonetheless help. This could happen when that center shares its information gathered from various sources amongst those same sources, that is, between academia, the news media, NGOs and international organizations. Those sources, by learning more about each other and their information, might increasingly work together to press for early action.

And if that action is early enough, months or years before a genocidal crisis erupts in earnest, the situation can be handled between governments by assistant secretaries of state and by deputy foreign ministers, or even by ambassadors, embassy *chargé d'affaires*, consuls, and attachés. Unlike many of their national leaders, they are the foreign policy professionals of their governments, seasoned by experience and often quite knowledgeable about the regions wherein they work. They may not possess the full political power of their president or prime minister, but at that much earlier time, when events are still fluid, they enjoy considerable authority and flexibility. They thus have more chance of guiding the situation down a more peaceful path before that society becomes too polarized by its rising hatreds, and before too many political moderates are either killed or politically marginalized. That is what a genocide early warning center should be designed to facilitate.

But with what tools? How can outsiders influence a genocidal crisis? In the United Nations' 1985 study on how to better enforce the Genocide Convention, the following options were offered as possible responses:

On an early warning alert being received, the steps to be taken could include: the investigation of allegations; activating different organs of the United Nations and related organizations, both directly and through national delegations, and making representations to national Governments and to interregional organizations for active involvement; seeking support of the international press in providing information; enlisting the aid of other media to call public attention to the threat, or actuality, of genocidal massacre; asking relevant racial, communal and religious leaders, in appropriate cases, to intercede, and arranging the immediate involvement of suitable mediators and conciliators at the outset.

Finally, there are the possibility of sanctions which could be applied with public support by means of economic boycotts, the refusal to handle goods to or from offending States, and selective exclusion from participation in international activities and events. Representations would also be made to Governments to enlist their support in the application of sanctions.[20]

Most of the remaining chapters of this book will explore the feasibility, as well as the advantages and disadvantages, of these and other options.

NOTES

1. Israel W. Charny and Chanan Rapaport, "Toward a Genocide Early Warning System," *How Can We Commit the Unthinkable? Genocide: the Human Cancer* (Boulder, CO: Westview Press, 1982), pp. 283-331. Also, Israel W. Charny (editor-in-chief), "Genocide Early Warning System (GEWS)," *Encyclopedia of Genocide* (Santa Barbara, CA: ABC-CLIO, Inc., 1999), pp. 253-261.

2. UN Doc. E/CN.4/Sub.2/1985/6, by Special Rapporteur Benjamin C. G. Whitaker (of the United Kingdom). Quoted in the entry "Genocide" in Edward Lawson (editor), *Encyclopedia of Human Rights* (New York: Taylor & Francis, 1991), p. 668.

3. Robert M. Gates, *From the Shadows: The Ultimate Insider's Story of Five Presidents and How They Won the Cold War* (New York: Simon & Schuster, 1996), pp. 217-218.

4. Edward R. Girardet, "Reporting Humanitarianism: Are the New Electronic Media Making a Difference?" in *From Massacres to Genocide: The Media, Public Policy, and Humanitarian Crises* (Cambridge, MA: The World Peace Foundation, 1996), p. 57.

5. "Committee on Elimination of Racial Discrimination expresses deep concern at persisting grave situation in Democratic Republic of Congo," OHCHR Press Release HR/CERD/99/66 (August 25, 1999)

6. A good example is Frank Chalk and Kurt Jonassohn, *The History and Sociology of Genocide: Analyses and Case Studies* (New Haven, CT: Yale University Press, 1990).

7. Michael Chege, "Africa's Murderous Professors," *The National Interest* (Winter 1996/97), pp. 32-40.

8. Gillian Sandford, "Anti-Milosevic revolt planned in army," *Irish Times* (October 9, 2000), p. 14.

9. Samuel P. Huntington, *The Soldier and the State: The Theory and Politics of Civil-Military Relations* (Cambridge, MA: Harvard University Press, 1957), p. 78.

10. Quoted in Robert Edwin Herzstein, "The Enslavement of the Army," *The Nazis* (Alexandria, VA: Time-Life Books, 1980), pp. 178-179.

11. See "Iran's Army: Don't Count On Us, Ayatollah," *The Economist* (August 27, 1994), p. 34. Also, "Letter from Officer X," *Time* (January 23, 1995), pp. 48-49.

12. John L. Davies and Ted Robert Gurr (editors), *Preventive Measures: Building Risk Assessment and Crisis Early Warning Systems* (Totowa, NJ: Rowman and Littlefield, 1998), in particular Chapter 5 by Barbara Harff, "Early Warning of Humanitarian Crises: Sequential Models and the Role of Accelerators."

13. For a description of the role of national honor in calculating vital national interests, see Donald Kagan, "Our Interests and Our Honor," *Commentary* (April 1997), pp. 42-45.

14. Hitler, according to Albert Speer, issued such an order in early 1945. See Albert Speer, *Inside the Third Reich* (New York: Macmillan Company, 1970), p. 440.

15. The Dalai Lama, "Critical Reflections: Human Rights and the Future of Tibet," *Harvard International Review* (Winter 1994/95), pp. 46-80.

16. Ibid.

17. Ingvar Carlsson, Han Sung-Joo and Rufus M. Kupolati, *Report of the Independent Inquiry into the Actions of the United Nations during the 1994 Genocide in Rwanda* (New York: United Nations Department of Information, dated December 15, 1999). Available online at: www.un.org/News/ossg/rwanda_report.htm

18. Philip Gourevitch, "The Genocide Fax," *The New Yorker* (May 11, 1998), pp. 42-46.

19. Ibid.

20. UN Doc. E/CN.4/Sub.2/1985/6, by Whitaker. Quoted in Lawson, *loc. cit.*

5

Forms of Nonviolent Pressure: Diplomacy, Economic Trade, and Nonviolent Resistance

> When one is faced with any conflict, we believe it is more useful to think about a good *process* for handling a flow of problems than to think about "solving" a particular problem once and for all. In fluid and turbulent times, it is better to think in terms of coping with conflicts than resolving them. . . . We are not looking for a perfect solution. We do not assume that all conflicts can be settled peacefully or that all negotiations will—or should—lead to agreement.
>
> — Roger Fisher, Elizabeth Kopelman, and Andrea Schneider
> *Beyond Machiavelli: Tools for Coping with Conflict*, 1994

Every form of nonviolent pressure at some level involves negotiations. But to negotiate effectively requires prerequisites that do not always exist, including having enough time to negotiate. As this chapter's introductory quote illustrates, various negotiation experts believe in, first, structuring a process and bargaining back and forth within that process.[1] But as a genocide massacres people, there may be little time to prepare and follow such a process. Even if the genocide's perpetrators are willing to talk, which may not mean they are willing to actually negotiate, will they pause their killings in the meantime? If the killings still continue, should the talks continue?

These questions reflect but a few of the many dilemmas and frustrations involved in trying to stop a genocide through nonviolent means alone. Warren Zimmermann, the last U.S. ambassador to the old (and rupturing) Yugoslavia of the early 1990s, issued this advice in his memoirs:

Those who practice diplomacy need constantly to be reminded of the human damage their efforts, or lack of them, can cause. For three years of the Bosnian War, the Western countries had attempted to rebuff the Serbian aggressors, bloated by their use of force, without making them fear that force would in turn be used against them. Western diplomacy was reduced to a kind of cynical theater, a pretense of useful activity, a way of disguising a lack of will. Diplomacy without force became an unloaded weapon, impotent and ridiculous.[2]

That said, various forms of nonviolent pressure can be used as tools against genocide. But their use should respect their limitations.

DIPLOMATIC PRESSURE

Forms of diplomatic pressure range from quiet diplomacy to public statements. What are presented here are some diplomatic methods and tactics.

Quiet Diplomacy

What is sometimes called *quiet diplomacy* tries to modify a regime's behavior by appealing to all three categories of its vital interest criteria, namely, national honor, ideology, and survival of the government. In deference to the regime's sensitivity to national honor, the applied pressure is "quiet" (inconspicuous) and "diplomatic" (respectful). To be persuasive, the pressure is often cast in the regime's own ideological language and deliberately connected in some (perhaps minor) way to the regime's survival. The pressure applied is to do something or not, in exchange for something or not. The reward must exceed the perceived cost of the compromising sacrifice. If that sacrifice is not tangible in material terms, what is its value? How much is a life worth? How much do the parties trust each other? Will the deal be kept? Will the reward be paid?

When quiet diplomacy is used to oppose a genocide, such efforts are rarely sufficient by themselves. Once a regime has chosen to commit genocide, or is even merely considering it, that regime has perceived, however subjectively, a serious threat to itself. The arrival of some low-profile foreign diplomats urging peace, compromise, and reconciliation may be seen as nothing more than an annoyance, a display of foreign ignorance and interference.

Before attempting to dissuade a regime from committing genocide, perhaps the first question worth asking is: What does the regime want? Such a regime usually wants what it should not get: military equipment, wealth, territory, and the destruction of the group it has targeted. Whom does that regime trust? It may trust very few allies, none of whom may be inclined to press the issue of human rights. For example, it is difficult to imagine how Nazi Germany could have been persuaded to stop the Final Solution after quietly receiving a delegation of Japanese envoys, especially after Japan's barbarous treatment of occupied China. What could Japan offer to Nazi Germany? Finland, another Nazi ally, might have been a better moral advocate. (The Finnish government did refuse Hitler's demand that Finnish Jews be deported to the Nazi death camps.) Yet it seems doubtful that even Finland's Carl-Gustav von Mannerheim, a martial leader so tall and intimidating that Hitler reportedly held him in awe, could have persuaded Hitler to stop exterminating Jews throughout Nazi-occupied Europe.

When should quiet diplomacy be applied? It is best applied before any genocide begins. To apply it during a genocide is to assume that an immense killing system, probably running on enormous bureaucratic momentum, will abruptly stop because of a few words from a foreign envoy. It also assumes that the genocide is centrally controlled. Against a more decentralized genocide, perpetrators at almost every level of the slaughter would need to be persuaded.

Even if a secret deal with a genocidal regime can be arranged, that deal may not be sustainable if the other party is a democratic government. This is because democratic governments are notoriously inconsistent, and open, about how they conduct their foreign policy. Chief executives offer one thing, legislatures enact another. Elected leaders change. How can an agreement with a genocidal regime be guaranteed? How can a democratic consensus to support that deal be built amid the inherent secrecy of quiet diplomacy?

Verbal Maneuver

What can be described as *verbal maneuvering* attempts to modify a regime's behavior by expressing statements more openly than does quiet diplomacy. If attempted in a slipshod manner, however, it can inadvertently escalate a delicate situation out of control.

One example of verbal maneuver is for a foreign government, an ally of the genocidal regime, to publicly reassure that regime that its own survival is not endangered because its ally will protect it. Such open reassurance can backfire, however, if the genocidal regime interprets that support as blanket permission to pursue whatever policies the regime wants. It is therefore essential to clarify, through quiet diplomacy, just how far the support will go.

A genocidal regime might be encouraged to improve its behavior by being verbally entangled in higher public expectations for it. A prominent ally could proclaim, for instance, that a genocidal regime's "gentle" ruler has "too much honor and dignity" to behave cruelly. The ally could even claim (falsely) to have received solemn reassurances from that ruler that a deadly crackdown is neither planned nor contemplated, neither now nor ever.

But would such public reassurance or verbal entanglement actually work? If Cambodia's Khmer Rouge had been reassured by their Communist Chinese ally that the "killing fields" genocide was "unnecessary" because the Chinese regime would safeguard the Khmer Rouge, would the Khmer Rouge have refrained? If China's leader Mao Zedong, or subsequently Deng Xiaoping, had publicly called Cambodia's ruler Pol Pot as "a gentle, kind ruler who has personally reassured me he would never permit such a thing," would the genocide have been curtailed? Probably not. Any genocidal regime that does not depend on outside support for its survival can probably inflict almost anything it wants upon its own country.

A "Friendly" Warning

A powerful ally of a genocidal regime could express a veiled threat, perhaps even a polite threat, that the regime must cease its uncivilized behavior *or else*.

When combined with quiet diplomacy, this "friendly" warning adds credibility to the quiet message by investing it with public awareness and scrutiny. If this tactic is used too frequently, however, the warnings can become perceived as hollow.

There is also the problem of *or else*. Or else what? To be credible, the warning must be plausible. To be effective, it must threaten something that the regime considers to be more important than whatever the regime perceives it is defending itself against by committing genocide. If, in the late 1980s, the Soviet Union's Mikhail Gorbachev had expressed a "friendly" warning to Romania's Nicolai Ceaucescu, or to Iraq's Saddam Hussein, would either of those Soviet client-rulers have improved their behaviors? Perhaps some token improvements would have resulted, but anything more seems unlikely.

An Unfriendly Warning

If the relationship between two governments is normally good and valued by both, an "unfriendly warning" denotes genuine seriousness. If their relationship is deteriorating but still valued, a quiet diplomatic overture can complement an unfriendly warning as part of a nuanced reward/punishment "carrot-and-stick" approach. If their relationship is poor but the warning is still credible—i.e., if provoked, dreaded punishment will occur—the warning may be effective. But what tangible thing does the warning threaten? How would adhering to an unfriendly foreign warning compensate the genocidal regime for not committing a genocide it may perceive as "necessary"? If the relationship between the two governments is so poor that any warning is essentially a bluff, an unfriendly warning might make matters worse by emboldening the genocidal regime.

Symbolic Support to an Opposition

Another unfriendly tactic is to express "moral support" for a regime's opponents. This tactic can involve public statements of support to the opposition, official and "unofficial" visits to the regime's opponents at their homes, official invitations to allow opponents and dissidents to speak abroad, as well as better relations with neighboring countries unfriendly to the regime. Whenever an opposition figure, such as a dissident, is empowered by foreign celebrity status and thereby gains the relative protection of that fame, he or she can use that fame to encourage more public scrutiny of the regime. Otherwise, however, this tactic may have little effect against a genocide.

Open Material Support to an Opposition

Open material support to a regime's opposition—help which is more than symbolic—can keep an otherwise deteriorating opposition alive and perhaps give it a struggling chance to succeed. Here the emphasis is on open material support, not secret support (which is addressed in Chapter 6). The disadvantages of open material support may outweigh its usefulness, however. This tactic is a form of foreign subversion, something a genocidal regime can point to via its propaganda to undermine its opponents' domestic credibility. Even under the best of conditions, open material support may not curtail an ongoing genocide very quickly, if at all.

Breaking Diplomatic Relations

Short of declaring war, the most extreme form of diplomatic protest is to break diplomatic relations. Unless those official ties are deeply valued by the regime, however, breaking diplomatic relations cannot, alone, curb a genocide. Breaking them can even do more harm than good. Without a working embassy inside that country, its persecuted people cannot be issued exit visas. Nor can a closed embassy gather intelligence about the genocide. Any opportunities to influence events using that embassy will be missed by default.

PUBLICITY

One of the most popular of nonviolent tactics is to publicize the horror to encourage a popular outcry against it. Scholars and political activists generally point to two historical cases: the so-called T-4 "euthanasia" program in Nazi Germany and, decades later, the plight of Baha'i followers in Iran. The first is an example of domestic publicity, the second of international publicity.

Domestic Publicity

The T-4 program was a Nazi campaign to exterminate Germany's mentally retarded children and adults ("life unworthy of life" in the Nazi mind-set) as supposed mercy killing.[3] Begun in late 1939, it was the first Nazi program to use poison gas to murder its victims. Although officially secret, it gradually raised the suspicions of the German public after patient deaths at particular psychiatric institutions became mysteriously common. Grieving families were warned by the Gestapo secret police not to ask prying questions, a warning that probably fueled their worst fears. Even some lower ranking members of the Nazi Party became suspicious. And upset. Eventually some courageous German clergymen, Christian Protestants and Catholics alike, denounced the T-4 program from their church pulpits; many, subsequently, were thrown into concentration camps. Yet in spite Germany's tightly controlled news media, one clergyman became so popular in his outspokenness—Count Clemens von Galen, the Roman Catholic Bishop of Munster—that the Nazi regime proved hesitant to remove him lest he become a martyr. Therefore, to stem the growing outcry to an embarrassingly open secret, the Nazi regime unceremoniously ended the T-4 program in August 1941.

But the Nazi murder of retarded Germans, especially children, continued, becoming less state-centralized than state-encouraged. No longer gassed, the victims were injected with deadly overdoses of serum by Nazi physicians in hospitals or, if children, deliberately starved to death. More German retarded children were murdered after the T-4 program than during it.

Today, the German public's opposition to the T-4 program is sometimes compared to the Final Solution with the assertion that since ordinary Germans stopped the T-4 genocide, they could and should have stopped the Holocaust.

The truth is more complex. Even if the killings of retarded people had ended with the T-4 program, which they did not, the T-4 program still lasted for nearly two years and murdered over 70,000 people, perhaps as many as 100,000.

International Publicity

The Constitution of the Islamic Republic of Iran, adopted under the rule of Ruhollah Khomeini, formally protects Iranian Jews and Christians but omits mention of, and thus protection for, Iran's largest religious minority: more than 300,000 Baha'is.[4] The Baha'i faith is related to Islam, much as Islam is related to Christianity and Judaism. Under Khomeini's rule from 1979 to 1989, Iranian Baha'is suffered for their faith in ways ominously similar to German Jews in the first years of Hitler's regime: Their businesses were confiscated, their temples desecrated and closed, they were dismissed from jobs, denied property and university schooling, arrested, and some killed. Furthermore, like anti-Semitism in Germany, persecutions of Baha'is in Iran are not new. During the 1840s and 1850s, over 20,000 Baha'is were executed as heretics. But whereas Hitler's Germany treated Jews as vermin and wanted them to leave, Khomeini's Iran treated Baha'is as wayward Muslims and wanted them to stay and "repent."

Thousands of Iranian Baha'is were imprisoned in the 1980s and nearly two hundred were executed—mostly community leaders, but also teenage girls, executed for teaching their religion to children. Fears spread that, eventually, tens of thousands might be executed. Afraid of provoking Khomeini's regime, however, many Iranian Baha'i leaders proved reluctant to publicize their own plight. But abroad many Baha'i communities did publicize it, in some cases hiring respected public relations firms to help. In the United States the publicity included supportive coverage in the *New York Times* and the *Washington Post.* Official resolutions supporting the Iranian Baha'is were passed by the UN General Assembly, by the U.S. Congress, and by the parliaments of Australia, Germany, Fiji, and Canada. The Baha'i International organization also lobbied to have the Genocide Convention amended to include a special commission to investigate allegations of genocide anywhere in the world.

By 1991 about 25,000 Baha'is had been allowed to leave Iran, and fewer than ten remained in jail. There had been no executions since 1988, leaving the execution toll since 1979 at 210. Baha'is who remained in Iran were allowed to reopen their shops, and their children could receive primary and secondary education. Baha'is were still denied the university level, however.

Did the international pressure upon Iran's regime prevent a genocide? It is difficult to know for certain and, if that pressure did work, it is difficult to know why. Ruhollah Khomeini was growing old; he died in 1989. Perhaps his senility, if he suffered any, was a factor in his regime's behavior. What is known for certain is that, in 1991, the post-Khomeini regime adopted the recommendations of a secret internal memorandum later smuggled to a UN human rights official and subsequently publicized by Baha'i International in 1993. On how to treat the Iranian Baha'is, that secret memorandum said:

They can be enrolled in schools provided they have not identified themselves as Baha'is. Preferably, they should be enrolled in schools which have a strong and imposing [Islamic] religious ideology. They must be expelled from universities . . . once it becomes known that they are Baha'is.

A plan must be devised to confront and destroy their cultural roots outside the country. . . . To the extent that it does not encourage them to be Baha'is, it is permissible to provide them the means for ordinary living in accordance with the general rights given to every Iranian citizen, such as ration booklets, passports, burial certificates, work permits, etc. Deny them employment if they identify themselves as Baha'is. Deny them any position of influence, such as in the educational sector, etc.[5]

The memorandum was signed by Ali Khamenei, Iran's president at that time. When contrasted against the more positive developments in the Baha'i situation, this clouds more than clarifies whether any outside pressure upon Iran's regime actually worked.

During the rest of the 1990s, vivid news coverage of genocide in Bosnia, Rwanda, Kosovo, and East Timor encouraged various international efforts, but not every genocide everywhere was covered as intensely, Sudan's for example. While most reporters want to expose such crises to public attention, the overall news media must also contend with commercial marketing factors. Visually shocking genocides are easier to televise and, for better or worse, tend to get better market ratings than do genocides-in-preparation. Vivid broadcasts can also distort the perceptions of the television audience, ignoring the importance of local history, context, and the relative size of the crisis. Good journalists try to correct these misperceptions, but the pressure to describe such a news story with simplistic sound bites can be intense. Submission deadlines must be met, and broadcast time is short.

Moreover, in recent years America's major commercial television networks, including their news departments, have merged into ever-larger conglomerates and corporate joint ventures, causing some reporters to fear that market-driven concerns may affect their news coverage even further. Television journalists themselves warn that television news should only report on, not make, foreign policy, which means that television news should not be relied upon to detect and cover every genocide. ABC News anchor Ted Koppel has emphasized:

We in the media tend for the most part to be willows in the wind—shifting direction with each passing breeze, focusing not on the national interest, but rather on what appears to interest the nation at any given moment. You cannot and should not expect the media to take the lead in determining how or whether the national interest is served by the continued existence of NATO or by unilateral U.S. intervention in Bosnia.[6]

Coverage by the print media tends to be more extensive than television's, but it is also less capable of reaching and swaying the general public as passionately. And it, too, is subject to commercial pressures. Those pressures, warns veteran journalist Edward Girardet, have now merged with cybertechnology to the added detriment of accurate news coverage:

Journalists in the field, particularly foreign correspondents, are, by and large, sympathetic to those involved in humanitarian plights. . . . They are usually more than willing to report a situation with as many dispatches as it takes to put the issue across. It is often their editors who are not willing to allow them the necessary scope. For reasons of competition, publicity, or ratings, news organizations increasingly want to be able to claim that they have a "body" on the spot, yet they do not really care how in-depth or consistent the information is. They also want the information instantly, supported by appropriate and uncomplicated cliched images.

This obsession with immediacy is giving journalists less time to fully research and understand the issues at hand. It encourages laziness and an overreliance on existent data. A considerable risk has already emerged of replicating mistakes and unreliable information (which gets reproduced again and again) gleaned from Nexus, CompuServe, America Online, the Internet, and other resource bases because of the temptation not to go out and do the reporting oneself.[7]

Negative publicity may indeed discourage a genocide; the tactic is certainly worth attempting. However, the numerous variables that influence it, ranging from the willingness of people to try it to those willing to take action because of it, make publicity alone an unreliable option.

ECONOMIC PRESSURE

Economic trade is the most common and, at least in peacetime, perhaps the most important activity between countries. It involves powerful constituencies, including banks, corporations, state-run enterprises, unions, and trade lobbies. Economic pressure can therefore be applied at multiple pressure points: trade negotiations, tariffs, development aid, loans, the freezing of financial assets, and trade sanctions. Trade sanctions can be tailored to include, exclude, or focus on almost anything traded, including arms transfers, nuclear-related technology, civilian/military "dual-use" technologies, petroleum, strategic minerals, medicine, and food.

Nevertheless, economic pressure has its limits. Do the trading partners have enough trade to seriously affect the offender? Who will feel the loss of trade more: the targeted country, or those denying the trade? Least likely to sacrifice may be those trading partners with the most trade at stake. The value of it can be immense; for example, by adhering to UN-imposed trade sanctions against Serbia during the Bosnian War, the already weak economies of Romania, Ukraine, and Hungary each suffered trade losses estimated at $1.5 billion per year, while Bulgaria lost an estimated $3.5 billion per year.[8] Studies of trade sanctions suggest they may need at least two years to achieve their intended political goal—and there is no guarantee of success. Some trade sanctions have remained politically ineffectual for decades.[9] But patience is rare in politics, rarer still in economics. Will the most important social and financial constituencies allow the intended economic pressure, which is only gradual, cause the desired political change? Or will that gradual pressure be lifted prematurely, supposedly because it failed? Whatever the answer, throughout those sanctions' duration a genocide can rage unhindered. And companies inside that country, sealed off by the trade embargo, can exploit that country's consumers by reaping monopoly profits within that closed, sheltered market.[10] Who will feel the pain of trade sanctions more: the country's leader, his security forces, the business community, or the poor?

Selectively targeted sanctions also take time to hurt, perhaps more than even all-inclusive sanctions. Against imports of conventional arms, for example, they become painful only after the regime's existing weaponry wears down and spare parts become scarce. Months or even years may pass, during which a black market can develop or even a domestic arms industry. The regime may be inconvenienced, but will it be inconvenienced enough to cease its genocide?

How receptive is the regime to political change? When South Africa was punished with trade sanctions for its apartheid racial policies, its white minority government became very receptive to change because, within racial limits, that government was still elected. Trade sanctions worked against South Africa because that country's white business community, as well as multitudes of white voters, could demand change and get it.

A regime far less receptive to change has been Saddam Hussein's in Iraq. In August 1990 the UN Security Council imposed economic sanctions against Iraq in response to Iraq's invasion of Kuwait. After Kuwait's independence was restored in 1991, the Security Council declared that the sanctions would remain in effect until Hussein's regime fully complied with every UN resolution his regime agreed to after the Gulf War, including that all of Iraq's "weapons of mass destruction" (chemical, biological, and attempted nuclear weapons) be destroyed. Years before, in the late 1980s, Hussein's regime had used chemical weapons against Kurdish villages in Iraq itself, killing as many as 100,000 Iraqi-Kurds with poison gas bombs.

Rolf Ekeus, an arms control expert from Sweden, was the first chair of the UN inspection commission established to verify that Iraq no longer possessed such weapons. Throughout his term, from 1991 to 1997, his many inspectors were harassed, stymied, lied to, and presented with so many incomplete reports by Hussein's regime, one after another—each report labeled Iraq's "full, final, and complete disclosure"—that this seemingly final label became an ongoing acronym, referred to as Iraq's first FFCD, its second FFCD, its third FFCD, and so on. No report was ever full, final, and complete, though they were all labeled as such. Ekeus recalled some typical incidents:

They blocked us at three locations. They delayed us once seven hours, once five. When [a] high Iraqi official arrived [to give us permission to enter a particular site], he waited until the site commander cleaned out the place and then said, "You can go in." [11]

These obstructive tactics were repeated during the term of Ekeus' successor, Richard Butler of Australia. Moreover, as late as 1995, several years after the trade sanctions were imposed, Hussein's regime was still illegally experimenting with a chemical nerve agent known as VX. One of deadliest poison gasses ever concocted, a mere droplet of VX on the human skin is fatal. At first Hussein's regime told the UN that Iraq had never had any VX. "Of course, we had found documents and had investigated, so they couldn't deny it," Ekeus explained. "Then we managed to detect a huge amount of imports of certain chemicals, so-called *precursors*, which could not be used really for anything but VX production." When the regime was asked why it had imported the precursors and where they were now, it replied it had destroyed the precursors in secret.

"They come up with a new explanation every time," Ekeus recounted. "They are very very innovative. This is frustrating and irritating sometimes, but also amusing, highly amusing. They tell the most incredible stories. It is like the *Thousand and One Nights,* where every night they tell a different story to save themselves." [12]

What is not amusing is the often-overlooked fact, monstrous though it is, that Hussein deliberately starved his own country. For despite common myths to the contrary, the UN trade sanctions against Iraq have never prohibited its import of food and medical supplies. Indeed, food and medical supplies were deliberately exempted from the trade sanctions when the Security Council first imposed them with its Resolution 661, on August 6, 1990:

The Security Council . . . decides that all States shall prevent . . . the sale or supply . . . of any commodities or products, including weapons or any other military equipment, whether or not originating in their territories, *but not including supplies intended strictly for medical purposes, and, in humanitarian circumstances, foodstuffs*, to any person or body in Iraq [emphasis added].

Throughout the subsequent decade, the Security Council insisted that, if the Iraq regime wanted to buy food and medical supplies, it must submit its foreign trade to UN inspection to verify that food and medical supplies were indeed being purchased, rather than armaments. But Hussein replied that any UN monitoring would violate Iraq's national sovereignty (even though, legally, it would not), so he refused to let Iraq import almost anything at all—not even food and medicine. Later the Security Council offered Iraq "oil-for-food" deals, allowing Iraq to export an amount of oil to purchase humanitarian supplies, again subject to UN conditions and verification. For four years, however, noted a report to the UN Human Rights Commission in 1998, the Iraqi regime, instead of accepting any oil-for-food deal to ease the plight of its famished population, "decided to rely only on domestic production"—in a largely desert country—"to meet the humanitarian needs of its people, preferring to let innocent people suffer while the Government maneuvered to get sanctions lifted." [13] This is because the oil-for-food deals help to debunk Hussein's propaganda that the sanctions supposedly starve Iraqi children and should therefore be lifted entirely, presumably to allow the Iraqi regime to import arms and related technologies.

The West and the UN do share some blame for the Iraqi people's misery, because more could have been done to help. If an American citizen in the 1990s tried to send food and medicine to the Iraqi people as a free gift, something the UN sanctions allowed, that charitable action was nonetheless prohibited by U.S. law. This is because the particular U.S. statutes used to enforce the UN sanctions were older and more rigid than the Security Council's Resolution 661 but were not updated to allow for the resolution's humanitarian exemptions. The United States and other countries could have sent food and medical supplies into Iraq free of charge, thereby denying Hussein any new money or weaponry. Such a humane policy has a precedent: When North Korea's people faced starvation in the 1990s, the United States and other democracies sent food aid into that totalitarian state.

The Iraqi sanctions case stands as a warning about the limits of economic pressure. Iraq, prior to the UN trade sanctions, suffered through eight years of devastating war with Iran, bankrupting Iraq so severely that Kuwait became its tempting prey. Moreover, because Iraq had so little of value besides oil exports, it was probably as vulnerable to trade sanctions as any country could be. And indeed, by 1998, Iraq suffered an estimated $130 billion in lost revenues. Yet, throughout the decade of the Nineties, Hussein's regime not only survived the UN trade sanctions but made their effect upon ordinary Iraqis monstrously worse. His regime turned scarcity and starvation into coercive tools, to further control the Iraqi nation.

Against any such genocidal regime, how can trade sanctions alone convince it to stop inflicting its genocide? If shortages and inflation mean so little to it, how can their gradual effect be measured in terms of political change? How much gradual change is required before the entire endangered population is slaughtered?

Too often trade sanctions masquerade as a policy where there is no policy, because there is no strategy. They can make a genocide less convenient to continue, but they cannot stop it. Are trade sanctions, therefore, the wrong approach? More than three decades of U.S. trade sanctions against Cuba did not topple its regime. Two decades of Western trade with post-Maoist China helped to transform its regime from one utterly totalitarian to one, arguably, only authoritarian. Moreover, as a response to genocide, are trade sanctions morally enough? The principles of free trade are no excuse for moral indifference, but to expect that trade sanctions alone, implemented as one's only tangible response, can somehow stop a genocide and thereby satisfy one's moral responsibilities accordingly may well be a mere delusion.

NONVIOLENT RESISTANCE

Many pacifists believe that the only ethical response to violence, including the violence of a genocide, is nonviolence. Nonviolent resistance was endorsed in a UN report on how to better enforce the Genocide Convention, listing it as one response among many:

As a further safeguard, public awareness should be developed internationally to reinforce the individual's responsibility based on the knowledge that it is illegal to obey a superior order or law that violates human rights. Although some Governments may be reluctant to agree, such a concept has been an honored tradition in many different parts of the world. Gandhi's and Martin Luther King's ideas on civil disobedience to unjust laws were developments of the earlier thinking of people such as Thoreau, who went to prison rather than acquiesce in the forced return of runaway slaves to their owners. . . . All these people followed their conscience, at personal danger. The safeguarding of human rights in the final resort will always need to depend upon such integrity and courage.[14]

Many of the Roman Empire's first Christians faced persecution with pacifism. Although many were murdered, the impressive stories of their martyrdoms encouraged multitudes of new conversions among the living. Despite several campaigns of genocide against early Christianity, the Roman Empire was eventually transformed. That transformation took about three hundred years, however. Moreover, in the early 1600s, the harrowing martyrdoms of Japan's first Christians did not transform feudal Japan. Instead, in a genocide waged by the ruling Japanese families against all Western influences, Christianity in Japan was virtually exterminated. Only in secret did the religion survive.

The Philosophy of Mohandas Gandhi

Mohandas Gandhi of India transformed the generally passive nonviolence of early Christianity into a form of active resistance. Though a Hindu by birth and by conviction, Gandhi said his tactics were inspired by Jesus' Sermon on the Mount. Gandhi taught that an individual's personal behavior and dignity are more important than any material things that person can possess:

It is not because I value life low that I can countenance with joy thousands voluntarily losing their lives for *Satyagraha* [i.e., for nonviolent resistance], but because I know that it results in the long run in the least loss of life. And, what is more, it ennobles those who lose their lives and morally enriches the world for their sacrifice.

Men can slaughter one another for years in the heat of battle—for then it seems to be a case of kill or be killed. But if there is no danger of being killed yourself by those you slay, you cannot go on killing defenseless and unprotesting people endlessly. You must put down your gun in self-disgust.[15]

In colonial South Africa and later in colonial India, the oppressors whom Gandhi and his followers faced were British authorities, authorities who faced the criticism of Great Britain's free press and elected parliament. Gandhi knew there were major differences between the British Empire and Nazi Germany. Nevertheless, even before the Final Solution officially began in 1942, Gandhi as early as 1938 recommended the use of nonviolent resistance to German Jews facing Nazi harassment:

If I were a Jew and born in Germany and earned my livelihood there, I would claim Germany as my home even as the tallest Gentile may, and challenge him to shoot me or cast me in the dungeon; I would refuse to be expelled or to submit to discriminating treatment. And for doing this, I should not wait for the fellow Jews to join me in civil resistance but would have confidence that, in the end, the rest are bound to follow my example.

The calculated violence of Hitler may even result in a general massacre of the Jews. . . . But if the Jewish mind could be prepared for voluntary suffering, even the massacre I have imagined could be turned into a day of thanksgiving and joy that Jehovah had wrought deliverance of the race even at the hands of the tyrant. For to the God-fearing, death has no terror. It is a joyful sleep to be followed by a waking that would be all the more refreshing for the long sleep. . . . [This] will be then a truly religious resistance offered against the godless fury of dehumanized man. The German Jews will score a lasting victory over the German Gentiles in the sense that they will have converted the latter to an appreciation of human dignity.[16]

In Gandhi's view the spiritual and material realms intertwined, which is why he conceived of nonviolent resistance as an act of religious devotion as much as a practical behavior. "If Hitler is unaffected by my suffering, it does not matter," he declared. "Hitherto [Hitler] and his likes have built upon their invariable experience that men yield to force. Unarmed men, women and children offering nonviolent resistance without any bitterness in them will be a novel experience for them. Who can dare say that it is not in their nature to respond to the higher and finer forces? They have the same soul that I have." [17]

Yet even as he abhorred violence, Gandhi believed that an endangered people do have a right to spontaneous self-defense, even if expressed violently. Gandhi explained this apparent contradiction in his philosophy after Poland was invaded by Nazi Germany in 1939:

If a man fights with his sword single-handed against a horde of dacoits armed to the teeth, I should say he is fighting almost nonviolently. Have not I said to our women that if, in defense of their honor, they used nails and teeth and even a dagger I should regard their conduct [as] nonviolent? . . . Suppose a mouse fighting a cat tried to resist the cat with his sharp teeth—would you call that mouse *violent?* In the same way, for the Poles to stand valiantly against the German hordes vastly superior in numbers, military equipment and strength, was almost nonviolence. . . . You must give its full value to the word *almost*. . . . The Poles were unprepared for the way in which the enemy swooped down upon them.[18]

At that time the word *genocide* did not exist. With the devastation of the First World War still in common memory, war itself was generally considered the worst evil human beings could collectively commit. More than a year before the Second World War began, Gandhi openly declared:

The German persecution of the Jews seems to have no parallel in history. The tyrants of old never went so mad as Hitler seems to have gone. . . . If there ever could be a justifiable war in the name of and for humanity, a war against [Nazi] Germany, to prevent the wanton persecution of a whole race, would be completely justified. But I do not believe in any war.[19]

The Rosenstrasse Protest

Later, in Nazi Germany in the winter of 1943, a nonviolent protest against the Final Solution actually worked. In Berlin in late February, the Gestapo secret police rounded up approximately 10,000 German Jews still residing openly in the Third Reich's capital to "deport them to the East"—to Auschwitz. Among them were about 1,700 Jewish men married to "Aryan" non-Jewish German women, a legal status which, until then, had protected them while the Nazi regime had busied itself with exterminating millions of other Jews. As word spread of the Berliner Jews' sudden arrest, their worried wives were referred by local police stations to check a holding center located on a street named Rosenstrasse.

That holding center was surrounded by guards who, after checking their lists of the Jews inside, confirmed to the women that their husbands were indeed there. Some guards were SS and Gestapo officials; others were local policemen. None of them had apparently expected to face a growing crowd of "Aryan" women demanding information about Jewish husbands. A few guards later even delivered small amounts of food and warm clothing to the prisoners from their wives outside.

Over the next six days, what had begun as individual pleas for information became a vocal crowd of several hundred women demanding that their husbands be released. Joseph Goebbels, the Nazi propaganda minister who was also the *Gauleiter* (dictatorial mayor) of Berlin, was not in Berlin when this protest began; nor was Hitler. For days Goebbels was not even informed of the protest, his underlings hoping that the women, shivering in the winter cold and facing the intimidating might of the Nazi regime, would eventually lose heart and leave. But they did not.

The Rosenstrasse Protest seems to suggest that a nonviolent protest can arise spontaneously, for in outward appearance this one did; but its participants were a rather unique group. Very few of them had expected to protest anything; daily survival in Nazi Germany had taught them to be inconspicuous. Yet for an entire decade, ever since the Nazi regime began, all of them had been publicly ostracized, harassed, and economically impoverished simply because they were married to Jews and had stubbornly refused to divorce their husbands. By remaining married to Jews for so long in Nazi Germany, they were already longtime nonconformists. They also lived in Berlin, the most tolerant and liberal city in Germany prior to the Nazi era. Berlin's historic tolerance was gone—or was it? The following two quotes are from two of the Rosenstrasse protesters:

One has to remember that we too could have been arrested. And it appeared to us to be more diplomatic to just get together in small groups and walk back and forth. And always we looked up toward the windows and called out in a chorus. We waved and hoped that [our husbands] would look out and see us.[20]

[Whenever the guards] threatened to shoot, we ran in separate directions so that they couldn't get all of us at once, or would think that we really went away. But after five or ten minutes we all appeared again, got together, and began calling out, *"We want our husbands!"* But only that; we didn't call out anything else.[21]

Six days into the protest, Goebbels decided to release the 1,700 Jews. In an official statement, he declared: "I will commission the security police not to continue the Jewish evacuations [*sic*] in a systematic manner during such a critical time"—that is, after Nazi Germany's recent military disaster at the Battle of Stalingrad. "We want to, rather, spare that for ourselves until after a few weeks; then we can carry it out that much more thoroughly."[22]

Fortunately for the Rosenstrasse Jews, no subsequent roundup ever included them. Goebbels had them reclassified as "protected Jews"—members of a select group of Jews exempt from persecution on the personal orders of Goebbels, Hitler, or Herman Goering. They were even ordered to remove the otherwise obligatory Star of David patches from their clothing, used by the Nazis to stigmatize other Jews throughout occupied Europe.

Hitler agreed with Goebbels' decision to release the Rosenstrasse Jews. Decades afterward, some answers as to why were supplied by Leopold Gutterer, Goebbels' chief deputy in the Nazi propaganda ministry:

These women were persons there. Anyone could recognize who they were. They demonstrated openly and risked their existence. They were very courageous, yes? No doubt about that. . . . But if one or [another of the them] had had a pistol along, then the police would have had to shoot. Of course there was an investigation to find out whether someone was instigating this, but nothing was found. If so, one could have hindered it. [It] wasn't organized but spread by word of mouth. It was a spontaneous reaction. A protest against the system never existed. These women didn't want a revolution.

That [protest] was only possible in a large city, where many people lived together, whether Jewish or not. In Berlin were also representatives of the international press, who immediately grabbed hold of something like this, to loudly proclaim it. Thus news of the protest would travel from one person to the next.

Goebbels released the Jews in order to eliminate the protest from the world. That was the simplest solution: to eradicate completely the reason for the protest. . . . There was unrest and it could have spread from neighborhood to neighborhood. . . . Why should Goebbels have had [the women] all arrested? Then he would have only had even more unrest, from the relatives of these newly arrested persons.[23]

The Rosenstrasse Protest succeeded because a multitude of chance variables happened to coincide: (1) The women were in love; (2) having been ostracized for a decade, they were also persistent; (3) their husbands were arrested as a group; (4) the local police were willing to tell the women where their husbands were; (5) their husbands were in one place, at an accessible location; and (6) the Nazi regime was unprepared for a protest there. Indeed, in the aftermath of its enormous defeat at Stalingrad, the Nazi regime was afraid of almost any public protest anywhere in Germany, especially in Berlin, a capital once known for its mass protests and bold political expression—and where foreign journalists still had a presence. Furthermore, (7) the demands of the women, even though their husbands were Jewish, epitomized the supposedly Nazi virtues of family and motherhood. The women were vocal, unarmed, and unwilling to stop protesting unless they got their husbands back; and (8) they wanted only 1,700 Jews. Meanwhile, over 8,000 Berliner Jews seized in that same roundup were deported to their deaths. By releasing 1,700 Jews, the Nazis could later re-arrest them as individuals.

Finally, (9) the Final Solution was supposed to be a state secret. Although many Germans throughout the Third Reich did suspect that something terrible was happening to Jews, the fact that some Aryan women were openly yelling and crying about it in the middle of Berlin advertised those suspicions far too bluntly for the Nazi regime to ignore. Too many ordinary Germans might start asking, *If vast numbers of Jews are really being "evacuated for resettlement"*— as the Nazi regime so claimed—*then why should the regime not release 1,700 Berliner Jews if their Aryan wives so desperately want them to stay?* Faced with a public question like that, the Nazi regime was trapped in its own secrecy.

Could mass protests throughout Nazi Germany have prevented the Final Solution? Perhaps, but the most favorable time was long before February 1943. The notorious Nuremberg Laws, which stripped German Jews of their most basic rights, including their citizenship, were enacted in 1935. That year, if not earlier, is when most Germans should have spoken out. Even in those early years, mass protests would have been difficult to stage in Nazi Germany. But as one participant in the Rosenstrasse Protest explained: "We acted from the heart, and look what happened. If you had to calculate whether you would do any good by protesting, you wouldn't have gone. But we acted from the heart." [24]

Contemporary Nonviolent Campaigns

Since Gandhi's time, nonviolent resistance tactics have appeared in countless other human rights movements, including those led by Martin Luther King in the United States and by Aung San Suu Kyi in Myanmar (Burma). Nonviolent "people power" revolutions transformed the Philippines in 1986, most of Eastern Europe in 1989, the Soviet Union in 1991, and Serbia in 2000—although Serbia changed only after Milosevic's four wars. Ibrahim Rugova in Kosovo led his fellow ethnic Albanians in a ten-year campaign of nonviolence throughout most of Milosevic's reign. Rugova's campaign did not prevent the Kosovo War, but it might have if Milosevic had been overthrown earlier, something that Serbian public protests nearly did in 1996. Elsewhere, a triumvirate of nonviolent leaders—Jose Alexandre "Xanana" Gusmao, Jose Ramos Horta, and Carlos Ximenes Belo, a Roman Catholic bishop—led East Timor to independence after almost twenty-five years of struggle against Indonesia. The final price of that independence, in 1999, included destructive reprisals by pro-Indonesian militias. However, if East Timor's independence movement had not been predominantly nonviolent, East Timor might not have received as much of the world's active sympathy and support as it did, especially in the United Nations.

Nonviolent tactics were also evident, despite a tragic outcome, in the Chinese pro-democracy rallies in Beijing's Tiananmen Square and in other Chinese cities in 1989. It is towards today's Chinese Communist regime that a nonviolent movement is still being used to oppose a gradual genocide against Tibet's native culture. The Fourteenth Dalai Lama, Tibet's exiled political and spiritual leader, has repeatedly declared his willingness to negotiate according to a joint Chinese-Tibetan agenda that does not include talk of full Tibetan independence. "My concern," he explained in 1994, "is the welfare of the ... Tibetans living in Tibet and the protection of their rights, freedoms and distinct culture." Beijing did hold exploratory talks with some Tibetan delegations in 1982 and 1984, but since then the prospects for direct talks have dwindled. In 1987 the Dalai Lama made public what he had proposed to Beijing:

I proposed that Tibet become a demilitarized zone of peace, a notion that continues to be the basis of my future vision for Tibet. . . . I have called this a zone of *Ahimsa,* or nonviolence. This idea is not merely a dream: it is precisely the way Tibetans tried to live for over a thousand years before Tibet was ruthlessly invaded by China in 1949-50.

For at least the last 300 years, Tibet has had virtually no army; Tibet gave up war as an instrument of national policy.

I cannot continue to simply hope and wait for a positive signal from Beijing when the continuation of the present situation only enables China to complete the colonization and absorption of Tibet. I have, therefore, called for concerted efforts by the international community to press the Chinese leadership to enter into substantive negotiations with us. . . . My commitment to nonviolence, however, is fundamental, and there will be no deviation from this path under my leadership.[25]

National, ethnic, and religious groups are not the only ones using nonviolent tactics. Two longstanding principles of United Nations peacekeeping operations are mediation and avoiding the use of force. Where democratic reform has been troubled, such as in El Salvador and Guatemala, human rights groups have provided election observers and human rights monitors. Some of these groups are native-born; others, such as International Peace Brigades, emphasize a spirit of transnational charity. Some peace groups have tried to attract international attention by physically interposing themselves between countries about to commence armed hostilities.[26]

Preventing a Rwandan-style genocide is a much more difficult problem, however, than protecting an election campaign or inhibiting a frontline-oriented war, especially if the massacre sites are scattered throughout an entire country. While in theory a few representatives from, say, the International Red Cross, could permanently post themselves at concentration camps and elsewhere to actively watch for any war crimes, this strategy depends on several factors. Will enough of those monitors be allowed into the country? Will they be able to locate and reach where any atrocities are ongoing, or could occur? Can they enter, or at least get near, any heavily guarded facility which they need to, such as a prison camp? And can those monitors favorably influence the killers, if necessary with nonviolent resistance? As clever and as committed as some nonviolent resisters are, some perpetrators of genocide can be equally clever and committed to slaughtering people.

It was in British-ruled colonial South Africa that Gandhi first practiced nonviolent resistance. Decades later, another advocate of human rights in South Africa, Nelson Mandela, related, however sadly, his own belief that Gandhi's techniques and those of Martin Luther King have their limits. While still in prison for his human rights activities, Mandela was asked by two journalists why South Africa's antiapartheid movement had resorted to violence. In his later memoirs, Mandela explained:

I told them that the conditions in which Martin Luther King struggled were totally different from my own: the United States was a democracy with constitutional guarantees of equal rights that protected nonviolent protest (though there was still prejudice against blacks); South Africa was a police state with a constitution that enshrined inequality and an army that responded to nonviolence with force. I told them that I was a Christian and had always been a Christian. Even Christ, I said, when he was left with no alternative, used force to expel the moneylenders from the temple. He was not a man of violence, but had no choice but to use force against evil.[27]

Gandhi might not have agreed with Mandela's answer, but today many people would agree with Mandela. Gandhian nonviolence may be a noble pursuit, but Mandela's answer illustrates that many morally decent people do not wholly subscribe to it. In fairness to today's proponents of nonviolent action, most do not advocate the most extreme form of pacifism that Gandhi advocated. Instead, they advocate the practice of nonviolent alternatives sooner rather than later—preferably much sooner, since "later" usually means too late. In the words of one such scholar, Duane L. Cady:

Unfortunately, pacifists get asked for their suggestions well after believers in violence have spread weapons and war throughout the region. Very often the asking is an attempt to reduce pacifism to absurdity when war has already shown itself to fail.

Pacifists no more have instant solutions to situations like those in Bosnia or Rwanda than do warists. When conditions deteriorate to the levels of shelling civilians or hacking neighbors with machetes, all options are inadequate. The challenge is creating and sustaining conditions where life may flourish, where order is internalized, cooperative and respectful of human rights, rather than conditions of misery where order is imposed, exploitative, domineering, and abusive.[28]

NOTES

1. Introductory quote from Roger Fisher, Elizabeth Kopelman, and Andrea Schneider, *Beyond Machiavelli: Tools for Coping with Conflict* (New York: Penguin Books, 1994), pp. 4-5.

2. Warren Zimmermann, *Origins of a Catastrophe* (New York: Times Books, 1996), pp. 230-231.

3. For a description of the T-4 program, see Robert Jay Lifton, *The Nazi Doctors: Medical Killing and the Psychology of Genocide* (New York: Basic Books, 1986), pp. 45-102.

4. Katharine R. Bigelow, "A Campaign to Deter Genocide: the Baha'i Experience," in Helen Fein (editor), *Genocide Watch* (New Haven, CT: Yale University Press, 1992), pp. 189-196.

5. Baha'i International Community, *The Baha'i Question: Iran's Secret Blueprint for the Destruction of a Religious Community (An Examination of the Persecution of the Baha'is of Iran 1979-1993)* (New York: Baha'i International Community Publications, 1993), pp. 38-39.

6. Ted Koppel, "The Global Information Revolution and TV News," *Keynote Address from the Managing Chaos Conference (Peaceworks No. 3)* (Washington, DC: U.S. Institute of Peace, 1995), p. 15.

7. Edward R. Girardet, "Reporting Humanitarianism: Are the New Electronic Media Making a Difference?" in Robert I. Rotberg and Thomas G. Weiss (editors), *From Massacres to Genocide: The Media, Public Policy, and Humanitarian Crises* (Cambridge, MA: The World Peace Foundation, 1996), pp. 59-60.

8. M. Dinu, "Address to the Economic Committee." Paper presented at the 40th General Assembly of the Atlantic Treaty Association (The Hague, 27 October 1994).

9. U.S. General Accounting Office, *Economic Sanctions: Effectiveness as Tools of Foreign Policy* (GAO/NSIAD-92-106, February 1992) (Washington, DC: GAO, 1992). Also, Peter A.G. van Bergeijk and Charles van Marrewijk, "Why do sanctions need time

to work? Adjustment, learning and anticipation," *Economic Modelling* (April 1995), pp. 75-86.

10. Peter A.G. van Bergeijk, "The Impact of Economic Sanctions in the 1990s," *World Economy* (May 1995), pp. 443-455.

11. Quoted in Barbara Crossette, "Iraqis Still Defying Arms Ban, Departing U.N. Official Says," *New York Times* (June 25, 1997), pp. A-1 and A-3.

12. Ibid.

13. Barbara Crossette, "1,500 Executions Cited for Iraq In Past Year, Mostly for Politics," *New York Times* (April 14, 1998), pp. A-1 and A-9.

14. UN Doc. E/CN.4/Sub.2/1985/6, by Special Rapporteur Benjamin C. G. Whitaker (of the United Kingdom). Quoted in the entry "Genocide" in Edward Lawson (editor), *Encyclopedia of Human Rights* (New York: Taylor & Francis, 1991), p. 668.

15. Mahatma Gandhi, *Non-Violence in Peace and War* (2nd edition, Ahmedabad: Navajivan, 1944), p. 49. Rashmi-Sudha Puri, *Gandhi on War and Peace* (New York: Praeger, 1987), p. 157.

16. Martin Green (editor), *Gandhi in India in his own words* (Hanover: University Press of New England, 1987), pp. 262-265.

17. Ibid, p. 260.

18. Puri, p. 150.

19. Green, p. 262.

20. Nathan Stoltzfus, *Resistance of the Heart: Intermarriage and the Rosenstrasse Protest in Nazi Germany* (New York: W. W. Norton & Company, 1996), p. 230.

21. Ibid, p. 227.

22. Ibid.

23. Ibid, p. 244-246.

24. Ibid.

25. The Dalai Lama, "Critical Reflections: Human Rights and the Future of Tibet," *Harvard International Review* (Winter 1994/95), pp. 46-80.

26. Thomas Weber, "From Maude Royden's Peace Army to the Gulf Peace Team: An Assessment of Unarmed Interpositionary Peace Forces," *Journal of Peace Research* (February 1993), Vol. 30, No.1, pp. 45-64. Also, Yeshua Moser-Puangsuwan, "Grassroots Initiatives in Unarmed Peacekeeping," *Peace Review* (1996), Vol. 8, No. 8, pp. 569-576.

27. Nelson Mandela, *Long Walk to Freedom: The Autobiography of Nelson Mandela* (New York: Little, Brown and Company, 1994), pp. 453-454.

28. Duane L. Cady, "Pacifist Perspectives on Humanitarian Intervention," in Robert L. Phillips and Duane L. Cady, *Humanitarian Intervention: Just War vs. Pacifism* (Lanham, NH: Rowman & Littlefield Publishers, Inc., 1996), p. 73.

6

Covert Action Against Genocide

Sure, I get scared sometimes. But I don't have a choice. I took on this mission and now I could never go back to Stockholm unless I knew inside myself that I'd done everything to save as many Jews as possible.

> — Raoul Wallenberg, Swedish diplomat and secret U.S. operative, credited with saving tens of thousands of Jews during the Holocaust

I know a person will betray me before they know it themselves.

> — Saddam Hussein, who survived countless assassination attempts

Covert action is one of several terms used to describe operations designed to influence events in a foreign country while allowing the instigator to plausibly deny direct involvement.[1] Other terms include *active measures*, *special activities*, and even *dirty tricks*. Since the idea of covert action enjoys an exotic mystique among the general public, it can be an almost romantic way to fight genocide. Only under very particular conditions, however, is covert action a truly practical option. It tends to be most effective when it only supplements other activities, ranging from domestic nonviolent resistance to foreign military intervention. Alone, it is rarely sufficient.

This chapter, to emphasize the limits of covert action, examines it as an option used in isolation.

SECRETLY ARMING THE IMPERILED

During the Bosnian War there were loud calls to supply the endangered Bosnian-Muslims with weaponry so they could defend themselves against "ethnic cleansing." This might well have balanced the relative forces in Bosnia, but in general the basic option of smuggling arms to an endangered people involves several problems. Until the Bosnian War forcibly separated Bosnia's intermixed Serb, Croat, and Muslim communities, arming only the Muslims was virtually impossible. Even if an imperiled people can directly receive enough smuggled weaponry, arranging that delivery network requires time and money, particularly a secret network delivering untraceable weapons. And more time and money, and advisors as well, could be needed to train the imperiled people how to use those weapons. Marksmanship, how to clean and repair weaponry, the proper care of ammunition—such training should not be left to guesswork, especially for machine guns, antitank missile launchers, or any type of artillery piece.

There is also the problem of recruitment. There could be plenty of volunteers, but should the recruits include boys and girls as young as fifteen years old? As young as twelve? Or nine? Since 1978 a protocol to the Geneva Conventions states:

The Parties to the conflict shall take all feasible measures in order that children who have not attained the age of 15 years do not take a direct part in hostilities and, in particular, they shall refrain from recruiting them into their armed forces. In recruiting among those persons who have attained the age of 15 years, but who have not attained the age of 18 years, the Parties to the conflict shall endeavor to give priority to those who are oldest.[2]

Child soldiers become commonplace in desperate times, but should their recruitment be encouraged by spreading firearms, whatever the justification? Will the great majority of them, and their elders, behave themselves? Will they all respect the various Geneva Conventions? Or will they avenge atrocities with their own atrocities? Should their outside suppliers of weaponry impose any standards?

Should the infirm and elderly be armed? What about the women, young and old, who want only to care for their children and siblings? Should they, too, be armed? In many war-ravaged places a nutritional disparity exists between the combatants, who are well fed, and the noncombatants, who are often underfed. This disparity exists because the people with guns have guns. To counter this, should the noncombatants be armed?

During the 1980s the United States secretly armed the *mujahedin* guerrillas of Afghanistan to fight that country's Soviet military occupation. That weaponry may have prevented a number of Soviet atrocities, but no one knows how many. What is known is that the war lasted for almost a decade, produced more than 4 million refugees, and left Afghanistan less tolerant and less governable than it was before the war. Many of those secretly funneled weapons have since gone to militant anti-Western groups, including terrorists. Any such "failed state" awash in weapons poses a vexing international problem even after the worst fighting stops. Moreover, elsewhere, lethal weapons are not necessarily the weapons of choice. The resistance movements of Tibet and Myanmar (Burma), for example, have been avowedly nonviolent.[3]

Whenever an imperiled people plead desperately for weapons, is there a moral obligation to supply them? Perhaps or perhaps not, but either way the romantic notion of a gallant underdog fighting against evil should not obscure the harsh reality of what too often happens. The Warsaw ghetto uprising of 1943 was a bold display of Jewish courage and tenacity against the Nazis, but it failed to even pause the Nazis' Final Solution. And the Warsaw ghetto was annihilated.

PHYSICAL SABOTAGE

Foreign commandos or native partisans might be able to sabotage key sites of whatever physical infrastructure is directly used by a genocide, as railways were to transport Jews to the Nazi death camps. Sabotage is still a difficult and dangerous option, however, only feasible when that genocide is indeed sustained by a vulnerable physical infrastructure. Such vulnerability is perhaps more true of centrally controlled genocides than for decentralized ones. A decentralized genocide might have some physical vulnerability, such as a radio or television station broadcasting hate propaganda, but destroying that one target might not stop the genocide, nor even pause it. There are also the practical difficulties of finding, training, equipping, and transporting enough saboteurs to and from their targets. Any supposed romance associated with the idea of sabotage should not obscure its practical constraints, its limited applicability, and its many physical and political risks.

ASSASSINATION

The idea of assassination may seem notorious in the abstract, but it gains in popularity when a notorious leader such as Adolf Hitler or Saddam Hussein is suggested as the target. As a practical option against genocide, however, it is extremely unreliable. For an assassination to be both feasible and beneficial, two preconditions must exist: The human target must be vulnerable, and his assassination must not bring to power someone similar or worse.

The first precondition is often sufficient to discourage the effort. Leaders who perpetrate genocide know they risk being assassinated, and so they take elaborate precautions to minimize their vulnerability. "I quite understand why 90 percent of the historic assassinations have been successful," boasted Hitler to his staff in 1942. "The only preventive measure one can take," he explained, "is to live irregularly: to walk, drive, and travel at irregular times and unexpectedly. . . . As far as possible, when I go anywhere by car, I go off unexpectedly and without warning the police." [4] For years Saddam Hussein slept in a different house every night, chosen at random from several confiscated for that one evening from Iraqi families placed in a hotel. Hussein used surgically altered doubles of himself for exposed public appearances. And he insisted on receiving only photocopies of his letters, lest the originals be coated with secret toxins. Despite the hazards of being a target, leaders such as Hitler and Hussein usually survive. Between 1991 and 1998, Hussein survived at least twenty attempted *coup d'etats* against him. "I know a person will betray me before they know it themselves," he remarked. [5]

The second precondition—a target not likely to be replaced by someone similar or worse—can be even more prohibitive. Genocides are not committed by one leader acting alone. The leader rules a regime, he is not the regime itself. A genocide employ masses of people to murder masses of people, so killing one one murderous leader will not guarantee a good successor will always emerge, or that the genocide will truly end. Indeed, amid the often violent politics of a genocidal regime, as well as the inevitable rumors of foreign involvement after any assassination attempt, the odds of a good outcome from an assassination are not very high. Perhaps the number of bad successors can be reduced through multiple assassinations, but these need to occur almost simultaneously to avoid alerting the other targets. Unless the targets are all expected to gather together at the same time, however, planning and executing multiple assassinations can be enormously complicated.

SECRET NON-LETHAL MATERIAL SUPPORT

Secret material support does not have to involve supplying firearms or combat training. During the later months of the Holocaust, the U.S. War Refugee Board smuggled basic survival supplies to thousands of endangered Europeans, including money, forged documents (identity cards, work permits, birth and baptismal certificates, ration cards, etc.), as well as small items such as soaps and cheap watches, which, because of their scarcity in Axis-controlled countries, could be used to bribe border officials and policemen.[6] Such help takes time to arrange, however, especially if it is to be done secretly. It also cannot stop a genocide very quickly, if ever. Therefore, it may be most appropriate against a gradual genocide.

PSYCHOLOGICAL OPERATIONS

Psychological operations, abbreviated as PSYOP or *psyop*, are a form of propaganda. The U.S. government defines *psyop* as:

Planned operations to convey selected information and indicators to foreign audiences to influence their emotions, motives, objective reasoning, and ultimately the behavior of foreign governments, organizations, groups and individuals. The purpose of psychological operations is to induce or reinforce foreign attitudes and behavior favorable to the originator's objectives.[7]

The psychological power of radio, television, booklets, and leaflets can be used to discourage a genocide even as its perpetrators try to incite the genocide with their own propaganda. Adolf Hitler, in his book *Mein Kampf,* asserted that every propagandist should "endeavor to upset [the public's] confidence in the convictions they have hitherto held. In order that such propaganda should have a backbone to it, it must be based on an organization."[8] With this remark Hitler expressed, however unintentionally, both the main strength and main weakness of an outside-based *psyop* campaign against a genocide. Its main strength is that the *psyop* campaign needs only to debunk the regime's propaganda to have some effect. Its main weakness is that the presence of the campaign in the target country—that is, its organization there—may consist of only illegal broadcasts and underground literature. Genocidal propaganda, by contrast, has a human presence on the scene: vocal enthusiasts urging the killers on, issuing orders, and inciting people through mob violence, terror, zeal, and peer pressure.

Genocidal regimes are also masters of the "Big Lie"—*say something often enough and people start to believe it.* Describing the Big Lie, Hitler explained: "At first all of it appeared to be idiotic in its imprudent assertiveness. Later on, it was looked upon as disturbing, but finally it was believed." [9] This imbedded mind-set of the Big Lie is what a *psyop* campaign faces in trying to discourage a genocide.

The credibility of any message depends as much on the credibility of its source as upon the plausibility of its content. When the message is declared by a powerful foreign government, even by an elected one, its credibility may not be much better than if it had come from a biased dictatorship because many people simply do not trust governments, elected or otherwise. Moreover, any hint of hypocrisy can arouse an eloquent counterattack by rival propagandists—and, for their source material, every democratic country has some past embarrassments. For example, a book written by some young Chinese writers in 1996 declared:

Those who criticize the fact that "America bashing" has become fashionable in China ignore the fact that "China bashing" has always been fashionable in America. The younger generation in China can't stand America's disingenuous preachiness on human rights—haven't we all seen the video of Rodney King, or the immigrant workers being mercilessly beaten by police in Riverside, California?—or its irresponsible threats on trade sanctions and Taiwan. [10]

"The art of propaganda," asserted Hitler, "consists precisely in being able to awaken the imagination of the public through an appeal to their feelings, in finding the appropriate psychological form that will arrest the attention and appeal to the hearts of the national masses." [11] Effective propaganda, in other words, builds upon an emotional appeal to a group identity. Many people who commit genocide sincerely believe that their group identity provides them with meaning as human beings, and that their acts of genocide are necessary to defend that meaning. Unfortunately, intellectual reasoning may not be very effective against such a passionately held delusion, at least not against its most zealous believers.

Luckily, not everyone will succumb to this delusion. "What amazed me was how many Yugoslavs resisted the incessant racist propaganda," recounted retired U.S. Ambassador Warren Zimmermann about the early 1990s. Though many other Yugoslavs were swayed by ethnic-based fears and hatreds promoted by state-controlled television, Zimmermann recalled that "Most of the people my wife and I met in six years in Yugoslavia were peaceful and decent, without a trace of the hostility which nationalism feeds." [12]

To oppose a genocide, therefore, towards whom should a *psyop* campaign be directed? Towards the perpetrators? The victims? The bystanders? What is it, precisely, that we want them to do? How are they supposed to do it? Can they be encouraged to act by some compelling reason or feeling? The campaign should be based on at least some understanding of the target audience's culture, the genocidal regime, and the genocide itself. A practical knowledge of human psychology and mass media communications, both overt and covert, are also valuable.

The *psyop* campaign can resort to deception, but at some risk. It could plant the rumor, for instance, that an outside military intervention against the genocide is imminent and therefore the perpetrators will soon be punished whereas anyone who protects the persecuted will soon be rewarded. Depending upon which "source" is considered most credible, this *psyop* effort could masquerade as a commercial broadcasting news station, an official information service, or a rebel group supposedly operating inside the target country. During World War II, Allied *psyop* broadcasters posing as a German resistance group inside the Third Reich actually duplicated the regional accents and social idioms specific to the particular German audiences they sought to influence.[13]

If the deceptive rumor is widely believed, it might save some lives. But for how long? Is the target audience supposed to revolt while the persecuted are still being killed? Or is the target audience supposed to hide the persecuted and in the meantime act inconspicuous? Such behavior could inadvertently help the regime by appearing to be public acquiescence. As the bitter truth of the *psyop* lie becomes known when no intervention occurs, feelings of disappointment, betrayal, and resentment could result—and the persecuted-in-hiding could feel the backlash. If, from the safety of our political and physical distance, we employ a *psyop* campaign to incite others to risk themselves to save a persecuted people, what obligation do *we* incur? If we succeed in only pausing the genocide instead of truly stopping it, do we have a moral obligation to intervene with troops to finish what we began ending with our own propaganda?

RESCUERS OF THE PERSECUTED

A *rescuer* is someone who actively helps one or more persecuted persons to survive, even in ways personally dangerous to the rescuer. In the Holocaust there were at least 13,618 rescuers of Jews—the number of "Righteous Gentiles" individually honored by Yad Vashem in Jerusalem in 1995.[14] Yet that number is only a minimum. Estimates of the total vary widely, from 50,000 to perhaps as many as half-a-million. Unfortunately, even half-a-million rescuers, if true, represented only a tiny portion of the approximately 300 million Europeans under Nazi rule at its height.[15] For every 600 non-Jewish bystanders, if not for every 6,000, there was but one rescuer of Jews worthy of being called a "Righteous Gentile." [16] To be a rescuer was to be exceptional, in more ways than one. Yet such exceptional people seem to exist amid every genocide. After the Rwandan genocide of 1994, one visitor noted:

I stumbled upon individual [Tutsis] who somehow managed to survive, sometimes with the help of an ethnic Hutu neighbor. In Nyamata, a young Hutu named Jean-Paul took it upon himself to save thirty-two Tutsi neighbors. Jean-Paul's own father was a local leader who helped coordinate the massacres in that area. It was clear in my interviews that Jean-Paul is deified by those thirty-two survivors, no less than Oskar Schindler is revered by the 1,000 or more persons on his list fifty years ago.[17]

An expert at Yad Vashem estimated that perhaps as many as 250,000 Jews were saved by rescuers.[18] Some rescuers operated as individuals, saving several Jews each. Other rescuers, often members of the same family, worked in teams to save as few as one Jew. Although the number of Jews saved is dwarfed by the 6 million who were murdered, 250,000 Jews saved is still a sizable figure. In a future genocide, could the number and influence of rescuers be encouraged artificially? The answer may depend in part on the specific type of rescuer. Rescuers can be categorized as either *native rescuers* or *foreign rescuers*.

Native Rescuers

A *native rescuer* is someone who lives where the genocide rages but is, him or herself, comparatively safe, or at least less persecuted. When the conditions they face are relatively favorable, native rescuers can accomplish remarkable feats. During a three-month period in Nazi-occupied Denmark, Danish native rescuers smuggled out all but 600 of Denmark's 8,000 Jews to safety in neutral Sweden, mostly in fishing boats. But Denmark's situation was unique, for in addition to being one of Europe's most tolerant democracies before the war, Denmark experienced the mildest occupation of any Nazi-occupied country. It was a sympathetic German official who tipped off the Danes that a Nazi roundup of Danish Jews was imminent.

Holland was another of Europe's most tolerant democracies before the war, and during the Holocaust there were many Dutch native rescuers. But because Holland's experience with Nazi occupation was far worse than Denmark's, rescue activities in Holland were nevertheless much more difficult. Yet at least in both countries the general population abhorred anti-Semitism. In too many other Nazi-occupied countries, such as Poland and France, anti-Semitism was so widespread that the general population could endanger a native rescuer of Jews as much as the Nazi regime did.

One of the most colorful of native rescuers during the Holocaust was Oskar Schindler, a German businessman and a member of the Nazi Party, though secretly disenchanted with it. More typical of native rescuers was Miep Gies, the Dutchwoman who secretly funneled supplies to Anne Frank and her family until they were discovered in hiding in 1944. "There is nothing special about me," Gies later wrote. "I was only willing to do what was asked of me and what seemed necessary at the time," she explained. "It was not enough." [19]

She may seem modest in describing herself, but Gies was being honest. Survey studies of native rescuers reveal that whereas they did something exceptional under exceptional circumstances, otherwise they are ordinary people living ordinary lives. Some are religious, others are not. A few are religious fanatics, others are avowed atheists. All of them have a helpful personality, but that willingness to help others, even heroically, is not always obvious, not even to the native rescuers themselves—not even *after* the fact. "If someone wanted to give me a million dollars today, I could not do it," explained one rescuer many years later. "But back then, it was life and death." [20]

According to rescuers' own testimonies, their transformation from bystanders to native rescuers was almost always an act of impulsive kindness rather than a long-pondered dilemma. Explained one Dutch rescuer who, with her husband, hid over thirty Jews:

My husband and I never sat down and discussed it or said, "Let's go help some Jews." . . . It was a spontaneous reaction, actually. Such things, such responses depend on fate, on the result of your upbringing, on your general love for people. . . . There was also a kind of nonchalance and optimism about it. I would say to myself, *Oh c'mon, you can do that.*[21]

The motives of another rescuing couple, both Poles, can be gleaned through this testimony of the husband's broken English:

When I am going to the [Warsaw] ghetto, I get stiff, I not believe, what was there, so many children was laid down, already dead. You walk blocks and blocks, dead children, dead and they covered by paper, just. They so skinny, the children, and the men stay and the women sit down, like ready to die, the fly eat from the nose, from the mouth. I was there, I, I, I, I never believed it can be like that. . . . And the Jewish children tag at your jacket, "Hey mister give me something, give me something." Then my friend say, "Hey, don't give nothing, because they no got a chance." But I say, "How can you not give?" How much money I had, I not remember, but I [give] everything. After I come home and I explain for my wife. My wife say, "You know, maybe me take a child from somebody."[22]

As the above testimony reveals, having personal contact with the people being persecuted, even if only a passing acquaintance, was an important factor. One native rescuer with a psychology background explained a few other factors:

It also helped very much to have a happy marriage, because when you feel strong at home you can be strong for other people. A lot of people did not have these advantages. I ask myself whether I can blame the people who said, "No, I can't do it." Some of those people lived in very unhappy homes where they quarreled all the time and didn't trust each other.

    People also knew that when they helped others they would endanger the people with whom they lived, as well as the people they were hiding. Some had family members who were very sick and needed help. Some people were in a location where it was absolutely dangerous.

    If you were to know the circumstances of all the people who did not help, you might be thankful that some of them didn't get involved. Some believed it would end in disaster and failure for them, as well as for the people who were hiding. These people lacked self-confidence which, in many instances, blocked their ability to help.[23]

Several studies of rescuers were conducted by Samuel P. Oliner and his wife Pearl. Samuel, a sociologist by training, was as a young Jewish boy saved by a native rescuer in Nazi-occupied Poland. In their research, the Oliners found:

Rescuers' parents were more likely to have disciplined them by reasoning and explanation of the consequences of their misbehavior than by verbal or physical punishment, which was common among nonrescuers. . . . While none of the more than fifty studies of rescue have arrived at a single reason for rescue, nearly all concur that such motivation is most often associated with a particular type of socialization experience and moral climate in which ethical behavior was molded by a significant other, such as a parent. This may help account for the frequently reiterated statements made by rescuers that helping Jews was simply the moral thing to do.[24]

Not all Holocaust-era rescuers acted out of moral convictions, but most did, according to the research of social psychologist Eva Fogelman. Of this group, which she described as *moral rescuers,* she wrote:

They did not leap at every opportunity to correct wrongdoing. On the contrary, moral rescuers rarely initiated action. Unlike rescuers with other types of motivation (such as people who were propelled by hatred of the Third Reich), moral rescuers typically launched their activity only after being asked to help or after an encounter with suffering and death that reawakened their consciences. For the most part, when asked to help, moral rescuers could not say no.[25]

If a person's childhood nurture, as well as chance experiences during the genocide itself, are so important in the formation of a native rescuer, a *psyop* campaign may find it very difficult indeed to simply "incite" or "persuade" them into existence. Historically, most *psyop* campaigns have attempted to simply undermine an enemy's morale. Inducing people to purposely become native rescuers is a much more action-oriented goal, one that outside persuasion alone —pitted against genocidal tyranny and terror—may only rarely achieve.

Perhaps a *psyop* campaign should therefore attempt to influence a genocide's intended victims. By warning them a genocide against them is either impending or ongoing, they could encouraged to seek out their own native rescuers. Such a warning may not always be possible, but very often it is. Furthermore, as one survivor asked rhetorically, "Would anybody get me alive to Auschwitz if I had *had* this information? Would thousands and thousands of able-bodied Jewish men send their children, wives, mothers to Auschwitz from all over Europe if they *knew?* " [26] One of the problems with simply warning people is that the institutions that could best issue warnings often face considerable political and bureaucratic pressures to keep silent, not least because such warnings would self-impose a moral obligation to do something more than only warn people.

Native rescue is, typically, a tedious, unglamorous, emotionally draining experience. It involves innumerable dirty tasks, including the routine and yet inconspicuous disposal of human waste from the hiding place. For days, months, or even years, the rescuer must find and deliver supplies to his/her people in hiding, probably in a land where food is rationed and shortages abound. And throughout this stressful period the native rescuer must present an image of normalcy to everyone else, including to friends, family members, and suspicious neighbors. During the Holocaust one particular mother and her grown daughter visited each other's homes every weekend; throughout those years, neither told the other each was hiding Jews.[27]

Perhaps a *psyop* campaign could lessen this emotional stress by transmitting sympathetic broadcasts. Native rescuers could be reminded by television or programs that they are not alone and their sacrifices not in vain. Perhaps the testimonies of rescuers from earlier genocides could be aired, revealing how they coped. Such broadcasts do entail risks, however. By noting the hazards and complexities of native rescue, such broadcasts could inadvertently deter people from becoming native rescuers. And any information aired will also reach the killers, so the aired information must be specific enough to help native rescuers and yet not specific enough to help the killers. Even some off-hand advice could be dangerous if aired. If, for example, a broadcast recommends the use of a particular medicine to treat some rising ailment in the country (such as flu, scurvy, or dysentery), there could be a suspiciously sudden demand for that particular medicine after the broadcast, inadvertently exposing native rescuers in their collective enthusiasm. All native rescuers begin as amateurs and, as amateurs, they can commit some tiny yet perilous mistakes.

Foreign Rescuers

A *foreign rescuer* is a foreign emissary, usually a diplomat, who exploits his or her official position and stature to save lives. The most famous of foreign rescuers during the Holocaust was Raoul Wallenberg. More typical, however, was Chiune Sugihara.

In late 1939 and early 1940, after Poland was invaded and subdivided between Nazi Germany and the Soviet Union, masses of terrified Jews fled into nearby Lithuania. Stranded between two totalitarian anti-Semitic empires, those Jews rightfully feared for their lives. Chiune Sugihara, the Japanese diplomatic consul in Kovno, Lithuania, willingly issued them transit visas by considerably stretching his own government's official rules, allowing the Polish Jews to cross Soviet territory en route to Japan and, from there, to anywhere they wished. Before the Japanese government reassigned him, Sugihara issued some 4,500 visas, many of them handwritten, and he did not stop issuing visas until literally the moment before his train carried him out of Kovno. His visas were also easy to counterfeit. Combined with those forgeries, Sugihara's efforts may well have saved some 10,000 Jews.[28]

Chiune Sugihara was but a minor diplomat, authorized to issue transit visas under very limited circumstances. He knew the Japanese government in Tokyo might bring serious legal charges against him, or worse, if either the Soviet regime complained too loudly or he fell out of favor amid the complicated and often violent power struggles that characterized Tokyo at that time. Yet Sugihara felt that the desperate refugees he saw had to be helped regardless. He later explained:

It is the kind of sentiment anyone would have when he actually sees the refugees face to face, begging with tears in their eyes. He just cannot help but sympathize with them. Among the refugees were the elderly and women. They were so desperate that they went so far as to kiss my shoes—yes, I actually witnessed such scenes with my own eyes. Also, I felt at that time that the Japanese government did not have any uniform opinion in Tokyo. Some Japanese military leaders were just scared of the pressure from the Nazis, while other officials in the Home Ministry were simply excited. . . . But I myself thought this would be the right thing to do. There is nothing wrong in saving many people's lives. If anybody sees anything wrong in the action, it is because something "not pure" exists in their state of mind.[29]

What Sugihara might have accomplished if his own government had fully supported him can be only imagined. What he did accomplish illustrates what one foreign rescuer with some diplomatic credentials can do. When diplomats are empowered to issue visas at their own discretion, at least during times of genocidal danger, they can become foreign rescuers with little or no effort. And since genocides are, by definition, inflicted against entire populations, those populations usually include large numbers of dedicated workers and skilled professionals who, as refugees, can invigorate the economy of the receiving country. But, today, accepting refugees is not a widely popular policy among democratic governments, and certainly not an unconditional policy. Even countries that have historically welcomed refugees now strictly limit whom and how many refugees they will accept.

The Method of Raoul Wallenberg

Raoul Wallenberg was an officially minor diplomat assigned to Sweden's small legation in Budapest, Hungary. A legation is an embassy of lesser status because it lacks an ambassador. Sweden was officially neutral in World War II. Hungary was an ally of Nazi Germany. Wallenberg, with the permission of the Swedish government, was secretly employed by the U.S. War Refugee Board for a special mission in Hungary: *save Jews*. And he did. From July 1944, when he arrived in Budapest, until January 1945, when Budapest was captured by advancing Soviet troops, Wallenberg saved as many as 100,000 Jews by some estimates.[30]

How did he do it? And could his method be used again? It all depended upon a set of circumstances that may never exist again, but his method does deserve a review.

By 1944, Hungary's wartime alliance with Nazi Germany against the Soviet Union was an increasingly reluctant one. On the eastern front German and Hungarian troops were in retreat, albeit slowly, as the Red Army inched its way towards Budapest and Berlin. For the government of Hungary's leader, Admiral Miklos Horthy, this worrisome situation raised the specter that a defeated Hungary could become a Soviet satellite unless Hungary gained some friends among the other Allied Powers, particularly the United States and Great Britain, neither of whom Hungary was officially at war with. But Hitler, meanwhile, wanted to exterminate Hungary's 725,000 Jews, a Nazi obsession likely to antagonize the American and British governments if Horthy acquiesced. While anti-Semitism did exist in Hungary as a cultural prejudice, it was not the racial extermination-oriented ideology of Nazism. Horthy, in a face to face meeting with Hitler in 1943, bluntly told him: "The Jews cannot be exterminated or beaten to death."[31]

Hitler thought otherwise and soon lost patience with Horthy. But he also calculated that the old admiral might still be useful to him. In early 1944 Hitler ordered German forces to occupy Hungary but to keep Horthy's government minimally in power.

It is important to note how relative Horthy's anti-Semitic prejudice was, because between his prejudice versus Hitler's obsession with extermination is where Wallenberg's method emerged and maneuvered. Three quotes illustrate how narrow that margin was. This first quote is from Joseph Goebbels, written in his personal diary:

The Hungarian state is permeated with Jews, and the Fuehrer did not succeed during his talk with Horthy in convincing the latter of the necessity of more stringent measures. . . . [Horthy] gave a number of humanitarian counterarguments which, of course, don't apply at all to this situation. You just cannot talk humanitarianism when dealing with Jews. Jews must be defeated. The Fuehrer made every effort to win Horthy over to his standpoint but succeeded only partially.[32]

This next quote comes from the war crimes trial testimony of Edmund Veesenmayer, Nazi Germany's plenipotentiary representative to Hungary:

Horthy himself told me that he was interested only in protecting those prosperous, the economically valuable Jews in Budapest, those who were well off. However, as to the remaining Jewry—and he used a very ugly term here—he had no interest in them and was quite prepared to have them go to the [Third] Reich or elsewhere for labor.[33]

The last quote is from Horthy himself, as told to Laszlo Baky, a Hungarian Fascist who later played a major role in the mass extermination of Hungary's Jews. Horthy told him:

Baky, the Germans have cheated me. Now they want to deport the Jews. I don't mind. I hate the Galician Jews and the Communists. Out with them! Out of the country! But you must see, Baky, that there are some Jews who are as good Hungarians as you and I— for example, [the industrialist Ferenc] Chorin and [the parliamentarian Jeno] Vida. Aren't they good Hungarians? I can't allow these to be taken away. But they can take the rest.[34]

By mid-1944, perhaps really believing that Hungarian Jews could somehow survive as Nazi slaves, Horthy's government emptied Hungary of hundreds of thousands of them and deported them on Nazi trains. Most died in Auschwitz. Horthy ended the deportations in July after an apparent change of heart, telling his government ministers, "The deportation is merely a cruel solution and does not coincide with the Hungarian character." [35] Only the Jewish community in Budapest remained intact: about a quarter-million people.

Before Wallenberg arrived that same July, the Swedish legation in Budapest had already stretched the limits of international law by issuing out some 700 "provisional passports" to Hungarian Jews with family or business ties in Sweden. Normally such passports were issued only to Swedish citizens to replace their original passports if they lost them abroad. Wallenberg, within a day of his arrival, devised a new document to issue to Hungarian Jews: the Swedish "protective pass." It had official Swedish markings, an approval signature, a photo of the bearer, some personal data, and the following text, printed in both Hungarian and German:

The Royal Swedish Legation in Budapest confirms that the above-mentioned person will travel to Sweden in the course of repatriation as authorized by the Royal Swedish Ministry of Foreign Affairs. The name of the person in question is covered by a collective passport. Until his departure, the above-mentioned person and his home are to be regarded as protected by the Royal Swedish Legation in Budapest. The validity of this document expires two weeks after arrival in Sweden. The journey to Sweden can only be undertaken on a collective passport, which is the only one to be furnished with a visa.

Under international law, *this document had no legal standing whatsoever.* Yet Wallenberg personally managed to convince Horthy to officially recognize it, and what it proposed, as one of several less severe ways of solving Hungary's "Jewish problem" than with what the Nazis were trying to do. Armed with Horthy's approval, Wallenberg then gained the acquiescence of the German forces in Hungary, playing upon their tendency to respect any official-looking document. The Nazis did realize that this strange document might cause them some inconvenience, but they reasoned that their respect of it would be an easy way to satisfy the squeamish consciences of neutral diplomats in Budapest— while the rest of the city's Jews remained conveniently unprotected.

The Hungarian government authorized Wallenberg to issue no more than 4,500 passes, a limit that compelled him, at least officially, to enforce an extremely selective eligibility criteria. Applicants had to prove they had either a close family relative in Sweden, at least a first cousin, or a significant business connection there, one of some years' standing. Documentation was required, such as letters with Swedish postmarks or Swedish tax forms. Since only a tiny fraction of Budapest's Jews could prove either of such ties, the first few passes went mainly to the very wealthy or well connected. The passes were distributed, one per family—Wallenberg hoped one per family would be enough—through an elaborate processing section run by prominent Jewish-Hungarian businessmen, hired by Wallenberg after Hungary's rising anti-Semitic fervor had left them all unemployed.

Soon the other neutral legations in Budapest began copying Wallenberg's idea, issuing their own protective passes, all of which Horthy's government agreed to honor. Switzerland, Spain, Portugal, the Holy See's Papal Nuncio, even the honorary consul of El Salvador issued protective passes, although their eligibility requirements tended to be even more restrictive than Sweden's. (The Spanish legation restricted its passes to the descendants of Jews expelled from Spain in the sixteenth century.) But Wallenberg's idea had nonetheless started something. Even the International Red Cross issued protective passes, although its passes had no governmental backing at all.

Soon forgeries began to appear—by the thousands. Since forgeries protected more Jews, especially Jews too poor or untraveled to qualify for a genuine pass, Wallenberg secretly approved. And to aid those forgery efforts, he deliberately disorganized his own accounting system with random pass numbers to make the exposure of phony passes more difficult. And he encouraged the other legations to do the same.

As thousands of Hungarian Jews now suddenly came under official Swedish protection, Wallenberg sheltered them in buildings he acquired near the Swedish legation and later in buildings he acquired all over Budapest. He also tried to ensure that, in spite of wartime food shortages, his Jews were fed. Unlike the Jews hidden by native rescuers, Wallenberg's Jews were not hidden: They were "protected" by Swedish flags hung outside their buildings, in another dubious stretch of diplomatic immunity. Once again his idea was copied by the other neutral legations and the Red Cross, and eventually hundreds of buildings were "protected" this way. When Soviet troops entered Budapest in January 1945, they found so many foreign and Red Cross flags hanging throughout the city that a Soviet field marshal remarked, "Apparently I have come to a Swiss or Swedish city, not a Hungarian one." [36]

Months before the Soviets arrived, however, disaster struck Hungary's Jews. In October 1944, a sudden Nazi-inspired *coup d'etat* overthrew the government of Admiral Horthy and replaced it with a far more brutal, Nazified regime, that immediately resumed the deportations of Jews to Auschwitz. To continue saving Jews in this dire situation, Wallenberg exploited two legacies inherited by that new regime: The protective pass system and the Hungarian bureaucracy.

When Horthy's government had accepted the protective pass system, it established a legal precedent—one the neutral legations in Budapest insisted the new regime honor. Whenever that regime tried to renounce the protective pass system, as it sometimes did, it immediately encountered diplomatic outrage that it felt obligated to calm. So frequently did it renounce and then reinstate the protective pass system that its own bureaucrats and policemen became confused, keeping the system alive because they were not sure it was dead. Wallenberg, in this confusion, secretly dropped his rigid criteria for pass eligibility, ultimately distributing more than twice as many Swedish passes as Horthy's government had authorized him.

Meanwhile, as Hungary's wartime situation became increasingly desperate, Hungarian officials became increasingly nervous, especially when Wallenberg threatened them with war crimes trials whenever they obstructed his plans. His threat was more of a bluff than a certainty, even in late 1944, but on occasion his bluff worked. He was also lavish with bribes, paying off countless bureaucrats, policemen, and soldiers with almost anything: scarce goods, Swedish protective passes to escape the advancing Red Army, promises of favorable mention in a future war crimes trial, and money—lots of money. Funded by the U.S. War Refugee Board and by private Jewish groups, Wallenberg held sizable financial resources and he cared little who he paid off. He once said he would bribe the Devil himself if that might save lives. Wallenberg paid off so many people, including secret contacts, informants, con artists, and forgers, that his network rivaled almost any espionage ring in wartime Europe.

Today, it is unlikely that even a wealthy government would permit one of its diplomatic agents to bribe literally anyone at will, as Wallenberg did. It is simply too expensive. Most intelligence agencies prefer to bribe one particular individual, turning him into a long-productive "spy," than attempt to bribe great multitudes of people for only short-term gains. To stop a genocide today, would any elected government be willing to bribe the foreign murderers? To bribe multitudes of them? If a free press uncovered this mass bribery, would it allow such bribery to continue unexposed? Would today's taxpayers approve?

Yet through bribery, persuasion, coercion, and on occasion even a moral argument, Wallenberg rescued small groups of Jews here and there even as the new regime tried to deport them all. One of his most valuable contacts was the wife of the new regime's foreign minister. She prevailed upon her husband to keep the protective pass system valid in Hungary, and for some weeks he did. The regime also craved at least the illusion of broad international acceptance. Wallenberg, to gain a small concession here and there, fed that illusion with as much official flattery as he could gush—at least when he was not objecting to one or another of the regime's anti-Semitic policies. Today, however, most genocidal regimes seem less likely to become so addicted to the charm of foreign diplomats. Furthermore, in view of Wallenberg's many illicit activities in Budapest, it seems remarkable that he was not declared *persona non grata* ("person unacceptable") and expelled back to Sweden.

Wallenberg was also able to exploit a necessary step in the Nazi system of genocide: the deportations. Flaunting his diplomatic credentials, he would push is way through to the Nazi death trains just before their departure and thereupon rescue some Jews. When confronted by any SS or Hungarian guards, he would suddenly spout some convenient ruse with an intimidating ferocity:

This is an outrage! *An outrage!* How *dare* you threaten a diplomatic representative of the Kingdom of Sweden! *And this, too, is an outrage!* I have it on good authority that among those arrested by you for deportation are Jews protected by the King of Sweden! How *dare* you rob them of their freedom! *Release them at once! AT ONCE!!! OR I'LL LODGE A FORMAL DIPLOMATIC PROTEST WITH YOUR SUPERIORS!!!* [37]

When the guards were sufficiently intimidated—which they usually were, facing an utterly self-confident Nordic diplomat screaming at them in fluent German—Wallenberg pressed his ruse even further. He would, for example, scan the condemned crowd, pretend to recognize particular Jews, and hand them passes. On at least one occasion he announced to a condemned crowd that he had Swedish protective passes for those on his "list"—actually a blank page in his accounting book, "from" which he called out the most common of Jewish surnames—and soon dozens of Jews stepped forward into safety. Wallenberg was a master of such ruses. But he could not have saved as many Jews as he did without the Nazis' preference for deportation, a routine he could exploit. When random pogroms later erupted in Budapest itself, not even the agile Wallenberg could be everywhere at once.

The darkest and most tragic aspect of Wallenberg's method was that, to save at least some of Budapest's Jews, the others had to die, or at least fend for themselves. This was because if every Jew in Budapest were issued an authentic protective pass, Wallenberg's already dubious pass system would have lost all credibility. Forced to choose between saving only some Jews versus saving none at all, Wallenberg chose to save some. "I want to save you all," he once whispered to a condemned crowd, "but they will only let me take a few. So please forgive me, but I must save the young ones because I want to save a nation." [38]

According to some estimates, Wallenberg did rescue as many as 100,000 Jews. Could seven Wallenberg-type diplomats have rescued 700,000 Hungarian Jews? Probably not, because Admiral Horthy was simply not interested in helping any Jews who did not live in Budapest—and without the cooperation of his government, no Wallenberg-type diplomat could save them. Moreover, it is unlikely that any foreign diplomat, except perhaps from Nazi Germany, could have received the Hungarian government's permission to roam throughout wartime Hungary beyond Budapest. Wallenberg squeezed out about as much cooperation as he probably could from Horthy's government, even getting it to accept a strange protective pass system without any validity under international law. Without that legacy of Horthy's cooperation and its legal precedent, along with the Nazis' own centralized system of genocide, Wallenberg could not have saved as many Jews as he later did under the more Nazified regime that replaced Horthy's. And none of Wallenberg's efforts could have succeeded without the constant pressure of the Soviet Red Army inching ever closer towards Budapest —a pressure that spurred a fearful incentive among at least some Hungarian officials to refrain from assisting the Nazis' genocidal efforts so devotedly.

The personal story of Raoul Wallenberg ends mysteriously, although almost certainly tragically. After the Red Army captured Budapest in January 1945, Wallenberg was arrested by the Soviet secret police, the NKVD. The fact that Wallenberg was a Swedish diplomat and in the secret employ of the USSR's wartime ally, the United States, did not help him. Indeed, those facts may have hurt him, because his American connections almost certainly marked him as a foreign spy in the suspicious eyes of the NKVD, an organization that treated all foreign spies as dangerous. Wallenberg disappeared into the GULAG; whether he died in prison soon after his arrest, or years later, or even decades later, may never be known for certain. Conflicting stories abound even today.

In 1981 the United States Congress bestowed honorary U.S. citizenship upon Raoul Wallenberg; at that time the only other honorary U.S. citizen was Winston Churchill. A permanent exhibit is devoted to Wallenberg and his rescue efforts at the U.S. Holocaust Memorial Museum. The museum itself is located near the central Mall in Washington, D.C., at 100 Raoul Wallenberg Place.

NOTES

1. Sound, scholarly, nonsensationalist books about covert action can be difficult to find. An excellent book written since the Cold War is: Roy Godson, *Dirty Tricks or Trump Cards: U.S. Covert Action and Counterintelligence* (London: Brassey's, 1995).

2. Excerpt from Article 77 of Protocol I, Additional to the Geneva Conventions of 12 August 1949, Relating to the Protection of Victims of International Armed Conflicts; opened for signature on June 8, 1977 and came into legal force on December 7, 1978.

3. In the 1950s and 1960s, the Tibetan resistance movement did receive some armaments and military training from the U.S. Central Intelligence Agency (CIA). The Dalai Lama, in his autobiography, related what resulted. See Tenzin Gyatso, *Freedom in Exile: The Autobiography of the Dalai Lama* (New York: Harper-Collins, 1990).

4. Quoted in William L. Shirer, *The Rise and Fall of the Third Reich: A History of Nazi Germany* (New York: Simon and Schuster, 1960), p. 1027n.

5. Melinda Liu and Alan Zarembo, "Saddam's Secret World," *Newsweek* (March 2, 1998), pp. 38-40.

6. David S. Wyman, *The Abandonment of the Jews: America and the Holocaust, 1941-1945* (New York: Pantheon Books, 1984), p. 232.

7. From Joint Pub 1-02, as quoted in the U.S. Armed Forces' *Joint Task Force Commander's Handbook for Peace Operations* (Fort Monroe, VA: Joint Warfighting Center, 28 February 1995).

8. Adolf Hitler, *Mein Kampf* (Boston: Houghton Mifflin, 1971), p. 321.

9. Ibid., p. 111.

10. Zhang Xiaobo and Song Qiang, "The China that can say No to America," *The National Times* (February 1997), pp. 25-26.

11. Hitler, p. 108.

12. Warren Zimmermann, *Origins of a Catastrophe* (New York: Times Books, 1996), p. xi.

13. Godson, p. 157.

14. Figure from Berel Lang, "For and Against the 'Righteous Gentiles,'" *Judaism* (Winter 1997), p. 91.

15. Eric Silver, *The Book of the Just: The Unsung Heroes Who Rescued Jews from Hitler* (New York: Grove Press, 1992), p. 2.

16. David P. Gushee, *The Righteous Gentiles of the Holocaust: A Christian Interpretation* (Minneapolis, MN: Augsburg Fortress Press, 1994), p. 9.

17. Roger Winter, "Rwanda, Up Close and Horrible" (Commentary), *Washington Post -- National Weekly Edition* (June 13-19, 1994), p. 23.

18. Gushee, *loc. cit.*

19. Miep Gies, *Anne Frank Remembered* (New York: Simon & Schuster, 1987), p. 11.

20. Eva Fogelman, *Conscience & Courage: Rescuers of Jews During the Holocaust* (New York: Anchor Books, 1994), p. 85.

21. Carol Rittner and Sondra Myers (editors), *The Courage to Care: Rescuers of Jews during the Holocaust* (New York: New York University Press, 1986), p. 27.

22. Quoted in Gushee, p. 114.

23. Rittner and Myers, pp. 25-26.

24. Samuel P. Oliner, "Rescuers of Jews during the Holocaust: A Portrait of Moral Courage," in Michael Berenbaum and Abraham J. Peck, *The Holocaust and History: The Known, the Unknown, the Disputed, and the Reexamined* (Bloomington, IN: Indiana University Press, 1998), pp. 678-690.

25. Eva Fogelman, "The Rescuer Self," in Berenbaum and Peck, pp. 663-677.

26. Wyman, p. 335.

27. Russell Miller, *The Resistance* (Alexandria, VA: Time-Life Books, 1979), p. 146.

28. Hillel Levine, *In Search of Sugihara* (New York: The Free Press, 1996).

29. Quoted in Levine, p. 259.

30. One of the more complete descriptions of Wallenberg's rescue activities is: Frederick E. Werbell and Thurston Clarke, *Lost Hero: The Mystery of Raoul Wallenberg* (New York: McGraw-Hill Book Company, 1982).

31. Quoted in Gay Block and Malka Drucker, *Rescuers: Portraits of Moral Courage in the Holocaust* (New York: Holmes & Meier Publishers, Inc., 1992), p. 213.

32. Quoted in Randolph L. Braham, *The Politics of Genocide: The Holocaust in Hungary, Volume I* (New York: Columbia University Press, 1981), p. 241.

33. Ibid.

34. Ibid., p. 379.

35. Quoted in Moshe Y. Herczl, *Christianity and the Holocaust of Hungarian Jewry* (New York: New York University Press, 1993), p. 216.

36. Werbell and Clarke, p. 189.

37. Ibid., p. 110.

38. Ibid., p. 105.

7

Ethical Principles of Humanitarian Intervention

Nations no longer have the right to be indifferent. The principles of nations'
sovereignty and of non-intervention in their domestic affairs—which remain
valid—nonetheless cannot be construed as a screen behind which one can
torture and assassinate.

— Pope John Paul II, 1992

State sovereignty in its most basic sense is being redefined by the forces of
globalization and international cooperation. The State is now widely
understood to be the servant of its people, and not vice versa. . . . Nothing in
the Charter [of the United Nations] precludes a recognition that there are
rights beyond borders.

— UN Secretary-General Kofi Annan, 1999

The term *humanitarian intervention* generally refers to an operation undertaken
in a foreign country to alleviate suffering caused there by a natural disaster or a
man-made emergency, such as a war or a genocide. The most controversial type
of humanitarian intervention involves the use of military forces, whether in the
form of combat forces or with units generally considered less violent, such as
transport, engineer, medical, security police, or civil affairs units (trained to help
a civil society rebuild itself). Many critics of humanitarian intervention decry it
as little more than a naïve attempt to undertake international "social work" using
the tools of power politics—something lofty in principle but perhaps ill advised
in practice. Other critics fear humanitarian intervention could become a form of
contemporary imperialism pursued under the guise of doing good, but ominously
similar to the "white man's burden" excuses of colonial times past.

In 1999 this controversy reached then-unprecedented heights when the NATO
alliance, led by the United States, waged a war against Slobodan Milosevic's

Yugoslavia to oppose genocidal "ethnic cleansing" by his regime against ethnic Albanians in Serbia's Kosovo province. NATO, calling its actions a humanitarian intervention, nevertheless did not invoke the Genocide Convention to justify its actions legally. Nor did NATO get—nor even seek—any direct approval from the UN Security Council in the form of a legal mandate. If NATO had tried to solicit the Council's approval, either Russia or China, or both, would almost certainly have vetoed it.

In September, three months after NATO won the war, UN Secretary-General Kofi Annan opened the UN General Assembly's fifty-fourth session with a provocative speech. Neither condemning NATO's actions as a violation of the UN Charter, nor downplaying the episode, Annan related it to the core of his speech: the occasional necessity for humanitarian intervention. With poignant experience, he told the assembled delegates:

To those for whom the greatest threat to the future of international order is the use of force in the absence of a Security Council mandate, one might ask, not in the context of Kosovo, but in the context of Rwanda: *If, in those dark days and hours leading up to the genocide, a coalition of States had been prepared to act in defense of the Tutsi population but did not receive prompt Council authorization, should such a coalition have stood aside and allowed the horror to unfold?*

To those for whom the Kosovo action heralded a new era when States and groups of States can take military action outside the established mechanisms for enforcing international law, one might ask: *Is there not a danger of...setting dangerous precedents for future interventions without a clear criterion to decide who might invoke these precedents, and in what circumstances?*

Just as we have learned that the world cannot stand aside when gross and systematic violations of human rights are taking place, so we have also learned that intervention must be based on legitimate and universal principles if it is to enjoy the sustained support of the world's peoples.[1]

Are there legitimate and universal principles for humanitarian intervention? By exploring some relevant schools of thought, this chapter offers some possible candidates.

AMID DIVERSITY, COMMONALITY

One argument raised against the very idea of humanitarian intervention is that different cultures have different concepts of what is right and wrong, of what is morally acceptable and what is not. But how true is this? In 1994 the spiritual leader of Tibetan Buddhism, the Fourteenth Dalai Lama, wrote in a published essay:

Some governments contend that the standards of human rights defined in the Universal Declaration of Human Rights are Western concepts and, therefore, do not apply to Asia and other parts of the Third World, both of which have experienced different patterns of cultural, social and economic development than the West.

I do not share this interpretation of human rights, and I am convinced that the majority of the world's population does not support it either. General standards of human rights apply to the people of all countries because, regardless of their cultural background, all humans share an inherent yearning for freedom, equality and dignity. Democracy and respect for fundamental human rights are as important to Africans and Asians as they are to Europeans and Americans. . . . Moreover, since those deprived of their rights are often those least able to speak up for themselves, the responsibility for the protection of universal human rights rests with those who already enjoy these freedoms.[2]

Perhaps not surprisingly, Kofi Annan, born in Ghana, agreed. In an address to a predominantly American audience in 1997, he declared:

There is no single model of democracy, or of human rights, or of cultural expression for all the world. But for all the world there must be democracy, human rights, and free cultural expression. Human ingenuity will ensure that each society, within its own traditions and history, will enshrine and promote these values. I am convinced of that. That is why I speak in Africa of human rights as "African rights"—as rights that must find expression in the language of the people they protect. It is never the people who complain of human rights as a Western or Northern imposition. It is too often their leaders who do so.[3]

Different cultures do express the nuances, the outward appearance, of basic morality somewhat differently. For example, in the Greco-Roman tradition of Western civilization, the human body has been called something "made in the image of God," so beautiful that human nudity has appeared in Western art for centuries. But no such nudity appears in Islamic art because Islam forbids the making of graven images. Yet the moral core of the two traditions, rooted in the universal values of justice, compassion, charity, and forgiveness, is the same. People may disagree over how to interpret those universal values taught by their respective religions—"Does the Biblical commandment to *Love Thy Neighbor* mean I must love literally everyone?"—but the universal values are there.

In the case of Islam, its reputation among non-Muslims has long been hurt by militant stereotypes. Islam does have a military heritage, beginning with the Prophet Mohammed himself, but it is no more brutal than Christianity's. In an interesting comparison, in medieval times Spain's Muslim-ruled city of Granada was conquered by Christian armies less than forty years after Muslim Turkish armies conquered the Christian city of Constantinople. In the newly conquered Granada, the entire Muslim population was either driven out, executed, or forced to convert to Christianity. Constantinople's Muslim rulers, by contrast, allowed the city, renamed Istanbul, to remain the seat of several branches of East Orthodox Christianity, churches hosted by Istanbul even to this day.

Islam preaches opposition to injustice, tempered with mercy. The Islamic holy book, the Quran, commands:

If two parties of believers take up arms against the other, make peace between them. If either of them commits aggression against the other, fight against the aggressors until they submit to God's judgment. When they submit, make peace between them in equity and justice; God loves those who exercise justice. (Surah 49:9-10)

The Prophet Mohammed himself established many of Islam's humanitarian customs for wartime. Agreements are to be honored, treachery is to be avoided, wounded prisoners must not be mutilated, nor the dead disfigured. Newly conquered women, children, and old people must not be killed, nor orchards, crops, or sacred objects destroyed. These are not the customs of genocide.

Despite these customs, far too many atrocities have still been committed in the name of Allah, though usually for reasons more rooted in the local culture than in Islamic values. Islam has a nonviolent tradition as well, epitomized in the mid-twentieth century by Abdul Ghaffer Khan. A charismatic, Gandhi-style leader who also knew Gandhi personally as a close friend, Ghaffer Khan was a devout Muslim pacifist who led a 100,000-person "Army of God" in nonviolent resistance against British colonial authorities in what is today Pakistan. Both Ghaffer Khan and Gandhi saw Islam, Hinduism, and other religions as mutually compatible. The nonviolent tradition of Islam was continued in the late twentieth century and into the twenty-first by leaders such as Ibrahim Rugova of Kosovo and other, lesser known Muslims.

The ethical declarations of Roman Catholic Christianity's Pope John Paul II, like those of Tibetan Buddhism's Dalai Lama, illustrate how fervently opposed to any genocide most major religious leaders are. At an international conference on nutrition in December 1992, the Pope declared:

It is imperative that wars between nations and internal conflicts not be allowed to condemn defenseless citizens to starvation because of egotistical or partisan motives. . . . The conscience of humankind, sustained henceforth by its liability to international human rights, asks that humanitarian interference be rendered mandatory in situations which gravely compromise the survival of entire peoples and ethnic groups. This is an obligation for both individual nations and the international community as a whole.[4]

This endorsement of humanitarian intervention surprised his international audience, but John Paul II emphasized his moral stand. "Nations no longer have the right to be indifferent," he said. "The principles of nations' sovereignty and of non-intervention in their domestic affairs—which remain valid—nonetheless cannot be construed as a screen behind which one can torture and assassinate." As for humanitarian intervention's legal aspects, the Pope added, "The lawyers ought to look into this new reality and refine its contours."[5]

Later, during the Rwandan genocide in 1994, the Vatican's official newspaper called for a humanitarian intervention to stop the slaughter, comparing the killings to the Biblical "slaughter of innocents" in ancient Bethlehem, when infant boys were murdered in an effort to kill the baby Jesus.[6] The killings in Rwanda also spurred a conference of Roman Catholic bishops from throughout Africa; in a joint statement, they urged the United Nations to thwart genocide throughout the entire continent through the establishment of permanent, locally available UN troops for rapid intervention.[7]

HUMANITARIAN INTERVENTION AND THE "JUST WAR"

The Fourteenth Dalai Lama has not endorsed military intervention for humanitarian purposes—he prefers demilitarization—but every major religion, including Buddhism, has used ethical criteria to consider what constitutes a morally just war.[8] The details vary, but the overall guidelines are remarkably similar.

Islam's doctrine of the *jihad* is probably the most misunderstood. *Jihad,* an Arabic word sometimes translated as "holy war," was originally defined by the Prophet Mohammed as referring to two different human struggles, one greater than the other. The lesser *jihad*, the only definition most non-Muslims know of, is the Muslim struggle against an outside enemy. The greater *jihad*, and for Muslims the more important, is the personal struggle against the enemy within oneself. A Muslim should not wage a *jihad* against others until and unless he has conquered hatred within himself, for otherwise his faith can be manipulated. Saddam Hussein tried to manipulate that faith during the Gulf War of 1990-1991 by calling for a *jihad* against the international coalition arrayed against him—a coalition that included most of the Muslim world. Even discounting Hussein's own (atheistic) Baathist ideology, he had no legitimate religious authority to declare a *jihad.* He was neither a cleric nor an Islamic scholar.

Christianity has one of the oldest "just war" doctrines. Generally attributed to Saint Augustine in the fifth century, its prerequisites for a just war remain the ethical standard of Western civilization and are closely paralleled in Islam for an authentic *jihad* (the lesser form). In the early 1990s Father J. Bryan Hehir, a leading Roman Catholic theologian at the Harvard Divinity School, suggested that, with some modification, the original prerequisites of the Christian just war doctrine could be applied to when and how a humanitarian intervention could be ethically decided upon.[9] He later criticized the methods of NATO's war against Yugoslavia because they were inconsistent with this doctrine.

The Christian just war doctrine starts from a presumption that nonintervention should be the world's ethical norm; that is, foreign invasions are generally wrong. This obligation to not interfere is, however, considered *prima facie*— that is, the ethical presumption requiring it can be "overridden" (suspended). To do so, six preconditions for an ethically based intervention must be satisfied. First, the intervention's basic intention must be just. Second, only a legitimate authority can decide when that intervention is necessary; in past centuries that authority was the Pope himself. Third, the intervention cannot be launched for immoral reasons under the guise of doing good; in other words, the actual intent of that intervention—its underlying motives—must also be just. Fourth, the intervention must be a last resort; all peaceful alternatives must have been exhausted. Fifth, the intervention must have a reasonable chance of success. Sixth, the intervention's expected cost must not exceed the importance of its outcome; the means and ends must be proportional. Only when all six of these preconditions are met can there be *jus ad bellum,* the moral justification for war.

Ironically, however, if the purpose of a humanitarian intervention is to stop a genocide, adhering to these six preconditions could do more harm than good. For whereas the first precondition may seem easy to satisfy—*what moral cause could be more just than to stop a genocide?*—the decision makers themselves may not be completely objective. Watching the genocide from afar, what if they refuse to intervene because they do not want to become involved? What if they claim the slaughter does not constitute a true "genocide" as defined by the

Genocide Convention of 1948? This excuse was actually used with regard to the Rwandan genocide in 1994, when the Clinton Administration in particular deliberately chose not to describe those killings as "genocide" for fear that the term might incite pressure by the American public to act.

The other five preconditions can confuse matters even further. For instance, to fulfill the second precondition, who possesses the legitimate authority to order an intervention against a genocide? The UN Security Council? If the Council fails to act and the genocide rages on, who has the authority then? Must every motive and intention of an antigenocidal intervention be morally pure, as the third precondition requires, or will any less than pure motives suffice? Instead of intervening early on, should negotiations with the genocide's perpetrators be attempted? If so, for how long? When is a last resort too late? When planning to fight, what constitutes a reasonable chance of success? What price is "proportional" to ending a genocide? Even when the risk of "failure" is high, how many civilian lives can be saved? Is the life of one intervening soldier worth the life of one rescued civilian? Is the life of one soldier worth the lives of two rescued children? Are the lives of an intervening battalion, brigade, or division worth the lives of a foreign town, city, or nation? What is a civilian population worth? What is a child's life worth? Can such a life, or lives, be measured financially? $1 billion? $10 billion? $100 billion?

The Christian just war doctrine does not end with *jus ad bellum*. For an intervention to remain morally justified, there must also be *jus in bello*, moral conduct in war. This means that throughout the intervention two tenets must be obeyed: respect for *noncombatant immunity* and *proportionality*. *Noncombatant immunity* means that innocent people must never be targeted for deliberate harm. Inadvertent harm, which in military parlance is called "collateral damage," is in the Christian just war doctrine called a "double effect" because the effects of the harm afflict both combatants and noncombatants. *Proportionality* means that each of the intervention's lesser objectives, such as the capture of a city, are to be achieved only with tactics that minimize harm to noncombatants and property. It is not morally proportional to destroy a city to "save" it. If these two tenets of *jus in bello* cannot be followed consistently, the intervention is not considered justified. If this is realized beforehand, the intervention must not be undertaken, even if the six preconditions for *jus ad bellum* are satisfied.

It was with regard to *jus in bello* during the Kosovo War that Father Hehir objected to NATO's "bombing only" strategy. In a published editorial, he explained:

The cause may be just, but that does not mean NATO should feel free to use any methods at its disposal to achieve its objectives. . . . NATO is now using "dumb bombs" (which do not have precision guidance) and cluster bombs. To use these quite indiscriminate weapons in proximity of civilian neighborhoods is simply not responsible. . . . While troops should not be put in danger without the gravest reasons, there are moral consequences in protecting our troops at the cost of the opponent's civilians.[10]

Earlier, during the Bosnian War, a moral dilemma arose when lightly armed UN troops were used to escort the delivery of humanitarian supplies to needy civilians throughout Bosnia-Herzegovina. Critics charged, with considerable evidence, that the very presence of those UN troops made them potential hostages to the warring sides, a fear which hindered the Security Council from opposing the war more assertively, inadvertently prolonging the war and its "ethnic cleansing". Yet the UN's alternative was to let needy civilians suffer and die from starvation, exposure, and a chronic lack of medical supplies. In such dilemmas any calculation of "proportionality" is likely to be controversial.

The Christian just war doctrine has, over its many centuries of history, been repeatedly revised and worked, arguably, about as well as imperfect Christians have allowed it to. It has its merits from its long scholarship and because its non-Christian equivalents, such as Islam's *jihad,* are so alike in their guidelines. The doctrine was devised to discourage the evils of war by imposing some moral prerequisites upon war. Yet genocide is arguably worse, and because it is worse, it confounds the prerequisites of the traditional just war doctrine. If the doctrine is to be revised to oppose genocide, its doctrinal essence might have to become in principle what the just war doctrine has already become largely in practice: a set of moral guidelines, not moral absolutes.

SECULAR PERSPECTIVES

In the public debate over if, when, and how to conduct a humanitarian intervention, theologians have plenty of company. Politicians are also involved. Soon after the Kosovo War, Britain's Prime Minister Tony Blair said proudly that NATO had "fought for a fundamental principle necessary for humanity's progress: that every human being, regardless of race, religion, or birth, has an inalienable right to live free from persecution." Germany's Chancellor Gerhard Schroeder declared that "the weak have in NATO a strong friend and ally, ready and willing to defend their human rights." And U.S. President Bill Clinton annunciated what has become called the Clinton Doctrine: "If somebody comes after innocent civilians and tries to kill them en masse because of their race, their ethnic background or their religion, and it is within our power to stop it, we will stop it."

Clinton's was a sweeping statement, perhaps too much so. In a later speech to the same UN General Assembly addressed by Kofi Annan a few days before, Clinton used more flexible language:

When we are faced with deliberate, organized campaigns to murder whole peoples, or expel them from their land, the care of victims is important but not enough. We should work to end the violence. Our response in every case cannot or should not be the same. Sometimes collective military force is both appropriate and feasible. Sometimes concerted economic and political pressure, combined with diplomacy, is a better answer, as it was in making possible the introduction of forces in East Timor.

Of course, the way the international community responds will depend upon the capacity of countries to act, and on their perception of their national interests. NATO acted in Kosovo, for example, to stop a vicious campaign of ethnic cleansing in a place where we had important interests at stake, and the ability to act collectively. . . . We cannot do everything everywhere. But simply because we have different interests in different parts of the world does not mean we can be indifferent to the destruction of innocents in any part of the world.[11]

The Western leaders who led NATO in the Kosovo War—Clinton, Blair, Schroeder, and others—are mostly identified with the political Left, but on occasion politicians on the Right have also advocated humanitarian intervention, even those sometimes accused of isolationist tendencies. One such politician, U.S. Senator Jesse Helms, chairman of the powerful Senate Foreign Relations Committee, was invited to address the UN Security Council in January 2000. With his characteristic zeal, yet mixed with the mannerisms of an old Southern gentleman, he told the Council:

The Secretary-General recently delivered an address on sovereignty. . . . "The last right of states cannot and must not be the right to enslave, persecute or torture their own citizens. The people of the world," he said, "have rights beyond borders." And I wholeheartedly agree with that. What the Secretary-General calls "rights beyond borders" we in America call *inalienable rights*.

The sovereignty of nations must be respected, but nations derive their sovereignty—their legitimacy—from the consent of the governed. Thus it follows that nations lose their legitimacy when they rule without the consent of the governed. They deservedly discard their sovereignty by brutally oppressing their people. Mr. Milosevic cannot claim sovereignty over Kosovo when he murdered Kosovar people and piled their bodies into mass graves. . . . Nor can Saddam Hussein defend his oppression of the Iraqi people by hiding behind phony claims of sovereignty. And when the oppressed peoples of the world cry out for help, the free peoples of the world have a fundamental right to respond.

And it's a fanciful notion that free peoples need to seek approval of an international body, some of whose members are totalitarian dictatorships, to lend support to nations struggling to break the chains of tyranny and claim their inalienable God-given rights. The United Nations, my friends, has no power to grant or decline legitimacy to such actions. They are inherently legitimate.[12]

Not every American conservative is an internationalist, nor every liberal an interventionist. Even within their respective political camps, there are diverse opinions. This is particularly true among academic scholars, many of whom have worked at high levels of government. The rest of this chapter provides samples of their views.

Michael Walzer, co-editor of the liberal/left journal *Dissent,* earned his credentials as an intellectual authority on humanitarian intervention back in 1977 when he published a now oft-cited book, *Just and Unjust Wars: A Moral Argument with Historical Illustrations.* In late 1994, after the genocide in Rwanda had ended but the Bosnian War still raged, Walzer publicly reaffirmed his view that "the presumption against intervention is strong. We on the Left especially have reasons for it which derive from our opposition to imperial politics and our commitment to self-determination, even when the process of self-determination is something less than peaceful and democratic. . . . Still, nonintervention is not an absolute moral rule; sometimes what is going on locally cannot be tolerated. Hence the practice of humanitarian intervention—

much abused, no doubt, but morally necessary whenever cruelty and suffering are extreme and no local forces seem capable of putting an end to them." [13]

Walzer conditioned his support by declaring that humanitarian interventions are not morally justified "for the sake of democracy or free enterprise, or economic justice, or voluntary association, or any other of the social practices and arrangements that we might hope for or even call for in other people's countries." But to stop acts of genocide, yes. He explained:

I don't mean to abandon the principle of nonintervention—only to honor its exceptions. It is true that right now there are a lot of exceptions. The vast numbers of murdered people: the men, women and children dying of disease and famine willfully caused or easily preventable; the masses of desperate refugees—none of these are served by reciting high-minded principles. Yes, the norm is not to intervene in other people's countries; the norm is self-determination. But not for *these people:* the victims of tyranny, ideological zeal, ethnic hatred—who are not determining anything for themselves, who urgently need help from the outside.[14]

In 1999 Walzer endorsed NATO's intervention against Yugoslavia, even though the operation lacked a UN mandate:

In some parts of Kosovo the harsh realities of ethnic cleansing were already visible before [NATO's] decision to hit the Serbs with missiles and smart bombs was made. And given the Serbian record in Bosnia, and the mobilization of soldiers on the borders of Kosovo and the refugees already on the move, military intervention seems to me entirely justified, even obligatory.

Many people on the Left yearn for a world where the UN, and only the UN, would act in all such cases. But given the oligarchic structure of the Security Council, it's not possible to count on this kind of action. . . . Nor am I convinced that the world would be improved by having only one agent of international rescue. The men and women in the burning building are probably better served if they can appeal to more than a single set of firefighters.[15]

Ernest Lefever, a neoconservative writer on ethics and world politics, shares this view of intervention and of the UN. He has asserted:

International action enjoys no special moral status over unilateral action. The twentieth century has seen many examples of destructive multinational behavior, from the League of Nations' flaccid and ineffectual effort to stop Mussolini's rape of Ethiopia in 1935, to the Warsaw Pact's crushing of the Hungarian Uprising of 1956 and the Prague Spring in 1968. The number of actors is morally irrelevant. It is the intention and consequence of the action that counts.

All military action, indeed all foreign policies, should be subjected to the traditional just war criteria. Is the intention just? Are the means just and proportional? And if the effort succeeds, will the chances for justice and peace be enhanced?[16]

The traditional just war criteria of Saint Augustine, antiquity's Bishop of Hippo, also requires that only a legitimate authority can authorize a military action. When asked about this in 1998, Lefever replied:

In the contemporary world, I regard this requirement as too legalistic. In a real sense, and I believe the Bishop of Hippo would agree, any man, organization, or agency (including the state) that has the capacity to stop or mitigate genocide has the moral authority to do so.

[As regards Rwanda's genocide in 1994,] this holocaust should have been stopped by any agency that had the capacity to—always preferably in cooperation with an agency representing the actual or potential victims. Where was the UN Security Council, the USA, Belgium, or the International Red Cross? In any event, Washington could have provided logistical and humanitarian assistance before matters got wholly out of hand.[17]

Richard Falk, a law professor at Princeton University, has expressed a very different view of humanitarian intervention. "Intervention as I define it is never good foreign policy, no matter how appealing the overall humanitarian case seems to be for changing political structure," he wrote in the left-wing journal *The Nation* in 1993. "It is not that intervention can *never* work, but that it will almost never succeed unless a costly, prolonged occupation is an ingredient of the commitment; even during the Cold War this seemed to be too high a price to pay." Falk acknowledged that to watch a genocide from afar with passive indifference is intolerable, but noted that "there are other ways to help the victim population" than with a military-type intervention. "One [such way] is to give expanded support and visibility to relief efforts without compromising their independence." In particular, he has called for more use of emergency relief organizations such as the Office of the UN High Commissioner for Refugees. "These ideas are not meant as panaceas," he admitted, but emphasized that "the situations being addressed are tragic in their depth and complexity." [18]

Views remarkably similar to this, though much further to the political Right, can be found at the libertarian conservative Cato Institute. In March 1999, Cato Senior Fellow Douglas Bandow questioned the entire rationale for NATO's Operation *Allied Force* even as the operation threatened to commence. Bandow asked:

What is the standard for making war? That is, what justifies the extreme step of unleashing death and destruction on another people? Traditionally it has been a military threat against the U.S. Yet Yugoslavia has done nothing against America or any of its allies. Grant that Serbian treatment of Kosovars has been atrocious. So has . . . the behavior of two score other governments in a variety of conflicts around the globe. Is war the right remedy in these cases?

Although America need not act everywhere if it desires to implement a policy of humanitarian intervention, some objective standards to determine when are necessary. . . . By any normal standard events in Kosovo are less important than those in many other nations around the world. . . . Ensnaring the U.S. in the tragedy would only make the situation more tragic.[19]

One of academia's strongest advocates of humanitarian intervention is Stanley Hoffmann, a professor at Harvard University. Hoffmann has asserted that to treat "these cases according to the natural disaster model—equating massacres with floods or ethnic cleansing with earthquakes—is a form of evasion, and may end up prolonging the agony: *Sarajevans are kept alive so that snipers can pick them off.*" Hoffmann advocates not only the early introduction of a humanitarian intervention, but if necessary the early use of coercive force as well. In a typical essay, he wrote:

My own criterion [for a humanitarian intervention] would be massive violations of human rights, which would encompass genocide, ethnic cleansing, brutal and large-scale repression . . . as well as the kinds of famines, massive breakdowns of law and order, epidemics and flights of refugees that occur when a "failed state" collapses.

There are situations in which a quick, early use of force may well be the best method and the only one capable of preventing a further aggravation of the crisis, as in Yugoslavia at the time of the Serb shelling of Dubrovnik, or Haiti after the military coup of 1991. . . . All that is required is the view that the peace of the graveyard is not true peace and that it is in the long-term "interest" of all not to settle for a world "order" in which such abuses are overlooked.[20]

Without necessarily disagreeing, Joshua Muravchik, a Resident Fellow at the American Enterprise Institute and a frequent contributor to the conservative journal *Commentary*, has nonetheless advised caution. "We must be very chary of spending American lives in humanitarian missions," he urged, "not because American lives are more valuable than others, but because an implicit premise of our national polity is to value ourselves before others and because the burdens are not equally shared among us. The men and women who volunteer for service in our armed forces know that their ultimate job is to kill and risk being killed, but the rest of us owe it to them not to risk their lives lightly." [21] At the same time, Muravchik warns that 'caution' ought not become "tantamount to consistent inaction in the face of crises that have humanitarian but not security dimensions. In specific, we ought to have intervened in Rwanda—a case of indisputable genocide—because the humanitarian issues were so unusually grievous."[22]

Jeane Kirkpatrick, a former U.S. Permanent Representative to the United Nations, has emphasized that "In the international community in general, actors must do what they say they are going to do in order to establish credibility and resolve crises in an optimal way. The failure to enforce UN resolutions in Bosnia, for example, was one of the reasons that the situation deteriorated into a military affair. I think that we would make significant progress if we established a few simple principles clearly and firmly." One such principle she urged is that governments never starve their citizens to death as a matter of policy. "Siege and starvation have been used regularly as instruments of war in Bosnia," she noted poignantly. "The international community cannot accept that and expect to have credibility. That is one of the reasons I have been terribly frustrated and disappointed with the response to the Bosnian crisis. . . . It will be impossible to establish credibility on such issues if we stand by and permit genocide." [23] She was a vocal supporter of NATO's actions against Yugoslavia in 1999. "The conduct of the Serb government in regard to Kosovo is unacceptable and uncivilized," she declared. "This has been an assault on civilization." [24]

Henry Kissinger, former Secretary of State, National Security Adviser and Harvard professor, has been portrayed as the quintessential embodiment of the

Realist school of thought, as someone who insists that a nation's foreign policy must pursue national interests narrowly defined by *realpolitik*. Yet even Kissinger, a Jewish refugee from Nazi Germany in his adolescent years, has asserted that U.S. foreign policy must have a moral side to it. In a television interview in 1998, he commented upon some of the world's places of genocide and what he felt the U.S. response ought to have been. Kissinger lamented:

At least in Bosnia we did something—maybe too late—but in Rwanda hundreds of thousands were killed. [Rwanda] is not a country of strategic importance for the United States; you cannot define a national interest that would take us there. And yet, there, I tend to think I personally would have supported an intervention.

It would have been a violation of what ordinarily is my principle. Ordinarily I feel you should not risk American lives for objectives where you cannot explain to the mothers why you did it. . . . [Yet] my instinct tells me we should have done it in Rwanda.

But then there are lots of killings—we cannot intervene against every unjust killing somewhere in the world. We cannot right every injustice in the world. But we should have a sense when something gets beyond a certain point that we ought to do something.[25]

Later, in the aftermath of the Kosovo War, Kissinger wrote an editorial to express some warnings and advice about future humanitarian interventions:

Those who sneer at history obviously do not recall that the legal doctrine of national sovereignty and the principle of noninterference—enshrined, by the way, in the UN Charter—emerged . . . to inhibit a repetition of the depredations of the seventeenth century, during which perhaps 40 percent of the population of Central Europe perished in the name of competing versions of universal truth. Once the doctrine of universal intervention spreads and competing truths contest, we risk entering a world in which, in G. K. Chesterton's phrase, virtue runs amok.

No more important task confronts [NATO] than to bring the rhetoric of its leaders in line with realistic choices. . . . [To do this there are] four principles of humanitarian intervention with which I generally agree: having a just cause in the eyes of others; proportionality of means to ends; high probability of success; and, whenever possible, reinforcement of the humanitarian cause by the existence of other strong national interests. Thus more narrowly defined, the rhetorical distinction between humanitarian and national interests erodes.[26]

Chester Crocker was the U.S. Assistant Secretary of State for Africa during the presidencies of Ronald Reagan and George Bush, Sr. On deciding whether or not to intervene, the former Georgetown professor offered this:

A crucial step, easily overlooked in popular commentary, is analyzing how the "least bad" form of intervention compares with the price of doing nothing at all. Experience in such places as [the former Yugoslavia] suggests that it is too easy for decision makers to adopt a narrow view of the choices before them and thereby overlook the political and economic consequences of inaction. At root, this is a political question: How can we encourage bureaucratic and political structures to measure the known price of sticking their neck out and doing something against the less tangible and measurable costs associated with having to pick up the pieces later—human casualties, loss of political prestige, famine and refugee relief, economic reconstruction, and peacekeeping? [27]

Drawing on his experience with the U.S. and UN humanitarian interventions into Somalia in 1993-1994, Crocker offered these recommendations:

Success in [humanitarian interventions] can be measured at two levels: saving lives, and creating a political basis for resolving the issues that put lives at risk in the first place. The absence of strong prospects for the second level of success should not become an excuse for doing nothing to protect people when something can be done at an acceptable cost to the intervenors. But humanitarian action makes so much more sense when conceived as a bridge to a political process that can provide the best basis for a successful exit. This was one of the missing ingredients that undercut the impact of U.S. and UN intervention in Somalia.[28]

In 1995 two professors at Yale University, Paul Kennedy and Bruce Russett, co-authored an essay about reforming the United Nations and offered this recommendation:

UN standing forces, sent to a crisis zone on the resolution of the Security Council alone, could quickly carry out an array of peacekeeping and humanitarian actions. The Secretary-General would not have to beg governments for peacekeeping contingents on an *ad hoc* basis, and governments would not be periodically confronted with the delicate choice of whether or not to commit national units. Critics raise objections about costs (a standing force of 10,000 could cost $500 million a year) and logistics (*Where would it be stationed?* for instance). But the greatest obstacles are political. Are governments willing to let the world organization have its own army of peacekeepers, making it appear to have acquired one of the attributes of statehood? [29]

Kennedy and Russett warned that to only have national units earmarked on a "standby" status for whenever the UN asks for them is but a halfway measure. Hesitant governments can, and have, refused to send those units when a crisis does erupt, even after they pledged those units earlier. Even if, eventually, those units are provided, their contributing governments will consume precious time until then pondering the UN's urgent request. Moreover, Kennedy and Russett noted, "as [those] separate national units grapple with language and coordination problems during the operation, they will still be subject to constant scrutiny by their home governments, which naturally will want a say in [their] operational decisions. A UN standing force would be far preferable." [30]

Richard Haass of the Brookings Institution, and a former member of the Bush Administration's National Security Council, considered the idea of a UN standing force in his book, *Intervention: The Use of American Military Force in the Post-Cold War World*, published in 1994. While acknowledging that a UN standing force could be available (at least in theory) on short notice and used in a variety of small peacekeeping or limited peace enforcement missions, Haass nevertheless listed several problems:

In addition to matters of expense (salaries, training, logistics, and so on), questions include availability (far from assured, since Russia and China wield a veto in the Security Council) and military capability. Such a small force could easily be overwhelmed. [UN] member-states, particularly the United States, would then come under pressure to act, not simply to deal with the situation at hand, but to save the credibility of the United Nations.[31]

Haass urged care in deciding both where and how to intervene, but he was not opposed to humanitarian interventions *per se.* On the contrary:

It is now widely held that the international community was wrong in not doing more to thwart the efforts of Hitler in Germany or Pol Pot in Cambodia, who by their behavior forfeited the normal benefits and protection of sovereignty, and that it was right in intervening on behalf of Iraq's Kurds in 1991 and in Somalia in 1992.[32]

The risk that an interventionary force may encounter dangers worse than it can handle can never be eliminated completely. Yet to forsake all humanitarian intervention solely because of that risk, however small, incurs a severe risk of its own, especially when the crisis involves genocide. And timely interventions can succeed. In 1964 a British force of 5,000 troops, with the prior approval of local civilian leaders in Africa, intervened at six places in three countries—Kenya, Uganda, and what is now Tanzania—to reverse local mutinies, deter *coup d'etats,* and restore civilian control. In each case the intervention succeeded, with minimal casualties.[33] More recently a former foreign minister of France remarked, albeit not very diplomatically, that Africa was a continent where France could still "change the course of history" with only 500 men.[34]

In 1999, Kofi Annan told the UN General Assembly:

It is important to define intervention as broadly as possible, to include actions along a wide continuum from the most pacific to the most coercive. A tragic irony of many of the crises that continue to go unnoticed and unchallenged today is that they could be dealt with by far less perilous acts of intervention than the one we witnessed recently in Yugoslavia. . . . It is also necessary to recognize that any armed intervention is itself a result of the failure of prevention. As we consider the future of intervention, we must redouble our efforts to enhance our preventive capabilities—including early warning, preventive diplomacy, preventive deployment and preventive disarmament.[35]

The next few chapters will examine the practice of peacekeeping and peace enforcement, the use to oppose genocide of national military forces vis-à-vis multinational forces, and the feasibility of some alternative forces.

NOTES

1. Kofi Annan, "Secretary-General presents Annual Report to General Assembly," United Nations Press Release SG/SM/7136—GA/9596, dated 20 September 1999.

2. The Dalai Lama, "Critical Reflections: Human Rights and the Future of Tibet," *Harvard International Review* (Winter 1994/95), pp. 46-80.

3. Kofi Annan, "'Ignorance, not knowledge . . . makes enemies of Man,' Secretary-General tells Communications Conference at Aspen Institute," United Nations Press Release SG/SM/6366, dated 20 October 1997.

4. Quoted in Renô Coste, "View From the Vatican: The Moral Dimension of Intervention," *Harvard International Review* (Fall 1993), pp. 28-67.

5. Ibid.

6. Stephen Zinzer, "European Leaders Reluctant to Send Troops to Rwanda," *New York Times* (May 25, 1994), pp. A-1 and A-12.

7. Reuters, "Bishops urge West to stop arms shipments to Africa," *Boston Globe* (May 7, 1994), p. 6.

8. The exploits of the Buddhist monks of China's Shaolin monastery provide a popular example. For other examples in Buddhism, see Lawrence P. Rockwood, "Apology of a Buddhist Soldier," *Tricycle* (Spring 1996), pp. 71-76.

9. For a summary of his original proposal, see J. Bryan Hehir, "Religion and International Affairs," *Nieman Reports* (Summer 1993), pp. 39-55.

10. J. Bryan Hehir, "What Makes a War Just? NATO's Laudable Goals and Questionable Means," *Washington Post* (May 16, 1999), p. B-3.

11. Bill Clinton, "Remarks by the President to the 54th Session of the United Nations General Assembly," Office of the White House Press Secretary, press release dated 21 September 1999.

12. Jesse Helms, "In the Words of Helms: A Lack of 'Gratitude'," *New York Times* (January 21, 2000), from the NYT website.

13. Michael Walzer, "The Politics of Rescue," *Dissent* (Winter 1995), pp. 35-41

14. Ibid.

15. Michael Walzer, "Kosovo," *Dissent* (Summer 1999), pp. 5-7.

16. Ernest W. Lefever, "Reining in the UN: Mistaking the Instrument for the Actor," *Foreign Affairs* (Summer 1993), pp. 17-20.

17. Personal correspondence with Ernest Lefever, letter dated September 5, 1998.

18. Richard Falk, "Intervention Revisited: Hard Choices and Tragic Dilemmas," *The Nation* (December 20, 1993), pp. 755-764.

19. Douglas Bandow, "The U.S. Role in Kosovo," in testimony before the U.S. House International Relations Committee (March 10, 1999).

20. Stanley Hoffmann, "The Politics and Ethics of Military Intervention," *Survival* (Winter 1995-1996), pp. 29-49. Also, Stanley Hoffmann, *The Ethics and Politics of Military Intervention* (Notre Dame, IN: University of Notre Dame Press, 1996).

21. Joshua Muravchik, "Beyond Self-Defense," *Commentary* (December 1993), pp. 19-24.

22. Personal correspondence with Joshua Muravchik, letter dated September 8, 1998.

23. Jeane J. Kirkpatrick, "A Critical Appraisal: The Making of Foreign Policy in the 1990s," *Harvard International Review* (Fall 1995), pp. 50-87.

24. Quoted in Bennett Roth, "War in the Balkans/Ground campaign is a necessity, foreign policy experts claim," *Houston Chronicle* (April 1, 1999), p. 19.

25. Henry Kissinger, from an interview on the PBS television program *Charlie Rose,* on April 16, 1998.

26. Henry Kissinger, "The End of NATO as We Know It?" *Washington Post* (August 15, 1999), p. B-7.

27. Chester A. Crocker, "The Varieties of Intervention: Conditions for Success," in Chester A. Crocker and Fen Osler Hampon (editors), *Managing Global Chaos: Sources of and Responses to International Conflict* (Washington, DC: U.S. Institute of Peace, 1996), pp. 183-195.

28. Ibid.

29. Paul Kennedy and Bruce Russett, "Reforming the United Nations," *Foreign Affairs* (September/October 1995), pp. 56-71.

30. Ibid.

31. Richard N. Haass, *Intervention: The Use of American Military Force in the Post-Cold War World* (Washington, DC: The Carnegie Endowment for International Peace, 1994), p. 147.

32. Ibid., p. 13.

33. Crocker, *loc. cit.*

34. Quoted from Adekeye Adebajo and Michael O'Hanlon, "Africa: Toward a Rapid-Reaction Force," *SAIS Review* (Summer-Fall 1997), pp. 153-164.

35. Annan, UN Press Release SG/SM/7136—GA/9596.

8

Peacekeeping and Peace Enforcement

> Peacekeeping is not a job for soldiers, but only a soldier can do it.
>
> — An oft-quoted insight generally attributed to
> Dag Hammarskjold, UN Secretary-General, 1954-1961

> Peacekeeping requires a referee, peace enforcement demands a player. The referee can be strict or easy-going, authoritative or ineffectual—but he will always be a referee. The player may be good, bad, orderly or disorderly—but he will always be a player. There is no middle ground that lies between player and referee—he can only be one or the other. If he tries to be both at the same time his performance of one will prejudice the status of the other. So it is with the peacekeeper and peace enforcer.
>
> — British Lieutenant Colonel Charles Dobbie,
> a contributor to the UN's *Peacekeeper's Handbook*

Since 1956, when soldiers from different countries first put on blue helmets with UN markings, most soldiers under the direct control of the United Nations have been called "peacekeepers." That label is generally accurate, but it has also been associated with soldiers performing operations very different from traditional *peacekeeping* as the concept is understood among experts. Misunderstandings were especially acute during the Bosnian War, when UN soldiers, mistakenly called "peacekeepers" by the news media, were deployed into a conflict where there was no peace to keep. By displaying an avowedly neutral behavior, those UN troops were criticized for not trying to forcibly stop the war and its genocidal "ethnic cleansing." Critics wanted them to literally enforce peace in Bosnia-Herzegovina, a mission known as *peace enforcement*.

Peacekeeping, which is not peace enforcement, can nonetheless play an important role in genocide prevention by precluding the need for a larger, costlier, more forcible intervention later. But for peacekeeping to be effective requires, at a minimum, an informed understanding of peacekeeping theory and practice.

PEACEKEEPING

One popular myth about peacekeeping is that it is merely a subtle form of peace enforcement, supposedly only a lower point on some spectrum of coercive tactics imposed for laudable purposes. But peacekeeping is not imposed, which makes it very different from peace enforcement. Whereas peace enforcement can resort to coercion, peacekeeping is always limited to persuasion. The U.S. Army's field manual FM 100-23, *Peace Operations*, emphasizes this difference:

[*Peacekeeping* and *peace enforcement*] are not part of a continuum allowing a unit to move freely from one to the other. A broad demarcation separates these operations. They take place under vastly different circumstances involving the variables of consent, force, and impartiality.

[*Peacekeeping* involves] military or paramilitary operations that are undertaken with the consent of all major belligerent parties. These operations are designed to monitor and facilitate implementation of an existing truce agreement and support diplomatic efforts to reach a long-term political settlement.[1]

The UN Organization defines *peacekeeping* as "the deployment of a United Nations presence in the field, hitherto with the consent of all the parties concerned, normally involving United Nations military and/or police personnel and frequently civilians as well."[2]

Notice that both the U.S. and UN definitions of peacekeeping stress the importance of *consent*—the willingness of the antagonists to accept a foreign force into their midst, a force whose very presence could reduce the antagonists' opportunities to do as they please. A peacekeeping force cannot deploy into an area unless those antagonists agree to accept it, and it operates there only as long as they permit it. If either of the antagonists orders the peacekeeping force to leave, the peacekeepers must leave. Sir Brian Urquhart, one of the pioneers of UN peacekeeping and its director for many years, explained this in his memoirs:

Peacekeeping depends on the non-use of force and on political symbolism. It is the projection of the principle of nonviolence onto the military plane. It requires discipline, initiative, objectivity, and leadership, as well as ceaseless supervision and political direction. It takes time to develop the full effectiveness of a peacekeeping operation and to secure the confidence and cooperation of the conflicting parties with which it is dealing.

Although military commanders often want them, I have always been strongly opposed to UN peacekeeping operations having offensive or heavy weapons. The real strength of a peacekeeping operation lies not in its capacity to use force, but precisely in its *not* using force and thereby remaining above the conflict and preserving its unique position and prestige. The moment a peacekeeping force starts killing people it becomes a part of the conflict it is supposed to be controlling, and therefore a part of the problem. It loses the one quality which distinguishes it from, and sets it above, the people it is dealing with.[3]

The principles of UN peacekeeping are listed in the *Peacekeeper's Handbook,* published by the UN's International Peace Academy:

1. Negotiation is the primary means of finding solutions.
2. Suggestion, advice and objective response to courses of action taken by the parties to the dispute rather than direction, imposition and coercion are the methods by which the Force's mandate is fulfilled.
3. Armed force is not a means of achieving the solutions. Armed force can only be used in self-defense and protection of UN property against attack, or as a last resort in carrying out the Force mandate.
4. Armed force should not be initiated in the first instance by the UN Force.
5. Impartiality without favor or affection is required of all members of the Force, along with restraint and patience at all times when dealing with all parties to the dispute.
6. It is important that the authority of the government(s) of the host country(s), on whose territory the Force is stationed, is recognized by members of the Force.[4]

A peacekeeping force's most important document is its *mandate,* which specifies its official mission and its international legal authority to perform that mission. In some cases, particularly when a force is run by the UN Organization directly, its mandate may also authorize the number of troops the force is allowed. The *Peacekeeper's Handbook* defines the word as follows:

Mandate. This is the sole authority under which a Peacekeeping Force can operate. It is devised by the Security Council and forms the basis of the Security Council resolution which establishes the Force. In order to ensure a consensus, resolutions and thereby the mandate are broadly phrased to meet the requirements of all members of the Security Council, but especially the requirements of the five permanent members, so that the possibility of a veto can be averted. Mandates, therefore, tend to be in vague terms, sometimes to the point of ambiguity. It is this vagueness that often handicaps UN Peacekeeping Forces in achieving total effectiveness; on the other hand, the peacekeeping operations might very well not take place were the resolutions to be phrased in more definitive terms.

The Force/Mission cannot exceed the provisions of its mandate but must comply with it in all respects at all times. The mandate can only be changed or modified by the Security Council.

Over the decades, through painful trial and error, UN peacekeepers have learned how far they can push, cajole, and assert their Security Council-given mandates. Urquhart elaborated:

There have been times when the peacekeeping function was more like that of an attendant in a lunatic asylum, and the soldiers had to accept abuse and harassment without getting into physical conflict or emotional involvement with the inmates. The feelings and reactions of peacekeepers must be kept under rigid control and must always come second to those of the afflicted. Thus they must often turn the other cheek, and never, except in the most extreme circumstances, use their weapons or shoot their way out of a situation. But they must also be firm and assert their authority in violent situations.[5]

When asked to describe when the practice of peacekeeping works best and when it does not, Urquhart explained:

It works best as a buffer between two conflicting governments that wish to have peace between them. A perfect example was the disengagement on the Golan Heights that [Henry] Kissinger arranged in 1974 between Syria and Israel. It was greatly to the advantage of both countries—a classic situation. And not more than fifty miles away, in [1980s] Lebanon, you see a totally imperfect situation: within the boundaries of one country, no governmental authority, but a mishmash of irregular bands of soldiers, so that there is no authority with which a peacekeeping force can come to agreement. This tends to produce civil wars, tribal wars, general anarchy—a nightmare.[6]

PEACE ENFORCEMENT

Peacekeeping was born at a time when governments dominated international relations. Their dominance did not make peacekeeping easy, but its practice was easier than in the absence of stable governments and cohesive societies. If a conflict erupts where the government is not stable or the society is not cohesive, where the locally preferred method of maintaining order is to scapegoat, target, and terrorize a particular civilian group, there is little that classic peacekeeping can do to stop the killing. In response to this situation the concept of *peace enforcement* was devised. It is a relatively benign form of foreign military occupation. According to the U.S. Army's FM 100-23:

[*Peace enforcement*] is the application of military force or the threat of its use, normally pursuant to international authorization, to compel compliance with generally accepted [international] resolutions or sanctions. [Its] purpose . . . is to maintain or restore peace and support diplomatic efforts to reach a long-term political settlement.[7]

Despite sounding so peaceful, peace enforcement can include harsh police duties or even combat:

Military forces may be employed to restore order and stability within a state or region where competent civil authority has ceased to function. They may be called upon to assist in the maintenance of order and stability in areas where it is threatened, where the loss of order and stability threatens international stability, or where human rights are endangered.

With the transition to combat action comes the requirement for the successful application of warfighting skills. Thus, in a theater of operations, both combat and noncombat actions may occur simultaneously. . . . The first phase may involve the insertion of rapidly deployable combat forces in order to establish a significant and visible military presence. Subsequent phases will involve the transition from a military presence to support for the development of competent civil authority.[8]

Peace enforcement operations in the 1990s included the UN-authorized, U.S.-led interventions into Somalia in 1992-1995, into Haiti in 1994-1995, into Bosnia-Herzegovina to implement the Dayton peace accords of late 1995, and into Serbia's Kosovo province after the war there in 1999. The operations in Bosnia and Kosovo were managed by the NATO alliance with Russian participation. The forces of any peace enforcement operation are, though prepared for combat, nonetheless encouraged to avoid it. FM 100-23 advises:

Commanders should always seek to de-escalate and not inflame an incident or crisis whenever possible. Alternatives to force should be fully explored before armed action is taken. They include mediation and negotiation. . . . Simple face-saving measures to preserve a party's dignity may serve to relax tension and defuse a crisis.

In all cases, force will be prudently applied proportional to the threat. In peace operations, every soldier must be aware that the goal is to produce conditions that are conducive to peace and not to the destruction of an enemy. The enemy is the conflict. . . . The unrestrained use of force will prejudice subsequent efforts at achieving settlement.[9]

A peace enforcement operation is a directly coercive way of halting mass atrocities with military power. Preparing such an operation can require days, weeks, or even months. Tens of thousands of troops may also be required, along with their equipment, much of it heavy, supported by a network of supply bases and various means of transportation whose grand totality can be immense. A peace enforcement operation is similar to going to war; indeed, sometimes it is going to war, albeit under a different label.

SOLDIERS AND REPORTERS: ALLIES AGAINST GENOCIDE?

One essential, even integral, factor that all peace operations must contend with is news coverage. In democratic countries both the military and the news media see themselves as guardians of democracy, even as they treat information in almost opposite ways. The military prefers to conceal key information, the news media prefers to reveal it. Peace operations hold the potential to reconcile these two extremes, at least to some extent and in spite of the emotional baggage of the Vietnam and Gulf Wars. This is because both the military and the news media seek to expose the atrocities that the peace operation was sent to stop. News media exposure may dissuade the perpetrators, and the military seeks that result.

To reporters, a humanitarian peace operation can appeal to an idealism that many of them feel but rarely see in practice. Most of them want the operation to succeed and, when they are treated with honesty and respect, most of them are willing to give the intervening military the benefit of the doubt. They also prefer to have the military's cooperation, because they can produce better news stories with it than without it. A peace operation can extend across an area the size of Bosnia, Kosovo, or East Timor, and sometimes only the military has the swift reliable transportation that reporters need, along with the military's expertise in military subjects, area knowledge, and physical security.

Peace operations also require fewer operational secrets than do other military operations. With fewer secrets to worry about, military personnel can be more forthcoming with reporters. "We don't win unless CNN says we win"—a blunt admission by the Chairman of the U.S. Joint Chiefs of Staff in 1994. In 1995 the U.S. commander of Operation *Uphold Democracy* in Haiti co-authored an article with his Public Affairs Officer (PAO), Lieutenant-Colonel Timothy Vane. In the U.S. Army's journal *Military Review*, they wrote:

The media constantly needs news. They must file stories and will do it with or without the military's help. It is in the military's best interest to assist the media, because there are many good stories that can be told. Therefore commanders and PAOs must plan a media event each day to gain and maintain the initiative. These events cannot be manipulative, misleading or contrived. Media events must be real, enlightening, and accurate. Credibility is too fragile an asset to waste on an unworthy or disingenuous news story. Exposing units, individuals, and events to media coverage can benefit everyone.

Military leaders should also know the media can be trusted if the military's explanation of events is valid and makes sense. The proof? Of all the reporters briefed on the operation plan prior to the start of *Uphold Democracy,* there were no leaks. None. Reporters understood the ground rules and knew that a story released ahead of time could endanger U.S. forces. Conversely, the media came away from this deployment with a new appreciation for the U.S. military's quality and professionalism. Many reporters were impressed with Operation *Uphold Democracy's* complexity and the detailed knowledge troops had of the plan.

There will always be healthy tension between the military's right to operations security and the media's right to ask questions and report stories. But there can be a middle ground.[10]

The co-authors told of a U.S. brigade commander who initially did not want any reporters covering his unit in Haiti because he had had some bad experiences with reporters elsewhere. He consented to hosting one reporter in Haiti. Within a week he was hosting four reporters; within two weeks, he was happily hosting eight. By being with them in daily contact he developed a better appreciation of the reporters' profession, while they reported on his unit favorably and accurately. "Letting reporters into my unit was the smartest thing I ever did," he said. If reporters share the same hardships as soldiers, he explained, reporters deserve to be treated with respect and given access.[11]

In October 1997 the commander of that Haitian operation, General Henry Hugh Shelton, became Chairman of the U.S. Joint Chiefs of Staff. Unfortunately, his openness with the news media did not reappear during the Kosovo War in 1999; instead, he and his boss, Defense Secretary William Cohen, reduced the military information usually made available to the news media, explaining that information security had become too lax. And a competent enemy can indeed deduce secrets from openly available news reports, especially when the reporters do not realize the collective military value of the tidbits they have reported. But there are also dangers in over-restricting military information, even in wartime, and not only because incompetence and war crimes can be concealed in official secrecy. In the Information Age a democracy's voters will not long support the military if they are left ignorant and suspicious, especially when a war is being fought, not for national self-defense, but to help distant foreigners such as the Kosovar-Albanians. The American people deserve to know why and how well their sons and daughters in uniform are helping a foreign population threatened with genocide.

In a future humanitarian intervention, documenting that genocide could be as important as curbing it. To do that, a truly sincere partnership between the news media and the military is essential. After seeing a Nazi concentration camp for the first time, General Dwight D. Eisenhower recounted:

I have never felt able to describe my emotional reactions when I first came face to face with indisputable evidence of Nazi brutality and ruthless disregard of every shred of decency. Up to that time I had known about it only generally or through secondary sources. I am certain, however, that I have never at any other time experienced an equal sense of shock. I visited every nook and cranny of the camp because I felt it my duty to be in a position from then on to testify at first hand about these things in case there ever grew up at home the belief or assumption that "the stories of Nazi brutality were just propaganda." Some members of my visiting party were unable to go through the ordeal. I not only did so but as soon as I returned to Patton's headquarters that evening I sent communications to both Washington and London, urging the two governments to send instantly to Germany a random group of newspaper editors and representative groups from the national legislatures. I felt that the evidence should be immediately placed before the American and British publics in a fashion that would leave no room for cynical doubt.[12]

Scores of Allied correspondents did record the newly liberated concentration camps and other aspects of the Holocaust in elaborate detail. Their films and interviews were later used in war crime trials and still referenced by historians and educators today. In a future documentation effort the news media will need the military's scope of access, learning where to look to record the genocide's details. The military, meanwhile, will need the news media to expose it to the world.

THE GENESIS OF PEACE OPERATIONS

The practice of peacekeeping began in 1956, when the UN Organization deployed a multinational observer force along the Egyptian-Israeli border under the guidance of then-UN Secretary-General Dag Hammarskjold. Interestingly, the word *peacekeeping* does not appear in the UN Charter. Its legal basis exists somewhere unspecified between the Charter's Chapter Six, on the peaceful settlements of disputes, and Chapter Seven, on breaches of the peace.[13] This legal ambiguity caused Hammarskjold himself to joke that UN peacekeeping is a "Chapter Six-and-a-half" activity, a description still used today.

The first time UN peacekeeping troops were used to curb an ethnic conflict was in 1960-1964, in the former Belgian colony of the Congo. Soon thereafter, in 1964, UN peacekeepers were sent to the Mediterranean island of Cyprus, a decade before Turkey's invasion of the island's north. The Congo was a newly independent African country when the first UN troops arrived. Cyprus had been an independent country for barely four years. The governments of both countries requested the UN's assistance and, in both countries, the mandate of the UN forces was to restore and maintain order.

Ensuring civil order by preventing riots is not the same as waging a war, an extreme the UN troops sought to avoid. They limited their activities to patrols, advertising their presence at important sites, and emphasized local mediation. They were also unnumbered. To cover the Congo, a country the size of Western Europe, the UN troops numbered less than 20,000. In Cyprus, they numbered less than 6,500.[14]

The Congo operation has since been criticized for what it did not do for Congolese human rights. The Congo was ravaged by a very brutal civil war, afterwards falling under the plunderous rule of the dictator Mobutu Sese Seko for over three decades. But the UN troops never had a Security Council mandate to convert Congo into a parliamentary democracy, and indeed the Congolese lacked experience in national self-government, democratic or otherwise. In Africa's second largest country, the UN force was mandated to bring order with fewer troops than are fielded by the city-state of Singapore. Only through their presence, negotiating efforts, mediation, and with some good luck was the Congo held together despite a secessionist movement in its Katanga province, various foreign pressures, and many mettlesome mercenaries. The Congolese civil war was bloody, but the UN troops themselves suffered fewer than 240 killed.[15]

Of the later Cyprus operation, the *Peacekeeper's Handbook* referred to it to illustrate the following advice for future peacekeepers:

Listen first and speak afterwards is wise counsel and can be supported by the corollary, *Speak in moderation but listen exceedingly*. A peacekeeper or a peacemaker needs to have infinite patience. Never should he expect quick results or solutions but rather he should evaluate repeatedly his achievement in the context of his aim.

In Cyprus, the daily yardstick for success was for there to have been no renewal in fighting during the 24-hour period, despite the continuing violent tensions. Every day between 1964-68 violence threatened and often violence occurred, but by means of physical contact and the use of tact, quiet diplomacy and patience, none but a very few of the incidents brought about a renewal of the fighting.[16]

To encourage the Greek-Cypriots and Turkish-Cypriots to build up some mutual trust, Urquhart recalled that the UN peacekeepers tried to find them mutual tasks that were mutually advantageous and yet not politically sensitive. "Unfortunately," he recalled, "on Cyprus reason and common sense all too easily gave way to hatred, fear, and fantasy, which often spilled over in preposterous accusations against United Nations personnel, who were in any case limited in the nature and scope of the actions they could take." They were prohibited from performing any governmental services, from forcibly disarming anyone, and from dictating any solutions. "They could only help those who really wished to find a peaceful solution to their problems," Urquhart explained, "and sometimes such people seemed few and far between." [17] Eventually the ethnic fighting was quelled, however, years before Greece and Turkey forcibly intervened in 1974.

THE 1990s: THE DISTINCTION BLURS

What was difficult about peace operations in the 1960s became very difficult in the 1990s. For in those first few years after the Cold War, wrote then-UN Secretary-General Boutros Boutros-Ghali as early as 1992, "not all the parties are governments."

As a result, the peacekeepers have had to learn how to deal with a multiplicity of "authorities." The leaders of such groups are often inaccessible and their identity even unknown; chains of command are shadowy; armed persons who offend against agreements signed by their supposed leaders are disowned; discipline is nonexistent or brutal. And everywhere there is an evil and uncontrolled proliferation of arms.[18]

Bosnia-Herzegovina became one of the most notorious cauldrons of those problems, a place that presented the United Nations with a delicate yet daunting challenge: *Is there a role for UN peacekeepers before there is any peace to keep?*

The Security Council decided there was. During the war, international aid organizations under the auspices of the UN High Commissioner for Refugees (UNHCR) tried to provide humanitarian necessities to nearly 3 million civilians in Bosnia. Very often, however, UNHCR's roadbound convoys were harassed, attacked, looted, and turned back, while the intended recipients of the aid, often cold and hungry, remained cold and hungry. If nothing were done to protect the aid convoys, a great many innocent children and adults were in danger of freezing and starving.[19] Therefore, to escort the convoys, the Security Council established the United Nations Protection Force (UNPROFOR).

The name of the force sounded very impressive, indeed too impressive because the word *protection* implied that UNPROFOR was supposed to protect Bosnia's entire population, but that was not its mandate. Less a protection force than an escort force, UNPROFOR was designed to accompany UNHCR's relief convoys. Its mandate was later expanded to include the stationing of UN troops in six Bosnian cities, designated by the Security Council as "safe havens." UNPROFOR was also ordered to monitor whatever truces the warring parties might accept. Countless truces were arranged, though few lasted more than a few days, or even hours.

Furthermore, in addition to Bosnia-Herzegovina, UNPROFOR was ordered by the Security Council to maintain contingents in the neighboring countries of Croatia and Macedonia—leaving UNPROFOR chronically short of troops. Since its duty was very hazardous, none of UNPROFOR's many contributors sent it the very large numbers of troops that it really needed. One consequence is that the shortage greatly increased UNPROFOR's need for mutual consent—the consent of almost anyone empowered by a gun, including private armies, militias, and paramilitary groups. Yet the Security Council continued to mandate new tasks for the vulnerable, patchwork force to perform. Exclaimed one officer in UNPROFOR, "Instead of sending more troops, they are sending more work! It's unbelievable!"[20]

The line between peacekeeping and peace enforcement blurred confusingly and ultimately very dangerously. Anticipating this as early as 1992, Boutros-Ghali and his staff proposed the creation of UN peace enforcement units:

It happens all too often that the parties to a conflict sign a cease-fire agreement but then fail to respect it. . . . The purpose of peace enforcement units—perhaps they should be called "cease-fire enforcement units"—would be to enable the United Nations to deploy troops quickly to enforce a cease-fire by taking coercive action against either party, or both, if they violate it.

[Such units] would be impartial between the two sides, taking action only if one or other of them violated the agreed cease-fire. But the concept goes beyond peacekeeping to the extent that the operation would be deployed without the express consent of the two parties, though its basis would be a cease-fire agreement previously reached between them. UN troops would be authorized to use force to ensure respect for the cease-fire. They would be trained, armed and equipped accordingly; a very rapid response would be essential.[21]

Those proposed UN units were never created. As acts of "ethnic cleansing" continued in Bosnia, however, the Security Council increasingly pressured UNPROFOR to perform peace enforcement. To support this role the West's NATO alliance gave UNPROFOR the authority to order NATO-flown bombing raids in Bosnia, an aerial arrangement codenamed Operation *Blue Sword.* This option for UNPROFOR was relatively easy to arrange since three members of NATO—the United States, Britain, and France—were also permanent members of the Security Council. Britain and France, as well as other NATO members, also contributed troops to UNPROFOR.

Peace enforcement was a role that several commanders of UNPROFOR were willing to accept if they were granted enough troops and authority. They never were. Instead, their authority was severely constrained. Back during the Congo operation, the country's unreliable telecommunications network had left some UN units almost autonomous in their authority. In Cyprus, according to the Secretary-General's official guidance, "the operations of the Force and the activities of the United Nations Mediator are separate and distinct undertakings, and shall be kept so." But in Bosnia a variety of different, yet interrelated, UN activities required that UNPROFOR's operations fall under the strict oversight of the Secretary-General's Special Representative in the region, who was also a key mediator of the long-running Bosnian peace talks. In practice this meant that whenever a UN soldier wanted to order a NATO-flown air strike for some urgently defensive purpose, his desperate request had to be approved by his entire chain of command, up to and including UNPROFOR's commander in Bosnia, and then as well by the Secretary-General's Special Representative, a civilian diplomat.

Insiders called this cumbersome approval system the "dual key"—as though two different keys had to be turned by two separate people to open the same lock to initiate only one action. It existed because an air strike is a very violent use of force, something not suitable for a peacekeeping operation, nor something a UN mediator wanted to see hurt his delicate efforts at mediation. Since so many people could veto or delay a requested air strike, unanimous go-aheads almost never occurred. Even some UN mediators disliked this system because it largely negated their ability to warn, prod, or bluff the warring sides to make compromises for fear of what NATO or UNPROFOR might otherwise inflict. A mediator is supposed to be an impartial go-between, trusted by all sides. But because the "dual key" system made the UN mediators a decisive veto link in the chain-of-command, they became perceived as unnecessarily biased.[22]

UN mediators were tainted, air strikes were rare, UN troops were resentful and worried, and most NATO and UNPROFOR commanders became extremely frustrated. One UNPROFOR commander, French General Jean Cot, publicly likened UNPROFOR to "a goat tethered to a fence." Cot was removed for his angry remarks, but not before they were seconded by French Lieutenant-General

Philippe Morillon, a former commander of UNPROFOR's troops in Bosnia. "To be effective," said Morillon, "the force has to be feared, and that means having the means to combat snipers and artillery fire." Morillon was replaced by Belgian Lieutenant-General Francis Briquemont. Briquemont later quit after he, too, loudly complained about the constraints imposed upon UNPROFOR. "I don't read the Security Council resolutions anymore because they don't help me," he told reporters. "There is a fantastic gap between the resolutions of the Security Council, the will to execute those resolutions, and the means available to commanders." [23]

General Cot was replaced by General Bertrand de LaPresle, also of France. "If the political decision is taken to change the mandate [of UNPROFOR] to peacemaking or enforcement," warned de LaPresle, "then this present force should be completely reorganized." [24] In Bosnia, Briquemont was replaced by British Lieutenant-General Sir Michael Rose. Rose presided over a limited triumph for UNPROFOR: the orchestration of a "heavy weapons" ban in and around Sarajevo, enforced by the threat of NATO air strikes. But to initially monitor that ban, Rose had to withdraw troops from other Bosnian cities and towns—places where starvation loomed—and still had to request another 4,600 new UN troops for Sarajevo and 6,000 more for the rest of Bosnia-Herzegovina. The Security Council approved only 3,500 more, in total. [25] The consequence was an undermanned, selective ban around Sarajevo, and a fragile cease-fire that ultimately collapsed months later.

Rose was succeeded by Lieutenant-General Rupert Smith, also from Britain. By 1995 the Security Council's demands upon UNPROFOR to be more forceful in Bosnia were louder than ever. Mindful of the risks, however, Smith and his superior, General Bernard Janvier of France, proposed that UNPROFOR's widely scattered troops in Bosnia be redeployed towards the Sarajevo region, to reduce their vulnerability to being taken hostage in retaliation whenever air strikes were used. Janvier and Smith also proposed that the three or four most outlying Bosnian cities designated by Security Council as safe havens—each containing hundreds of UN troops, although not enough for a proper defense—instead keep only a few UN observers and forward air controllers, to call-in defensive air strikes if ever needed. Since those outlying havens were already maintained more with UN symbolism and mutual consent than with anything else, Janvier and Smith asserted that their vulnerability as safe havens would be no worse and even possibly improved with fewer UN troops on site. And a less vulnerable UNPROFOR overall, Janvier and Smith continued, would then allow UNPROFOR to pursue more peace enforcement. [26]

But the Security Council rejected this redeployment proposal as politically unfeasible. UNPROFOR in Bosnia, micromanaged by the Security Council in New York City, remained as vulnerable as ever.

Ultimately it was the Bosnian-Serb forces, ironically, who empowered UNPROFOR to become more forceful in Bosnia—when in July 1995 those forces eliminated the UN's outlying safe havens at Srebrenica and Zepa, expelling most of the occupants and massacring the rest. UN troops then abandoned their exposed positions in Gorazde, another outlying safe haven. Since the consent of the Bosnian-Serbs had been necessary to maintain Srebrenica, Zepa, and Gorazde as safe havens, by reneging on the deal the Bosnian-Serbs inadvertently lost most of their influence over UNPROFOR. Without any UN troops left exposed to retaliate against and take hostage, UNPROFOR now stood invulnerable. This enabled NATO to inflict a two-week bombing campaign against the Bosnian-Serbs, Operation *Deliberate Force*, made even more painful by the battles the Bosnian-Serbs were meanwhile losing to newly improved Bosnian-Muslim and Bosnian-Croat forces. Faced with the prospect of more defeats, the Bosnian-Serbs were finally persuaded to negotiate a lasting cease-fire. The Dayton peace accords—named for Dayton, Ohio, where the accords were arranged—were signed in December 1995.[27]

UNPROFOR began as an escort force too weak to protect itself as a whole. Pressured by the Security Council to undertake peace enforcement duties, UNPROFOR was nonetheless never empowered with enough troops, the proper equipment, nor even enough internal authority to operate effectively. Instead, the Security Council micromanaged UNPROFOR, often in contradictory ways, in an attempt to run a peace enforcement operation "on the cheap" both politically and militarily. These lessons from failure were heeded in the multinational force that replaced UNPROFOR in Bosnia, the Dayton peace accords' Implementation Force (IFOR), led by NATO. UNPROFOR at its largest had fielded barely 21,300 lightly-armed "blue helmets" in Bosnia. IFOR entered Bosnia with over 50,000 heavily-armed troops, with enough firepower to effectively impress all who saw it. As a peace enforcement force, IFOR was a force prepared for war.

DEADLY DELAYS IN RWANDA

In 1993, in central Africa, a peacekeeping force named the UN Assistance Mission in Rwanda (UNAMIR) deployed to monitor a new peace agreement negotiated between that country's ethnic Hutu-run regime and outlying ethnic Tutsi guerrillas. The agreement, signed in early August, had called for the peacekeeping force to deploy within five weeks, but the Security Council failed to decide UNAMIR's mandate for two months. To actually assemble and equip UNAMIR's lightly-armed force of 2,500 took another five months.

Soon after peacekeepers arrived in Rwanda, they uncovered ominous clues of political trouble brewing. "We had reports," a senior UNAMIR official later revealed, "that certain elements were distributing arms to civilians and training civilians to carry out atrocities. We informed New York and wanted to mount operations, but were told it was not in our mandate." Eventually those disturbing reports became so detailed that "we had information on the location of weapons, training camps, information on the distribution of arms." The commander of UNAMIR, Canadian Major-General Romeo Dallaire, became so concerned that he made a personal appeal in New York to get the UN's official authority to seize the weapons before a genocide erupted. Instead, Dallaire was "dissuaded, he was instructed, he was cautioned: *It was not in his mandate.*"[28]

To confiscate those weapons would have been an act of peace enforcement, an act that required a revised Security Council mandate. Although UNAMIR was not designed for peace enforcement, Dallaire and his men were willing to perform it. And during those first few months of the long-brewing crisis in Rwanda, UNAMIR was militarily strong enough to confiscate those stockpiles of weapons, most of which were simply machetes. To confiscate them might have hurt UNAMIR's relations with Rwanda's government, but whether it would have destroyed the consent that UNAMIR still needed to fulfill its peacekeeping mandate in Rwanda is unclear.

When the Rwandan genocide did erupt in early April 1994 after a bloody power struggle between Hutu political factions, Rwanda's new regime tried to expel UNAMIR. Without any peace to keep as the genocide raged, UNAMIR was ordered reduced by the Security Council to fewer than 500 personnel. By mid-May, however, global outcries against the genocide caused the Council to mandate a larger UNAMIR of 5,500 troops. Unfortunately, due to bureaucratic haggling and a lack of political will, UNAMIR's new larger size was not reached in actuality until the genocide was largely over. A UNAMIR officer later lamented:

With 450 men, we had our hands full. If we had had the 5,500 [troops that we were eventually authorized], instead of protecting 18,000 to 20,000 refugees in the [capital], we could have protected maybe 100,000 or 200,000. . . . We could have gone out to the churches where we knew people were trapped. We would have been able to protect them and deliver them food. There were hundreds of thousands of tons of food in the city, but we didn't have access because when we went to the warehouses, people would fire on us.[29]

THE LESSONS OF BOSNIA AND RWANDA

Some classic principles of military science were painfully relearned in the 1990s, namely, the importance of having enough military personnel, properly trained and equipped, at the right place at the right time. Rapid deployment is essential. The 1990s also revealed a dilemma, however, that military science cannot resolve on its own because the dilemma is political as much as military. It stems from needing mutual consent for peacekeeping but not necessarily for peace enforcement. This difference, and its psychological ramifications, are strongly stressed in the U.S. Army's FM 100-23:

Generally, a contingent that has been conducting operations under a [peace enforcement] mandate should not be used in a [peacekeeping] role in that same mission area, because the impartiality and consent divides have been crossed during the enforcement operation. Commanders must understand these key differences.[30]

Even among military professionals who accept this distinction, however, a controversy remains over what objective the peacekeepers should seek in an environment where there is little or no peace to keep. Canadian Major-General John MacInnis, a former deputy commander of UNPROFOR, expressed the following in the Canadian military journal *International Peacekeeping:*

Too often impartiality, ostensibly one of the guiding principles of peacekeeping, has been used as an excuse for inaction. . . . Brigadier Angus Ramsay, the eloquent and effective chief of staff to General Francis Briquemont, used the simile of the medieval church to describe peacekeeping in Bosnia. Like the monks, princes, and churchmen of old, peacekeepers operated out of separate and secure camps, distributing alms, providing succor and limited sanctuary when approached, moving among the local population but remaining aloof from their earthly squabbles and concerns. But even the princes of the early Church would not have stood back until the rape, pillage and torture had abated, as the unnamed advocates of total restraint would have us do. Humanitarian intervention has to be more than the delivery of foodstuffs and medicines—much more.

Both [Generals Bertrand] de LaPresle and Jean-Pierre Cot before him proclaimed what they called "constructive impartiality," which meant maximum contact, investigations, discussions and negotiations, and the submission of detailed reports, all in an effort to move slowly towards normalization. This worked well in some areas, particularly in Croatia, but had limited success in the more complex Bosnian situation.[31]

The ordeal of UNPROFOR in Bosnia revealed what happens when peace enforcement duties are demanded of a force too weak to perform them. The ordeal of UNAMIR in Rwanda revealed what happens when a peacekeeping force is denied the opportunity (a fleeting opportunity) to prevent a future crisis through some limited enforcement action, so limited that even a lightly armed peacekeeping force may be strong enough to perform it. A peacekeeping force that violates the "consent divide" between peacekeeping and peace enforcement may be, thereafter, too tainted politically and psychologically to remain as a peacekeeping force. Therefore, that "consent divide" should not be violated unless the looming danger is indeed worse than war itself: the danger of outright genocide.

NOTES

1. FM 100-23 *Peace Operations* (Washington: U.S. Department of the Army, 1994), pp. 4 and 12.

2. Boutros Boutros-Ghali, *An Agenda for Peace* (New York: UN Department of Public Information, 1992), p. 10.

3. Brian Urquhart, *A Life in Peace and War* (New York: Harper & Row, 1987), pp. 178-179 and 248.

4. International Peace Academy, *Peacekeeper's Handbook* (New York: Pergamon Press, 1984), p. 55.

5. Urquhart, p. 248.

6. Lance Morrow, "The Man in the Middle," *Soldiers for Peace* (Supplement to *Military History Quarterly/MHQ*) (Autumn 1992), pp. 24-27.

7. FM 100-23, pp. 6-7.

8. Ibid.

9. Ibid, p. 17.

10. H. Hugh Shelton and Timothy D. Vane, "Winning the Information War in Haiti," *Military Review* (November-December 1995), pp. 2-9.

11. Ibid.

12. Quoted in Israel W. Charny (editor-in-chief), *Encyclopedia of Genocide* (Santa Barbara, CA.: ABC-CLIO, 1999), Vol. I, p.296.

13. For an overview of the many legal issues involving UN peacekeeping, see Hilaire McCoubrey and Nigel D. White, *The Blue Helmets: Legal Regulation of United Nations Military Operations* (Aldershot, UK, and Brookfield, USA: Dartmouth Publishing Co., 1996).

14. UN troop figures from *The Blue Helmets: A Review of United Nations Peacekeeping* (New York: UN Department of Public Information, 1985 and 1990).

15. Ibid.

16. *Peacekeeper's Handbook*, p. 55.

17. Urquhart, p. 200.

18. Boutros Boutros-Ghali, "Empowering the United Nations," *Foreign Affairs* (Winter 1992/93), p. 91.

19. John Archibald MacInnis, "Lessons from UNPROFOR: Peacekeeping from a Force Commander's Perspective," *The New Peacekeeping Partnership* (Clementsport: Lester B. Pearson Canadian International Peacekeeping Training Centre, 1995), p. 179.

20. Reuters, "Bosnian Serbs Resume Halting U.N. Aid Convoys," *The New York Times* (March 6, 1994), p. 13.

21. Boutros-Ghali, "Empowering the United Nations," pp. 93-94.

22. Giandomenico Picco, "The UN and the Use of Force," *Foreign Affairs* (September-October 1994), pp. 14-18.

23. Roger Cohen, "Dispute Grows Over U.N.'s Troops in Bosnia," *New York Times* (January 25, 1994), p. A-8.

24. Kathleen Bunten, "Gen de Lapresle: guarding a fragile peace," *Jane's Defence Weekly* (June 11, 1994), p. 4.

25. Elizabeth Neuffer, "Question is How to Build Peace," *Boston Globe* (February 22, 1994), p. 1. Stephen Kinzer, "U.N. Seeks More Troops to Keep the Peace in Bosnia," *New York Times* (March 4, 1994), p. 3. Mary Curtius, "Clinton Lobbies for Airpower," *Boston Globe* (April 21, 1994), p. 1.

26. Jan Willem Honig and Norbert Both, *Srebrenica: Record of a War Crime* (New York: Penguin Books, 1996), pp. 151-153.

27. Bruce R. Pirnie and William E. Simons, *Soldiers for Peace: An Operational Typology* (Santa Monica: RAND, 1996), pp. 59-61.

28. John-Thor Dahlburg, "Why the World Let Rwanda Bleed," *Los Angeles Times* (September 10, 1994), p. A-1.

29. Ibid.

30. FM 100-23, p. 12.

31. John A. MacInnis, "Peacekeeping and International Humanitarian Law," *International Peacekeeping* (Autumn 1996), pp. 92-97.

9

Military Expedients Against Genocide

All sides in a conflict will typically use the wealth represented in disaster relief commodities—food, medicine, and relief infrastructure—as tools of war. . . . Guaranteeing access to victims under these conditions is no simple matter. Humanitarian organizations have shown little skill in dealing with this problem, since it frequently involves intervening militarily.

> — Andrew Natsios, Vice President of the World Vision relief organization and a retired U.S. Army Reserve officer, c. 1996

At Vukovar [during that city's siege in 1991], if we had put a relatively small amount of forces onto the ground at that time, we could . . . probably have stopped what has grown into an enormous [Balkan] crisis.

> — General John Galvin, NATO's Supreme Allied Commander Europe

In 1991, as the old Yugoslavia began to split apart, Serbian-led Yugoslav forces laid siege to the centuries-old Croatian cities of Dubrovnik and Vukovar, firing artillery on them with little apparent concern for civilian casualties. Meanwhile, monitoring the situation from Western Europe, U.S. General John Galvin, the NATO alliance's Supreme Allied Commander Europe (SACEUR), suggested to his superiors a possible Western response:

In the destruction of Dubrovnik, I believe we could have sent the U.S. Sixth Fleet, or we could have sent [NATO's] Standing Naval Force Mediterranean, into the Adriatic and—with very little military action—we could have shown the determination of Western nations and, indeed, of the United Nations, that this did not get out of hand.

At Vukovar, if we had put a relatively small amount of forces onto the ground at that time, we could again probably have stopped what has grown into an enormous crisis.[1]

Unfortunately, those decisive opportunities to quell the Balkan conflict early on were not taken for fear of being drawn into a possible military quagmire, epitomized by the U.S. experience during the Vietnam War. Recalled Lawrence Eagleburger, the U.S. Secretary of State in 1991-1992, "We had largely made a decision we were not going to get involved [militarily in Yugoslavia]. And nothing, including those [gruesome news] stories, pushed as into it. . . . I hated it, because this was condoning—I won't say genocide—but condoning a hell of a lot of murder." President George Bush, Sr., publicly alluded to the Vietnam War, explaining, "I do not want to see the United States bogged down in any way into some guerrilla warfare. We lived through that once." [2]

Eventually, albeit gradually, the United Nations did intervene with troops in the old Yugoslavia—to protect humanitarian aid convoys—and discovered that a tardy, understrength, haphazard humanitarian intervention can create a mix of benefits and consequences so intertwined that a straightforward cost-benefit analysis becomes impossible. Clearly in Bosnia-Herzegovina there were needy civilians who benefited from the humanitarian aid convoys escorted to them by troops from UNPROFOR. Yet the very presence of those UN troops, constantly vulnerable to being retaliated against by Bosnia's warring sides, hampered the Security Council's ability to compel those warring sides to cease their genocidal "ethnic cleansing." Critics assert that this vulnerability of UNPROFOR's, the consequence of a well-intentioned humanitarian intervention, inadvertently prolonged the Bosnian War—which it may have. Yet the counterargument has merits of its own. The Security Council chose to alleviate the war's suffering by feeding and protecting needy civilians. "As a result," a UN official pointed out, "a large number of people are alive, housed and safe today who would have been killed, or displaced, or in peril had UNPROFOR not been deployed." [3]

Throughout history, relatively few military interventions have been launched primarily to stop a genocide. The Allies fought World War II, for example, not to stop the Holocaust first and foremost, but primarily for their own national reasons. And whereas, in 1999, NATO's Operation *Allied Force* appeared to be waged primarily to stop Milosevic's genocide against Yugoslavia's Kosovar-Albanians, NATO to a considerable extent also blundered into that war. Its primary objective, critics say, was the preservation of NATO's own international credibility as a post-Cold War alliance, an alliance that showed little willingness to risk casualties among its own pilots and troops even while as many as 10,000 Kosovar-Albanians were being slain and more than 800,000 expelled.

When the stopping of a genocide is only the secondary objective of a military intervention, the genocide can continue even as that intervention goes on, until the primary objectives are first achieved. In other words, many more innocent victims can be murdered, because so little is being done *directly* to stop their slaughter.

This chapter examines a few expedient military tactics designed to prevent genocidal violence *directly*. Being expedient, however, these tactics are little more than hasty improvisations. Their limitations thus reflect the consequences of waiting too long, and doing too little, as a brewing crisis becomes a genocide.

USING AIRPOWER IN ISOLATION

Airpower can be a remarkably precise means of destroying physical targets. Airpower is also relatively inexpensive, politically as well as militarily, for whereas ground forces must rumble and march over roads, bridges, and open fields, their blatant presence etched in the ensuing memories of local spectators, airplanes by contrast merely fly through the air, barely leaving a trace of their speedy passing. Airpower achieved an awe-inspiring reputation during the Gulf War in 1990-1991. Later, during the Bosnian War of 1991-1995, airpower was frequently proposed as an alternative to sending more UN troops to contain the region's "ethnic cleansing." What the mostly aerial Kosovo War in 1999 showed, however, is that airpower is not a cure-all.

Airpower is only one component of military power. To achieve its maximum effectiveness, it must be used in concert with other components. When used in isolation—something often advocated for political reasons, too often without a full recognition of its military limitations—airpower almost always produces inadequate results. Airpower can indeed destroy a physical target, but that target must be both physical and identifiable. Most acts of genocide are not. During World War II, the Allies could have hindered the Final Solution by bombing the Nazi extermination camps and their relevant railways, but that bombing would not have ended the killings, because over 1 million Jews were murdered in ways not requiring extermination camps. Massacres perpetrated in forests are not easily stopped with airpower, a limitation re-encountered in the 1990s in both Bosnia and Kosovo. In Rwanda, and to some extent in East Timor, the acts of genocide occurred in towns and villages shaded by jungle.

Airpower did, eventually, help to end the Bosnian War. In mid-1995, after years of genocidal warfare, the changing local conditions finally enabled NATO to inflict a two-week bombing campaign, named Operation *Deliberate Force*, to pressure the warring sides to negotiate a peace settlement. Even then, bombing had its limits, as explained by NATO's U.S. Air Force General Charles Boyd:

Despite its appeal to the amateur strategist, a reliance on airpower alone—the strike option —in this type of terrain with these kinds of targets has never held any real promise of conflict resolution. . . . The use of "robust" airpower can have an effect on Serb behavior, particularly if it is used without regard for civilian casualties. But it cannot make the Serbs want to live as an ethnic minority in a nation they perceive to be hostile. It can only reinforce the paranoia that drives them to continue the fight.[4]

If an endangered people are located far enough away from their persecutors, airpower can help safeguard them in a designated *safe zone*. In 1991, soon after the Gulf War, the Allied Coalition used this technique to safeguard Iraqi-Kurdish and other Iraqi communities endangered by Saddam Hussein's regime, forcibly denying Hussein's air force entry into "no-fly zones" imposed over northern and southern Iraq. Using Allied airpower alone to enforce those zones, however, the results have been mixed. The Iraqi warplanes did stay out, but the zones did not prevent every episode of persecution. The same was true of another no-fly zone, Operation *Deny Flight*, imposed by the United Nations over the old Yugoslavia during the Bosnian War, in early 1993.

Later that year, in response to artillery shellings of Sarajevo in Bosnia, the UN forces there ordered that all artillery guns and howitzers within a designated zone, regardless of ownership, be withdrawn or placed under the watchful eyes of UN inspectors. To enforce this "heavy weapons" ban, the UN used the threat of retaliation by NATO-flown air strikes, and the ban soon produced a chilly but welcome peace in Sarajevo. But because relatively small firearms, such as rifles and machine guns, are extremely difficult to find and destroy using airpower, at least not without hitting the surrounding area, the ban did not extend to them. Consequently, Sarajevo was doused in sniper fire many times, shootings that eventually collapsed the city's shaky peace altogether.

That collapse of Sarajevo's peace illustrates that the apparent wonders of airpower cannot compensate for other military weaknesses. After the Security Council officially designated several Bosnian cities as UN-guarded *safe havens* for noncombatants, one UN officer, frustrated by UNPROFOR's continuing shortage of troops, told a reporter:

The safe havens were never properly defined and we were never given, and still do not have, the means to defend them properly. Even using airpower liberally, we need people on the ground—every military conflict has shown that—but we don't have them.[5]

Britain and France both contributed troops to UNPROFOR, and for two years their governments repeatedly blocked initiatives to use NATO's airpower to curb the war, afraid of the reprisals their soldiers in UN blue helmets might suffer if either NATO or UNPROFOR behaved too forcefully. And their fears were justified, for when NATO's airpower was eventually used more forcefully in Bosnia, hundreds of UN soldiers were taken hostage and chained to potential bombing targets.

Airpower is more than combat power; it is also air transportation. The most famous example of this is the Berlin Airlift of 1948-1949, a record of delivered tonnage actually surpassed during the Bosnian War by NATO's humanitarian resupply of Sarajevo, Operation *Provide Promise*. Air delivery usually requires a contingent of technicians on the receiving end; that is, unless the supplies are parachuted in. During two winters in 1993-1994, several Bosnian safe havens were resupplied by parachute drops, at least with the barest necessities: 18,000 metric tons worth, delivered by over 2,800 sorties flown by French, German, and American pilots.[6]

But parachuting-in supplies is still a risky endeavor, even without the threat of antiaircraft attacks. The parachuted supplies may fall into the wrong location or become damaged upon impact. Some falling supplies, even when slowed by parachutes, can literally crush people on the ground. For the Bosnian airdrops, NATO had to first drop warning leaflets, urging the recipients to stay away until the supplies had landed completely. This danger was reduced in East Timor, in 1999, through the parachuting of lighter supplies; consequently, however, not enough supplies were delivered to feed all the famished refugees. In any crisis, the supplies may be fought over by desperate crowds, or stolen by the wrong people. Air-dropping supplies is therefore an option best reserved for situations when and where trained personnel exist on the ground, ready to receive the supplies to distribute them properly. Simply dropping in bundles of food almost chaotically is a poor expedient against a genocide.

INTERPOSITION

The tactic of *interposition,* or *interposing,* is central to the practice of peacekeeping. It involves deploying peacekeepers between two groups, either because they are mutually belligerent or because one is dangerously vulnerable to the other. Due to this tactic's obvious crossfire hazards, peacekeepers rarely try it if the shooting has already begun. Nevertheless, in an emergency situation, it can be done in haste. The UN's *Peacekeeper's Handbook* explains:

Interposition can be a hazardous operation, but its value is in its capacity to separate two warring or potentially warring parties and to defuse sensitive and explosive situations—it is of little purpose if the size of the element used is such that it can be easily pushed aside or neutralized by either protagonist without the latter having to use force.

Speed is the crucial factor . . . The important consideration is to establish some degree of third party presence, however minimal, as quickly as possible and to build upon it. To wait until a sizeable element can be assembled before interposing it could increase the danger [as the situation] becomes uncontrollable and widespread fighting breaks out.

For the interposition to be credible, the principle permitting the use of force in self-defense and the defense of one's positions has to be firmly recognized by those who might attempt to attack or pass through the positions held by the peacekeeping force. Without such credibility, the interposition would be non-viable and non-effective.[7]

Once the interposition is deployed and local negotiations begin, the presence should be continuously reinforced with more and more peacekeepers, even as the negotiations continue, until the peacekeepers become "sufficiently strong to exercise a superiority over the local armed forces of the two protagonists" to thereby balance and deter them.[8]

PARTITIONING

Interposition is only an interim step against ethnic violence, not a solution. Yet in Cyprus an interposition has become apparently permanent, and this raises the issue of partitioning. Is the physical separation of groups, a separation either agreed to or coerced, a viable solution to some forms of genocide? Partitioning was an objective of the "ethnic cleansing" campaigns in the old Yugoslavia, as the rival ethnic groups expelled each other from conquered areas. Partitioning was also, for a time, an objective of the Nazis, waged by confining Jews inside overcrowded ghettos until, eventually, the Nazis switched to outright slaughter. Since partitioning is what many perpetrators of genocide seemingly want—or else they start killing people—it is politically problematic as a lasting solution and, at best, morally tainted. In an imperfect world, however, partitioning has been advocated by decent people in the name of pragmatism.

Partitioning may be pragmatic, but it is not simple. In 1947, when the Indian subcontinent was partitioned by the departing British colonial authorities into predominantly Muslim Pakistan (including East Pakistan, now Bangladesh) and Hindu India, at least 10 million Hindus and Muslims suddenly found themselves on the wrong side of the partition. Millions fled to reach the other side, and perhaps as many as 1 million died in the attempt. Nor did the partitionings of Ireland in 1920-1921 or of Palestine in 1948 leave legacies of durable peace.

Figuratively and literally, where do we draw the line? Physically intermixed ethnic groups are not easily partitioned into separate viable countries. Nor do individuals of a racial mix easily fit into this Nazi-style definition of the pure *nation*-state. What happens to someone born in Sarajevo of a Serbian mother and a Croat father, and who later marries a Muslim? What happens to someone classified as a Tutsi but with the physical features of a Hutu?

The main argument for partitioning is that, once rival groups suffer mass atrocities, their fears, suspicions, and hatreds are too inflamed to contain without first separating those groups, probably for years, and that means partitioning. Partitioning may not be easy, but, at some point, it can become the most feasible accommodation. The experience of India and Pakistan in 1947 may have been gruesome, but so too was Lebanon's in the 1970s and 1980s, when an ethno-religious civil war left that tiny country splintered into rival spheres of influence and fiefdoms ruled by warlords.

Cyprus is the quintessential example of an apparently permanent partitioning with peacekeepers. But the Cypriot case is not common. In 1974, Greece's then-ruling military junta tried to violently replace the Cypriot government with a pro-junta regime to unite the two countries. The scheme failed, but not before forces from Turkey invaded northern Cyprus, ostensibly to protect the island's Turkish-Cypriot minority from its Greek-Cypriot majority. Ten years earlier UN peacekeepers had arrived on Cyprus, not to divide the island, but to calm its ethnic troubles, and they were generally successful. However, with the forcible intervention of Greece and Turkey in 1974, those UN peacekeepers received a new mission: monitor the island's new *de facto* line of separation. They did, and have remained there ever since, because both sides want them there. They number fewer than 1,400 troops, which is not a high number to maintain, though even that number has gradually decreased as the peacekeepers' contributors tire of this decades-old mission. Since their number may someday shrink to zero, the rival Greek- and Turkish-Cypriot communities know they themselves must either (1) settle their dispute, (2) find someone else to patrol the dividing line, or (3) re-ignite an ethnic war after decades of relative peace. The Cypriot crisis will resolve itself someday.

Nevertheless, critics of peacekeeping warn that, even when it supposedly works, Cyprus shows what peacekeeping can become: a seemingly endless foreign entanglement, consuming outside money and troops that could be used elsewhere. Again, however, the Cypriot case is not a common case. For almost thirty years, Cyprus was a potential crisis spot of the Cold War, a place where the Soviet Union could have spread its own troublesome influence by exploiting an ethnic dispute on a geostrategic Mediterranean island, upsetting at least two members of NATO (Greece and Turkey) and probably a third (Great Britain) to conveniently distract an important fourth (the United States). That wider crisis was avoided, at far less cost than the alternative, though the price was the freezing of the Cypriot ethnic dispute with a decades-long partitioning. Rather than being synonymous with NATO's much larger, more expensive, post-Cold War peace enforcement operations in Bosnia-Herzegovina and Kosovo, the Cypriot case shows that a small peacekeeping operation—*if begun early*—can help quell a dangerously explosive ethnoreligious dispute, albeit imperfectly.

SAFE HAVENS

A *safe haven* is sometimes called a *safe area* or a *protected area*. It is a sanctuary of sorts, a place where persecuted people can go to survive. It should not be romanticized, however, because a safe haven is little more than a benign form of ghettoizing. It is not a place where the people can live a normal life.

For the conditions inside are almost always abominable. During the UN's Congo operation in 1960-1964, only about 50 peacekeepers could be spared to watch over a safe haven containing over 75,000 refugees from the Congolese Baluba tribe. Brian Urquhart, a UN official at that time, later wrote: "This square kilometer of red clay, constantly rained upon, was a microcosm of the urban problems of the world. Almost everything could be found in the Baluba camp— politics, mysterious cults, crime, witch doctors, bicycle chain gangs, and tribal rivalries." Until a UN platoon of guard dogs was brought in, many refugees were routinely robbed of their food rations by youth gangs.[9]

Politics can also interfere. During the Bosnian War, the Security Council designated six Bosnian cities as safe havens: Sarajevo, Tuzla, Bihac, Gorazde, Zepa, and Srebrenica. The last three, filled with Bosnian-Muslims but deep in Bosnian-Serb territory, completely depended on the consent of the surrounding Bosnian-Serb forces to even exist, let alone fed by the roadbound food convoys of international relief agencies. To the Security Council, the havens represented its own commitment to oppose "ethnic cleansing." To the Bosnian-Muslim government, the havens of Gorazde, Zepa, and Srebrenica represented its own land claim upon Bosnian territories otherwise occupied by eastern Serbs. To their refugee-occupants, the havens represented safety in the abstract but misery in practice.

Srebrenica's experience in particular reveals the limits of a safe haven whose existence utterly depends upon the consent of the hostile forces encircling it. Srebrenica was not a symbolic island of democracy and harmony in a sea of ethnic conflict. Srebrenica was a grim, miserable, unsanitary, overcrowded town-turned-city whose local leaders and criminal elements routinely exploited its hapless population, especially the refugees. On the best of days many people scavenged through trash dumps for edible garbage to eat. Others simply walked around, aimlessly. An internal UN report described the following conditions in Srebrenica in 1993:

Although safer from shelling than it has been in over a year, the social situation is worsening daily as basic survival needs are not met. Violence, black-market activities, prostitution, theft are becoming the only activities of the population. Tensions are mounting between the majority refugee population and minority local population. As always the women, children and elderly are most at risk. The enclave must now be recognized for what it is, namely a closed refugee camp of 50,000 persons without adequate facilities for more than about 15,000.[10]

Srebrenica was not a fortress; indeed, aside from some trenches, it was almost indefensible. In the original safe haven plan, it was supposed to have between 1,200 and 5,600 UN troops, but it never did. The most that it ever held were 570 Dutch UN troops beginning in March 1994, deployed as replacements for about 140 Canadian UN troops who left, utterly exhausted. The more troops that UNPROFOR put into safe havens such as Srebrenica, the more dependent those troops became upon the consent—that is, upon the limited goodwill—of the encircling Bosnian-Serb forces to permit needed supplies into those havens. The alternative for UNPROFOR was to airlift everything in, but that operation would have been difficult for Srebrenica, already considered too weak to withstand a determined attack. Although the Dutch troops had armored personnel carriers, heavy machine guns, and 81-mm mortars, most of their ammunition was not allowed in by the surrounding Bosnian-Serbs.

Srebrenica also had about 1,500 Bosnian-Muslim soldiers and a similar number of militiamen—ill-disciplined and armed with an odd assortment of light infantry weapons. Per the agreement with the Bosnian-Serbs, Srebrenica was supposed to be sealed and demilitarized, but it was clearly neither. Even worse, some Bosnian-Muslim troops assumed positions near the UN troops and sometimes fired at the outlying Bosnian-Serbs—hoping to provoke the Serbs into shooting back, and thus entangle the UN troops on the Muslims' side. "The Muslims are provoking the fighting," one astonished UN soldier wrote in a letter home.[11] The Muslim commanders of Srebrenica also enjoyed a brisk black-market trade: At night they launched small groups into the outside to barter and loot, returning the next morning with exchanged or stolen booty, including weapons. The few UN troops on night duty, having a very long perimeter to watch, could do little about this illicit activity except complain about it the next morning.

By 1995, the Bosnian-Serb forces had also acquired a reputation for violating agreements. Yet in view of what so many armed Muslims were doing from Srebrenica, the Bosnian-Serbs had some understandable reasons for wanting to eliminate the safe haven. They gradually denied the haven various supplies until ominous shortages appeared. In July, they attacked. Some 30 Dutch soldiers were quickly taken hostage as their still uncaptured commander pleaded via radio for a NATO-flown air strike. Eventually, after several delays, two Bosnian-Serb tanks were bombed. The Bosnian-Serb commander then threatened to kill his Dutch hostages unless all future air attacks were halted. Abroad, Holland's defense minister also called for a halt, fearing a repeat of what UNPROFOR had faced earlier that year, when several hundred UN troops had been taken hostage after NATO's air strikes near Sarajevo, later handcuffed by the Bosnian-Serbs to potential bombing targets.

Srebrenica was captured. Subsequently, the Bosnian-Serb forces expelled some 30,000 Muslims and mass executed an estimated 7,000 Muslim men and boys. Srebrenica, the former safe haven, witnessed the worst massacre on European soil recorded since the Second World War.

Why did Srebrenica fall so easily? Shashi Tharoor, an official in the UN's Department of Peacekeeping Operations, later wrote of the dilemma that faced all UN soldiers manning safe havens in Bosnia-Herzegovina:

The Security Council resolutions on the safe areas required the parties to treat them as "safe," imposed no obligations on their inhabitants and defenders, deployed United Nations troops in them but expected their mere presence to "deter attacks," carefully avoided asking the peacekeepers to "defend" or "protect" these areas, but authorized them to call in air-power "in self-defense"—a masterpiece of diplomatic drafting, but largely unimplementable as an operational directive.

The safe areas and the people inside them, including United Nations peacekeepers, could only be fed, supplied and maintained through Serb territory and with Serb consent; yet the world has cried for the UN to attack the Serbs for every transgression, a course of action that would simply end the cooperation without which the safe areas could not be maintained. It is no easy task to make war and peace with the same people on the same territory at the same time.[12]

Rwanda held a few *de facto* safe havens during its genocide in 1994. The largest of them was the Amahoro stadium in Kigali, the capital, commandeered by UN troops who turned the stadium into their headquarters and welcomed in any persecuted person who could reach it. It eventually held an estimated 10,000 civilians, mostly Tutsis. Efforts by genocidal *Interahamwe* militiamen to enter the stadium were blocked, though some hapless dwellers were killed by artillery rounds fired at the stadium. Many others suffered from dysentery and cholera, and everyone had to endure the nauseating stench of their own accumulating filth. Yet Amahoro somehow managed to hold out for three months, when the capital was captured by Tutsi guerrillas and the stadium saved. Meanwhile, a mere 500 UN troops manned some smaller safe havens in Rwanda. At the Milles Collines Hotel, for example, a few Tunisian soldiers protected about 600 people. Other UN troops protected people in the capital's King Faisal Hospital. As with the Amahoro stadium, those smaller havens held out just long enough to be rescued. They could not have held out indefinitely.

What would an "ideal" safe haven, defensively secure and sustainable over a prolonged time, require to be so? Barry Posen, a defense analyst and professor at the Massachusetts Institute of Technology (MIT), believes that the military requirements could be similar to those faced by the Khe Sanh outpost during the Vietnam War. During an intense three-month siege in 1968, about 6,500 U.S. Marines and South Vietnamese troops in Khe Sanh held out against 22,000 Communist Vietnamese troops encircling them. To blunt the siege, American and South Vietnamese warplanes dropped nearly 100,000 tons of bombs while Khe Sanh's own howitzers and heavy mortars fired off some 159,000 rounds. Yet even with all that firepower protecting them, Khe Sanh's defenders suffered hundreds of killed and many more wounded.[13] If Khe Sanh had been a safe haven, its civilian casualties could have been horrific. Posen also doubts whether the average place's local economy and infrastructure could a new safe haven's great multitude of refugees. "Even if water is locally available, chemicals and machinery will be required to keep it pure," he noted. "In all but tropical climates, blankets and shelter materials may be necessary. Some fuel may be necessary just to run basic humanitarian services; more could be necessary to provide warmth in the dead of winter. Rescuers' military units will require their own supplies, including fuel and munitions. . . . It is as if the Berlin Airlift and the siege of Khe Sanh were combined into one operation." [14]

SAFE ZONES

Within a country experiencing a genocide, a *safe zone* is a region rendered relatively free of the killing due to the presence, either in it or nearby, of foreign guardian forces. A safe zone is much larger than a safe haven, large enough to encompass several towns or even cities. For this reason, a safe zone's refugee-inhabitants can live a relatively normal existence, almost in a mini-state. Three safe zones were established in the 1990s: in northern Iraq, southwestern Rwanda, and the Serbian province of Kosovo.

Northern Iraq

The Kurds, a non-Arab ethnic group, live in communities scattered among Iraq, Turkey, Iran, and Syria. In the late 1980s, Saddam Hussein tried to exterminate many of Iraq's Kurds by having their villages attacked with poison gas bombs and massacring them on the ground; perhaps as many as 100,000 died, including women and children. In mid-1991, soon after the Gulf War, about half a million Iraqi-Kurds were attacked by Hussein's Republican Guard and chased northward into Iraq's mountainous frontier with Turkey. The Turkish government, meanwhile, was waging a war against Turkish-Kurd rebels and did not want any Iraqi-Kurds joining their Turkish-Kurd brethren. Consequently, the Iraqi-Kurds were kept out of Turkey, left cold and starving in the Iraqi mountains. Their plight was televised worldwide and, eventually, under a vague mandate from the UN Security Council, military forces from the United States, Britain, and France entered northern Iraq via Turkey and established a safe zone for them in Iraq itself, reinforced by the aerial Operation *Northern Watch*, a protective no-fly zone that banned Iraqi planes flying north of the 36th parallel latitude.

Every safe zone has a political quasi-sovereignty that helps the zone when its creators want to curtail the sovereignty of, and thereby politically undermine, the genocidal regime against which that safe zone exists; the zone exists to spite the regime. But that quasi-sovereignty can encourage the same problems in a safe zone common to sovereign states, including internal struggles for power. The Kurdish safe zone experienced both.

Hussein undoubtedly despised the establishment of a Kurdish safe zone on sovereign Iraqi territory, but he had to tolerate it because he did not want another military confrontation with the West so soon after Iraq's defeat in the Gulf War. Western military forces eventually left the safe zone, their presence replaced by ordinary UN security guards, deployed literally from the corridors of the UN's headquarters in New York City. Those UN guards, directly subordinate to the Secretary-General, posed a much weaker, largely symbolic barrier to Hussein's Republican Guard than had the Western troops before them, but Hussein still tolerated the safe zone, in part because Western warplanes continued to patrol the overhead no-fly zone.

Before their safe zone was created in 1991, the Iraqi-Kurds had cooperated with each other, despite their differences, because they had all felt imperiled by Hussein's regime. After their safe zone was created, however, the Iraqi-Kurds failed to stay united, despite their common hatred for Hussein. Two Kurdish political parties eventually dominated the zone, the Kurdistan Democratic Party (KDP) and the Patriotic Union of Kurdistan (PUK). The KDP collected illegal tolls on Turkish trucks ferrying diesel fuel from Iraq to Turkey in violation of the UN trade sanctions against Iraq. The PUK controlled the city of Irbil (also spelled Arbil) and about 70 percent of the zone's population. Rivalries between the two parties became so intense that, in 1994-1996, more than 4,000 Kurds died in fighting between them.

Iran, whose own forces sometimes entered the zone to attack Iranian-Kurdish rebels, tried to mediate between the KDP and the PUK. Hussein's regime also tried to mediate. The United States, objecting to any involvement by either Iran or Hussein, then mediated an agreement between the KDP and the PUK. But that agreement was never fully implemented, and fighting erupted again. The PUK received military aid from Iran. The KDP made a deal with Hussein and, in mid-1996, some 30,000 of his troops entered portions of the safe zone to help the KDP to capture Irbil. The sudden arrival of Hussein's troops prompted the U.S. government to evacuate some 5,000 Iraqis associated with a secret U.S. program in the zone intended to overthrow Hussein's regime, but not before 100 members of the Iraqi National Congress, an anti-Hussein organization, were hunted down and killed by his secret police.

Critics said the United States failed to smash an intrusion by Hussein's forces with the aerial punishment long threatened. The Clinton Administration did warn Hussein not to permanently reoccupy the safe zone, and launched cruise missiles against Iraq to emphasize this warning. Meanwhile, the PUK's forces rebounded against the KDP, although Irbil was not recaptured. American mediators negotiated another cease-fire.

The creation of the Iraqi-Kurdish safe zone in 1991 saved perhaps hundreds of thousands of people from genocide; in that sense the safe zone was a success. But another purpose of the safe zone was to help establish a federal Kurdish entity inside an eventually democratic Iraq, with a regional Iraqi-Kurdish capital at Irbil. If the history of the Iraqi-Kurdish safe zone is any preview of its future, that goal will be terribly difficult to achieve.

Southwestern Rwanda

In 1994, three months after the Rwandan genocide began, French military forces entered southwestern Rwanda to establish a safe zone there. It was a controversial intervention because for years the French government had actively supported Rwanda's Hutu extremist leaders. When those extremists faced defeat in 1994, despite the genocide they were inflicting, many people suspected the French government of trying to bolster the regime only because it was French-speaking and culturally French-oriented, whereas the winning Tutsi guerrillas were English-speaking, having bases in English-speaking Uganda. When the French government asked the UN Security Council to approve the proposed intervention, five Council members—New Zealand, Brazil, Nigeria, Pakistan, and China—were so disgusted by the choice of either approving it or else doing nothing to stop the genocide, that they all abstained. By sheer coincidence Rwanda also had a seat on the Security Council at that time—and Rwanda's delegate voted in favor of the French intervention into his own country. (His genocide-committing regime was, meanwhile, preparing to flee the advancing Tutsi guerrillas.) The mandate passed. Moreover, unlike the few UNAMIR peacekeepers already in Rwanda, whose mandate under the UN Charter's Chapter Six did not authorize any force except in self-defense, France's intervention was mandated under the Charter's more forceful Chapter Seven, authorizing the use of whatever force was considered necessary.

France's Operation *Turquoise* entered Rwanda with 2,500 troops, including French marines, commandos, and Foreign Legionnaires, as well as 700 vehicles (100 armored), an artillery battery of 120-mm mortars, ten helicopters (light and heavy), and twelve fixed-wing combat aircraft (mostly jets).[15] By African standards, *Turquoise* was an impressive force, but its quality could not entirely compensate for its lack of quantity. Rwanda is the size of Maryland or Belgium. *Turquoise* demarcated a safe zone in only its southwestern third, yet even that area was three times larger than Rhode Island or Luxembourg—a daunting expanse to cover with a mere 2,500 troops. The ratio of soldiers-per-inhabitants was, at best, only 1:1,000. Most democratic societies are policed even in the quiet of peacetime at ratio of, at least, 2:1,000. British forces in Northern Ireland, during its troubles, maintained a ratio of some 20:1,000.[16]

The Rwandan safe zone ultimately harbored some 3 million people, half of whom were the zone's original inhabitants, the others "internally displaced persons" (domestic refugees). The great majority of them were Hutu, not Tutsi. An independent study of *Turquoise* later concluded:

[The French soldiers'] mandate was to stop mass murders, yet they appeared only after the bloodletting had largely stopped. Taking up positions in the southwest, French soldiers remarked on how little killing was going on and how few Tutsis were visible, only to learn that most who were to lose their lives had already done so. . . . The "humanitarian safe zone" became, in effect, a safe [zone] for the very people suspected of perpetrating genocide.[17]

Many of the anti-Tutsi Hutus welcomed the French as saviors, a reception that increasingly unnerved the French troops as they discovered what had really happened in Rwanda. Spouted one soldier: "I am fed up with being cheered along by murderers."[18]

Could Operation *Turquoise* have entered southwest Rwanda as easily, gone as far, or performed as well, regardless of its reception? What if most Hutus had opposed the intervention? There is no certain answer to these questions. Even with their warm reception, however, the French discovered that they could not impose order throughout the entire zone. Though they did genuinely protect many thousands of Tutsis, for other Tutsis the "safe zone" was simply not safe. One critic of *Turquoise* later wrote:

When they found small pockets of hunted Tutsi, the French would often tell them that, because of their present lack of trucks, they would "come back the next day." There were too many useless armored cars and not enough trucks because the whole operation had been conceived as a fighting one, whereas *Turquoise* was mostly faced with a gigantic humanitarian problem. By the next morning the Tutsi the French had met the day before were usually dead.[19]

A full month after the French forces arrived, bands of genocidal Hutu militia still roamed the zone, plundering and killing. Reports later emerged of French troops who, upon seeing atrocities being inflicted on Tutsis, failed to stop them; instead, the French simply drove away, perhaps because they were outnumbered. There were also reports of continued military training in the zone by supporters of the old regime. Even the regime's notoriously anti-Tutsi radio station, Radio Mille Collines, relocated itself into the zone and continued to spout its hateful propaganda from mobile transmission sites.[20]

In fairness to the French, they readily admitted that their forces were overstretched and pleaded for large troop contributions from France's allies in NATO and Africa. The NATO allies all refused. The French-speaking African countries sent only a few token forces, all of which the French had to equip. Fortunately for the French, *Turquoise's* UN mandate was limited, both in its tasks and its deadline.

The French military did worked fairly well with most international relief organizations, providing them with enough security in the safe zone to allow those organizations to assist others. Whatever the ulterior motives of Operation *Turquoise,* the French forces never did clash with Rwanda's victorious Tutsi guerrillas. An independent study concluded:

In the short term, the number of lives saved, Tutsis as well as Hutus, was impressive, perhaps ranging into the tens or even the hundreds of thousands. Operation *Turquoise* also reassured the 1.5 million displaced people living in the protected zone that it was safe to stay, thus discouraging a more massive [Hutu] exodus to Zaire. . . . While French troops, acting with discipline and restraint, applied [coercive] force sparingly for preventive and protective purposes, their willingness to do was an effective deterrent. Having skilled troops who are able to use proportionate force proved indispensable.[21]

The study also quoted a Rwandan official of the new Tutsi-led government, who spoke on the condition of anonymity. "Without Operation *Turquoise,*" he said, "the situation would have been five times worse. It would have been better, however, to expand *Turquoise* to other parts in Rwanda." [22]

The French military maintained the safe zone for about two months, after which responsibility was transferred to UNAMIR, and in subsequent months over to Rwanda's new government.

Kosovo

For centuries the Serbian province of Kosovo was the center of Serbian East Orthodox Christianity and Serbian nationalism. By the late twentieth century, however, its population was less than 10 percent Serbian and over 90 percent ethnic Albanian. In 1989 the regime of Slobodan Milosevic took direct control of the province and disenfranchised the Kosovar Albanians, expelling them from the government, the police, the broadcast media, and the public education system. At first the Kosovar Albanians resisted in mostly nonviolent ways, but eventually an increasingly vicious guerrilla movement emerged, the Kosovo Liberation Army (KLA). Milosevic's regime combated the KLA with harsh policies, brutalizing and occasionally murdering innocent Kosovar Albanians in the process. Many villages were destroyed, often with but a moment's notice to evacuate. In 1998 the number of Kosovar Albanian homeless rose dramatically, to about 100,000. Late that year, the West tried to stop the harsh policies by compelling Milosevic to accept, under the threat of NATO air strikes, political autonomy for Kosovo, along with the presence there of unarmed "verifiers."

There were never enough "verifiers" to watch the whole province, however, and the atrocities soon resumed, demonstrating the danger of trying to create a safe zone "on the cheap." After the subsequent Kosovo War in 1999, Milosevic withdrew his forces from Kosovo (although not Serbia's official sovereignty over the province) as NATO and Russia occupied it a multinational force of 30,000 troops called the Kosovo Force (KFOR).[23] Kosovo had become a safe zone.

KFOR's first mission was to ensure the safe return of 820,000 Kosovar Albanians expelled by Milosevic's forces in 1999. It did so, safeguarding the fastest mass return of refugees in history. Its second mission was to safeguard the Kosovar Serb community, but at this, KFOR was far less successful. Within weeks more than 200 (mostly innocent) Serbs were murdered, numerous Serbian churches were destroyed, many Serbian homes were looted or taken over by returning Albanians, and the great majority of Serbs fled, many into *de facto* cantonments—Serbian neighborhoods, mostly near the rest of Serbia, with few if any ethnic Albanian inhabitants.

In trying to preserve an integrated, multiethnic Kosovo, KFOR and the new UN administration were frustrated by at least three factors. First, Kosovo (and Serbia in general) had very weak democratic institutions; principles of tolerance and individual rights, especially for people of a different language, culture, and religion, had been taught inconsistently. Though before the war there were many individuals who did respect the differences of others, during the war their number—and their activism—were reduced by the second factor: the gruesome atrocities inflicted upon Kosovar Albanians by Milosevic's forces as too many Kosovar Serbs ignored what was happening or even participated in it. The third factor emerged from and reinforced the other two: the emergence of some undemocratic, vengeful, power-hungry thugs among the Kosovar Albanians, many associated with the KLA, who targeted all Kosovar Serbs—even those who had helped ethnic Albanians during the war—for either murder or expulsion from Kosovo. Amid all the postwar hatred, most Kosovar Albanians were either too bitter or too intimidated to speak up for the now-endangered Kosovar Serbs.

Wherever and whenever any genocide rages, the creation of a safe zone may appear self-evidently necessary and even simple. What was discovered in the 1990s, however, is that to actually do so is not so simple. A safe zone can be very demanding of the foreign guardians' forces, daunting to arrange in the short time typically available, and, in a myriad of respects, very difficult to administer and sustain. Moreover, the average inhabitants of a safe zone are not angels; among them may be armed groups whose leaders are violent, power-hungry, and intolerant. These consequences of a safe zone may well be worth it, especially when the alternative is genocide, but there are consequences nonetheless. The very existence of a safe zone imposes a heavy burden of responsibility upon its foreign guardians, a burden that may not end until a very favorable change occurs in the country's genocidal government, a change that enables a future reconciliation.

NON-LETHAL WEAPONS

What are sometimes called *non-lethal weapons* (NLWs) are technologies designed to incapacitate an opponent without deliberately resorting to deadly force. NLWs include everything from rope nets to tear gas, as well as more exotic technologies such as super-adhesive sticky foam.

How can soldiers forcibly defend themselves without killing any nearby noncombatants? In other words, using the terminology of the military, how can they avoid any deadly *collateral damage?* In the terminology of the Christian just war tradition, how can they avoid a *double effect?* Non-lethal weapons offer one possible solution. Nevertheless, though labeled "non-lethal" because they are not designed to kill, NLWs can kill. Tear gas can kill a person afflicted with asthma or a weak heart, or cause a child to be trampled to death by a terrified crowd hit by tear gas. Other NLWs can seriously maim. Some types of non-lethal lasers can blind a person for life, an effect deemed so inhumane that, in 1995, their future development was banned by an international agreement. To glamorize NLWs neglects a very unpleasant fact: NLWs can be used to torture people, as anyone familiar with an electric-shocking "stun gun" can probably imagine. NLWs are tools, and tools can be abused.

Fortunately, when used properly, NLWs can be used to prevent genocidal violence. NLWs could, for example, give a sentry the means to incapacitate any hostile intruders of a safe haven without killing any unidentified people trying to flee into it for safety. Many NLWs are designed to quell potentially genocidal disturbances, such as riots.[24] To be most effect, however, NLWs must be part of a larger plan implemented by trained, disciplined, well-led soldiers or police. Merely using thugs to brutalize a crowd may disperse the crowd, but not without fueling widespread bitterness and future propaganda. Effective, well-disciplined riot control techniques do not come naturally to soldiers or police. These techniques must be taught and practiced repeatedly.

A disorganized riot arises from what is called *emotional contagion,* the mass adoption of violent behavior when individuals can hide their violence amid the violence of others. When a rioting mob inflicts itself upon a particular group (or group identity) by robbing, brutalizing, or even killing, that behavior becomes the apparent social norm. The most effective way to combat such a riot is to destroy its illusion of individual nonaccountability, preferably before the mob's contagion produces deadly results. Quite often the mob contains opportunists and agitators urging the other rioters on. A highly accurate NLW, such as a gun-fired rubber projectile, can incapacitate the agitators without killing them, leaving the riot leaderless and vulnerable. Other NLWs, such as tear gas or pepper spray, can enforce accountability more broadly, and yet still individually because the pain is individual. Such wide-area NLWs can be more effective than even riot batons because batons hit only selected people—"other people but not me" in the mind-set of a rioter. Every rioter has a different degree of personal commitment to the riot. By using escalating levels of non-lethal force, the rioters can be dispersed and the riot extinguished.

A seemingly ordinary yet well-organized crowd of protesters can also pose a genocidal danger. In some countries such crowds have numbered thousands of people. The crowd is an army of sorts, with a working chain of command, firearms, tactics, and a violent plan. At its core are its leaders and their cadre, often very well armed. Surrounding that core is a much larger group, typically equipped with clubs, sticks, knives, and perhaps spears. Another large group among the crowd may be unarmed, or limited to throwing only stones, but it forms a living screen around the other groups while shouting verbal taunts to unnerve and provoke the police-type opponents it faces. The crowd may have women, children, and old people displayed up front to deter attacks upon itself, even with non-lethal weapons. Some crowd members may also have cameras ready to record and exploit any incident for propaganda purposes; indeed, the crowd's real goal may be to provoke a harsh counterattack upon itself to gain some media publicity. Gunmen may hide among the crowd to shoot from it and toss grenades. Such a swirling mass of young and old people can inflict acts of genocide while still retaining the appearance of a legitimate protest.[25]

Such a crowd cannot be repelled without inflicting casualties, but NLWs can minimize their severity. A police-type force, interposed for peace enforcement, should first consider where such strife might locally occur. How large could a hostile crowd become? Hundreds of people? Thousands? Tens of thousands? Are the rival groups separated or intermixed? Entry into sensitive places can be discouraged with posted signs, barbed wire, barricades, and loudspeakers issuing warnings. Is the area of possible confrontation urban or rural? Urban crowds can be assembled quickly but are also limited, due to the city's buildings, to particular routes. Rural crowds may require a greater effort to assemble and, by lacking surrounding buildings to psychologically magnify their numbers, may also have less cohesion under stress.

In 1995, an eminent group of experts from American academia and the military theorized about how NLWs (including some NLWs not yet in existence, though technologically possible) might be used on a much grander scale, such as to stop a genocidal war. Using the Bosnian War as a model, they suggested shorting out a country's electric power, air control centers, telecommunications, and television transmissions. Four years later, during the Kosovo War, NATO actually did that to Serbia—and was criticized for destroying civilian facilities. The study group also suggested using "slickums" and "stickums" (non-lethal slick and sticky foams) as well as disorienting, obnoxious-smelling weapons to impede traffic and render the "ethnically cleansed" places uninhabitable until their original inhabitants are allowed to return. The study group discovered, however, that their proposed NLWs (many chemical-oriented) might be illegal under international law, including by the Chemical Warfare Convention.[26]

Non-lethal weapons might, someday, include non-chemical technologies that can incapacitate people on a vast scale, simultaneously. The most likely of these include microwave and acoustic (sonic) frequencies and electromagnetic waves. Microwave weapons can disrupt human body functions, impair memory, "stun" a person, cause fevers, burns, or cardiac arrest. Acoustic frequencies can cause motion sickness, vertigo, nausea, and muscle spasms. Electromagnetic wave radiation might be capable of causing people to fall asleep *en masse.*[27]

It might sound morally acceptable and even quaint to forcibly put people to sleep to prevent a genocide, but the reality may be much harsher. For what is non-lethal to a strong human body may kill a fragile human body. It is not safe to douse children and old people with tear gas; nor is it safe to disrupt their body functions with microwaves, or inflict them with acoustic-induced nausea. Even if multitudes of people could be caused to fall asleep to prevent a genocide, that strategy alone will not be sufficient. The site of the planned massacre must be occupied, soon, presumably with troops. The perpetrators must be disarmed, separated from their intended victims, and presumably imprisoned. Some of the people will need medical attention; indeed, after experiencing a sleep-inducing electromagnetic wave weapon, everyone may need medical attention. Are the rescuing forces supposed to roam from place to place, from one attempted massacre to another, putting people to sleep, imprisoning some people while freeing others, until the whole country is occupied? The reality may not be that easy.

The hope that war itself can be rendered non-lethal is something encouraged by the idea of non-lethal weapons, especially the exotic ones. Unfortunately, the deadly reality is that people wage war—and genocide—when they are willing to use almost any amount of violence to achieve their goals. NLWs cannot change that. Military deterrence need not be brutal, but even in a peace enforcement operation, it must be intimidating enough to dissuade opponents from fighting back. To sustain deterrence over time, the military's response must, sometimes, be deadly.[28] Moreover, no technological weapon, no matter how powerful or non-lethal, can dampen a genocide forever. To keep a genocide permanently prevented requires a sociopolitical solution, not an exclusively technological one.

ON SITE PSYCHOLOGICAL OPERATIONS

Chapter Six assessed the use of psychological operations (*psyop* or *psyops*) as a covert action implemented against a target country from the outside. It also emphasized that the most effective *psyop* campaign is an organized presence in the target country, a presence that is located on site.

Brian Cloughley, an Australian military expert who commanded Australia's psychological warfare unit during the Vietnam War, has openly advocated the use of psychological operations by the United Nations, including on site. He has written:

With the introduction of non-lethal weaponry and an increased reluctance on the part of national governments to place their armed forces in harm's way (especially when involved in United Nations operations), *psyops* has an even more important role to play. This is true in conflict and in the period before conflict begins. . . . However, the employment of *psyops* must be more skillful and more subtle than in the past. The UN should use *psyops* as it does diplomacy: as an interlocking tool that along with other means at its disposal— including force—can be used to limit casualties and assist in achieving aims set by the UN Security Council.[29]

Another advocate is Canada's Major-General Romeo Dallaire, the former commander of UNAMIR in Rwanda. He has declared:

The UN needs, quite literally, a TV UN, Radio UN, a UN newspaper and a UN News agency. It must have the ability to tap into the international media and present the facts on a situation and not be reacting to false reports, propaganda, hype or deliberate disinformation.   Since most of the international community's political, military, humanitarian, and therefore international, policy and reactions seem to be based on the media interest, the UN requires the means to provide accurate, overt and timely information. [In 1994] UN radio and newspapers could have been used to counter the propaganda of the Rwanda media that created and managed the hysteria that directly influenced the genocide, and at times targeted members of the UNAMIR force itself.[30]

Similar recommendations were made in a report by the UN's Institute for Disarmament Research (UNIDIR), an institute independent of the UN Secretary-General and his staff. That report quoted UNPROFOR's British General Sir Michael Rose: "If you can tell people what is going on and what you are doing for them, and what your limitations are, then you won't have this business of disappointed expectations created by propagandists. And there are a lot of propagandists in any war situation." [31] The UNIDIR report went on to say:

[Psychological operations] must not be seen as a "one-way street" in which leaflets are dropped and loudspeakers are directed at a passive population. This is particularly true for a peacekeeping operation whose outcome very often depends on the goodwill of the local population. The establishment of a dialogue [was, therefore, the goal of two call-in radio shows by UNPROFOR in Bosnia]. . . .These shows, which were never recorded and were aired only "live," were centered around two weekly shows, one in the Croatian-held town of Daruvar and one in Serb-held Okucani. Each show lasted for an hour or two and typically had about ten listeners calling to ask questions; between questions, music was played.

These UN call-in shows had a difficult start: initially, most callers were very hostile to the UN presence and used the opportunity to accuse UNPROFOR of corruption, trafficking, bias, etc. What was particularly difficult for the UN representatives was the fact that not all such accusations were completely unfounded; nevertheless, with diplomacy and forthrightness, even the more difficult questions were answered. Soon, however, the nature of the questions asked began to change [in favor of] information on refugees, pleas for assistance for persecuted relatives, inquiries on the possibility to correspond with relatives, or to visit them, or to attend a funeral in "enemy territory." The UN began providing a very valuable assistance and information service to the local population on both sides.[32]

UNIDIR's report emphasized that "truth is our best weapon" and suggested that the UN consider employing private experts on a contractual basis:

The civilian market offers a host of different companies which offer all types of services ranging from commercial advertisement, to public relations, to media relations. Competent consulting firms could assist the UN in determining its needs and the optimal ways to combine the capabilities of the market to address them.[33]

In postwar Bosnia, NATO's initial three years of *psyop* efforts meant to win over the locals' "hearts and minds" only revealed how clumsy and outdated its methods were—and remained through the Kosovo War in 1999. "Even in this CNN age," lamented a U.S. Army *psyop* officer in a military journal article, "*psyop* forces are too focused on the use of the traditional and less-powerful *psyop* tools of leaflets, loudspeakers and handbills" instead of using television and radio. He warned that NATO's *psyop* units, especially in the U.S. Army, displayed too little understanding of the local culture while NATO's higher levels expected *psyop* to overcome Bosnia's ethnic suspicions without properly incorporating *psyop* expertise and techniques into every level of their planning and operations.[34]

During the Kosovo War, NATO's *psyop* efforts consisted primarily of "Commando Solo"—an EC-130 turboprop airplane of the Pennsylvania Air National Guard flying near Yugoslavia, broadcasting about four hours a day of Serbian-language news and European pop music. Its news bulletins spoke of Serbian atrocities in Kosovo, the build-up of NATO's military strength against Yugoslavia, and that Milosevic was responsible for the suffering of the Serbian people. No video was broadcast, though audiotapes could be heard on Serbian television channel 21, accompanied by photographs, some of Kosovar Albanian refugees. Residents of Belgrade said the reception was occasionally fuzzy and the signal difficult to find. Almost no one on either side expected the broadcasts to change any minds.

NATO also dropped more than 19 million leaflets on Yugoslavia. One leaflet for Serbian soldiers in Kosovo showed a U.S. Army antitank helicopter with Serbian tanks in its crosshairs, the accompanying caption declaring *Don't wait for me!* On the leaflet's opposite side was a message, warning, "NATO forces will relentlessly attack you with many different weapons systems from many different nations, from the land, from the sea, and from the sky. Stop following Milosevic's orders to commit genocide and other atrocities against civilians in Kosovo . . . "

Another leaflet, meant for Serbian civilians, alluded to the plight of Kosovar Albanians. It declared:

In the last weeks, Serb military and police, under direct orders from Slobodan Milosevic, emptied the villages and cities of Kosovo-Metohija, and burned or bulldozed thousands of homes. Heads of families have been pulled from the arms of their wives and children and shot. Thousands of innocent and unarmed people are feared dead. Hundreds of thousands of refugees are fleeing Milosevic's pogrom. *Do not allow misguided patriotism to blind you to his atrocities.*

NATO will intensify its strikes until the forces used in the repression of civilians in Kosovo-Metohija are withdrawn, the refugees are allowed safe return, and your leaders resume meaningful negotiation. NATO remains resolved to Defend the Defenseless in Kosovo-Metohija.[35]

Meanwhile, Yugoslavia's Ministry of Information was broadcasting slick, visually impressive television programs equating NATO's bombing campaign with the Nazi bombings of Yugoslavia fifty years earlier. In one sequence, Hitler's face morphed into that of U.S. Secretary of State Madeleine Albright. While NATO was dropping leaflets and beaming in a few hours a day of slanted news coverage, Milosevic's regime was orchestrating an intensive, nationalistic propaganda campaign as technologically sophisticated as the nastiest negative ads found in a very dirty Western election campaign. Only on the Internet did the quality of NATO's efforts rival their Serbian counterparts, though web pages were unlikely to change many minds in Serbia.[36]

So disappointed was Brian Cloughley with NATO's *psyop* campaign that, in a published editorial, he urged immediate changes:

Put yourself in the mind of a Serb civilian. Milosevic is your leader. NATO is bombing factories and bridges, taking away your livelihood. You have done nothing wrong. Who do you support? . . . Even his former opponents are now behind him. This need not have been so, had a *psyops* plan been made before the bombing began.

If NATO could show that Belgrade's propagandists were serving up rubbish, then half of its job would be done. You do not do this by wiping out [Belgrade's] TV station, killing civilians in the process. . . . *Psyops* against Serbia's civilians has got to be positive. "This is what we have to offer you" rather than a lipsmacking "This is what we're gonna do to you." . . . It is essential that the advice of regional specialists, preferably native-born, is taken. A *psyops* campaign should be conducted in tandem with bombing military targets. It is worse than useless if civilian-related installations are destroyed.

Concentrate *psyops* on the proper target: the confused, largely innocent, and winnable civilian population of Serbia. They are the people who could bring down Milosevic.[37]

Cloughley's advice was not taken. Milosevic survived the war with his genocidal regime intact. And, at the start of the twenty-first century, NATO and the United Nations remained novices at harnessing the profoundly democratic, antigenocidal potential of the Information Age.

NOTES

1. Quoted in Anthony Lewis, "What Might Have Been," *New York Times* (January 10, 1994), p. A-17.

2. Quoted in Warren P. Strobel, "The Media and U.S. Policies Toward Intervention: A Closer Look at the 'CNN Effect'," *Managing Global Chaos: Sources of and Responses*

to International Conflict (Washington, U.S. Institute of Peace, 1996), p. 367.

3. Shashi Tharoor, "Should UN Peacekeeping Go 'Back to Basics'?" *Survival* (Winter 1995-96), p. 58.

4. Charles G. Boyd, "Making Peace with the Guilty," *Foreign Affairs* (September-October 1995), pp. 22-38. William Perry quoted in Michael R. Gordon, "U.S. Troops to Relieve Scandinavians for Bosnia," *New York Times* (March 11, 1994), p. 7.

5. See Roger Cohen, "Should U.N. Escalate or Back Off?" *New York Times* (April 17, 1994), p. 12. Roger Cohen, "U.N. Rebuffs NATO Plan on Bosnia," *New York Times* (May 24, 1994), p. 12.

6. Tim Ripley, *Air War Bosnia: UN and NATO Airpower* (Osceola, WI: Motorbooks International, 1996), p. 28.

7. International Peace Academy, *Peacekeeper's Handbook* (New York: Pergamon Press, 1984), p. 105.

8. Ibid.

9. Brian Urquhart, *A Life in Peace and War* (New York: Harper & Row, 1987), p. 187.

10. Jan Willem Honig and Norbert Both, *Srebrenica: Record of a War Crime* (New York: Penguin Books, 1996), p. 115.

11. Ibid., p. 136.

12. Tharoor, p. 60.

13. Cited from John Prados and Ray W. Stubbe, *Valley of Decision: The Siege of Khe Sanh* (New York: Dell, 1991).

14. Barry Posen, "Military Responses to Refugee Disasters," *International Security* (Summer 1996), pp. 98-104.

15. Larry Minear and Philippe Guillot, *Soldiers to the Rescue: Humanitarian Lessons from Rwanda* (Paris: Organization for Economic Cooperation and Development/OSCE, 1996), p. 95. Gerard Prunier, *The Rwanda Crisis: History of a Genocide* (New York: Columbia University Press, 1995), p. 291.

16. Taylor Seybolt, "Whither Humanitarian Intervention? Indications from Rwanda," *Breakthroughs* (Spring 1996), 19-26.

17. Minear and Guillot, pp. 104-106.

18. Prunier, p. 292.

19. Prunier, p. 293 (citation 24).

20. As reported in Seybolt, *loc. cit.*

21. Minear and Guillot, pp. 103 and 108.

22. Ibid.

23. Technically, the Russian brigade in Kosovo was not part of KFOR because KFOR was a NATO-run force, whereas the Russians preserved their national chain of command. However, the peace enforcement activities of the Russian brigade were so intertwined with those of KFOR, codenamed Operation *Joint Guardian*, that the two efforts were *de facto* the same.

24. For details, see FM 19-15 *Civil Disturbances* (Washington: U.S. Department of the Army, November 1985). Also, Jon B. Becker and Charles Heal, "Less-Than-Lethal Force: Doctrine must lead the Technology Rush," *Jane's International Defense Review* (February 1996), pp. 62-64.

25. Martin Stanton, "What Price Sticky Foam?" *Proceedings* (January 1996), pp. 58-60.

26. Report of an Independent Task Force, *Non-Lethal Technologies: Military Options and Implications* (New York: Council on Foreign Relations, 1995).

27. Douglas Pasternak, "Wonder Weapons," *U.S. News & World Report* (July 7, 1997), pp. 38-46.

28. Martin Stanton, "Nonlethal Weapons: Can of Worms," *Proceedings* (November

1996), pp. 58-60.

29. Brian Cloughley, "Peace in Mind: Will the UN give *psyops* a chance?" *Jane's International Defense Review* (March 1996), pp. 59-61.

30. Romeo Dallaire, "The Rwandan Experience," in Alex Morrison (editor), *The New Peacekeeping Partnership* (Clementsport, The Lester B. Pearson Canadian International Peacekeeping Training Centre, 1995), pp. 14-25.

31. Originally quoted in Tim Ripley, "Peacekeeping With a War Machine: Interview With General Rose," *International Defense Review* (January 1995), p. 11.

32. Andrei Raevsky, UNIDIR/96/31 *Managing Arms in Peace Processes: Aspects of Psychological Operations & Intelligence* (Geneva: United Nations Institute for Disarmament Research, 1996), pp. 25.

33. Ibid., pp. 11 and 29.

34. Steven Collins, "Army PSYOP in Bosnia: Capabilities and Constraints," *Parameters* (July 1999), pp. 57-70.

35. Matthew Kaminski, "Propaganda Push by NATO Gets Slow Start," *Wall Street Journal* (April 20, 1999). Paul Ames, "NATO seeks to counter Serb media image of Kosovo conflict," Associated Press (April 24, 1999). Ian Bruce, "Propaganda floats down," *The Herald* (April 28, 1999), p. 11

36. Fred Coleman, "'Commando Solo' debuts in propaganda war," *USA Today* (April 14, 1999), p. 5-A. Michael Satchell et al, "Captain Dragan's Serbian Cybercops: How Milosevic took the Internet battlefield," *U.S. News & World Report* (May 10, 1999), p. 42. "War on the Web," *The Economist* (May 15, 1999), p. 8.

37. Brian Cloughley, "Bullying is a losing battle: NATO's heavy-handed propaganda campaign is doing more harm than good in bid to win over Serbs," *The Herald* (April 24, 1999), p. 11.

10

The Limits of National Military Forces

One of the fondest expressions around here [in the Pentagon] is that we can't be the world's policeman. But guess who gets called when suddenly someone needs a cop?

— General Colin Powell,
Chairman of the U.S. Joint Chiefs of Staff, in 1990

Things should be quieted down in the world—so who will do it? Russia, in one part of the world? America, in another part of the world? It's wrong. It should be the United Nations.

— Yuri Vorontsov,
Russia's Permanent Representative to the United Nations, in 1993

National military forces have, on average, one national language, one common cultural background, one basic standard of military training, one basic military doctrine, one standard for discipline and military justice, one set of standard operating procedures, one standard for military equipment, and one operational chain of command running from the highest leader down to the lowest soldier.

Compared to the average multinational force, these otherwise inconsequential traits are major advantages. National military forces require, on average, far fewer decisions and less haggling for prepare to move out. National forces also tend to maintain themselves at a relatively high level of readiness. Multinational forces, burdened with having to coordinate two or more participating national contingents and the greater complexity that entails, find this task more difficult.

THE GREAT DISADVANTAGE

The great disadvantage of national military forces, at least for preventing genocide abroad, is, ironically, the very advantage that governments like most about national military forces: Each government controls its own. Preventing a genocide abroad is a charitable action, something that is not the first priority of the average national military force. Its first priority is the defense of its own country's vital interests, as determined by its government; only secondarily might its training include how to stop genocidal violence abroad, or how to care for multitudes of refugees, or how to conduct a competent peacekeeping operation. Different national militaries train for these secondary missions differently, if at all, because whatever effort and funding they devote to these missions inevitably detracts from their primary mission of national defense, measured by their own readiness for war.

Ordinary citizens in that country will also hold their government responsible if, in trying to balance the needs of national defense with secondary missions, anything goes terribly wrong. If their sons and daughters in uniform are killed on a secondary mission abroad, they will want to know why. If an operation lasts longer than they think it ought to, or becomes costlier than they first expected, they will want to know why. If not enough of them are satisfied with whatever answers their government declares, that government could face some serious domestic trouble, especially if that government is elected. This risk of having to face the public's wrath makes most governments, including among the Great Powers, very hesitant to oppose any foreign genocide with their own national military forces, at least not without allies. The exceptions to this tendency are the exceptions, not the overall tendency, and the former should not be mistaken for the latter.

GREAT POWERS: NOT WHAT THEY USED TO BE

There was a time when a country's relative strength could be measured by how much territory it covered on a world map. During the Second World War, for example, most of the world was ruled by only six Great Powers: the British and French empires, the Soviet Union, Nazi Germany, Imperial Japan, and the United States. Additionally, there were a few minor powers: the Dutch, Belgian, and Portuguese empires, the colonial holdings of Spain and Italy, and the widely admired, though militarily weak, civilizations of China, Turkey, and Persia (Iran). The rest of the globe lay in the sphere of influence of one or another of the Great Powers. The era of colonialism was harsh, but measuring power was relatively simple.

With the end of World War II, the colonial empires of Europe began to split into a myriad of Asian and African countries, even as the Cold War split the world into Communist and non-Communist blocs. Possessing raw territory was still prestigious, but because the ultimate weapons of the time were nuclear weapons, even a tiny country like Israel could be considered a major power. Industrial productivity was also important. Once again, however, countries as impoverished as China and India could, with nuclear weapons, be considered major powers. Indeed, as the lackluster economy of the Soviet Union gradually struggled to remain productive and ultimately failed to, it nonetheless retained its status as a superpower because it possessed nuclear weapons. By contrast, the power status of Germany and Japan was somewhat ambiguous—Were they major powers or minor powers?—because, despite being industrial powers, they did not have nuclear weapons.

In the years after the Cold War, the United States emerged as the world's sole superpower. The United States is not the world's largest territorial country. Its nuclear arsenal is shrinking. Yet by almost any other measure of power— military, political, economic, even cultural—the United States dominates the globe. In military terms alone, no other historical Great Power can fully match the United States: neither Russia nor China, nor France, Britain, Germany, or Japan, and certainly not Israel or India. If all those countries could somehow combine their military forces, they might just approximate the military strength of the United States. Or they might not.

Grasping the entirety of this new reality has been difficult for the average American, because it all appeared very abruptly. It is historically unprecedented, so much so that even some longtime experts in international relations have had difficulty adjusting their views and traditional theories to it. Many theories of international relations which well guided governments until the late twentieth century must now be reconsidered in today's unprecedented era. Theories of "balance of power" politics and of regional "spheres of influence" are especially questionable. As abstract concepts these theories are still valuable and, in some ways and places, still applicable in practice. But they should not be applied automatically without at least considering what assumptions they inherently depend on and whether those assumptions are still true. What was inherent in the dynamics of the recent past may not be inherent today. What worked in the past may not work today. When issues of war and genocide are at stake, the consequences of a misapplied theory can be catastrophic.

BALANCE OF POWER

Some experts in international relations believe that outbreaks of genocide can be prevented through an international balance of power. The classic argument for this theory is that, in the 1930s, if Britain, France, and other countries had contained Nazi Germany with better military deterrence, the Holocaust would not have spread across the European continent along with Second World War. If international relations were ever that simple, however, they no longer are. To understand why and why not requires a review of how an international balance of power works.

A so-called *balance of power* is a rough parity of forces between two or more rival groups, with a general equality nurtured between them to prevent any of them from gaining enough force to confidently attack the others. A stable balance of power depends on their mutual perception that a military stalemate exists between them, so if they want to survive they must learn to co-exist within their constrained circumstances.

International balances of power have existed in one form or another for centuries. Their long history and their elegance as theories have made them attractive to many diplomats and scholars. Whenever a few countries face a potentially genocidal threat, such as a militarily strong Iraq ruled by Saddam Hussein, prudence dictates that they should join together in some sort of alliance to deter and contain that threat; in other words, to create a balance of power. But balance of power theories should not be applied to situations where the feared threat does not objectively exist. Unfortunately, this is terribly easy to do if a gruesome history has left a collective legacy of bitterness and fear of a particular nation. If that nation is militarily weak and fears that its neighbors are organizing themselves against it, which is how their efforts to create a "balance of power" against it may appear, then that nation may react with hostility. For both sides, their mutual fear of the other becomes a self-fulfilling prophecy, inadvertently worsening the risks to both sides.

An example of this arose in the mid-1990s. Earlier, during the Cold War, the Soviet Union was widely regarded as a belligerent superpower, a totalitarian state responsible for the murder of millions. In late 1991, however, the Soviet Union broke apart and a somewhat smaller, more democratic Russia appeared. Yet the popular rhetoric of Russia's foreign critics frequently associated that new Russia with the defunct Soviet Union, and/or with the old Tsarist Russian Empire of nearly a century before. The fact that Russia in the 1990s was ruled by Western-style democrats made little or no apparent difference to those critics, and their rhetoric became the basis for the West's controversial enlargement of NATO, an alliance many Russians openly fear.

A few simple comparisons between the United States and Russia reveal how inappropriate most balance of power theories are when applied to today's Russia. During the Cold War's last years, the Soviet Union tried to maintain a military establishment about the size of its American rival—stronger in some respects, weaker in others—with a struggling Soviet economy only half the size of the American economy. For the United States, funding a military-industrial complex was economically painful. For the Soviet Union, funding a military-industrial complex drove it into virtual bankruptcy. Today, many years later, Russia is still trying to maintain the expensive remnants of that Soviet military establishment, with a Russian economy not even 15 percent of the American economy's size; in other words, for every dollar the United States can spend on defense, Russia can barely afford to spend 15 cents—for roughly the same-size establishment. Consequently, Russia's armed forces have fallen into a severe decay, in some cases literally. Many of its Soviet-era nuclear submarines are so rusty that they could break apart and poison the Arctic Ocean with nuclear contamination. Even Russia's most advanced post-Soviet submarines reflect the weaknesses of its troubled economy, as the ill-fated *Kursk* haplessly demonstrated when it sank with all hands aboard in August 2000, its design and maintenance inadvertently sabotaged by severe cost-cutting efforts.

Today's superpowerful United States, with its powerful European allies, all face a Russia so militarily downtrodden as to be almost pathetic. Yet there continue to be those who call for a new Western "balance of power" against Russia, as though Russia had much military power to balance against.

Wherever a balance of power is not objectively needed but a "balance" is nonetheless imposed, the danger exists that its participants will be too afraid to divert their national military forces to any other purpose than to that supposed balance of power. Self-deception blinds them to other problems they ought to address, such as preventing foreign genocides with humanitarian interventions.

Balances of power are usually associated with peace, albeit an armed peace, because an armed peace is what a balance of power is supposed to bring about. But balances of power can also be created in wartime, if a conflict's onlooking powers actively encourage a stalemate to preserve both sides. Such a stalemate is especially desirable for civilians when that conflict involves acts of genocide. In 1994, to stop the then-ongoing Bosnian War, former U.S. President Richard Nixon advocated such a balance of power. In his last book, *Beyond Peace*, he wrote:

Our failure to appreciate the diversity of the Muslim world and the genuine threats its populations face has already contributed to the tragedy in Bosnia-Herzegovina—one of the most disgraceful chapters of the post-World War II era. . . . The siege of Sarajevo can have a redeeming character only if the West learns two things as a result. The first is that enlightened peoples cannot be selective about condemning aggression and genocide.

The other lesson is that, because we are the last remaining superpower, no crisis is irrelevant to our interests. If the United States had been willing to lead, a number of steps short of the commitment of [American] ground forces—for instance, revoking the arms embargo [to arm the Bosnian-Muslims]—could have been taken early in the Bosnian crisis to blunt Serbian aggression. Our failure to do so tarnished our reputation as an evenhanded player on the international stage and contributed to an image promoted by extreme Muslim fundamentalists that the West is callous to the fate of Muslim nations but protective of Christian and Jewish nations.[1]

Today, most cases of genocide occur within countries, not between countries, a fact that leaves little room for international balance of power theories. A balance of power during the Cold War did not prevent genocides in Mao's China or Pol Pot's Cambodia. Nor did a regional balance of power in the Middle East prevent a genocide in Hussein's Iraq against the Kurds. Verbal condemnations and balance of power arrangements are not enough; sometimes what is needed is a humanitarian intervention.

SPHERES OF INFLUENCE

A *sphere of influence,* as the term is used in international relations, is a collection of countries dominated by one powerful country for the benefit of the latter's security, trade, and/or cultural ties. Great Powers in particular have militarily intervened with near impunity in their respective spheres. At the same time, Great Powers have generally avoided intervening in each others' spheres of influence. To do so, at least in colonial times, risked igniting a devastating war, probably spread around the globe because their spheres of influence were global. There have been some major exceptions, such as World War I, but the general tendency has been to leave one another's sphere of influence alone.

When the Cold War ended, the prime justification for Great Powers having spheres of influence shifted from self-interest to being in the supposed interest of the foreign populations inside them; each Great Power could, for instance, police its own sphere to prevent outbreaks of genocide. But whereas this idea might have been feasible when Great Powers ruled most of the globe, there are now very few spheres of influence left, nor Great Powers willing to police them.

The world's strongest Great Power, the United States, has a regional sphere of influence sometimes called "America's backyard." It covers North America, Central America, and the Caribbean Sea. The United States also has a global sphere of influence—and to describe the entire world as being within it is but a slight exaggeration. That global sphere extends from the Pacific Rim and parts of East Asia, across the entire Pacific Ocean, the entire Western Hemisphere, most of the Atlantic Ocean into some parts of Africa and most of Europe, and farther east into the Middle East and parts of Southwest Asia. This immense sphere, unprecedented in its size, has emerged due to the economic productivity of the United States, even without having foreign colonies, and because the United States has filled various regional power vacuums left by the demise of European colonialism and Soviet Communism.

Of the very few non-American spheres of influence still left, the countries of French-speaking West Africa are sometimes considered France's sphere of influence, while the non-Russian republics of the former Soviet Union are generally considered a sphere of influence of Russia, what some Russians call their "near abroad." Some Russians also view the Balkans as being in their sphere of influence. Aside from America's global sphere, however, no other Great Power has a sphere of influence as large as France's or Russia's. Even the British Commonwealth, an association that includes most of the former colonies of the British Empire, is not really a powerful sphere of influence as much as a nostalgic affiliation with the British crown. Germany and Japan, and to a lesser extent Italy, once ruled very large spheres of influence that reached their zenith during World War II. Today, however, none of these ex-Axis powers wants a classic sphere of influence, and neither do their wary neighbors. Sometimes a small former colonial power, such as Belgium or the Netherlands, becomes temporarily reinvolved in a past colony somewhere, but such events are unusual today.

When Communist China was ruled by Mao Zedong until his death in 1976, China's sphere of influence extended from North Korea to Indochina, west into Tibet, out to a disputed border with neighboring India. That extent is probably China's limit. Perhaps some day anti-Communist Taiwan will politically reunite with the Chinese mainland, but the non-Chinese populations of the Pacific Rim have long been suspicious of Chinese power. Even if China greatly strengthens its armed forces, it may never gain a sphere of influence that extends much beyond its current borders and coastline. An expert on China's military has written:

China's military is benefiting from impressive economic growth, but many Western observers have an exaggerated view of how rapidly it is developing because of an inadequate appreciation of the very low starting point of the People's Liberation Army (PLA). . . . Other than its potential to play missile diplomacy against [Taiwan], the PLA has a very limited ability to project force very far from its shores.[2]

China's Communist regime might be willing to discourage a genocide in its ally North Korea, but almost nobody else anywhere would trust it to be a sincere guardian of human rights and freedoms.

Does any country "deserve" a sphere of influence? Should military strength be the only requirement for it? What domestic mechanism exists to ensure that a powerful government manages its foreign sphere of influence responsibly? Does Hussein's Iraq deserve a sphere of influence? What about Khomeini's Iran? Or Milosevic's Serbia? Where should the line be drawn? Should we even draw lines between spheres? Is it better for a weak country to exist within a stronger country's sphere of influence? Or would that weak country be better off being outside of every sphere of influence, potentially vulnerable to domestic anarchy? Or would that country be safest in the overlap portion between rival spheres of influence? Cambodia has, either simultaneously or sequentially, found itself in the spheres of influence of Vietnam, China, France, Japan, the Soviet Union, and the United States. Has Cambodia been lucky or unlucky?

If the current justification for spheres of influence is to prevent outbreaks of foreign genocide, that justification ought to require a Great Power to sometimes forcibly intervene with its own national military forces. But when that sphere requires armed intervention to keep it safe and stable, even its privileged Great Power tends to dislike the arrangement. Great Powers prefer to intervene only when their vital national interests are threatened directly. Until then, a raging genocide in a sphere might be left to rage for quite a while.

Here the example of East Timor is worth noting. In a UN-supervised referendum on August 30, 1999, the native population of East Timor voted overwhelmingly for independence from Indonesia, nearly a quarter-century after Indonesia invaded and annexed the former Portuguese colony. In the weeks prior to that referendum, the vote campaign was marred by brutal intimidation, as militia gangs linked to the Indonesian Army tried to terrorize the natives into submission and from voting for independence. Most observers predicted even worse violence would follow the referendum, no matter what its outcome. A peacekeeping force was preemptively needed to preclude this ominous future, and there were many calls for one. But the government of Australia, the most powerful democracy in the region, refused to deploy one, in part because the Australian government feared endangering its economic and defense ties with Indonesia. Those reasons held sway even after the referendum, for days, as the militias vengefully devastated East Timor for its independence vote, burning most of its cities and forcing hundreds of thousands of natives to flee. Many East Timorese were murdered or starved, including infants and the elderly. The militias' favorite targets were priests and nuns of the Roman Catholic Church, whom they considered too sympathetic to the aspirations of the average East Timorese. Not until mid-September did the Australian government, pressed by television-induced outrage throughout Australia and around the world, lead a UN-approved intervention into East Timor, and then only with the permission of the Indonesian government.

Like Australia, most Great Powers today are extremely reluctant to risk casualties among their own troops to prevent a foreign genocide. Much of their reluctance is due, ironically, to what eventually pressed Australia to intervene, vivid television coverage, but with the fear that the voters might watch their own soldiers fight and die in politically embarrassing ways. Another reason for the reluctance could be that today's populations, especially of the Great Powers, may value the lives of their soldiers as individuals more highly than in times past. This theory was first suggested in 1994 by Edward Luttwak, an American defense analyst. Luttwak hypothesized that in the bygone era of larger families

when it was normal to lose one or more children to disease, the loss of one more youngster in war had a different meaning than it has for today's families, which have [only] two or three children, all of whom are expected to survive, and each of whom represents a larger share of the family's emotional economy. . . . To lose a young family member for any reason was no doubt always tragic, yet a death in combat was not the extraordinary and fundamentally unacceptable event that it has now become.

If [this theory] is accepted, it follows that no advanced low-birthrate countries can play the role of a classic Great Power anymore—not the United States or Russia, not Britain, France or, least of all, Germany or Japan. They may still possess the physical attributes of military strength or the economic base to develop such strength even on a great scale, but their societies are so allergic to casualties that they are effectively debellicized, or nearly so.[3]

And this, in Luttwak's opinion, was not an entirely welcome development.

The absence of functioning Great Powers is the cause of the world's inability to cope with all manner of violent disorders. The result is that not only groups of secessionists and aggressive small powers, such as Serbia, but even mere armed bands can now impose their will or simply rampage, unchecked by any greater force from without. . . .Unless the world is content to cohabit with chronic disorder and widespread violence, a synthetic version of law-and-order interventionism by Great Powers will have to be invented.

SHARING THE BURDEN, AVOIDING THE BLAME

Luttwak, to overcome the domestic political risks of using national military forces abroad, proposed two alternatives for the United States:

One scheme would be to copy the Gurkha model, recruiting troops in some suitable region, if not in Nepal itself. . . . The [second] alternative is to copy the foreign legion model, with units that combine U.S. officers and nonnative volunteers. . . . Under both schemes, political responsibility for any casualties would be much reduced, even if not eliminated. The United States, by the way, raised ethnic mercenary units in Indochina with rather good results, and it recruited individual foreign volunteers for Europe-based special forces. So neither scheme is as outlandish as it may seem.

Perhaps not outlandish, but Luttwak did admit that his two schemes had some "unpleasant moral connotations" that rendered them unlikely to be adopted.

Moreover, we live in an era of generally negative news coverage, with constant public opinion surveys and unrelenting election politics. Amid these pressures, would the existence of some "Americanized" Gurkhas or foreign legionnaires really give an American president enough political leeway to intervene more actively in places of only marginal U.S. national interest? Would that American president really be willing to intervene in such obscure places early on, in sizable numbers? Willing to intervene again and again, all over the world, without exhausting the patience of the U.S. Congress and the American people? To expect such assertiveness from any American president, simply because no "American" lives are at stake, might be expecting too much. Yet to combat genocide in these obscure places, such assertive interventions must come from someone.

Here a few comments concerning Russia's sphere of influence are merited. Contrary to some common rhetoric, not everyone in the Russian government wants to see a new pseudo-Tsarist empire carved out of the former Soviet Union, if only because Russia is not greatly enriched by occupying such ethnoreligious power kegs as Armenia, Chechnya, Dagestan, and Tajikistan. The Russians, within the limits of international law, have a legitimate right to be concerned with the stability of their federation and of nearby ex-Soviet republics, as well as with the treatment of Russian minorities inside those republics. In the 1990s some Russian military units were criticized, deservedly, for their brutal behavior in Russia's so-called near abroad and likewise in Chechnya, but there have been times when the Russian government has sought some international alternatives but was rebuffed.

In 1993, for example, the fragile government of ex-Soviet Georgia asked the United Nations for a 3,000-man UN peacekeeping force to help protect refugees returning to Georgia's separatist Abkhazia region. Only Russia offered troops to that UN force, though Russia did not want to be its only contributor. For seven months, Russia's UN Permanent Representative, Yuri Vorontsov, pleaded with the UN's members to create a multinational force to help keep the peace in Georgia. He failed. The result is that only Russian troops were sent to Georgia, though watched over by some UN observers under a Security Council mandate. Vorontsov, to gain that mandate, at one point threatened to withhold Russia's support for a then-contemplated U.S. intervention in Haiti unless the Clinton Administration returned the favor in advance. Even with that mandate, however, what emerged was not what Vorontsov really wanted nor what Georgia deserved: a truly multinational UN peacekeeping force. He later remarked, "Things should be quieted down in the world—so who will do it? Russia, in one part of the world? America, in another part of the world? It's wrong. It should be the United Nations." [4]

Edward Luttwak's schemes could be applied to the United Nations under the direct control of the Security Council, but that option is very controversial. Before exploring it, the next chapter will examine the more traditional option of using multinational forces to combat genocide.

NOTES

1. Richard Nixon, *Beyond Peace* (New York: Random House, 1994), pp. 141 and 154-155.

2. Russell E. Travers, "Challenging the Assumptions of U.S. Military Strategy," *The Washington Quarterly* (Spring 1997), pp. 97-114.

3. Edward N. Luttwak, "Where are the Great Powers?" *Foreign Affairs* (July-August 1994), pp. 23-28. Subsequent quotes by Luttwak are drawn from this article.

4. Colum Lynch, "Weary UN Letting Powerful Keep Watch," *Boston Globe* (July 29, 1994), p. 6. Reuters, "UN Endorses Russian Troops for Peacekeeping in Caucasus," *New York Times* (July 22, 1994), p. A-2.

11

The Limits of Multinational Forces

Nothing that I have ever been taught prepared me for the mental jump needed to go from being Chief of Operations in a NATO Army Group to being Chief of Staff of a UN operation where I had to bring together the staff from ten different nations and staff the deployment in less than three weeks from the Security Council Resolution.

— Major-General R. A. Cordy-Simpson of the British Army

Collateral damage drove us to an extraordinary degree. General [Wesley] Clark committed hours of his day to dealing with the allies and issues of collateral damage. . . . [Our] incidents of collateral damage were extraordinarily low for this type of a campaign, but the reaction to every incident, internationally, was just extraordinary. . . . [Our NATO allies would] say, "We cannot strike that target, our parliament or our government will not allow it, but certainly you can go on and strike it." The concern that we all had was when [an ally] wouldn't allow *anyone* to strike the target.

— Lieutenant-General Michael Short,
Commander of NATO's air campaign during the Kosovo War

Governments watching a genocide from afar rarely perceive that it endangers any vital national interests of their own. But many governments are willing to help pacify the violence they see being televised. One way to do so is with a humanitarian intervention by a *multinational force*. It can consist of a variety of national military contingents from several countries, perhaps along with some civilian physicians and relief-aid workers, gathered into an international mosaic to respond as a single force.

The United Nations Protection Force (UNPROFOR) was such a mosaic. In November 1993, in Bosnia-Herzegovina, while guarding the UN safe haven at

Srebrenica (almost two years before its tragic end), UNPROFOR's Canadian contingent there, exhausted, asked to be relieved. UNPROFOR's commander in Bosnia, Belgian Lieutenant-General Francis Briquemont, duly ordered one of his best units, the 700-man Nordic Battalion, to replace the Canadians. The Nordic countries have a distinguished history in UN peacekeeping operations. Denmark, Norway, Sweden, and Finland all run UN-affiliated training centers to prepare their soldiers accordingly. Few countries understand the mechanics of UN peacekeeping as well and accept its hazards so readily.

Therefore Briquemont was surprised as much as infuriated when Sweden's defense minister suddenly telephoned from Stockholm, ordering the Nordic Battalion's Swedish commander to disobey Briquemont and, in effect, ignore the Canadians at Srebrenica. Briquemont complained to his UN superiors, to no avail. Two months later, disgusted and exhausted by the mounting frustrations of his job, he quit.[1] Whereas a multinational force is supposed to have only one boss, its field commander, in truth it has several potential bosses—the force's contributors.

Worldwide, there is no international organization with sizable military forces of its own. What a very few international organizations do have are military forces on loan to them from their member-countries; and each of those members retains the right to decide how its own military forces may or may not be used. While it is rare for a government to interfere as blatantly as Sweden's defense minister did, such interference does sometimes happen in a multinational force because it can happen. Because it is legal.

MULTINATIONAL FORCES OF THE UNITED NATIONS

Some of the most famous multinational forces, especially in peacetime, are those of the United Nations. Contrary to some conspiracy theories, however, the UN does not have an army of its own. Whenever the UN Security Council orders a new mission requiring UN peacekeepers, the UN Organization, via its Secretary-General, can only ask, not order, its member-countries to provide those newly needed troops. Most of the UN's members are very stingy, and every contributor has the right to withdraw its own troops at any time, a right that many have invoked, sometimes with little advance warning.

Over the years this haphazard process has produced some very haphazard multinational forces. Those forces, in addition to mixing soldiers wearing different national uniforms, have a maddening variety of operating procedures, styles of training, equipment models, combat doctrines, and even peacekeeping doctrines. This metaphoric patchwork can be tolerated in a peacekeeping force when the two antagonists that peacekeeping force is deployed between both want the cease-fire between them preserved; they restrain the behavior of their own troops to avoid provoking the other side. The interpositioned peacekeepers are only mediators and observers, not coercive enforcers.

But the most demanding of military operations involve combat, or at least peace enforcement, and for these operations multinational forces are among the most problem-ridden forces conceivable. To be a patchwork force means poor cohesion and widespread incompatibility, problems that disrupt and weaken that force from within. UNPROFOR experienced these problems in Bosnia. It was not designed to be a combat force, though many people assumed otherwise. It was designed to escort, to accompany, the delivery of civilian relief supplies. It was later ordered to maintain a presence in a few UN-designated safe havens, such as Srebrenica, and to perform peacekeeping whenever and wherever a durable truce could be arranged.

UNPROFOR's Bosnia force alone had, in 1994, some 21,300 troops drawn from seventeen countries. From *France* came four infantry battalions and a fifth battalion intermixed with Belgian infantrymen, as well as a support battalion and a helicopter unit; the *United Kingdom* contributed two infantry battalions, an artillery radar unit, a headquarters unit, some engineers, and some reconnaissance troops in armored vehicles; *Belgium* provided a transport unit and the Belgian infantrymen in the mixed French battalion; the *Netherlands* contributed an infantry battalion and a transport battalion; *Pakistan* sent two infantry battalions; *Egypt, Canada, Malaysia, Russia, Spain, Turkey* and *Ukraine* each contributed an infantry battalion; plus there was the Nordic Battalion with infantrymen from *Denmark, Norway, Sweden,* and *Finland;* Denmark also sent a headquarters company while Norway sent a medical company, together forming a second Nordic battalion; and from *Jordan* came a radar unit.[2]

With so much diversity in UNPROFOR, the quality of its training, equipment, and personnel varied considerably from contingent to contingent, sometimes dramatically so. Although criminality is the exception in most multinational forces, the problem was serious enough in the mid-1990s that UN troops were assailed for it in a report by the human rights group Amnesty International. "UN troops," it warned, "must never be permitted to violate the UN's own hard-won standards or consider themselves outside the treaties which the UN calls upon governments worldwide to respect."[3] A few UNPROFOR troops were investigated for black-marketeering, arms smuggling, drug trafficking, rape, and for running prostitution rings. Whenever and wherever standards of military discipline vary so widely, as they do in a patchwork force, severe lapses like these can result, especially in a foreign environment where law and order have already broken down.

During the Korean War of 1950-1953 and the Gulf War of 1990-1991, UN multinational forces were used for combat. A major reason why they functioned relatively well in those conflicts, but not in Bosnia where the mission was supposedly easier, is because the former were largely contributed and directed by the United States. The UN bureaucracy was too small and too internationally fractured to manage them properly. Their sheer size in Korea and Arabia was immense, drawing from countries entire brigades (each comprising thousands of troops) and even divisions (with tens of thousands each).[4] In the future, though, multinational forces are more likely to consist of only companies, battalions, and regiments per country, numbering perhaps only a few thousand troops in total. Since companies, battalions, and regiments are much smaller than brigades and divisions, the smaller units must be integrated more intimately than the larger units, making the frictions of their diversity more acute.

For small composites of multinational forces to become effective enough for combat, they must develop an almost intangible quality called *unit cohesion*. Unit cohesion is a feeling of fraternal pride based on the unit's high competence and reputation. Unit cohesion can be enhanced when the unit's members share an experience of overcoming adversity together, a collective experience that can be produced by rigorous training designed to encourage a spirit of teamwork so intense that the members willingly sacrifice their individual self-interests to the needs of their comrades and their unit's honor. A multinational force, especially if assembled *ad hoc* amid the urgency of an international crisis, cannot develop this collective trust and devotion overnight.

The Rwandan crisis of 1993-1994 brought out many of the worst problems inherent in UN multinational forces, especially if little international willingness exists to face the risks of possible combat in an obscure, "unimportant" country. Canadian Major-General Romeo Dallaire, the commander of the United Nations Assistance Mission in Rwanda (UNAMIR), recalled that when UNAMIR was being established

> I was told that Rwanda was not really of strategic interest to any nation, so the mission was to be conducted on the "cheap." In fact, in the UN, the Secretary-General was ordered to seek economies in personnel and funding. Given the international community's frame of mind, several problems quickly manifested themselves almost from the very inception of the operation, causing several delays. . . . In sum, the UNAMIR operation lacked properly equipped military personnel, it had no [support] contracts, and it had virtually no budget after more than six months into the mission.[5]

All of these problems arose for a force of only 2,500 lightly-armed troops, equivalent to a mere two reinforced military police battalions. And yet, to find enough troops for this small force, UNAMIR had to accept contributions from fourteen countries: Austria, Bangladesh, Belgium, Canada, Congo (Brazzaville), Egypt, Fiji, Ghana, Malawi, Mali, Nigeria, Poland, Russia, and Senegal.[6]

Soon after UNAMIR arrived in Rwanda in late 1993, the peacekeepers uncovered ominous clues of a genocide being prepared, including training camps and the stockpiling of weaponry. But in spite Dallaire's efforts to get his mandate changed to authorize UNAMIR to address Rwanda's brewing crisis more forcefully, the Security Council failed to act. Rwanda was not considered important enough.

The genocide erupted on April 6, 1994. Among its first victims, all targeted by Hutu political extremists, was Prime Minister Agathe Uwilingiyimana, a Hutu moderate. Trying to protect her were ten Belgian soldiers from UNAMIR who were also killed, hacked to death with machetes. Their gruesome murder so shocked the Belgian government that it quickly withdrew Belgium's entire troop contingent from UNAMIR, virtually without warning. "This contingent, the best-equipped in UNAMIR . . . could have become an effective deterrent force had we been given the appropriate mandate and backing," Dallaire later lamented. Many Tutsis and Hutu moderates fled to the Belgian contingent's headquarters in Rwanda, hoping to receive the Belgians' protection—only to watch the entire contingent pack up and depart, leaving the imperiled Rwandans to their fate.[7]

The Belgians were not the only ones to leave. France temporarily sent in 600 troops to help evacuate over 1,300 non-Rwandans, including 450 French nationals. Most of UNAMIR soon evacuated as well, ordered by the Security Council to reduce itself to fewer than 500 troops; the goal was 270. The last remnant of UNAMIR was ordered to monitor the capital's airport and a hotel, as well as assist the Secretary-General's representative mediating the crisis. That was in mid-April.

By mid-May some 200,000 Rwandans lay murdered. Nearly 2 million others were homeless, hundreds of thousands of which were in makeshift refugee camps in Tanzania, Burundi, Uganda, and Zaire. And in Rwanda the genocide still raged. Only then did the Security Council reverse its evacuation order: UNAMIR's troop strength was ordered raised to 5,500 troops. But authorizing a higher troop figure is not the same as actually finding the troops' contributors. So severe were the bureaucratic and political delays that by September, after the genocide was over, UNAMIR's actual strength in Rwanda was still only 1,600; in other words, UNAMIR had fielded more troops prior to the genocide, under its originally low troop authorization, than it did during the genocide, under an officially much higher authorization.

Months earlier, in an effort to speed the assembly of new UN multinational forces, officials in its New York headquarters had compiled a list of countries whose governments said they were willing, whenever necessary, to contribute new troops and equipment. By March 1994 that list had pledges from thirty-one countries, including nineteen with pledges of troops, for a paper inventory of 70,000 potential peacekeepers and their equipment. When the genocide erupted in Rwanda, however, all of those pledges proved to be hollow.[8]

Later, at a press conference in late May, a frustrated UN Secretary-General Boutros Boutros-Ghali declared:

It is a genocide which has been committed! More than 200,000 people have been killed —*and the international community is still discussing what ought to be done!* I begged them to send troops. . . . Unfortunately, let me say with great humility, I failed. It is a *scandal!* I am the first one to say it, and I am ready to repeat it. It is a failure not only for the United Nations, it is a failure for the international community![9]

But the failure and frustration did not end in May. On June 8th, ten weeks into the genocide, the Security Council finally approved a new mandate for UNAMIR. The new force, named UNAMIR II, was to be manned by troop contingents from eight African countries. Canada agreed to provide it with communications gear. Airplanes and helicopters were to come from Italy, the Netherlands, and Russia. Armored vehicles were to come from South Africa and the United States. The new mandate emphasized that the force's mission was only humanitarian relief, not combat or peace enforcement. Yet even that less-ambitious mandate proved to be daunting. New troops from Ethiopia arrived in Rwanda with only their vehicles. New troops from Malawi arrived with only their rifles. New troops from Tunisia arrived without any equipment at all. "I need tents," Dallaire told reporters in early June. "I need kitchens, I need digging utensils, I need APCs, I need helicopters, I need communications equipment. I need the equivalent of a brigade here." [10] But new personnel and equipment only trickled in: medics from Australia, more infantry from Ghana, communications specialists from Canada, medics, engineers, and logisticians from the United Kingdom. [11] "One argument often used to explain these delays," Dallaire later explained, "was that those states that had the necessary equipment for the UNAMIR operation would not give some of it to those states that could provide the troops, but had no equipment." [12]

The United States, meanwhile, almost failed in its own obligation. Pledged to provide fifty obsolescent M-113 armored personnel carriers (APCs), the U.S. government refused to provide them for free; it wanted to sell them. The United Nations wanted to lease them. Yet either way, per U.S. government regulations, the APCs could be neither refurbished nor moved from their depots in Germany until a final contract was signed. Logisticians knew it would take two weeks to transport the APCs to Frankfurt for shipment, plus another eight days to fly them to Uganda for pickup. They knew that, once there, final movement of the APCs into neighboring Rwanda would depend, at least in part, upon how quickly the soldiers from Ghana assigned to drive them could learn to; such driver training can consume weeks. But, instead, the APCs simply sat in their depots, even past June 8th, as negotiators haggled over a deal worth about $10 million. It was later raised to $15 million after the U.S. Defense Department revised its own cost estimate and insisted that the UN also finance the vehicles' return flight to Germany. This bureaucratic squabbling and procrastination was soon reported by the *New York Times*—after which the contract's price quickly fell back to $10 million, the UN was allowed to return the APCs by ship instead of more expensively by air, and their initial delivery to Uganda was cut from eight days to five through the use of better cargo planes. And, as a bonus, the deal included another ten APCs in nearby Somalia. [13]

Delays like this are typical of UN multinational forces; their makeshift nature makes them so. Soon Boutros-Ghali was forced to announce that UNAMIR II, to become fully operational, would need another *three months*. Three months of more bickering, debate, planning, and preparation—during which the Rwandan genocide could continue unabated. The French government at last decided that these delays were intolerable; soon thereafter, French military forces entered southwest Rwanda to establish a safe zone there.

In fairness to the UN Organization, its problems are not solely its own fault. General Dallaire had to endure the UN's delays and difficulties more than most people, and yet after the Rwandan genocide his harshest criticisms were directed further afield:

Quite frankly, as with Rwanda, the UN is too often used as the scapegoat to cover the apathy, self-interest and collective impotence of the international community. . . . In my opinion, it is the international community that is at fault for denying the UN the means to react effectively to crises all over the world in this so-called "new era."

If I had had such a [5,500-man] force available to me while I was the UNAMIR Force Commander sometime in mid-April, we could have saved the lives of hundreds of thousands of people. As evidence, with 450 men under my command during this interim, we saved and directly protected over 25,000 people and moved tens of thousands between the combat lines. What could a force of 5,000 personnel have prevented? Perhaps the most obvious answer is that it would have prevented the massacres which took place in the southern and western parts of the country because they did not start until early May— nearly a month after the war had started.[14]

Dallaire also raised a more unsettling question:

Even today I wonder whether the international community would have reacted more rapidly and even more forcibly if it had been the Great Mountain gorillas of Rwanda—an endangered species—that were being slaughtered instead of human beings.[15]

Since then, many governments have thought about how to improve upon the Stand-by Arrangement System that failed so utterly in 1994. One such proposal is for a UN "Stand-by Forces High Readiness Brigade" (SHIRBRIG). As a multinational composite entity, it is not as cohesive as its name may imply, and it is not designed to undertake peace enforcement. A study in 1996 by Denmark with the help of ten other countries—Argentina, Austria, Belgium, Canada, the Czech Republic, the Netherlands, New Zealand, Norway, Poland and Sweden— explained:

Based on impartiality, the Brigade will operate with the consent of parties involved, and use of force will not be considered except in self-defense. . . . [The] Brigade should only be deployed for [peacekeeping] missions where the time factor is important, and when other peacekeeping forces cannot meet the United Nations' requirements. To secure maximum availability of the Brigade for rapid deployment, its use should be limited to deployments with a maximum duration of 6 months. . . . After these 6 months, the mission should either be terminated, or the Brigade must have been replaced by other peacekeeping forces. [16]

SHIRBRIG, being a composite force, remains vulnerable to the same basic weakness of UNAMIR and other such multinational forces: the reluctance of governments to put their own troops at risk in places of only negligible interest. "Since the last four hundred years," noted Boutros-Ghali after the Rwandan debacle, "public opinion accepts that a young boy will be killed to defend his homeland, his country. But to be killed to defend a concept like 'peace' in a far remote country under a strange flag of an international organization is something new. And the public can't accept that. It says, *We are not interested, we want to withdraw!*" [17]

THE NATO ALLIANCE

The world's most competent multinational forces are probably those fielded by the North Atlantic Treaty Organization (NATO). In 1995, air strikes in Bosnia by NATO's warplanes helped to pressure Bosnia's warring sides to negotiate a peace accord. In 1999, in response to "ethnic cleansing" in Kosovo by Slobodan Milosevic's regime, NATO waged Operation *Allied Force* against the Federal Republic of Yugoslavia. Milosevic agreed to NATO's demands within three months.

Fifty years earlier, NATO was established by the North Atlantic Treaty of 1949. The treaty's heart is Article 5: "The Parties agree that an armed attack against one or more of them in Europe or North America shall be considered an attack upon them all." The clause *in Europe or North America* was included because, in 1949, several European countries still ruled large colonial empires in Asia and Africa, but the founders of NATO wanted it to focus on defending the homelands of the West, not their colonies. Moreover, although the treaty does not overtly say so, NATO was designed to fulfill three purposes: (1) to deter a military attack against Western Europe or North America by the Soviet Union; (2) to politically connect the United States to Western Europe despite American isolationist tendencies; and (3) to give the West Europeans and North Americans some control over postwar Germany's military potential after the genocide and military aggression of the Nazi era. There is a not very tactful saying in NATO that, with regard to Western Europe, NATO was created "to keep the Russians out, the Americans in, and the Germans down."

Painstakingly organized and refined over decades, the NATO alliance is the most cosmopolitan integration of different national military forces ever created. Its internationalist spirit and structure may even come close to what the framers of the UN Charter originally had in mind for the United Nations; for in late 1945 those framers had intended to equip the new UN Organization as an alliance of sorts, armed with hundreds of thousands of troops, a large naval fleet, and a UN air force. Even the name *United Nations* was taken from what the Allies of World War II had sometimes called themselves.[18] Many Western generals, including U.S. General Dwight Eisenhower and British Field Marshal Bernard Montgomery, had expected that, after the war, they would help to organize the multinational forces of the new UN Organization. Instead, as the Cold War arose in the late 1940s, they found themselves organizing a new Western alliance called NATO.

By the time the Cold War finally ended in 1991, NATO had grown to sixteen members: the *United States* (which joined in 1949), the *United Kingdom* (1949), *France* (1949), *Italy* (1949), *Canada* (1949), *Iceland* (1949), *Portugal* (1949), *Belgium* (1949), the *Netherlands* (1949), *Luxembourg* (1949), *Denmark* (1949), *Norway* (1949), *Greece* (1951), *Turkey* (1951), the *Federal Republic of Germany* (1955, absorbing the ex-East Germany in 1990), and *Spain* (1982).

Since then, in the Cold War's aftermath, NATO has been pulled in two directions. One direction is from the past. NATO began as an alliance against a Communist Russian menace, and there are people who believe that NATO should always remain that, even if Russia is no longer Communist nor much of a threat, but only potentially so. Many East Europeans west of Russia, having bitter memories of Soviet dominance, want to join NATO to politically connect themselves to the West. To them, NATO represents safety.

Many Russians, however, have long viewed NATO very differently: as a Western military alliance aimed at Russia. In the eyes of many Russian military planners in particular, an expanding NATO is not only an anti-Russian alliance but in closer striking distance to Russia than ever before, with goals at least potentially belligerent. During World War II, tens of millions of people were killed on Russian soil by an invasion from Germany, a European Great Power that is now a key member of NATO. For many Russians whose backgrounds were shaped by the major events of the twentieth century, including by World War II and by the Cold War, what they perceive today feels humiliating, even terrifying. In 1997, in its large-scale training exercises, the Russian military postulated an attack upon Russia by NATO forces allied with pro-NATO forces in Lithuania and Poland, two of Russia's historical enemies. (Since then, Poland has joined NATO as a member.) In those fictional war-games, the Russians deemed their own armed forces to be so weak (as they are in reality) that they resorted to using Russian nuclear weapons to stop the NATO-led forces.[19]

The other, almost opposite direction pulling NATO after the Cold War is European peacekeeping and peace enforcement. This new direction began in 1991 when U.S. General John Galvin, NATO's Supreme Allied Commander Europe (SACEUR) at that time, suggested that the alliance could intervene in the then-fracturing Yugoslavia to end the Serbian artillery bombardments of Dubrovnik and Vukovar. NATO's members, appalled by the carnage they saw being televised daily, nonetheless held back. Yet, within two years, NATO was flying humanitarian aid supplies into Sarajevo as NATO's warships enforced a UN-declared arms embargo. By 1994, NATO's warplanes were striking targets in Bosnia-Herzegovina to assist the UN troops there.

NATO also announced its Partnership for Peace (PfP) program in 1994, a means by which non-NATO countries can militarily cooperate with NATO. To calm the Russians' fears, NATO refused to guarantee that any PfP participant would ever become a full NATO member—although, to the East Europeans, the PfP program was portrayed as a way through which they could eventually gain full membership. Twenty-seven countries soon enrolled, of which four were former political neutrals in Europe: *Switzerland, Austria, Sweden,* and *Finland*. Two other countries, *Slovenia* and *Macedonia,* were once republics in the old Yugoslavia. Seven countries, aside from the USSR itself, were once part of the Soviet-controlled and now defunct Warsaw Pact alliance: the *Czech Republic* and *Slovakia* (both once constituting the combined country of Czechoslovakia), plus *Poland, Hungary, Romania, Bulgaria,* and *Albania*. All fifteen republics of the former Soviet Union also joined: the Baltic states of *Estonia, Latvia,* and *Lithuania,* the Caucasus republics of *Georgia, Armenia,* and *Azerbaijan,* the predominantly Slavic countries of *Belarus, Ukraine, Moldova,* and the *Russian Federation*, and the Central Asian republics of *Kazakhstan, Turkmenistan, Uzbekistan, Tajikistan* and *Kyrgyzstan*.

There was a time when any NATO activity outside of Western Europe, even in neighboring Yugoslavia, was so unusual that NATO's official term for it reflected its peculiarity: *out-of-area operations*. Since the 1990s, however, the United States and other NATO members have conducted joint military exercises in places as far away as Kazakhstan in Central Asia. To encourage even more cooperation, NATO has since gradually merged its PfP program into its North

Atlantic Cooperation Council to form a new body, the Euro-Atlantic Partnership Council.

In December 1995, after the Bosnian War's peace accords were signed in Dayton, Ohio, some 50,000 NATO troops (including 20,000 American) went "out-of-area" into Bosnia to enforce the peace there, assisted by 10,000 troops from NATO's PfP partners—including from Russia, which contributed an entire brigade—along with contingents from a few non-PfP countries such as Egypt and Malaysia. This Implementation Force (IFOR) of the Dayton accords was larger and more powerful than any multinational force ever run by the UN Organization directly. IFOR, built around NATO's Allied Rapid Reaction Corps, included an air component headquartered in Italy with NATO-aligned air bases in Italy, Greece, Germany, Britain, and France. IFOR also had a naval component of destroyers, frigates, and patrol craft. IFOR's entirety was led by a U.S. general who, simultaneously, was NATO's Commander-in-Chief Allied Forces Southern Europe (AFSOUTH). His AFSOUTH headquarters was in Naples, Italy. His IFOR headquarters was in Sarajevo, Bosnia.[20]

Can NATO become a peace enforcement arm of the United Nations? Such a role is permitted by Article 43 of the UN Charter. Note the italicized portion:

All Members of the United Nations, in order to contribute to the maintenance of international peace and security, undertake to make available to the Security Council, on its call and in accordance with a special agreement or agreements, armed forces, assistance, and facilities. . . . The agreement or agreements shall be concluded between the Security Council and [UN] Members or between the Security Council and *groups of Members* and shall be subject to ratification by the signatory states in accordance with their respective constitutional processes.

Three of NATO's most powerful members hold permanent seats on the UN Security Council, each with a veto: the United States, Britain and France. Those three could become four or even five if Germany, a NATO member, gains a permanent seat on the Security Council, and/or if Russia, which already has a permanent Council seat, becomes a member of NATO. In 1996, in accord with a UN mandate, NATO's IFOR successfully enforced the peace in Bosnia for one year, after which it was replaced by a smaller but still competent Stabilization Force (SFOR) of 25,000 troops, also largely fielded by NATO.[21]

Part of this new direction for NATO is the NATO-Russia Founding Act. Signed in 1997 as an agreement, though not a formal treaty, the Act established a "NATO-Russia Permanent Joint Council" to allow the Russian government to raise its concerns with NATO and facilitate joint cooperation in peacekeeping, peace enforcement, and arms control. Some Western critics of the Act fear that the Permanent Joint Council could give the Russian government a veto over NATO's future activities, though the Act specifically prohibits any such veto. And indeed Russia was unable to veto NATO's war against Yugoslavia. What the Founding Act did establish were some principles for the still evolving relationship between NATO and Russia. The Act mentions that Russian troops have served alongside NATO troops in Bosnia to help implement the Dayton accords, and it declares that NATO and Russia have a "shared objective" in responding to a "persistent abuse of human rights and of persons belonging to national minorities" in Europe, an objective that obviously includes the curbing of genocide.

NATO's expansion into Eastern Europe has terrified the Russians. Poland, Hungary, and the Czech Republic joined NATO as full members in early 1999. France wants to invite Romania, with whom France has cultural and economic ties, while Italy wants to invite Slovenia. Bulgaria, too, has expressed its desire to join NATO, as have the Baltic states of Estonia, Latvia, and Lithuania—all of particular discomfort to Russia, since all four countries were once well within the Soviet-era sphere of influence. Likewise Ukraine, once ruled by Russia, has signed a "distinctive partnership" charter with NATO, an agreement similar to the Founding Act.

But if Poland, Hungary, and the Czech Republic joined NATO expecting to have peace, they were soon disappointed. Within weeks of their admission, NATO entered the Kosovo War. Ironically, if NATO had not expanded itself in apparent disregard for Russia's expressed insecurities, that war might have been avoided. Milosevic's "ethnic cleansing" of Kosovo was likely emboldened by Russia's pan-Slavic feelings towards Serbia. If NATO had not taken Russia's support for NATO's antigenocidal goals for granted, Milosevic could have been denied his strongest ally before the war even began. He might have capitulated to NATO's threats to retaliate with aerial bombing before it started.

Instead, NATO's bombing of Yugoslavia infuriated the Russians. When Russia tried to raise its objections in the Security Council, the Western powers vetoed any discussion of them. As anti-Western feelings rose throughout Slavic Europe, Russia froze its formal cooperation with NATO, including in the Permanent Joint Council, and tried to mediate a cease-fire—while using every opportunity to publicly criticize NATO's campaign. On occasion, Russia even threatened to militarily support the Serbs.

In the twenty-first century, Russia's fears of an expanding NATO will not be soothed as long as NATO tries to pursue two contradictory directions at the same time. The first direction is for NATO to remain an anti-Moscow alliance, despite the end of the Cold War. The second, newer direction is for NATO to be an alliance against political violence and genocide. If the common perception is that the East European countries are joining NATO to protect themselves, the logical question almost all Russians ask is: *To protect themselves from whom?* If the answer is, *Not Russia, but political violence and genocide in general*, then the Russians wonder, *Why is entry into NATO not open to everyone now? Why is membership in NATO so selective, so exclusive?*

"Our attitude toward the West over the past decade has been a long fall, from euphoria to disenchantment," explained Georgi Shakhnazarov, an advisor to Mikhail Gorbachev. "Everybody thought the West would help us, teach us, bring us into its superior way of life. Now increasing numbers of Russians believe the U.S. and other countries conspired to destroy the Soviet Union, to wreak our economy and reduce us to third-world status."[22]

In 1997, five years after his retirement as SACEUR, General John Galvin expressed his own views about NATO's two contradictory directions:

I do think that the new strategy of crisis management needs to be elucidated and emphasized. The old strategy of defense against attack, in other words Article 5, needs to be thrown out. However, NATO is sticking with that old strategy and trying to have a new strategy at the same time. You really can't have a strategy of crisis management that says you have no enemies whatsoever, and that your only enemy is instability, while also having a strategy of massive defense against an attack by Russia.

If we feel there's going to be an attack by the Russians, then we've never really left the Cold War. So we have to decide: *Are we out of the Cold War or are we in?* . . . If we mean the Russians, let's say so and say that we're back in the Cold War. If it's not the Russians, then let's clearly say that and sit down with the Russians and figure out what the security of Europe should look like.[23]

If NATO is to be an anti-Russian alliance, not even the most Westernized of Russian democrats should ever fully trust NATO. Nor should they trust the West. For, with the Soviet Union now gone, an anti-Russian NATO means that NATO was never truly an anti-Communist alliance. The Russian parliament has long delayed ratifying some of the most important U.S.-Russian disarmament agreements ever negotiated, including the START-II treaty that cuts back the Russian nuclear arsenal, because of the Russian parliamentarians' anger towards, and fear of, NATO. This Russian distrust of NATO has complicated U.S. policies not only in the Balkans but likewise towards Iraq, with whom Russia has important economic ties. The foreign policies of the United States are more internationally credible when they are endorsed by the UN Security Council. But those symbolic UN endorsements are jeopardized by strained U.S.-Russian relations.

It is sometimes said that the Russians are a product of their own history. But today's Russians are also influenced by the Information Age. If their limited exposure to a free press, market economics, and democratic processes have not influenced them as much as their critics would like, the solution is to further integrate Russia into that cosmopolitan world—and to make that integration benefit most Russians instead of only their most privileged. But to erect an ever encroaching armed barrier against Russia, as though a Tsarist/Communist lust for conquest is somehow in the Russians' genes, is dangerous because it fuels their worst fears. It is especially dangerous while the Russians still retain a large nuclear arsenal, retained largely because of NATO's expansion and because Russia's conventional forces have deteriorated so severely since the end of the Soviet Union.

How weak those conventional forces of Russia are, and will likely remain for some time to come, is something that NATO should consider as it forges its own future. During the 1990s, Russia's armed forces fought in many places—in ex-Soviet Georgia, in Tajikistan, and elsewhere in the former USSR—but they always had Soviet-era bases from which to operate, bases that already had Russian troops in them when the USSR split into fifteen new countries in 1991. This dependence upon Soviet-era bases is a severe operating constraint for the Russian military, because there are no Russian-occupied bases beyond the territory of the former Soviet Union. Even in the Russian Federation itself, the Russian military lost the Chechen War of 1994-1995 in a region only slightly larger than Connecticut, indeed half the size of Belgium. Russia's next war in Chechnya, begun in 1999, required an enormous focus of resources by the Russian military, in part due to its earlier losses and humiliation. If the West, prior to NATO's expansion and the Kosovo War, had been more receptive to the Russians' concerns, the Russians might have waged that second Chechen war far less brutally, more receptive to the West's concerns. Instead, when the West did object to how it was being waged, the Russians decried those objections as Western hypocrisy coming so soon after NATO's war against Yugoslavia.

NATO to a great extent still looks like a barrier alliance aimed at the USSR. NATO therefore needs to further reorganize its own internal structure. Critics of this may ask, *If an anti-Russian alliance is ever needed in Europe, why change NATO now if NATO can be that anti-Russian alliance today? Why not keep NATO structurally stable?* The answer to this is that NATO is already changing, and needs to change still further even as an anti-Russian alliance. For there is a difference between defending the once relatively short border between West Germany and Communist East Germany to defending, say, the extremely lengthy, open eastern frontier of Poland. To accommodate every new member that NATO adds, more upon more, NATO must change its organizational structure, its military planning, and innumerable other aspects. Meanwhile, there is an ongoing revolution in new military technologies, new doctrines, and new command structures, while Russia will need many years if not decades to build up a genuine invasion threat to Europe, if Russia ever can. To expect, therefore, that NATO must have itself structurally complete and ready for war at this present moment, to face a possible Russian invasion threat not realistically envisioned for many years at the earliest, is to be ignorant of the military facts. In 1990-1991, in preparation for the Gulf War's Operation *Desert Storm*, the Allied Coalition against Iraq organized an elaborate yet effective command structure within a matter of weeks. NATO can, if necessary, organize itself as quickly, although NATO is much more likely to have years of warning and preparation time.

Until then, NATO, having the capability to thwart genocide and other forms of severe violence in Europe, may still not always respond to such crises as much as it arguably should. In 1997, when Albania was swept by near anarchy after its economy collapsed, creating a nationwide food shortage, NATO was asked to intervene but refused. Civil order in Albania had to be restored by an Italian-led UN peacekeeping force of a mere 7,200 troops. Italy is a member of NATO, but Italy had to go to the United Nations to organize any help to assist its neighbor across the Adriatic.[24] And in 1999, during the Kosovo War, the great majority of NATO's forces were American, not European, an imbalance that so embarrassed the Europeans that they have sought to create a 60,000-man European Rapid Reaction Force (ERRF), or *Euroforce*, for future Kosovo-type crises. Composed of composite national units, the ERRF is being built around the Franco-German *Eurocorps* affiliated with the European Union (EU). But the ERRF will still take years to develop, which means that NATO's military forces will probably remain largely American for many years to come. And this means that, unless a future crisis attracts the active interest of the United States, it is unlikely to attract the active interest of NATO, even if it occurs in Europe.

NATO, like all international organizations, will do only what its member-governments allow it to do. Rather than intervene all over the Eurasian continent, something that most members of NATO would prefer that it not do, the most far-reaching contribution to genocide prevention that NATO may make could be quite mundane, namely, gradually transform the once Soviet-style militaries of Eastern Europe and other countries into Western-style militaries capable of doing peacekeeping and peace enforcement, all in scrupulous adherence to the Geneva Conventions. If NATO had developed a better relationship with Russia prior to 1999, in that year a NATO-reformed Russian military might not have behaved so brutally in Chechnya.

MULTINATIONAL FORCES OF OTHER ORGANIZATIONS

Could a global network of regional organizations, each with its own regional multinational forces, curb outbreaks of genocide? To some degree perhaps, but most regional organizations face some debilitating limits as "regional sheriffs." Very few of them have military bureaucracies developed enough to manage large multinational operations. And all of them, including NATO, face the same basic vulnerability of multinational politics, namely, that each organization can act only when enough of its member-governments participate accordingly, preferably with donations of troops. Very few governments are willing to do this. Even fewer donate enough troops beyond a token.

The Commonwealth of Independent States (CIS), led by Russia, is the regional military organization of the former Soviet Union. It was formed in late 1991 as the USSR was breaking apart. Many Soviet officers at that time wanted to preserve the entire Soviet military as a single united force to defend the entire post-Soviet landmass. The new CIS failed to achieve this, however, and instead the USSR's armed forces were divided up. Since then, having less ambitious goals, CIS-affiliated troops have deployed as peacekeepers and peace enforcers to ex-Soviet republics such as Georgia and Tajikistan under legal mandates from the UN Security Council, watched over by accompanying UN observers. Those CIS operations, considered essential by Moscow for Russia's national security, nonetheless involved only relatively small numbers of Russian troops (2,000 in Georgia, 6,000 in Tajikistan) and deployed only after the worst strife had ended. Likewise today, unless the Russian government perceives that its vital national interests are at stake, the CIS is unlikely to have either the will or the capability to intervene into every major episode of ethnic and religious violence in the former Soviet Union. As two wars in Chechnya in the 1990s revealed, the Russian Federation already has plenty of ethnic and religious problems within its own borders to contend with.

The Organization of American States (OAS) and the Association of South East Asian Nations (ASEAN) are, respectively, the main regional organizations of the Western Hemisphere and Southeast Asia. Neither organization has ever directly commanded any multinational forces and neither expects to. Most of their members, having experienced histories of foreign colonialism, are unlikely to want those organizations converted into pseudocolonial authorities armed with multinational forces capable of intervening against them, whatever the justification. The OAS did sponsor a U.S.-led military intervention into the Dominican Republic in 1965. In the 1990s, however, the OAS was using UN peacekeepers to supervise the peaceful disbanding of guerrilla armies in Central America. ASEAN is mainly a regional trade organization, with Indonesia as an important member. When Suharto's Indonesia forcibly incorporated the former Portuguese colony of East Timor in 1975 and committed genocidal human rights abuses there for more than two decades thereafter, ASEAN did little about it. In 1999, after East Timor voted for independence and was subsequently devastated by militia gangs linked to the Indonesian military, some Asian countries did participate in an Australian-led International Force for East Timor (INTERFET), a peace enforcement force endorsed by the UN and begrudgingly accepted by the Indonesian government. ASEAN, however, had nothing to do with it.

Africa, after witnessing the largely unhindered genocide in Rwanda in 1994, no longer views every outside intervention as an act of foreign imperialism. But the Organization for African Unity (OAU), Africa's largest international body, has little experience with fielding peacekeeping forces and none with fielding multinational forces for peace enforcement.

In West Africa, a regional organization called the Economic Community of West African States (ECOWAS) in the 1990s began fielding a multinational force called ECOMOG, attempting to quell civil wars in Liberia and later in Sierra Leone. ECOMOG experienced the same problems in Liberia common to almost all multinational forces: differing national agendas, different military doctrines and equipment, uneven standards of training and discipline, and a politically fractured chain of command. It sometimes performed peacekeeping in Liberia, at other times a very harsh peace enforcement, only to attempt peacekeeping again. It did some successes in Liberia; by restoring order and food deliveries within Liberia's capital, for instance, it probably saved thousands of lives. But ECOMOG arrived too late to quell Liberia's civil war easily, and it never had enough troops to finish the task.[25] It enjoyed more success in Sierra Leone where, in 1998, it restored an elected leader to power after dispelling the military junta that ousted him nine months earlier. Cheering crowds greeted ECOMOG's troops. Whether it can perform as well elsewhere is questionable, however. ECOMOG operates only in West Africa, not throughout the continent, and the regime it dispelled in Sierra Leone was little more than a collection of ragtag gangs and brutal thugs lacking any popular support.

In late 1996, the United States announced its African Crisis Relief Initiative (ACRI), devised by the Clinton Administration to create a Response Force of some 10,000 African troops supported by Western funding, training, and, if necessary, logistics for its transportation and resupply. At first many African and European governments viewed the ACRI program with suspicion. The Africans said that, being such a broad foreign initiative for their continent, it should have been proposed under at least the auspices of the United Nations, not by the United States acting alone. Many Europeans openly wondered whether the ACRI program was not really an attempt to spread U.S. military influence into Africa, a continent where France in particular has long maintained a sphere of influence.[26]

To overcome these first impressions, the United States tried to accommodate the Africans' and Europeans' concerns. In doing so, however, the ACRI program fell victim to the typical limitations of multinational forces. The Africans wanted, and got, a role in deciding when, where, and how their Response Force would be used; consequently, their governments are not obligated to include their troops in the Response Force in any actual crisis. Nor are the European governments obligated to fund and equip the Response Force for any operation they do not fully agree with; consequently, even if the mission is to quell a genocide, the Response Force, prior to its deployment, might be paralyzed by disagreements over how that mission should be carried out. Should the Response Force perform peacekeeping, peace enforcement, or both, or neither? To what extent should diplomats be involved? To what extent should international organizations, such as the UN and the OAU, be involved? When is an African crisis serious enough to warrant a humanitarian intervention? These questions would be contentious under any circumstances, but when a multinational force requires that the answers be broadly agreed upon before it even deploys, it may not deploy very quickly, nor be very beneficial by the time it gets there. The ACRI program does promote multinational exercises and joint military training, but because its Response Force is not an independent standing force, these contentious questions cannot be resolved beforehand.

As long as governments control the armed forces that they contribute, no multinational force can be a credible deterrent to genocide at all times. For when everyone is officially responsible, no one has to be responsible in practice.

NOTES

1. Thomas Post and Joel Brand, "Blues for the Blue Helmets," *Newsweek* (February 7, 1994), pp. 22-23. This incident regarding the Nordic Battalion was confirmed in an interview with the UN's Department of Peacekeeping Operations.

2. Figures from: International Institute for Strategic Studies, *The Military Balance 1994-1995* (London: Brassey's, 1994).

3. Quoted in Colum Lynch, "Amnesty International Assails U.N. on Peacekeeping Units," *Boston Globe* (January 26, 1994), p. 2.

4. For an assessment of the military problems of equipping the UN Organization with forces on the scale of Operation *Desert Storm,* see John G. Heidenrich, "Arming the United Nations: Military Considerations & Operational Constraints," in Fariborz Mokhtari (editor), *Peacemaking, Peacekeeping and Coalition Warfare: The Future Role of the United Nations* (Washington: U.S. National Defense University, 1994), pp. 41-56.

5. Romeo Dallaire, "The Rwandan Experience," in Alex Morrison (editor), *The New Peacekeeping Partnership* (Clementsport, The Lester B. Pearson Canadian International Peacekeeping Training Centre, 1995), pp. 14-25.

6. *The Military Balance 1994-1995,* p. 272.

7. Larry Minear and Philippe Guillot, *Soldiers to the Rescue: Humanitarian Lessons from Rwanda* (Paris: Organization for Economic Cooperation and Development/OECD, 1996), pp. 76-79.

8. Eric Schmitt, "15 Nations Offer Troops For U.N. Force of 54,000," *New York Times* (April 13, 1994), p. A-12. Also, Colum Lynch, "UN Planning a Standby Force of 70,000," *Boston Globe* (May 17, 1994), p. 18.

9. Paul Lewis, "Boutros-Ghali Angrily Condemns All Sides for Not Saving Rwanda," *New York Times* (May 26, 1994), pp. A-1 and A-10.

10. Associated Press, "US to send vehicles to help evacuate Rwanda refugees," *Boston Globe* (June 2, 1994), p. 10.

11. Minear and Guillot, *loc. cit.*

12. Dallaire, *loc. cit.*

13. Michael R. Gordon, "U.N.'s Rwanda Deployment Slowed by Lack of Vehicles," *New York Times* (June 9, 1994), p. A-10. Also, Michael R. Gordon, "U.S. Acting More Urgently To End Rwanda Slaughter," *New York Times* (June 16, 1994), p. A-12.

14. Dallaire, *loc. cit.*

15. Ibid.

16. *Report by the Working Group on a Multinational United Nations Stand-by Forces High Readiness Brigade* (Annex to a letter to the UN Secretary-General from Denmark's Permanent Representative to the United Nations, dated February 29, 1996). Available on the Internet: www.undp.org/missions/denmark/policy/rapid.htm . Also, www.shirbrig.dk/

17. Randolph Ryan, "UN Head Says Nations Lack Political Will," *Boston Globe* (December 15, 1994), p. 13.

18. For details, see Eric Grove, "UN Armed Forces and the Military Staff Committee: A Look Back," *International Security* (Spring 1993), pp. 172-182. Most relevant are Articles 42, 43, 45, and 47 of the UN Charter's Chapter VII.

19. Bill Gertz, "Russians practiced nuclear counterattack on NATO," *Washington Times* (July 8, 1997), p. 1.

20. International Institute for Strategic Studies, "NATO Implementation Force (IFOR) for Bosnia and Herzegovina," *The Military Balance 1996/97* (London: Oxford University Press, 1996), pp. 32-35 and 303-304. Also, International Institute for Strategic Studies, "Reforming and Enlarging NATO," *The Strategic Survey 1996/97* (London: Oxford University Press, 1996), pp. 110-120.

21. Ibid.

22. Quoted in Fred Weir, "Russia's uneasy place in Europe," *The Christian Science Monitor* (May 11, 1999), p. 6.

23. Quoted from "An Interview with John R. Galvin," *The Fletcher Forum of World Affairs* (Summer/Fall 1997), pp. 37-45.

24. Known as Operation *Alba,* this Italian-led UN humanitarian intervention into Albania involved a force of 7,200 troops, including 3,800 Italians. Other contributors included Austria, Denmark, Spain, France, Greece, Romania, and Turkey. At that time Austria and Romania were both in NATO's Partnership for Peace program. The other contributors were full NATO members.

25. ECOMOG's size varied between 2,700 and 12,500 troops: enough to secure Liberia's capital against rebel attacks, but not the entire country, a mission that officials speculated ECOMOG needed at least 20,000 troops for. See Herbert Howe, "Lessons of Liberia: ECOMOG and Regional Peacekeeping," *International Security* (Winter 1996-97), pp. 145-176. Also, Funmi Oloniskin, "UN Co-operation with Regional Organizations in Peacekeeping: The Experience of ECOMOG and UNOMIL in Liberia," *International Peacekeeping* (Autumn 1996), pp. 33-51.

26. Dan Henk, *Uncharted Paths, Uncertain Vision: U.S. Military Involvements in Sub-Saharan Africa in the Wake of the Cold War* (U.S. Air Force Academy, Colorado: USAF Institute for National Security Studies, March 1998), pp. 22-25. Also, Adekeye

Adebajo and Michael O'Hanlon, "Africa: Toward a Rapid-Reaction Force," *SAIS Review* (Summer-Fall 1997), pp. 153-164.

12

The Evolution of an Idea

I would remind you that as long ago as 1947, I was working over in the
Pentagon on the composition of the American contingent for the United Nations
Peace Force. This thing has always been up to the fore, most people believing
that if the United Nations is going to be truly effective in many instances, it
ought to have something of that kind. . . . [It] is one of those things that I think
has to develop and come about with the growth of common sense and a little
bit greater spirit of tolerance among nations. I think it is a very fine thing.

— U.S. President Dwight D. Eisenhower, 1958

It is not only the Balkans that can be saved from perpetual conflict; so can
other regions torn by ethnic or political violence. An African recipient of the
Nobel Prize has asked, *Why does the world ignore ethnic cleansing in Africa?*
And he is right—African genocide is no less a crime against humanity than
mass murder in the heart of Europe. . . . We must work toward a standing UN
force—an army of conscience—that is fully equipped and prepared to carve
out human sanctuaries through force if necessary.

— Retired U.S. President Ronald Reagan, 1992

If an elected government wants to stay out of another country's genocidal crisis,
it will find or invent enough reasons for itself to stay out. Even if its own voting
constituents would support sending a humanitarian intervention, that government
may not trust that the enthusiasm will last if those voters' own sons and daughters
in uniform start getting killed there.

Consequently, because the UN Security Council reflects the concerns of its
leading members—including their domestic political fears—its responses to
distant crises have not necessarily been decided by what is objectively needed.
One possible solution is to make their feared domestic price of a prudently early
humanitarian intervention less costly to the Council's members. This could

require that the Security Council be equipped with a small, independent peace enforcement unit of its own: an international legion of volunteers.

AN "ARMY OF CONSCIENCE"

In December 1992, former U.S. President Ronald Reagan delivered a speech at Oxford University one year after the Soviet Union collapsed. He began his speech by mentioning how he once told the British parliament that Marxism-Leninism would end up, in his words, on the "ash heap of history." "For my pains," he recalled, "I was called a dreamer and an ideologue, out of touch with reality. Some foreign affairs experts regarded me not unlike the way the German poet Heine described a certain ambassador, saying, 'Ordinarily, he is insane, but he has lucid moments when he is only stupid.' "

That humor was typical of Reagan. So, too, was his optimistic response: "Whenever I hear such comments, I know I must be onto something. At the very least, I'm encouraged to continue questioning conventional wisdom. For there are worse things than to be called a dreamer."

One such dream, he explained, was to end the horrors his speech subsequently described:

Let us be frank. Evil still stalks the planet. Its ideology may be nothing more than bloodlust, no program more complex than economic plunder or military aggrandizement—but it is evil all the same. And wherever there are forces that would destroy the human spirit and diminish human potential, they must be recognized and they must be countered. . . . If we are to fulfill the hope that the fall of Communism has presented us, the world's democracies must enforce stricter humanitarian standards of international conduct.

Reagan then spoke of the horrors of genocide, "ethnic cleansing" and other atrocities, urging international organizations to declare them totally unacceptable. "And we must be prepared to put weapons behind our words," he added, elaborating:

It is not only the Balkans that can be saved from perpetual conflict; so can other regions torn by ethnic or political violence. An African recipient of the Nobel Prize has asked: *Why does the world ignore ethnic cleansing in Africa?* And he is right—African genocide is no less a crime against humanity than mass murder in the heart of Europe.

Last year, largely in reaction to Iraq's murderous treatment of the Kurds, the UN changed the mandate of its World Food Program, enabling it to operate without the consent of host governments. I believe that precedent bears repeating, albeit on an even larger scale in sub-Saharan Africa. I believe it is not only right, but morally imperative, that the UN militarily intervene in Somalia.

But that is only the beginning of what must be done. We must work toward a standing UN force—an army of conscience—that is fully equipped and prepared to carve out human sanctuaries through force if necessary.

It was a controversial idea—a standing force for the United Nations, an "army of conscience." Critics would declare it a naively radical idea. Yet Reagan advocated it, and he explained his reasons:

As long as military power remains a necessary fact of modern existence, then we should use it as a humanitarian tool. At the same time, I believe that we should rely more on multilateral institutions, such as NATO, the UN, and other organizations, to sanction the reasoned and concerted use of power available.

I did not always value international organizations, and for good reason. . . . Their sole role seemed to be to blame the U.S. for the world's ills. In the past, the divided world of the Cold War paralyzed global organizations; it was virtually impossible to achieve global cooperation on most subjects. But with the end of the Cold War, the UN was also liberated. With the fall of the Soviet Union, obstruction has been replaced by more cooperation. And with it, the noble vision of the UN's founders is now closer to realization.

Reagan closed his speech with a challenge:

Your world is poised for better tomorrows. What will you do on your journey? As I see it, you have the opportunity to set and enforce international standards of civilized behavior. Does that sound unrealistic? It is not any larger a challenge than what my generation confronted.[1]

This speech proved to be one of Reagan's last, delivered only months before the debilitating onset of Alzheimer's disease. It received relatively little media attention, perhaps because its ideas were not so controversial in the fast-changing world of 1992. Yet the underlying Idealist sentiments expressed by Reagan, the quintessential conservative, reflected a new trend after the Cold War.

Previously, indeed throughout the Cold War, proponents of the Idealist "school of thought" in international relations were called liberals, or at least somewhere on the political Left, whereas advocates of the Realist "school of thought" were deemed to be conservatives, somewhere on the political Right. This traditional demarcation started to blur, however, during the Gulf War of 1990-1991, when many on the Right and Left jointly supported using military force to end Iraq's occupation of Kuwait, while others on the Right and Left jointly objected. This blurring continued over whether to send a humanitarian intervention into Somalia in 1992, and into Haiti in 1994. It continued throughout the 1990s over how to stop "ethnic cleansing" in Bosnia and Kosovo. Even today, this controversy has not been completely resolved.

The idea that Reagan advocated, an international legion of volunteers, has a long history, with fellow advocates and supporters spread all along the political spectrum. This chapter summarizes that history.

THE BIRTH OF AN IDEA

Reagan was not the first U.S. president to advocate that the United Nations have a standing force. Earlier it was proposed by President Franklin Roosevelt, in 1945, and even incorporated into the UN Charter, which is why Articles 42, 43, and 45 call on member-countries to make military forces available to the UN Organization for international enforcement purposes. The goal of the UN was supposed to be *collective security*, the defense of all countries by all countries

By 1948, however, the prospect that the UN, via its Security Council, would ever directly command an immense international military force became but one more casualty of the new Cold War. Recognizing this, the UN's first Secretary-General, Trygve Lie, proposed something much less ambitious. In 1948-1949, during the first Arab-Israeli war, fighting raged in Jerusalem despite a Security Council resolution calling for a cease-fire there. Since the Council's legal authority was being blatantly disregarded, Lie reasoned that this was an issue on which the Council's usually bickering members could agree. He proposed the creation of a small, standing UN "guard" force,

recruited by the Secretary-General and placed at the disposal of the Security Council and the General Assembly. Such a force would not be used as a substitute for the forces contemplated in Article 42 and 43. It would not be a striking force, but purely a guard force. It could be used for guard duty with UN missions, in the conduct of plebiscites under the supervision of the UN, and in the administration of truce terms. . . .It might also be called upon by the Security Council under Article 40 of the Charter, which provides for provisional measures to prevent the aggravation of a situation threatening the peace.[2]

Instead of emphasizing collective security, Lie proposed an early example of what is now called *cooperative security*, the encouragement of international peace through the joint efforts of the world's Great Powers. Whereas collective security is unabashedly idealist, cooperative security tries to pragmatically build on whatever common interests exist between governments that, otherwise, have very different agendas. Although few Realists may consider it a Realist idea, cooperative security probably owes as much to the Realist school as the Idealist.

The Cold War's first years involved so little trust between the Soviet Union and the West, sometimes not even in what ought to have been objective facts, that Lie's proposal went nowhere except into the archives. Since then, however, the basic idea of a UN guard force has often resurfaced in different incarnations.

THE EARLY SUCCESS OF UN PEACEKEEPING

One variant on Lie's idea is a UN peacekeeping force serving as a symbolic guard force. This concept became a reality during the Cold War because of the difference between voluntary cooperation and potential coercion, that is, between peacekeeping and peace enforcement. Although the UN did engage in peace enforcement on occasion, such as in Korea and the Congo, those situations were extremely unusual and case-specific. The multinational forces involved there were not standing forces but *ad hoc*, assembled with the specific permission of their participating governments in response to particular crises.

Nevertheless, since the Security Council could agree to field UN peacekeeping forces, the desire to quicken their assembly and deployment became a favorite theme of several American presidents. In 1958, President Dwight Eisenhower urged the creation of a UN "peace force" to render "prompt and effective action" in future crises. At a press conference, the former five-star general explained:

I would remind you that as long ago as 1947, I was working over in the Pentagon on the composition of the American contingent for the United Nations Peace Force. This thing has always been up to the fore, most people believing that if the United Nations is going to be truly effective in many instances, it ought to have something of that kind. . . . [It] is one of those things that I think has to develop and come about with the growth of common sense and a little bit greater spirit of tolerance among nations. I think it is a very fine thing.[3]

President John F. Kennedy in 1961 envisioned an even greater role for UN peacekeeping forces, with improvements in how they could be assembled, organized, and deployed. Kennedy told the General Assembly:

In the world we seek, the United Nations Emergency Forces, which have been hastily assembled, uncertainly supplied, and inadequately financed, will never be enough. Therefore, the United States recommends that all member-nations earmark special peacekeeping units in their armed forces—to be on call of the United Nations, to be specially trained and quickly available, and with advance provision for financial and logistic support.[4]

In 1973, U.S. Secretary of State Henry Kissinger expressed the frustrations and desires of the Nixon Administration concerning UN peacekeeping forces. Kissinger told the General Assembly:

In recent years, we have found ourselves locked in fruitless debates about the inauguration of the peacekeeping operations and over the degree of control the Security Council would exercise over peacekeeping machinery—an impasse which has insured only that permanent peacekeeping machinery would not come into being. Each peacekeeping unit we have formed has been an improvisation growing out of argument and controversy. We should delay no longer. The time has come to agree on peacekeeping guidelines so that this Organization can act swiftly, confidently and effectively in future crises.[5]

AN ERA OF CHANGE

At about the time of Kissinger's speech, the U.S. Permanent Representative to the UN was George Bush, Sr. Almost two decades later, as president, Bush seized opportunities offered by the Cold War's end to utilize the UN Organization as few U.S. presidents could before. Between 1988 and early 1993, the Security Council authorized as many new UN peacekeeping operations as it had authorized in the previous four decades. In 1990 there were 10,000 "blue helmets" on duty with the United Nations; by 1993, that figure had grown to 83,000. "Peacekeepers are stretched to the limit while demands for their services increase by the day," Bush told the General Assembly in 1992. "The need for monitoring and preventive peacekeeping—putting people on the ground before the fighting starts—may become especially critical in volatile regions."[6]

Meanwhile, in that same election year of 1992, then-presidential candidate Bill Clinton proposed that a UN "rapid deployment force" of volunteers be created for, among other missions, "preventing mass violence against civilian populations." This idea was one of the few foreign initiatives Clinton suggested in his campaign-era book, *Putting People First*.[7]

The newly elected UN Secretary-General, Boutros Boutros-Ghali, likewise suggested that the Security Council should, at long last, equip itself with peace enforcement units of its own. He explained:

Cease-fires have often been agreed to but not complied with, and the United Nations has sometimes been called upon to send forces to restore and maintain the cease-fire. This task can on occasion exceed the mission of peacekeeping forces and the expectations of [their] contributors. I recommend that the Council consider the utilization of peace enforcement units in clearly defined circumstances and with their terms of reference specified in advance. Such units would be available on call and would consist of troops that have volunteered for such service.[8]

Throughout 1992 and 1993, a flurry of proposals were offered and assessed. Three authors at the U.S. Naval Postgraduate School—Vice Admiral John Lee, Ambassador Robert von Pagenhardt, and Dr. Timothy Stanley—published one in a book they entitled *To Unite Our Strength.* They wrote:

Several experienced UN force commanders have . . . expressed the view that an integrated force of individual professionals who had trained together and had uniform equipment and doctrines would be more effective and have less cause for animosity [than a traditional multinational force]. . . . These problems confirm the utility of a military element that is not a unit of the military establishment of any country: a completely international standing UN legion, under the Secretary-General and immediately available to the Security Council without requiring national concurrences for its deployment (assuming no veto is exercised in the Council). It could be dispatched rapidly wherever needed, even as a deterrent in anticipation of trouble.[9]

The authors proposed that this UN legion have between 4,500 and 5,500 troops, organized into a combined-arms brigade task force with light infantry, light armor, and mechanized vehicles, augmented by helicopters and mobile artillery, with engineer, communications, and medical support. It would depend on one or more national air forces for its aerial transport, resupply, and combat air support. By using existing base facilities donated by various countries, along with unused surplus military equipment either donated or purchased at a discount, the authors estimated that the expense of a UN legion could be kept to less than $400 million per year in 1992 dollars.[10]

The idea of a UN legion also began to appear in the professional journals of the U.S. armed forces. One such essay, penned in 1993 by retired Lieutenant-Colonel Timothy Thomas of the U.S. Army's Command and General Staff College, appeared in the U.S. Army's *Military Review:*

The UN faces a set of operations that look very much like low intensity conflict, in which the major powers have little inclination to get involved. Such actions are, by their nature, protracted and may require long-term commitment of military power. In such circumstances, the UN may require the creation of its own legion—small, elite, mobile, professional and with its own military doctrine to provide a coherent center of gravity to UN operations.[11]

Sir Brian Urquhart, one of the pioneers of UN peacekeeping and its director for many years, in June 1993 publicly endorsed the concept of a UN legion. In an essay he entitled "For a UN Volunteer Military Force," Urquhart explained:

Clearly, a timely intervention by a relatively small but highly trained force [of volunteers], willing and authorized to take combat risks and representing the will of the international community, could make a decisive difference in the early stages of . . . low-level but dangerous conflicts, especially ones involving irregular militias and groups.

A UN volunteer force would not, of course, take the place of preventive diplomacy, traditional peacekeeping forces, or of large-scale enforcement action under Chapter VII of the [UN] Charter, such as *Desert Storm*. It would not normally be employed against the military forces of states. It would be designed simply to fill a very important gap in the armory of the Security Council, giving it the ability to back up preventive diplomacy with a measure of immediate peace enforcement. . . . The volunteer force would be trained in the techniques of peacekeeping and negotiation as well as in the more bloody business of fighting.

Any number of possible objections can be posed to the idea of a UN volunteer force. Until quite recently I myself, after a long association with UN peacekeeping, would have argued against it. The idea will certainly raise, in some minds at least, the specter of supranationality that has always haunted the idea of a standing UN army. If, however, the force can only be deployed with the authority of the Security Council, the necessary degree of control by member-governments is guaranteed. The main difference from peacekeeping will be the role, the volunteer nature, and the immediate availability of the force.[12]

Two months later, in August 1993, the staff of the U.S. Senate Foreign Relations Committee reported the following "finding" in a bipartisan study:

The creation of a permanent UN force with a rapid deployment capability has considerable appeal, [particularly] in a world where flash crises now appear the norm. . . . [Many] military officers currently serving in peacekeeping operations . . . believe that a small, well-equipped force trained in the nuances of peacekeeping could be usefully deployed in the early stages of a crisis, helping to defuse tensions, and thereby eliminating the need for a large peace enforcement mission. . . . Some have argued that a reinforced infantry brigade would be sufficient.[13]

Back in 1987, then-President Reagan signed legislation which ultimately established the bipartisan "U.S. Commission on Improving the Effectiveness of the United Nations." Six years later, in September 1993, the Commission released its final report with this recommendation:

Establish a rapid-reaction force, now often referred to as a UN legion, that could be deployed within hours after Security Council action. It should be under the control of the Security Council and consist initially of 5,000 to 10,000 highly trained soldiers.

The Commission believes that a UN rapid-reaction force is necessary because no nation likes to send its soldiers into potential combat zones when its own interests may not be directly affected by the outcome. Security Council actions too often come after the conflict has escalated beyond the control of a small force. The rapid-reaction force should be composed of soldiers supplied by member-states who have volunteered as individuals. . . . It could also be used to give the UN an immediate presence in a troubled region, while a larger force is formed using units contributed by member-nations.[14]

LOST MOMENTUM

By the time that President Bill Clinton was inaugurated in January 1993, rarely has such a far-reaching foreign policy idea—a UN legion—had so many advocates in and near the White House, including, on record, the President himself. In their respective confirmation hearings, both U.S. Secretary of State Warren Christopher and UN Permanent Representative Madeline Albright expressed support for formal U.S. compliance with Article 43 of the UN Charter —the article that calls for UN military forces. In 1992 William Perry, only months before he succeeded Les Aspin as Secretary of Defense, helped author a book on cooperative security wherein Perry, too, advocated strengthening the UN with a "relatively small permanent force, designed for peacekeeping duties."[15] James Woolsey, prior to becoming director of the Central Intelligence Agency, chaired a private study group that proposed establishing a small UN standing force.[16] The idea was likewise supported by various assistant secretaries in the Departments of State and Defense.

But the support did not last. Clinton as not very interested in foreign policy, at least not initially, and the momentum was lost. Support was not very firm outside of the Clinton Administration, either, despite the endorsement of Ronald Reagan. The blue-ribbon commission that recommended a UN rapid-reaction force had not done so unanimously; instead, its final report included a lengthy "statement of minority views" including the following:

Should the UN command an army of its own? The answer is no. The benefits claimed for such a rapid-deployment "UN legion"—on-site reconnaissance and [political] fire-fighting early on, before the conflagration spreads—can be accomplished more effectively by the ready forces of UN member-countries, and at far less cost. Recruiting, training and equipping a legion of even 5,000 to 10,000 personnel would cost at least $400 million annually—without provision for air- and sealift—and with nearly 80,000 "blue helmets" already in the field, a UN legion might not be adequate for as much as a single mission. Once initiated, a UN standing force would only grow.

In any case, there is no evidence at all that the lack of such a force ever has barred or even deterred effective UN action to keep the peace: first there has to be a Security Council resolution to deploy the required force, if force in fact is the answer, to accomplish a particular mission. And that decision must remain exclusively with the United States, its colleagues among the Permanent Five, and the other members of the Security Council. Once that decision is made, assembling a force never has been a major problem.[17]

Unfortunately, less than a year later, during the genocide in Rwanda, abundant evidence emerged that assembling a UN force can indeed be a major problem. But that debacle had yet to happen; at the time the commission released its final report, whatever attention most Americans devoted to Africa was focused, not on Rwanda, but on Somalia.

SOMALIA: MURDER THROUGH ANARCHY

By 1992, a civil war in Somalia had turned food into a weapon as warring clans denied food to anyone not under their respective control. The UN Security

Council, watching in horror, urged them to allow food to reach the general population, much of which was starving to death. Not until August, however, did the two main Somali clans agree, in principle, to allow a neutral UN force to secure Mogadishu's ports for food deliveries and to escort that food's distribution throughout the capital. An advance party of 500 Pakistani UN troops arrived in September, part of what was supposed to be a 3,500-man UN escort force. But that total force took too long to assemble. The Pakistani troops in Mogadishu, meanwhile, were too few and too outgunned to make much of a difference by themselves.

By late November, after the famine in Somalia had reached catastrophic proportions, President George Bush, Sr., proposed that a massive humanitarian intervention, led by the U.S. military, be sent into the country. The Security Council agreed. Bush explained:

Our mission is humanitarian, but we will not tolerate armed gangs ripping off their own people, condemning them to death by starvation. General Hoar and his troops have the authority to take whatever military action is necessary to safeguard the lives of our troops and the lives of Somalia's people.[18]

Codenamed Operation *Restore Hope*, the American-led Unified Task Force (UNITAF) entered Somalia in December to pause the civil war and feed the country's starving multitudes. Intimidated by the sudden appearance of U.S. military firepower, the warring Somali leaders soon agreed to a cease-fire. Food flowed into the desperately ravenous nation. An estimated 250,000 Somalis, if not more, were saved from imminent starvation.

Their relief was only temporary, however, because UNITAF would someday have to leave Somalia and everybody knew it. Many Somalis wanted the clans and gangs disarmed because, without their weapons, overall power in Somalia would become more democratic. But disarming a society awash in firearms is a very dangerous endeavor, especially when the people possessing them insist on keeping them. UNITAF did persuade the Somali clans to remove their heaviest weapons from Mogadishu. Otherwise, however, no Somali clans were ever disarmed by UNITAF, not even after the clans formally agreed to disarm under an accord they themselves negotiated and signed in March 1993. UNITAF was powerful enough to enforce that convenient agreement. But, instead, to avoid any possible American casualties, the predominantly American UNITAF departed Somalia as quickly as it could. The disarmament problem was left to a UN-run force scheduled to replace UNITAF.

Several experts now believe that delay was a mistake. UNITAF had 35,000 well-armed, well-organized, highly trained troops, most of them U.S. soldiers and Marines with recent experience from the Gulf War. The incoming UN force, known as the "United Nations Operation in Somalia II" (or UNOSOM II; the first UNOSOM had been the original 500 Pakistanis), was a patchwork of some 19,000 troops from Pakistan, India, Egypt, Zimbabwe, Malaysia, Bangladesh, Nigeria, and Botswana. Their organization was haphazard, their quality varied, and their contributors had somewhat different agendas. Even before their staff arrived in Mogadishu, most of UNITAF's staff had already left. What should have been an orderly transfer of duties, procedures, and advice was, instead, two dangerously disconnected operations, leaving UNOSOM II largely unprepared for what it was supposed to do.[19] An already tense relationship with the Somali clans became even tenser as UNOSOM II tried to disarm them, ordered to by both the Security Council and the new Secretary-General, Boutros Boutros-Ghali.

On June 5, 1993, twenty-four Pakistani UN soldiers were slain by an ambush. The killings were blamed on the clan of General Mohammed Farah Aideed and so infuriated American and UN officials that a manhunt was launched against Aideed himself. When he proved himself to be too elusive, a raid was launched against his closest subordinates. That raid occurred on October 3, 1993. It cost the lives of eighteen American soldiers.

One of the tragedies of the Somali crisis is that if a brigade-size UN legion of volunteers had existed in 1992, it could have deployed to Somalia instead of the mere 500 Pakistanis. A UN legion could have secured Mogadishu's seaport and airport to receive food, and likewise escorted the food's delivery throughout the capital: all the duties the Somali clans had agreed that a multinational UN force of 3,500 could do without their interference—but only 500 Pakistanis arrived. The entirety of the later U.S. intervention into Somalia could have been avoided: the deployment of UNITAF's 35,000 troops, the later deployment of UNOSOM II's 19,000 troops, the notorious Mogadishu raid, the killings of Americans, Somalis, and others—all avoided if a UN legion of volunteers had existed.

THE MOGADISHU RAID AND ITS MYTHS

What actually happened in the Mogadishu raid of October 1993 contradicts much of the political rhetoric that has, for years since, influenced U.S. policies toward the United Nations. Myths about it have grown into arguments against ever fielding a UN standing force. As long as those myths persist, a UN legion will never receive the support of the United States.

The first myth is that, in 1993, the UN Organization was an aspiring world government run against U.S. interests by the UN Secretary-General. The truth is that, while one may reasonably disagree with what actions the UN took against Aideed and his clan, the United States did have a decisive say in those actions from beginning to end. The UN's policy in Somalia was ordered, not by the Secretary-General, but by the Security Council, dominated by its most powerful member, the United States. The UN's policy towards Somalia was shaped by U.S. policy towards Somalia, not vice versa. UNOSOM II was commanded by an American, U.S. Army Major-General Thomas Montgomery. And the man to whom Montgomery reported, the UN Secretary-General's Special Assistant in Somalia, was also an American, retired U.S. Navy Admiral Jonathan Howe, a former deputy national security adviser in the Bush Administration.

The second myth surrounding the Mogadishu raid is that it resulted from a UN effort known as *nation-building*—trying to replace anarchy by encouraging the establishment of basic political institutions. Critics charged that nation-building by UNOSOM II was a more ambitious goal, too ambitious, than what UNITAF had done, feed people but little else. But the reality is that UNITAF, too, had tried to rebuild some semblance of a Somali state, such as by pressing the Somali clans to negotiate a common government. At this, UNITAF was more successful than UNOSOM II because UNITAF was stronger.

Critics say another problem with UNOSOM II was "mission creep"—the addition of new duties and responsibilities for which the force was not designed. In Bosnia, for instance, "mission creep" did afflict the UN Protection Force. In Somalia, however, UNOSOM II's original mandate from the U.S.-prodded Security Council was to: (1) "assume responsibility for the consolidation, expansion, and maintenance of a secure environment throughout Somalia"; (2) "take appropriate action against any faction that violates or threatens to violate the cessation of hostilities"; and (3) "seize the small arms of all unauthorized armed elements." It was a mandate so broad that, to accomplish it, UNOSOM II probably needed more troops, but that was not a case of "mission creep." The force's troop shortage was due to the Security Council's unwillingness to fund any more troops, despite the need.

A third myth about the Mogadishu raid is that "foreign" officials in the UN Organization ordered American troops into combat and, under UN command, those Americans got killed. The facts are dramatically different. Although UNOSOM II was involved in the UN's campaign against General Aideed and his supporters, it was a campaign in line with both U.S. policy and the views of the Secretary-General's (American) Special Representative in Somalia, Admiral Howe. UNOSOM II was commanded by Major-General Montgomery, not by a non-American. The raid itself was undertaken by elite U.S. Army Rangers. If the raid had been commanded by UNOSOM II—that is, by the United Nations —those Rangers would have been commanded by Americans at several levels: at their own unit-level, at the level of General Montgomery, and likewise higher at the level of Admiral Howe.

Yet the raid was *not* commanded by the UN. Montgomery did authorize the raid, but, to preserve its operational secrecy, the Rangers' chain of command remained strictly within the U.S. military system. The Rangers were commanded by Major-General William Garrison, a U.S. Army Special Forces officer who reported directly to the U.S. Central Command at MacDill Air Force Base in distant Florida. In other words, there were two chains of command: a UN chain, commanded by Americans, and a U.S. chain, also commanded by Americans. The Rangers were commanded within the U.S. chain.

The fourth myth is that the raid was a failure; in fact, it succeeded. Its objective was to capture some of Aideed's closest supporters, to weaken Aideed politically, and it accomplished this without any serious harm to the Rangers during its actual capture phase.

So why did the Mogadishu raid become so notorious? After the successful capture of Aideed's supporters, a nearby U.S. Army helicopter was shot down. Some Rangers fought their way to it to rescue its pilot, suffering casualties as they went, only to discover that their pilot friend was dead and that his body could not be extracted from the wreckage. Refusing to leave his body behind, the Rangers radioed for help, hunkered down, and waited. Defending a corpse may seem strange, but Army helicopter pilots and Rangers have very close emotional bonds because they rely on each other. When another helicopter was shot down, two more Rangers died trying to rescue its pilot. (He was captured by Aideed's clan and later released.) Civilians may equate these deaths with failure, but U.S. soldiers are taught that *The mission comes first—always*, and that whatever casualties they suffer, while tragic, are nonetheless secondary. Measured against that harsh standard, the Mogadishu raid did succeed.

What upset the Pentagon was not that any Americans were under foreign command—they never were—but that UNOSOM II was so disorganized when something unexpected went wrong. When Montgomery was notified that the Rangers needed help, a U.S. infantry company in UNOSOM II was sent to rescue them; but because that infantry company lacked armored vehicles, it could not reach the Rangers. A stronger force needed to be organized, *ad hoc*, without any prior planning or practice. Fortunately the Rangers could afford to wait, for they had established themselves in a relatively defensible position. And wait they did: UNOSOM II took seven hours to organize the *ad hoc* rescue force. An entire U.S. infantry battalion was called upon, along with four Pakistani tanks and twenty-eight Malaysian armored personnel carriers, many of them painted white with black "UN" lettering. The Pakistanis objected to having their tanks placed up front, facing the most danger. Time was also spent trying to find enough Malaysian drivers who spoke English. When this *ad hoc* rescue force finally moved out, it displayed such a chaotic, amateurish appearance that one senior U.S. officer called it "a three ring circus."

Nevertheless, that force did rescue the Rangers.

AFTER THE MOGADISHU RAID

The American public reacted to the Mogadishu raid with bewilderment and horror. Only months earlier, U.S. troops had been televised distributing food to grateful Somalis; now eighteen U.S. soldiers were suddenly dead, the near naked corpse of one was televised being dragged through Mogadishu's streets by an ecstatic Somali mob. Many longtime American critics of the United Nations blamed the UN, calling it callous and incompetent, apparently believing that American troops had died under foreign command. The Clinton Administration, new and inexperienced, failed to correct these misperceptions; instead, it quickly announced that most U.S. forces would be withdrawn by March 1994. The UN's operation in Somalia was left to fend for itself, which it could not. It collapsed.

Even before the Mogadishu raid, Clinton ceased to support what he had once called for as a candidate. In a speech to the UN General Assembly in September 1993, a week before the raid, he neither proposed nor even mentioned the idea of establishing a UN rapid deployment force of volunteers. Instead, he called upon the United Nations to "prepare UN peacekeeping for the twenty-first century"— with a criteria that sounded less internationalist than a bit rigid:

We need to [bring] the rigors of military and political analysis to every UN peace mission. . . . *Is there a real threat to international peace? Does the proposed mission have clear objectives? Can an end point be identified for those who will be asked to participate? How much will the mission cost?* From now on, the United Nations should address these and other hard questions for every proposed mission before we vote and before the mission begins. The United Nations simply cannot become engaged in every one of the world's conflicts. If the American people are to say yes to UN peacekeeping, the United Nations must know when to say no.[20]

The outcome of the Mogadishu raid so embarrassed the Administration that it rewrote its own guidelines for deciding future humanitarian interventions. The result was Presidential Decision Directive (PDD) 25, formally entitled *The Clinton Administration's Policy on Reforming Multilateral Peace Operations.* In addition to stressing the importance of budgetary efficiency in future peace operations, PDD-25 also declared, "The U.S. does not support a standing UN army, nor will we earmark specific U.S. military units for participation in UN operations." When UN officials in New York sought to compile of list of countries willing to loan the Organization new troops and equipment for future peace operations, the United States, when asked, declined. Explained a senior UN official, "My American friends, each time I talk with them, [assume that] I'm looking for a standing army, which is not the case."[21]

By a fateful coincidence, the adoption of PDD-25 occurred at about the same time that Rwanda experienced its genocide in 1994. Consequently, the Clinton Administration viewed that sudden crisis as the first test of PDD-25's guidelines for humanitarian intervention. PDD-25 had set forth:

The U.S. will support well-defined peace operations, generally, as a tool to provide finite windows of opportunity to allow combatants to resolve their differences and failed societies to begin to reconstitute themselves. Peace operations should not be open-ended commitments but instead linked to concrete political solutions; otherwise, they normally should not be undertaken. To the greatest extent possible, each UN peace operation should have a specified timeframe tied to intermediate or final objectives, an integrated political/military strategy well-coordinated with humanitarian assistance efforts, specified troop levels, and a firm budget estimate. The U.S. will continue to urge the UN Secretariat and Security Council members to engage in rigorous, standard evaluations of all proposed new peace operations.

What may sound reasonable in theory can be perilous in practice, and in the case of Rwanda this is what happened. PDD-25's qualifiers could be interpreted so rigidly that any of them could stymie a peace operation before it even began: *well-defined, finite, concrete political solutions, greatest extent possible, specified timeframe, integrated political/military strategy, well-coordinated, specified troop levels, firm budget estimate, rigorous standard evaluations.* Unless a rapidly deployable UN force is already available, ready to go, these prerequisites cannot be fulfilled without spending, and losing, precious time in bureaucratic haggling and diplomatic maneuvers. Eventually even the Clinton Administration, with the benefit of hindsight, admitted that its own rigid interpretation of PDD-25 had done Rwanda more harm than good.

AFTER RWANDA'S GENOCIDE

Even during the genocide itself, *The Economist,* the respected conservative British newsmagazine, declared in a blunt editorial:

Never has intervention been needed more quickly than in Rwanda; never has it materialized more slowly. . . . Yet even now, as autumn approaches, the world's governments, acting through the UN, are barely finished with humming and hawing, counting pennies and wondering whether joint intervention is in their national interest. Their foot-dragging over Rwanda is the best argument yet for the UN to have a small, flexible peacekeeping force of its own.[22]

Upon his return to his native Canada, Major-General Romeo Dallaire, UNAMIR's commander, likewise became a vocal supporter of a UN legion. There was a need, he said, "for military units which could be deployed almost instantly as soon as the UN Security Council has mandated an operation. . . . If I had had such a force available to me while I was the Force Commander for UNAMIR sometime in mid-April 1994, UNAMIR could have saved the lives of hundreds of thousands of people."[23]

Soon the entire Canadian government became interested in a UN legion. So, too, did the Dutch government. In a speech in late 1994, Hans van Mierlo, the Dutch foreign minister and former defense minister, told the General Assembly:

The human tragedy in Rwanda will always remain a shame for the international community. Collectively we must acknowledge that we had ample warning of impending disaster and that we could have done more to prevent the genocide. . . . If the deployment of a brigade could have prevented the indiscriminate slaughter of many hundreds of thousands, what then prevented us from doing so?

The reason was that, under the circumstances, no government was prepared to risk the lives of its citizens. The physical danger was considered too high. . . . Either we act upon our feeling of horror and indignation, or we stop moralizing. If member-states are not in a position to provide the necessary military personnel, will it then not become unavoidable for us to consider the establishment of a full-time professional, at all times available and rapidly deployable UN brigade for this purpose? An all-volunteer "fire brigade" may enable the UN to save lives in situations such as Rwanda.[24]

The Dutch and Canadian governments subsequently began feasibility studies. Meanwhile, the idea gained more endorsements. Former prime ministers of Sweden and Japan endorsed it. Jacques Delors, the influential former president of the European Union, likewise endorsed it. It was endorsed in general terms by the governments of France, Russia, Denmark, even Egypt. Explained Nabil Elaraby, Egypt's Permanent Representative to the UN: "This would not be a fighting army of the sort that could throw Iraq out of Kuwait. But it would be the sort of army that could enter Rwanda and separate the people who would otherwise massacre each other."[25]

Several private studies were also done. One of the most widely referenced was *Vital Force: A Proposal for the Overhaul of the UN Peace Operations System and for the Creation of a UN Legion,* produced in 1995 by Carl Conetta and Charles Knight. Later, in 1996, *Peace Operations by the United Nations:*

The Case for a Volunteer UN Military Force, by MIT professors Carl Kaysen and George Rathjens. Drawing on the work of Conetta and Knight, Kaysen and Rathjens also consulted experts at Harvard University, the U.S. National Defense University, the U.S. Army War College, and research institutes. Christopher Bellamy, a British defense analyst, devoted an entire book to the idea, entitling it, *Knights in White Armour: The New Art of War and Peace*. The year ended with an editorial by William F. Buckley, the eloquent American conservative, published in his journal, *National Review:*

In Zaire/Burundi/Rwanda we see gestating in direct view of CNN's cameras the threat of a return to butchery on a scale that should appall. Over 1 million Tutsis and Hutus have slaughtered each other in the last two years. . . . Rwanda and Burundi have forfeited the authority inherent in sovereign states. The world needs an organization modeled on the French Foreign Legion, organized and (substantially) financed by the superpower, with contributions expected from other civilized nations. In the tradition of the French Foreign Legion, we might, after five years' faithful service, grant citizenship to applicants. It is this Legion, not U.S. Army troops, which would now be headed for Rwanda.[26]

The year 1997 began with another endorsement, from *U.S. News & World Report*. Declaring that the United Nations had failed to prevent mass civilian slaughters in places such as Rwanda and Bosnia, the newsmagazine noted that the UN had to reply on its member-states to supply its soldiers. The solution, asserted its editorial, was to create a highly professional, strictly apolitical UN rapid-reaction force, for which it proposed the famed Gurkhas of Nepal, long recruited by the British Army as some of the fiercest, most respected soldiers in the world. The editorial concluded:

The idea of a Gurkha UN rapid reaction force is not new: It comes up every time Western powers find themselves caught in a military morass they can't avoid and won't win. British Prime Minister John Major put the idea before the UN in 1991, but it was deemed too expensive. Since that time, Bosnia, Somalia, Rwanda, Haiti, and now Zaire have proved how much cheaper prevention is than cure.[27]

More reports and studies followed, as did more endorsements. In December 1997, the Carnegie Commission on Preventing Deadly Conflict published its final report. Among the Commission's members were former Norwegian Prime Minister Gro Harlem Brundtland, former U.S. Secretary of State Cyrus Vance, as well as Gareth Evans, General Sahabzada Yaqub-Khan, and Shridath Ramphal, the respective ex-foreign ministers of Australia, Pakistan, and Guyana. Their report declared:

The Commission supports the establishment of a rapid reaction force of some 5,000 to 10,000 troops, the core of which would be contributed by members of the Security Council. . . . The Commission offers two arguments for such a capability: first, the record of international crises points out the need in certain cases to respond rapidly and, if necessary, with force; and second, the operational integrity of such a force requires that it not be assembled in pieces or in haste. A standing force may well be necessary for effective prevention. . . . The force would be under the authority of the Security Council and its deployment subject to a veto by any of the permanent members. . . . [The] problem is less one of early warning than of early action.[28]

The 1990s ended with two more genocidal crises that a standing UN legion could have quelled. In Kosovo in 1998-1999, prior to NATO's Operation *Allied Force*, Milosevic refused to allow any armed NATO troops into the province to safeguard its ethnic Albanian and Serbian communities and to insure its political autonomy. But Milosevic was willing to allow unarmed OSCE observers into Kosovo. Later, just before NATO's intervention, he claimed a willingness to let UN peacekeepers into Kosovo. Since creating a UN force would have involved more months of delay as Milosevic continued to "ethnically cleanse" Kosovo, his preference for UN troops was likely a stalling tactic. However, the existence of an armed, standing UN legion could have foreclosed this tactic; his Russian allies might have even pressured him to accept that legion's deployment. If a UN legion had existed, NATO might not have had to intervene.

Likewise in Indonesian-ruled East Timor, during the run-up campaign to its independence referendum in August 1999, a UN legion could have suppressed the violent intimidation tactics of pro-Indonesian militias. Instead, after the voters overwhelmingly chose independence, those militias devastated East Timor while the Indonesian Army looked on and even secretly participated. The Indonesian government refused to allow any UN force into East Timor until the devastation had become widespread. However, that government faced less international pressure than it might have faced if a standing UN legion had existed, ready to deploy. Earlier, before the run-up campaign began, the Indonesian government did allow some unarmed contingents of UN Civilian Police (CIVPOL) into East Timor to help oversee the referendum's pre-vote preparation. Deploying a UN legion could have been justified (albeit with Indonesia's permission, preferably) as a mere augmentation of CIVPOL. But no such UN legion existed.

RELIEF WORKERS SPEAK OUT

Today, about 75 percent of the world's humanitarian relief activities are performed by seven major non-governmental organizations (NGOs): CARE, Catholic Relief Services, *Medicines Sans Frontieres* ("Doctors Without Borders," abbreviated in French as MSF), Oxfam, the International Committee of the Red Cross (ICRC), Save the Children, and World Vision. Each has a long history of political neutrality and, in some cases, of outright pacifism. In 1992, MSF opposed the American-led UN humanitarian intervention into Somalia because military forces were used. Likewise, during the Bosnian War, MSF opposed the use of UN "blue helmet" troops to escort humanitarian relief convoys.

Since the Rwandan genocide of 1994, however, these seven NGOs have had to reconsider their long-held beliefs, and MSF was among the first to do so. When the genocide began, MSF, for the first time in its history, publicly called for an international military intervention to stop the slaughter. "MSF had a presence in Rwanda throughout the period, but you cannot stop a genocide with doctors," it explained in a public statement.[29] Later, when the perpetrators fled into neighboring Zaire and Tanzania, they pulled along more than 1 million Hutu bystanders as new refugees. Most of those reluctant refugees wanted to return to Rwanda, but the perpetrators forced them to stay in overcrowded refugee camps. "And in order to ensure food distributions" within those camps, explained MSF's Secretary-General Alain Destexhe, "aid workers have to work through the Hutu leaders, who are often the same people who instigated and carried out local massacres of Tutsis in Rwanda." Consequently, he noted, "international aid has become the currency of power within the camps and is reinforcing the influence of criminals."[30]

Destexhe also noted that, in 1979, when the Khmer Rouge were driven from Cambodia by advancing Vietnamese troops, the Khmer Rouge also pulled along multitudes of bystanders into refugee camps, in Thailand. By dominating those camps and controlling the NGOs' distribution of food aid, the Khmer Rouge were able to build up a power base from which the Rouge recruited new members and waged a guerrilla war into Cambodia for years. The perpetrators of Rwanda's genocide clearly wanted to pursue the same strategy.

MSF, increasingly appalled by the Rwandan refugee situation, ultimately broke with another of its longstanding traditions. In the midst of a crisis, its doctors and staff packed up and left. MSF explained:

There must be a point at which to draw the line, and the difference between most situations and the one with which we are currently faced is genocide: the worst of the crimes against humanity. Moreover it is the aid itself which permits this [refugee camp] structure to exist. To remain silent on this issue is to be an accomplice to this system of manipulation and control.[31]

Destexhe offered a proposal that has since become very popular among relief workers:

The best way for the international community to prepare for early intervention in such crises would be to create a UN standing army. Unlike the blue helmets, such a force could be rapidly mobilized and transported where needed. Under the current system, the UN calls upon countries to provide troops and equipment from their national armies. Some countries offer troops and no equipment, others equipment and no troops. That laborious process wastes time and often results in a poorly equipped, under-staffed UN force.[32]

There was time when the official neutrality of relief-aid NGOs gave them access to the needy. In the 1990s, however, relief workers themselves became targets of attack. In 1992, workers employed by UN agencies such as UNICEF were killed on an average of one per month; by 1997, the average was one per week. In 1998, for the first time in its history, the UN suffered more civilian employees killed than peacekeepers killed. "Most dangerous," explained one aid worker, "are the killers who simply don't want witnesses to the terrible things being done." The International Red Cross, whose history spans more than a century, experienced its worst loss on record in December 1996, when six of its physicians and nurses were murdered in a hospital in Chechnya—although only six months earlier three Red Cross workers were murdered in Burundi. CARE suffered 44 killed in Somalia alone. "Today, security is on everyone's mind," admitted Oxfam-America's President, Raymond Offenheiser. "We're pulling out of places that have simply become too dangerous." [33]

"Basically, we're powerless," observed a CARE employee. "Without some serious support from the outside world, a relief operation can be shut down by a handful of 14-year-olds with Kalashnikov rifles." Or the perverse opposite can occur, explained an MSF worker. "In Liberia, when one of the factions needs food or supplies, they just capture a village and start starving people. They say, 'We know you aid people will come with food, which we will seize and eat.' And guess what: *they're right!* We've got situations where aid is like some soup kitchen for mass murderers and thugs!" A Red Cross official elaborated, "Military operations can stop the killing, control violence, secure corridors, and police cease-fire agreements. Neutral humanitarian activity can do none of these things." [34]

"The issue of armed intervention is tearing the aid community apart," Offenheiser confessed. "There is a sea change going on in attitude, with a recognition that, in some cases, a military operation is necessary, is desirable, is good. Still, it is weird to hear groups dedicated to healing wounds of war saying, 'Bring in the air strike!'" [35]

Sadako Ogata, the UN High Commissioner for Refugees (UNHCR) through the 1990s, has said that refugee issues have become "indivisible from questions of international peace and security." In 1997, her agency was responsible for the care of more than 13 million foreign refugees, 4.7 million internally displaced persons, and almost 5 million other victims of conflict. Since the world's Great Powers are generally unwilling to engage directly in "areas where their strategic interests are thin," she has recommended that they equip the UN Organization with, as she puts it, "a rapid military deployment capability" of its own, with forces mandated to protect emergency relief missions as well as to "separate and disarm armed elements in civilian refugee camps." This idea is not impractical, though she admits it is politically controversial. "I do not have ready-made answers," she confessed. "What I do know is that a business-as-usual approach is totally inappropriate." [36]

NOTES

1. Quotations cited from Ronald Reagan, "The Work of Freedom . . . An Unending Challenge," *Washington Times* (December 14, 1992), p. E-1.

2. Quoted in Dick Leurdijk (editor), *A UN Rapid Deployment Brigade: Strengthening Capacity for Quick Response* (The Hague, NL: Netherlands Institute of International Relations 'Clingendael', 1995), p. 23.

3. Dwight D. Eisenhower, "News Conference of August 20, 1958," *Public Papers of the Presidents: Dwight D. Eisenhower, 1958* (Washington: U.S. Government Printing Office, 1959), Item 213 (pages 623-624).

4. John F. Kennedy, "Address to the United Nations General Assembly on September 25, 1961," *Public Papers of the Presidents: John F. Kennedy, 1961* (Washington: U.S. Government Printing Office, 1962), Item 387 (page 622).

5. Delivered before the UN General Assembly on September 24, 1973. Cited in I. J. Rikhye, M. Harbottle, and B. Egge, *The Thin Blue Line: International Peacekeeping and*

its Future (New Haven, 1974), p. 1.

6. George Bush, "Address to the United Nations General Assembly (September 21, 1992)," *Public Papers of the Presidents: George Bush, 1992-93,* Volume II (Washington: U.S. Government Printing Office, 1993), pp. 1599-1600.

7. Bill Clinton and Al Gore, "National Security: Share the Burden," *Putting People First: How We Can All Change America* (New York: Times Books, 1992), p. 135. Clinton quote from Elaine Sciolino, "New U.S. Peacekeeping Policy De-Emphasizes Role of the U.N.," *New York Times* (May 6, 1994), pp. A-1 and A-7.

8. Boutros Boutros-Ghali, *An Agenda for Peace* (New York: UN Department of Public Information, 1992), p. 26.

9. John Lee, Robert von Pagenhardt, and Timothy Stanley, *To Unite Our Strength: Enhancing the United Nations Peace and Security System* (Lanham: University Press of America, 1992), pp. 44-48.

10. Ibid, and pp. 114-117.

11. Timothy L. Thomas, "The U.N.'s Vietnam?" *Military Review* (February 1994), pp. 47-55.

12. Brian Urquhart, "For a UN Volunteer Military Force," *New York Review of Books* (June 10, 1993), pp. 3-4.

13. Staff, U.S. Senate Committee on Foreign Relations, *Reform of United Nations Peacekeeping Operations: A Mandate for Change* (Washington: U.S. Government Printing Office, 1993), p. 63.

14. James A. Leach and Charles M. Lichenstein (Co-Chairs), *Final Report of the United States Commission on Improving the Effectiveness of the United Nations* (Washington: U.S. Government Printing Office, September 1993), p. 20.

15. Ashton Carter, William Perry, and John Steinbruner, *A New Concept of Cooperative Security* (Washington: The Brookings Institution, 1992), p. 28.

16. Leach and Lichenstein, p. 63.

17. Ibid, pp. 56-57.

18. George Bush (Sr.), "Humanitarian Mission to Somalia: Address to the Nation, Washington, D.C., December 4, 1992," *U.S Department of State Dispatch* (December 7, 1992), Vol. 3, No. 49.

19. For details, see Chester A. Crocker, "The Lessons of Somalia: Not Everything Went Wrong," *Foreign Affairs* (May/June 1995), pp. 2-8. Also, John L. Hirsch and Robert B. Oakley, *Somalia and Operation Restore Hope* (Washington: U.S. Institute of Peace, 1995).

20. Bill Clinton, "Confronting the Challenges of a Broader World," *U.S. Department of State Dispatch* (September 27, 1993), Vol. 4, No. 39, pp. 649-653 (esp. 652).

21. Eric Schmitt, "15 Nations Offer Troops For U.N. Force of 54,000," *New York Times* (April 13, 1994), p. A-12. Also, Colum Lynch, "UN Planning a Standby Force of 70,000," *Boston Globe* (May 17, 1994), p. 18.

22. Editorial, "Learning from Rwanda," *The Economist* (August 20, 1994), pp. 13-14.

23. Romeo Dallaire, "Military Aspects," in Leurdijk, pp. 47-54.

24. Hans van Mierlo, Annex I: "Speech by the Netherlands Minister of Foreign Affairs Hans van Mierlo at the 49th UN General Assembly, New York, September 27, 1994," quoted in Leurdijk, p. 71.

25. Bob Mantiri, "Eminent Experts Endorse Standing U.N. Army," *International Press Service* (June 7, 1994). (Author), "Hata Says Japan Should Back Proposed U.N. Forces," *Japan Economic Newswire* (August 19, 1994). Dave Todd, "Russia, Canada Make Strides on UN Reform Plans," *Calgary Herald* (October 7, 1994), p. A-18. Also, Moira Farrow, "Ambassador urges speedy UN army," *Vancouver Sun* (August 2, 1994), p. B-3.

26. William F. Buckley, Jr., "On being involved with Mankind," *National Review*

(December 23, 1996), p. 63.

27. Jonah Blank, "Want peacekeepers with spine? Hire the world's fiercest mercenaries," *U.S. News & World Report* (December 30, 1996-January 6, 1997), pp. 42-43.

28. Carnegie Commission on Preventing Deadly Conflict, *Preventing Deadly Conflict: Executive Summary of the Final Report* (Washington, DC: Carnegie Commission on Preventing Deadly Conflict, 1997), pp. 11 and 18.

29. Fiona Terry, *Rwanda: The Limits and Ambiguity of Humanitarian Aid* (Paris: Medecins Sans Frontieres, January 1995).

30. Alain Destexhe, "The Third Genocide," *Foreign Policy* (Winter 1994-95), pp. 3-17.

31. Terry, *loc. cit.*

32. Destexhe, *loc. cit.*

33. Quotes and statistics from Colin Nickerson, "Relief workers shoulder a world of conflict," *Boston Sunday Globe* (July 27, 1997), pp. A-1 and A-24 to A-26.

34. Ibid.

35. Ibid.

36. Edward Mortimer, "UN needs its own forces, says Ogata," *London Financial Times* (April 4, 1997), p. 6.

13

Feasibility Options for an International Legion of Volunteers

> To strengthen the UN's peacekeeping and peace enforcement capabilities, the Commission proposes the creation of a 5,000- to 10,000-blue helmet rapid reaction force of volunteers. The Commission believes such a force would be useful in containing conflicts before they escalate out of control or in deterring them altogether.
>
> — U.S. Presidential blue-ribbon Commission on Improving the Effectiveness of the United Nations, September 1993

> The creation of a standing rapid deployment brigade is by no means a panacea. Nevertheless, it offers a solution to a number of specific problems which arise in the broader framework of UN peacekeeping operations. As such, it is an important option that needs to be considered when discussing the improvement of the UN's rapid reaction capacity.
>
> — *A UN Rapid Deployment Brigade: A Preliminary Study,* produced by the Dutch government, April 1995

Very little about an international legion of volunteers employed in the service of the United Nations would be truly unprecedented. Peacekeeping is not new. Peace enforcement is not new. Protecting noncombatants from harm is not new. Deploying UN forces into a crisis early on is not new. Using military personnel, policemen, or civilian guards in an operation mandated by the Security Council is not new.

Even the overseas deployment of UN guards directly subordinate to the Secretary-General is not new. It happened in 1991, after the Gulf War, when ordinary UN security guards were deployed into northern Iraq to symbolically guard and help monitor the new Iraqi-Kurdish safe zone there. They were all volunteers, all subject to the Secretary-General's direct control, and yet none of them were from any troop contingent "on loan" to the United Nations from the UN's member-countries.

The only thing unprecedented about a UN legion of volunteers is that most of these already existing precedents would be combined into a single standing unit, available to the Security Council for relatively small scale but still risky missions of importance.

WHAT'S IN A NAME?

The idea of a UN legion or its private equivalent may sound dangerously akin to a force of mercenaries, soldiers of fortune in blue helmets, fighting on behalf of a world government. But that is not what this chapter proposes.

The word *mercenary* is so emotionally loaded that it is sometimes used when it is not technically true, and not used when it is technically true. The British Army in World War I was composed entirely of volunteers and for this reason their German enemies across the battlefield, German soldiers who were drafted, derisively called those British volunteers "mercenaries." Technically that label was not true. During World War II, large numbers of individual Germans and Austrians, many of them Jews, enlisted in the armies of the Allies to fight Nazi Germany. Those anti-Nazi Germans and Austrians were, arguably, mercenaries. Yet in the contemporary democracies of Germany and Austria, they are now remembered as heroes.

The Vatican hired mercenaries during the European Renaissance and, in deference to that tradition, still does. They are called the Swiss Guards, the armed guardians of the Pope, and though they wear colorful Renaissance costumes and hold ceremonial pikes, they are actual soldiers whose arsenal includes machine guns and armored cars.

According to Webster's New English Dictionary, the word *mercenary* has definitions. As an adjective, it means "inspired merely by a desire for gain." As a noun, it refers to "a hired soldier serving a country other than his own." These two definitions can overlap, but they do not always in practice. International law therefore has a more specific definition for what constitutes a *mercenary*; it appears in a protocol to the Geneva Conventions added in 1977, and likewise in the International Convention Against the Recruitment, Use, Financing and Training of Mercenaries, a treaty that opened for national signatures in 1989:

A *mercenary* is any person who: (a) is specially recruited locally or abroad in order to fight in an armed conflict; (b) does in fact take a direct part in the hostilities; (c) is motivated to take part in the hostilities essentially by the desire for private gain and, in fact, is promised, by or on behalf of a Party to the conflict, material compensation substantially in excess of that promised or paid to combatants of similar ranks and functions in the armed forces of that Party; (d) is neither a national of a Party to the conflict nor a resident of territory controlled by a Party to the conflict; (e) is not a member of the armed forces of a Party to the conflict; and (f) has not been sent by a State which is not a Party to the conflict on official duty as a member of its armed forces.[1]

In this legal sense, the members of a UN legion, or members of its private equivalent, would not be mercenaries because their mission would be to protect noncombatants from harm, not to fight in the conflict. Moreover, they would receive a specific international legal mandate from the UN Security Council, to whom they would ultimately report.

COMPOSITION, SIZE, AND RECRUITMENT

Can a unit of soldiers composed of a variety of nationalities, ethnic groups, and religions, yet fully integrated, function effectively? It historically has. One of the most elite units of World War II was the First Special Service Force, a light infantry brigade of Americans, French-Canadians, and Anglo-Canadians. Originally trained for Arctic warfare in Norway, it fought with distinction from Italy to France and was the first Allied unit to enter Rome. It still holds an honored place in the official lineage of the U.S. Army's elite Special Forces, more commonly known as the Green Berets. Hollywood dramatized the First Special Service Force in its 1968 motion picture *The Devil's Brigade,* starring William Holden and Cliff Robertson.

Another famed international unit is the French Foreign Legion. Manned by non-French volunteers and led by French officers, it has a long and proud history, including duty in Bosnia-Herzegovina and Rwanda in the 1990s. Christopher Bellamy, a British defense analyst and proponent of a UN legion, has described the French Foreign Legion as follows:

The 8,500-strong French Foreign Legion is a unique organization. It is recruited from foreigners, many of whom have served in other armies, but its officers are French—some of the very best. It is largely self-contained, with one light tank battalion, one parachute battalion, six infantry, and a regiment of engineers. It is admirably configured for rapid deployment anywhere in the world, come from every corner of the globe. They do not recruit criminals, and are very selective. Their motto—*Legio patria nostra* ("The Legion is our country")—tells of their identity, divorced from their parent states, and in the service of France.[2]

And their salaries are meager, to deflect criticisms that they are "mercenary" soldiers of fortune. Furthermore, despite its elite reputation, the capabilities of the French Foreign Legion are limited by its relatively small size and light weaponry, as well as by its dependence on the transport and resupply capacities of France. In 1994, to intervene into a mere one-third of Rwanda, the Legion needed the use of French bases throughout Africa, including a temporary base in Zaire, as well as French aerial transports, and supported by French national forces. One argument sometimes raised against a proposed United Nations "foreign legion" is that it might militarily threaten the United States or a U.S. ally, presumably in spite of America's immense political and budgetary influence in the United Nations. The weakness of this argument is illustrated by the limits of the French Foreign Legion, an elite unit that cannot pose a threat to anyone without the transport and resupply capabilities of France, capabilities beyond the Legion's control.

After the Rwandan genocide of 1994, the governments of Canada and the Netherlands conducted feasibility studies on how to improve the UN's response capabilities. The Canadian study, *Towards a Rapid Reaction Capability for the*

United Nations, made several recommendations, the most controversial to create a small but rapidly deployable vanguard force. If such a small force could be introduced quickly into an escalating crisis, the Canadian study asserted, that force could help calm the situation while a larger, more traditional multinational peacekeeping force is assembled and eventually deployed.

The Dutch study, later incorporated into an international report entitled *A UN Rapid Deployment Brigade: Strengthening the Capacity for Quick Response,* assessed the idea of a UN legion more directly. Neither the Dutch nor Canadian studies recommended anything larger than a relatively small UN legion, perhaps a brigade of about 5,000 troops, drawn from a permanent pool of 15,000 personnel, all volunteers. The personnel pool would permit a rotation practice wherein, for every soldier deployed with the brigade, a replacement soldier could spend the time preparing to deploy while a third soldier recuperates from a previous deployment. The UN legion would be lightly armed, requiring outside assistance for its overseas transport and resupply. It could militarily oppose rag-tag militias or a poor quality army, but not much more.

There is no guarantee that, having helped to calm a crisis and then departed, the UN legion would never be needed in that country again. Nor is there any guarantee the UN legion would always prevail on its own, though the odds are better if it deploys early during a crisis. There is also no guarantee that, during two simultaneous crises, the UN legion would not be requested for both. But these uncertainties ought not be decisive reasons not to create a UN legion, no more than reasons not to hire a sheriff or constable to quell small disturbances in a neighborhood.

Returning to the issue of international diversity within a military unit, such diversity can inhibit a unit's cohesion. The UN legion should therefore be very careful about the individuals it recruits. They should be psychologically mature and culturally tolerant, as well as intelligent and physically fit. Trained together thereafter, intensely, in a single unit under good leadership, a solid cohesion and *esprit d'corps* can be built despite the international variety of their backgrounds.

David Owen was a peace negotiator during the Bosnian War, a British envoy acting on behalf of the European Union. After the war he, too, advocated the creation of a UN rapid-reaction brigade. Unlike many other advocates, however, he strongly opposed the idea of recruiting its volunteers directly instead of being "on loan" from governments. "My fear," he wrote in 1995, "is that a directly recruited UN Brigade would widen the gap in the Security Council between rhetoric and reality and increase the divorce between power and responsibility." Owen elaborated:

We have seen in recent years how major governments escape their responsibilities as soon as something goes wrong. In Somalia, when the American-led UN operation crossed the "Mogadishu line" between peacekeeper and combatant, responsibility was barely acknowledged by the U.S. administration, who had run the whole operation; it became the UN's fault. . . . How much easier would it be for the Security Council member-states to evade their responsibility if a directly recruited, instantly deployable UN Brigade ran into difficulties?

Only when the Security Council members accept, as part of the obligation associated with membership in the Council, making a contribution from their own armed services to a permanent, instantly deployable UN Brigade will power and responsibility come together on the Council. . . . To believe there should be no such linkage is to use the arguments that many have advanced down the centuries for deploying mercenaries.[3]

During the Bosnian War, the Security Council did indeed order UNPROFOR to undertake missions for which the force was not well designed and therefore could not perform well, if at all. The performance would have gone better, Owen contended, if every Security Council member had contributed soldiers to a multinational UN Brigade.

If their ambassadors voted, for example, for something like the creation of "safe havens" in Bosnia-Herzegovina with a force of only 7,500, knowing that the UN military advisers had recommended 35,000, they would all have to justify the decision in the knowledge that, if the force were inadequate, they would be putting at risk by immediate deployment some 300-700 of their own nationals.[4]

However, there is an inherent assumption in Owen's proposal for a UN legion: Whenever a genocidal crisis requires the UN's intervention, the Security Council will act forcefully sooner rather than later. Unfortunately, the Council's past procrastination in response to the crises in Bosnia, Rwanda, and elsewhere does not bear this out. Furthermore, with regard to the distastefulness of using mercenaries, Owen himself proposed something arguably mercenary as means to include the United States in a multinational UN brigade. He wrote:

U.S. Congressional resistance [to America's participation in a UN Brigade] could be reduced by the U.S. government contribution being met by their government employing civilian pilots and chartering planes and ships for logistical support from private companies in much the same way as the UN and the U.S. Army increasingly contract out their logistic back-up. The fact that they were not in U.S. uniform and were not part of the troop contingent would not substantially weaken the sense of U.S. involvement, for logistical support is not risk-free, as we saw with the pilots flying in and out of [the besieged] Sarajevo airport.[5]

The Dutch study for a UN rapid deployment brigade proposed:

Recruitment for the Brigade could follow a procedure which is analogous to the one which applies at present to the recruitment of personnel for the UN Secretariat, whereby the Member-States act as intermediaries between the UN and the candidates. . . . This intermediary role for Member-States in the recruitment of personnel for the Brigade is specifically intended to warrant that a UN Brigade will not turn into a mercenary force which mainly attracts "soldiers of fortune." [6]

Obviously the Dutch were also concerned about the mercenary label. But to involve the UN's member-governments so closely in the process of personnel selection for a UN legion could create problems of its own. Individual merit ought to be the decisive factor in selecting people to become UN legionnaires. If governments can offer up the only candidates available, however, they may use a very different criteria, such as political or family connections, national chauvinism, bigotry, absolute loyalty to the candidate's government, the desire to send away a politically unwanted individual, or, conversely, to protect and render more "respectable" a candidate guilty of an atrocious crime.

Even a selection process based solely on individual achievement would be questionable. For achievements are not necessarily the same as merit, especially in countries where soldiers can attain high rank through political connections alone. Would the officers of a UN legion, including the legion's commander, have the practical power to refuse, dismiss, or retire anyone they considered incompetent? The Dutch study did not offer a solution, but it did at least hint at the problem:

For political and symbolic reasons, a sufficiently representative geographical distribution should be applied as a criterion when recruiting for the Brigade. For practical reasons, however, it will not be feasible to have all nations proportionally represented in it. Prudent recruitment will have to produce a geographical distribution which is equitable as well as practical.

Another option would be to have a fully homogeneous Brigade, or fully homogeneous battalions, on condition that the troops would not come from one of the major powers.[7]

A "fully homogeneous" unit means recruiting it from a single ethnic group or nationality, such as the martially renown Gurkhas of Nepal. In an interview in 1992, Brian Urquhart, one of the pioneers of UN peacekeeping, talked about idea of a UN legion manned with Gurkhas:

I am always receiving proposals, especially from old [British] generals who had some service in India, who say, "They are hereditary soldiers and there is no real place for them in the modern world. Why not use them as a UN rapid deployment force?" It's an interesting idea, though the force would have to be much more representative of other nations. But the Gurkhas are pretty impressive. I know—I had two battalions of Gurkhas in [the Congolese province of] Katanga in 1961. After the first experience of them, we had only to breathe the word *Gurkhas* and everybody would calm down and go about their business without any more nonsense.[8]

Gurkha troops have traditionally depended on British officers to lead them, though in the 1990s Nepal did send a couple of mostly Gurkha contingents, each numbering a few hundred troops, on some UN assignments, including with UNPROFOR in Croatia. Nevertheless, training the Gurkhas, including Gurkha officers, up to a standard the Security Council will accept, especially suspicious France, Russia, and China, could take a considerable period of time. The UN legionnaires should be proficient not only in combat skills but likewise in local negotiation skills, foreign cultural awareness, patience in the face of repeated foreign insults, and able to work well with both the UN bureaucracy and with countless non-governmental organizations. If the UN legion consists of Gurkha troops led by British officers, it could appear very akin to a form of British colonialism, which is not the impression a UN legion should project. And since the Gurkhas are not representative of all countries and cultures, that fact alone may offend some governments and groups.

MISSION, ORIENTATION, WEAPONRY, AND UNIT STRUCTURE

A UN legion intended for both peacekeeping and peace enforcement must reconcile two contradictory orientations. A force designed for peacekeeping is only lightly equipped, typically, because such a militarily weak force might be the only international force that two warring sides will allow to be deployed between them once they agree to a cease-fire. By contrast, a force equipped for peace enforcement, that is, a heavily armed force, might not be allowed in unless that force fights its way in because its mission is to, in effect, impose a local military occupation. Being heavier, it is more difficult to transport and resupply over long distances and cannot deploy as rapidly. The Dutch study warned:

A light infantry brigade requires a limited logistics capacity. A fully motorized infantry brigade needs a 3-to-5 times larger logistics capacity. For a mechanized unit, the required capacity increases by a factor of 10, and for a helicopter mobile unit by a factor of 100. In addition, supplies have to be available to enable the Brigade to be logistically self-sufficient for 90 days. [9]

Where the unit is to be home-based complicates matters further. If the UN legion is based at several sites worldwide, some portions of the legion could be deployed to particular locations faster than to more distant ones. But having so many bases, the Dutch study warned, would diminish the UN legion's training, experience, and cohesion as a whole. For reasons ranging from unit training to financial efficiency, the better option seems to be to home-base the UN legion at one single location; but then the problem is reversed. The Dutch study explained:

When based in a single location, it will not be attainable for the [UN] Brigade to reach every possible area of deployment within the span of a few days. The time required for deployment of troops is dependent on (1) the time required to prepare the troops for their expected duties and to make them ready for departure, (2) the time required for the transportation (by air or by sea) of personnel and equipment, and (3) the time required for preparations in or near the area of operations. Normally, the time required for (1) and (3) together is around 14 days. [10]

Fourteen days could become a bloody long time, literally, for a UN brigade to enter a hazardous area to undertake a peace enforcement mission, perhaps having to fight its way in if uninvited. Peacekeepers, by contrast, are invited. That permission, and the local safety it provides, combined with the relative lightness of their unit during transport can enable a vanguard of peacekeepers to deploy very quickly. In 1960, some 3,000 UN troops deployed to the Congo in three days of the Security Council's authorization. Canadian troops arrived in Cyprus in 1964 within twenty-four hours of the Council's authorization. But will classic peacekeeping alone be enough to calm a genocidal crisis, especially without a cease-fire? In 1996, Canadian Major-General John MacInnis, a former deputy commander of UNPROFOR, offered the following advice to future UN peacekeepers:

A true peacekeeping operation . . . acts as an impartial third-party in the day-to-day relations with and between the former belligerents. When there is no peace to keep, however, impartiality must take on a different meaning. This is doubly true if the mandate given is related to the plight of the victims of the conflict rather than to the conflict itself.

It may well be necessary and appropriate to treat the parties to the conflict differently: impartiality would come to mean nondiscrimination in carrying out the peacekeeping mandate itself. This in turn demands that, as far as UN peacekeeping is concerned, the enabling [Security Council] resolutions clearly mark the line in the sand which defines the crossover between acceptable and unacceptable behavior. Still better would be a universal code of conduct for peacekeepers, plus a new standing doctrine for peacekeeping which demands zero tolerance for noncompliance with the more widely accepted international legal instruments [such as the Geneva Conventions].

Such a situation would require peacekeepers to be fully capable of, and prepared to use, force, while remaining noncombatants. This demands the ultimate in knowledge, wisdom, restraint and discipline in order to know when to intervene and how much force, and not to turn a blind eye to misbehavior. I firmly believe that the use of force when justified, impartial, and commensurate with the provocation, contributes to credibility and acts as a deterrent against future provocation.[11]

Can a peacekeeper enforce peace and still remain a peacekeeper? Generally the answer is no, but in specific situations the answer may depend more on how much enforcement is actually imposed. Consent and cooperation are essential to peacekeeping, but who gives the consent—and to what degree—are not always straightforward. Sometimes one "side" consists of more than one party, but rather a collection of militia groups, gangs, private armies, and various other groups. Much as in a civil society wherein only a few policemen can maintain the peace by acting against only the most blatant troublemakers, peacekeepers might also enforce the peace by acting against only its most blatant violators. But the risks inherent in this ambiguous overlap between peacekeeping and peace enforcement are still severe. Using weapons only somewhat more powerful, at best, than those carried by lightly armed peacekeepers, the soldiers involved must also be peace enforcers.

The soldiers most suitable for this combined peacekeeping/peace enforcement mission are probably Military Police (MP). In the U.S. Army, for instance, MPs do more than guard prisoners and direct traffic. They operate as small units of motorized infantry, coordinated by radio, equipped with all-terrain vehicles, and armed with heavy machine guns among other weapons. In addition to their combat missions, they quell riots, fight crime, serve as local counterterrorist forces on Army installations, and have a major role in peacekeeping operations. They sometimes joke that their acronym of MP stands for "Multi-Purpose."

The psychological maturity that American MPs are expected to display is considerably high relative to how young most of them really are. For example, most U.S. soldiers in peacetime are rarely given access to live ammunition, and those few occasions are highly controlled. This is true for infantrymen, tank crews, and artillerymen. Yet almost everyday, for several hours each day, American MPs as young as 19 years old are issued live ammunition with their pistols and are expected to handle those deadly weapons responsibly. And pistols are not the only weapons for which American MPs are responsible; they also guard the U.S. Army's nuclear weapons. Whether as guards, policemen, peacekeepers, or local peace enforcers, they are expected to show initiative and good judgment in complex situations. Only because of their training, discipline, and psychological maturity do they perform these duties as well as they do. Many say their discipline and maturity are due to their training.

A UN legion of military police would have several advantages. It could be transported and resupplied about as easily as a peacekeeping force of similar size. If equipped with light armored vehicles, infantry weapons and police equipment (such as field surveillance devices and non-lethal weapons for riot control), the unit could perform peacekeeping and, at a low level of trouble, some limited peace enforcement. If such a UN legion had been deployed into the fragmenting Yugoslavia in 1991, its presence might have discouraged the brutal sieges of Dubrovnik and Vukovar and helped to avert the subsequent Bosnian War. In other cases, such as in refugee camps, UN MPs could disarm domineering thugs and gangs. For two years this was desperately needed in the Rwandan refugee camps in Zaire and Tanzania after the 1994 genocide. Indeed, prior to the genocide, if a UN legion of military police had reinforced (or served as) the UN force in Rwanda, they could have closed down Rwanda's regime-run genocide training camps and confiscated the many weapons being stockpiled in preparation. In 1999, a UN legion might have averted the worst violence that befell both Kosovo and East Timor.

Terms such as *military police, military constabulary, gendarmerie, security police,* or *emergency police* have a connotation not as harsh as *combat force* and yet not as meek as *peacekeeping force.* Many governments that might otherwise refuse to allow a heavily-armed UN force onto their territory might be willing to allow in UN MPs. Likewise, many governments might be more willing to help finance a UN legion of MPs than a UN legion of almost anything else. The label "UN military police" would also remind the Security Council, as well as the general public, of what missions the UN legion can realistically perform or not perform. It can perform military police duties. It can fight for a limited time in a combat environment. It cannot wage a war.

The unit structure of a UN legion of MPs could be based on what the Dutch government proposed for a UN infantry brigade: approximately 5,000 troops organized into three infantry battalions, one engineer battalion (with construction, mine clearing, and demolition capabilities), one medical company, one logistics company (for transportation and resupply), one maintenance company, and a headquarters company. Each of the brigade's companies would have about 200 personnel. Each of the brigade's three infantry battalions would consist of three infantry companies and a service company, the infantry companies subdivided each into three infantry platoons, a fourth platoon with antitank weapons, and a fifth platoon with antiaircraft weaponry. The brigade's three service companies, in addition to having medical, maintenance, and supply platoons, would each also have a reconnaissance (scout) platoon and a platoon armed with mortars.

The Dutch proposal left as undecided whether the UN brigade should be dismounted (the infantry on foot), or motorized, mechanized, or a combination thereof. To reconfigure this model into a military police brigade, ideally the entire brigade should be lightly armored (with armored cars or armored tracked vehicles), or at least motorized (that is, trucks). Including an engineer battalion is probably prudent since the brigade must operate autonomously. Instead of infantrymen, the UN brigade would have military police troops.

The extra weaponry of the UN brigade (that is, its antitank weapons, anti-aircraft weaponry, mortars, etc.) is more politically problematic. Unless those weapons are available for use early in a troublesome situation, they will not be sufficient to enforce any peace after the situation has deteriorated further. In other words, the UN legionnaires should be, as peacekeepers, relatively well armed in case their situation deteriorates. But the antagonists may not want them so well armed. Perhaps the solution is to make their extra weaponry literally inseparable from the rest of the UN brigade: mounted on, bolted into, or embedded within the brigade's armored cars and other necessary vehicles. The weaponry would then not be "extra" because it would not be removable. The UN military police, along with their vehicles and their vehicle-borne weapons, would be a complete package—either everything must be deployed or nothing will be deployed. Although the UN brigade might have to deploy as smaller disconnected units, for instance as separate MP battalions or companies to different locations on the globe simultaneously, those smaller units would never go without their most powerful weapons literally attached to their vehicles, inseparable, and thus always available.

Some proposals for a UN legion have advocated equipping it with much more powerful weaponry, such as field artillery larger than mortars, for stronger fighting capabilities in major combat situations; that is, for peace enforcement at the middle or higher end of the combat spectrum, not at the lower end where MPs would suffice. Most governments, however, are unlikely to permit on their own territory any UN-controlled force with so much firepower. No matter how theoretically attractive a truly independent, very powerful UN force for global peace enforcement may appear, the idea is simply too ambitious to expect its attainment anytime soon.

HIGHER COMMAND AND INTERFACE

Forces under the direct command of the UN Organization receive their missions and mandates from the Security Council, but they are managed day to day by the Secretary-General and his Secretariat staff. Some experts fear that placing a UN standing force under the Secretary-General's control could make his position overly powerful and, during a crisis, taint his neutral impartiality and that of the UN mediators he appoints.

The evident solution is to exclude the Secretary-General and the Secretariat from any control over a standing UN legion. Instead, the UN legion could serve the Security Council directly. But this arrangement, though promising, poses some problems of its own. If the Secretariat does not manage the UN legion, who will? The legion would have to manage itself, which as a standing force it could do, perhaps even quite efficiently since its administrative needs would not be as diverse and broad as those of the entire UN Organization.

A more sensitive problem is who should have the power to order the legion's resort to coercive force. The Security Council could give it a mandate that authorizes possible force, or pass resolutions that encourage or even demand its resort to force, but at the actual time and place the actual use of force will be ordered by an official who serves the Council. Who should that official be? The UN legion's commander? If so, should he be allowed to order some limited peace enforcement (such as the forcible disarmament of an unruly group) without first consulting with the Security Council? If he is that assertive, he may not be properly supported by the Council's members if something goes wrong, even if he acted within the Council's mandate. This is because David Owen had a point: The Security Council has sometimes created mandates for UN forces that, when something later went wrong, the Council's members simply evaded their responsibility for it by unfairly blaming the hapless UN force or the UN as a whole.

To gain the durable support of the Security Council could necessitate monitoring its members' diverse, shifting moods. To do this, the UN legion's commander may have to spend more time with the Council in New York City than abroad with his own UN legionnaires. If not him, someone else must function as the UN legion's liaison with the Council. Whoever holds the job should be militarily knowledgeable enough to understand the legion's special needs, so as to give competent advice to the Council, as well as politically savvy enough to dissuade the Council from being too demanding or micromanaging the legion. Subordinates in any military organization deserve the loyalty of their superiors as much as those superiors deserve the loyalty of their subordinates. The New York-based official would exist to encourage this two-way loyalty between the Security Council and its subordinate UN legion. The job will be emotionally pressured and probably thankless, but it is utterly essential.

FINANCING

The expense of a UN legion would be a form of global insurance, especially against genocide. In 1995, General Dallaire told an international conference:

Let me point out that UN peace support operations deployed during the early stages of a crisis make good economic sense. For example, in Rwanda, we estimated the 22-month mission required about $200 million in August '93. We received only a fraction of that amount. Compare those costs with the billions which have and continue to be sent to the same country in humanitarian aid, rebuilding destroyed infrastructure, and military security operations.[12]

Those costs included the feeding of more than 1 million Rwandan refugees languishing in camps in both Zaire and Tanzania for over two years, costs that could have lasted for years longer if a chance change had not occurred in 1996.

Using U.S. dollar figures in 1995, the Dutch study estimated the following expenses per year for a UN brigade of 5,000 troops:

Personnel (salaries)	$ 150 million
Personnel (allowances, food, clothing)	$ 40 million
Basing and upkeep of quarters	$ 20 million
Maintenance	$ 40 million
Procurement (annualized)	$ 50 million
Total	$ 300 million

The initial procurement of equipment and other "start up" costs might total about $550 million in that first year. The annual cost of a UN military police brigade would likely be similar, between $300 million and $400 million a year. The Dutch government did not calculate the cost to maintain a UN legionnaire manpower pool. Funding a manpower pool large enough to man one brigade three times over, thus allowing the brigade to be replenished through a rotation cycle of rest and refresher training, could triple the cost to about $1 billion per year. Depending upon how many items of heavy equipment are to be purchased three times over, or not, the initial start up costs could be anywhere from $550 million to $1.65 billion.

These costs, when presented out of context, may appear very large, but in global terms they are not so immense. The U.S. defense budget in 1995 was about $270 billion. The defense budget of the city-state of Singapore was about $4 billion. Even the U.S. Coast Guard had a budget of $3.7 billion, higher than the entirety of UN peacekeeping operations in 1995, when about $3 billion was spent funding 54,000 "blue helmet" troops worldwide.[13]

The cost of a UN legion could be shared among the UN's membership. The United States could pay about 20 percent of the total, roughly commensurate with its proportion of the world economy. Annually, therefore, the U.S. share could amount to about $200 million (expressed in 1995 dollars), roughly equal to the price of four F-15 fighter jets (at $55 million each). Other countries' shares could be paid in various ways, such as with donations of equipment, free use of national facilities and bases, the lending of special instructors, or permitting UN legionnaires to attend desired national military schools and staff colleges.

"Two days of *Desert Storm*," noted Brian Urquhart after the Gulf War, "would comfortably pay for all UN peacekeeping operations worldwide for one year. If you want to do something, you can pay for it." [14]

ALTERNATIVE OPTIONS

Aside from the multinational and unilateral options described in previous chapters, there are three basic alternatives to employing a UN legion:

A *De Facto* Legion

Through extensive planning and preparation, the services of various NGOs, volunteer groups, and private companies could become a *de facto* legion for peacekeeping missions, and possibly even for limited peace enforcement. To gain the legal symbolism of the United Nations, this collective entity could be granted a conditional mandate by the Security Council. Regional international organizations could do something similar. The idea of forming a *de facto* legion was suggested by Brian Urquhart. "Until governments are more amenable to a UN volunteer force," he told an international conference in 1995, "we should perhaps work, among other things, on a rapid-reaction group as a first step." [15] He elaborated:

Some of the elements of a mixed-discipline rapid-reaction group already exist in different parts of the UN system. The UN Field Service, which has existed since 1948, is a uniformed service trained in security and communications functions and with a long and distinguished record of operating effectively in confused and violent situations all over the world. The [UN] Secretariat routinely supplies political, legal, and administrative officers for field missions. Many of these officials have developed skill and ingenuity in dealing with unexpected, and sometimes dangerous, situations. The High Commissioner for Refugees and UNICEF have long and varied experience in dealing at very short notice with emergency humanitarian situations. Outside the UN system, there is a wide range of non-governmental organizations with a long record of dealing with humanitarian emergencies. Many of these elements could be brought together as the initial core of an established rapid-reaction group.[16]

One controversy of a *de facto* legion could be what military-type personnel are to be employed on commercial contracts. Those personnel could be accused of being more "mercenary" than those of a regular UN legion. The need to have them will exist, however, whether they are contracted for or not. Explained Urquhart: "Personally I believe that such a [rapid-reaction] group must have a hard shell of military and police personnel so that it can operate in violent conditions without harm or intimidation, and this will require some new elements." He noted that a number of private firms offer security services on very short notice, adding, "It might be wise to consider how such elements could be brought together and made ready to deploy at any time." [17]

The most ambitious of these firms are private military companies (PMCs) and, though their critics decry them as new-fashioned mercenaries, they became increasingly respectable in the 1990s. Among the most well-known is Sandline International, founded by Timothy Spicer, a former British lieutenant-colonel on the staff of UNPROFOR's commander in Bosnia. Sandline's Internet website declares:

The business was established in the early 1990s to fill a vacuum in the post-Cold War era. Our purpose is to offer governments and other legitimate organizations specialist military expertise at a time when Western national desire to provide active support to friendly governments, and to support them in conflict resolution, has materially decreased, as has their capability to do so.

Sandline is privately managed by a number of senior ex-military personnel from the U.K. and U.S. armed forces. This management team is supported by access to a pool of consultants with extensive commercial and legal expertise. Sandline personnel are highly professional, often former military, police and government employees, recruited from a number of countries. They are the best available, and have extensive experience of all levels of conflict, but are tuned to the nuances and political sensitivities in the world today.[18]

In 1998, after Sierra Leone's elected president was deposed by an unpopular military junta, Sandline helped the West African ECOMOG multinational force restore him to power, providing logistical, aerial, and intelligence support. The British *Sunday Times* later asked Spicer to write an op-ed piece about private military companies. Under the headline "Why We Can Help Where Governments Fear to Tread," he wrote:

It's not so much that we can do things better than sovereign governments. . . . It's that we can do it without any of the spin-offs that make military intervention unpalatable to governments; casualties among PMCs do not have the same emotive impact as those from national military forces. And we can act quickly. Too often politicians won't make a decision to intervene either at all or until it is too late.

PMCs are not casual mercenaries. . . . Unlike the "dogs of war" to whom people like to compare us, once contracted and deployed PMCs operate as a military hierarchy with associated discipline, observance of the laws and customs of the host nation and, finally, adhering to the principles of the Geneva Conventions and the international law of armed conflict. . . . The real problem comes when you get a country where the insurgents are in the right. We can't work for them because if we did we would be helping to overthrow [UN-]recognized governments. That type of dilemma could be solved by regulation, something we would welcome.

It is a question of deciding what kind of world we want. People wrung their hands over the genocide in Rwanda but who did anything about it? Yes, we expect to be paid, but we are a lot less costly than a sovereign or UN military force, and maybe far more effective. Yes, we apply commercial values; what if we do? Surely it is better to prevent death, destruction, and hardship than turn your back on it, especially if private military companies are the last and only resort.[19]

Sandline's desire for respectability-through-regulation led the company to propose how to regulate PMCs, whether by their parent countries, the UN, or other international organizations. Some excerpts from Sandline's proposal:

Very few PMCs would object to the attachment of an observer team deployed alongside them in the field. . . . By being present throughout the deployment and operational planning phases, the observer [team] will be fully conversant with the overall objectives, chain-of-command, directives and orders that are issued, and the conduct of operations, thereby creating accountability for all actions of the PMCs.[20]

In some paragraphs Sandline sounded more like a critic of PMCs rather than one itself:

PMCs must be willing to open themselves up for inspection and make their businesses transparent beyond the requirements of company law. . . . This is an essential factor in establishing acceptability and credibility in the eyes of the international community. If these companies want to continue to conduct business without having to constantly and retrospectively fend off the suspicions of the press and the public, this is part of the price they must be willing to pay.[21]

More notorious than Sandline was Executive Outcomes (EO). Most of EO's more than 1,000 employees were formerly soldiers of the apartheid-era South African Defence Force, three-quarters of them black. To EO's credit, it did take several steps to break with its racist past, becoming licensed as a regulated PMC by Nelson Mandela's government. "The fastest thing that would get us out of business," an EO executive said, "is human rights violations."[22]

EO in 1992-1996 was hired by Angola's government to help fight rebels once actively supported by South Africa's regime, a reversed relationship whose irony was not lost on EO's employees, but they fulfilled the contract. A UN peacekeeping force was later sent to maintain Angola's new stability, a stability

that EO claimed some credit for. In 1995-1997, EO helped train Sierra Leone's army to fight that country's notoriously brutal rebels. It was so successful that a government official admitted, "The government of Sierra Leone believes EO can do a better job than the Sierra Leone Army." [23]   Indeed, one of the rebels' conditions for a peace agreement was that EO leave Sierra Leone. EO left—and within four months the rebels rebounded and overthrew Sierra Leone's elected government, which Sandline helped to restore some months later.

EO's fee in Angola was about $40 million a year, compared to $135 million budgeted for the later UN peacekeeping force in 1996-1997. The UN also budgeted $47 million for an eight-month peacekeeping force for Sierra Leone before the situation deteriorated again in 1997; EO, for its earlier twenty-two month stay, cost the government of Sierra Leone about $35 million.[24] At least fourteen EO employees were killed in Angola, as well as two in Sierra Leone, but in both countries the company stayed and fulfilled its contracts. Executive Outcomes dissolved itself as a company in late 1998. Its former employees now operate with less attention from the news media.

Various PMCs have the personnel, training, and equipment to perform the military police duties needed by a *de facto* legion. Some companies have small numbers of military helicopters and armored personnel carriers. A few employ Gurkhas: "We employ former U.K. Army Gurkhas," one firm explained, "as a result of their exemplary performance, high personal standards, loyalty, pleasant nature, versatility, and determination. As a result, they would be ideal for any organization requiring these talents." [25]

What PMCs do not have are enough soldiers in any single firm to field a 15,000-man *de facto* legion or even only a 5,000-man unit. Therefore, several PMCs would have to be hired, requiring an overarching supervisory authority to organize them into an integrated, cohesive whole. When combined with the many NGOs, volunteer groups, and other private companies that a rapid-reaction group ought to include, a *de facto* legion could be an administrative nightmare for the UN or for whatever regional international organization is in charge.

If not run by an international organization, a *de facto* legion could be run by one or more countries' governments. Those governments would have to fund it alone and they would have articulate some plausible public reason why "their" legion is not really pursing a selfish national agenda under a noble guise. In 1994, when the French government wanted to intervene in Rwanda during the genocide, Zaire was the only country whose government granted the French forces permission to operate from its adjacent territory. The governments of neighboring Burundi, Uganda, and Tanzania all refused because they all distrusted the French, despite the French having gained a UN mandate. If Zaire's government had refused as well, France's intervention into Rwanda would have been nearly impossible. As the French government discovered, securing some international goodwill can be essential to oppose even a genocide.

An *Ad Hoc* Legion

An *ad hoc* legion would be a patchwork of NGOs and private entities, hastily gathered together to address an urgent crisis, much as a multinational force is a patchwork of different national contingents contributed by governments. The problems of an *ad hoc* legion would not be identical to those of a multinational force, but they would be similar and considerable. The hasty compression of different organizations, different styles, and perhaps different agendas into an *ad hoc* legion would almost certainly hamper its effectiveness and budgetary efficiency. The result may not even approximate what Brian Urquhart deemed necessary for a rapid-reaction group:

The UN needs a highly-trained, flexible, immediately available group, with modern communications and other technical advantages, ready to go at 24-hours notice. Such a group must develop *esprit d'corps* and a reputation for excellence. Its effectiveness will, of course, depend on early warning and the willingness of the Security Council to act on early warning. There is a lot of useful work that could be done to make this first step.[26]

An *ad hoc* legion would not have much if any *esprit d'corps*. Yet this was the option the international community preferred in the 1990s, even though many elements could not work together efficiently and could not be ready in 24 hours.

An NGO Legion

In today's era of global privatization and free markets, an inherently cohesive legion that is also a non-governmental organization could be created. Such an NGO legion could be equipped with police-type capabilities, including armored cars. Available for hire only by the Security Council, it might still be accused of being more "mercenary" than a UN legion organic to the UN Organization. Under the Council's oversight, however, it could also incorporate some special features.

It could have, for example, a section devoted to forecasting and reporting on places of potential trouble, an international early warning center for genocide. Through consistent accurate reporting, it could become a credible source for the news media. As a monitored crisis gets worse, the NGO legion could publicize more and more urgent warnings, in effect pressuring hesitant governments to respond. The warning reports would repeatedly emphasize the growing costs of waiting too long. Some quality assurance could also be designed in through a bit of healthy competition. As each warning report is issued, two separate teams of experts could devise response recommendations. If the crisis worsens, and more warnings are issued, their subsequent recommendations will likely call for more involvement, such as larger peacekeeping forces, more active diplomacy, more public attention upon the crisis, and so forth. Such a trend, both of the crisis itself and of the recommendations to quell it, might encourage onlooking governments to act sooner rather than later.

Unfortunately, the cost of funding an NGO legion, if it is have at least 5,000 police-type personnel, could be relatively expensive by the standards of NGOs.

WHAT WILL THE WORLD ACCEPT?

The UN Organization has long opposed the use of mercenaries, perceiving them as soldiers of fortune, as neocolonial oppressors of the natives, as arrogant racist thugs. Plenty of evidence exists to support that perception, but there are exceptions, especially among legitimate private military companies. Their critics, notably in the UN, say that governments hire PMCs to perform tasks that those sovereign governments ought to be performing themselves as a responsibility of sovereignty. To assert this criticism is assert a value judgment, however. Even Western governments, whose sovereignty is envied, now hire private military companies to perform tasks that those governments once performed themselves.

In a speech at the U.S. Holocaust Memorial Museum, Sadako Ogata, the UN High Commissioner for Refugees, noted that, for two years after the Rwandan genocide, "the Rwandan refugee camps in Zaire and Tanzania were controlled by armed men, many of whom were probably guilty of genocide. We asked for international help in getting these people out of the camps. No country offered to get involved. My staff had to continue feeding criminals as the price for feeding hundreds of thousands of innocent women and children." [27]

Is the hiring of mercenaries to oppose genocide so much worse than what those humanitarian aid organizations had to do? Is the hiring of private military companies, or their nonprofit equivalent, so much worse than new multitudes of refugees and internally displaced persons? Or worse than new multitudes of murdered victims?

NOTES

1. Quoted from Article 47 of Protocol I, "Additional to the Geneva Conventions of August 12, 1949, Relating to the Protection of Victims of International Armed Conflicts"; adopted on June 8, 1977 and came into force on December 7, 1978. Also quoted from Article 1 of the "International Convention Against the Recruitment, Use, Financing and Training of Mercenaries"; opened for signature on December 4, 1989.

2. Christopher Bellamy, *Knights in White Armour: The New Art of War and Peace* (London: Random House, 1996). Also, Douglas Porch, *The French Foreign Legion: A Complete History of the Legendary Fighting Force* (New York: HarperCollins Pub., 1991).

3. David Owen, *Balkan Odyssey* (New York: Harcourt Brace & Company, 1995), pp. 361-363.

4. Ibid.

5. Ibid.

6. From Dick A. Leurdijk (editor), *A UN Rapid Deployment Brigade: Strengthening Capacity for Quick Response* (The Hague: Netherlands Institute of International Relations 'Clingendael', 1995), pp. 87-88.

7. Ibid.

8. Lance Morrow, "An Interview: The Man in the Middle," *Soldiers for Peace* (supplement to *MHQ: The Quarterly Journal of Military History,* Autumn 1992), p. 27.

9. Leurdijk, p. 84.

10. Ibid, p. 89.

11. John MacInnis, "Peacekeeping and International Humanitarian Law," *International Peacekeeping* (Autumn 1996), pp. 92-97.

12. Romeo Dallaire, "Military Aspects," in Leurdijk, p. 49.

13. Figures from International Institute for Strategic Studies, *The Military Balance 1995/96* and *The Military Balance 1996/97* (London: Brassey's, 1995 and 1996).

14. Morrow, *loc. cit.*

15. Brian Urquhart, "Prospects for a UN Rapid Response Capability," in Leurdijk, pp. 21-22.

16. Brian Urquhart & Francois Heisbourg, "Prospects for a Rapid Reaction Capability: A Dialogue," in Olara A. Otunnu and Michael W. Doyle (editors), *Peacemaking and Peacekeeping for the New Century* (Lanham: Rowman & Littlefield Pub., 1998), p. 194

17. Ibid.

18. See Internet website www.sandline.com

19. Tim Spicer, "Why we can help where governments fear to tread," *Sunday Times* (24 May 1998).

20. From Sandline white papers entitled, "Private Military Companies: Independent or Regulated?" and "Should the Activities of Private Military Companies Be Transparent?" on the Sandline International website: www.sandline.com

21. Ibid.

22. Kevin Whitelaw, "Have gun, will prop up regime," *U.S. News & World Report* (20 January 1997), pp. 46-48.

23. Whitelaw, *loc. cit.*

24. David Shearer, "Outsourcing War," *Foreign Policy* (Fall 1998), pp. 68-81.

25. From an e-mail correspondence with Securewest International Limited & Gurkha Manpower Services, at securewestmanpower@compuserve.com

26. Urquhart in Leurdijk, *loc. cit.*

27. Quoted in Lionel Rosenblatt and Larry Thompson, "The Door of Opportunity: Creating a Permanent Peacekeeping Force," *World Policy Journal* (Spring 1998), pp. 36-42.

14

The Future Belongs to You

We, the Reis-ul-Ulema of the Islamic Community of Bosnia-Herzegovina, the responsible representatives of the two Christian churches (Serbian Orthodox and Roman Catholic) and the President of the Jewish Community of Bosnia-Herzegovina, recognize that our Churches and Religious Communities differ from each other, and that each of them feels called to live true to its own faith. As the same time we recognize that our religious and spiritual traditions hold many values in common and that these shared values can provide an authentic basis for mutual esteem, cooperation and free common living in Bosnia-Herzegovina.

Specifically, we condemn: (i) acts of hatred based on ethnicity or religious differences—we express our especial concern at the burning of houses, the desecration of religious buildings, and the destruction of graveyards; (ii) the obstruction of the free right of return; (iii) acts of revenge; and (iv) the abuse of the media with the aim of spreading hatred. . . . Finally, we call on all people of good will to take responsibility for their own acts. Let us treat others as we would wish them to treat us.

> — Signed in Sarajevo by the leaders of the Muslim, Jewish,
> Roman Catholic and East Orthodox Christian faiths
> of Bosnia-Herzegovina, on June 9, 1997

Even as genocide has occurred throughout the history of human civilization, throughout that same history the overwhelming majority of human beings have never killed another human being. For being as much as a legal and ethical crime, genocidal mass murder is an innate crime, repugnant to the basic nature of our species. To attribute this crime's cause to something supposedly nebulous and uncontrollable, such as "bad" genes, is to excuse its worst perpetrators and render them unaccountable. It is also an all-too convenient excuse for our own indifference when the crime afflicts other people.

WHAT GENOCIDE IS

A group identity begins as a group whose members psychologically identify their own personal meaning and purpose as human beings as being members of that group. They may then categorize other people, regardless of those others' individuality, into other groups and, in effect, create other group identities. The crime of genocide is an attempt by a group identity's members to destroy another group identity, a group typically defined by a national, ethnic, racial, or religious criteria. The perpetrators proclaim and may even believe that the targeted group is a malevolent enemy that must be destroyed for the common good. Theirs is a mind-set akin to paranoia—the addiction of the zealot, the violent fanatic. Such people may number only a tiny few at first, but in a hyperpressured society they can increase their ranks enough to dominate a passive majority.

This is because every culture has at least some elements of bigotry. Bigotry by itself, however, will not necessarily produce mass murder. Bigotry is only the kindling. The fire is politics. Genocidal violence may appear chaotic, but at its core the violence is premeditated, prepared for, organized and orchestrated by an ambitious leadership. For genocide is a manifestation of tyranny, employing propaganda to increase fear and enflame bigotry by exploiting the language of the society's prevailing culture, religion, or ideology, portraying the genocidal victimizer as a victim. The self-labeled "good" group, the propaganda declares, has suffered terrible injustices at the hands of the "evil" group, a scapegoat, demonized and dehumanized as the supposed instigator of a grand conspiracy to inflict even worse atrocities unless that scapegoat is destroyed *as a group*.

If enough people are receptive to this emotionally charged message, the message will spread, along with its insidious hatred, eventually reinforced by acts of violence by opportunists and militant believers. And after each violent episode, after each outburst of hateful propaganda, more and more people may feel compelled to join a side to physically protect themselves and their families, even if this choice means identifying themselves with a group identity that may have meant little or nothing to them before the violence began. Once a genocidal crisis reaches this level of intensity, it is extremely difficult to quell. And its consequences will haunt generations to come.

THE NECESSITY FOR EARLY ACTION

Fortunately, genocide is preventable. Most people around the world want to live in harmony with their neighbors, no matter how different those neighbors are. Reaching those ordinary people while they still believe in some degree of tolerance, while there are still enough political moderates among them able to compete with the extremists and opportunists seeking power through hateful "identity politics"—that is when a genocidal trend is easiest to reverse. Even if a regime of would-be perpetrators is already in power, an early effort can engage that regime when it feels strong enough to compromise but not brazen enough —at least not yet—to massacre people openly. That is the time when quiet diplomacy, focused publicity, verbal political pressure, and nonviolent resistance can be most effective. It is when resident diplomats have the most leeway to influence the situation largely unencumbered by their home countries' domestic politics. It is when the regime might be most willing, however grudgingly, to accept an international peacekeeping force on its territory, a force capable of performing some very limited peace enforcement if necessary. Such a presence can discourage violence by the rival groups, help safeguard political moderates, and preserve a general sentiment among the public that prefers peace. But unless this window of opportunity is acted upon, the opportunity will slip away.

If democratic governments would rather not intervene abroad with their own military forces to uphold the most elementary of human rights—*the right of a population not to be mass murdered*—then an alternative force is needed. A rapid-reaction unit of about 5,000 international volunteers, either directed by the United Nations or merely given a UN legal mandate, could be fielded, a unit that is specially designed not to be overly encumbered by the domestic politics of governments far from the crisis. Being more police-oriented than military, such a UN legion, or its equivalent, could enhance the national security of democratic countries by helping to free up their national military forces for their respective national defense. It could help address what are currently costly distractions of Western, especially American, military power. Albeit, there is no guarantee that such a small specialized force will always prevail in every mission it receives, but its present lack of existence currently imposes an enormous moral obligation upon the Western democracies to intervene in genocidal crises in forcible ways they have traditionally shown little earnest desire to perform. The early action needed rarely occurs.

Early action requires early warning. Early warning, in turn, requires a global monitoring effort by dedicated experts funded sufficiently. This is a permanent expense, repeatedly difficult to justify to some accountants. Yet the costs of an unhindered genocide, deliberately unanticipated, allowed to erupt through sheer neglect, are far more expensive and burdensome. When constant monitoring and early warning are both treated seriously, they become cost-effective because they pay for themselves. Treating them seriously means institutionalizing them as intellectual disciplines with their own staff and methods. In a bureaucracy of multiple departments and priorities, a genocide early warning center may always have a relatively small staff, producing ominous predictions that are not meant to come true because they are warnings, not prophecies. Consequently, that center may always be vulnerable to testy budget-cutters. For its experts to do their jobs properly, the very high officials whom that center serves must shield it against bureaucratic encroachment and promote its work in spite of the envy and resistance of other departments.

THE CONSEQUENCES OF PROCRASTINATION

The longer the delay before a genocidal crisis is quelled, the more daunting are the difficulties in mounting a humanitarian intervention against it. Sensing the world's indifference, the horror's perpetrators typically become ever bolder and deadly, worsening the magnitude of the crisis as well as its lasting hatreds. The second half of this book has described not only the military tactics available to a humanitarian intervention but the limitations of those tactics against a very determined genocidal killer. Procrastination, whether as outright inaction or as a gradual, timid intervention, usually proves disastrous.

Covert action alone is rarely very effective against a genocide. Whether it involves assassination, physical sabotage, or secretly arming an imperiled group, covert action requires elaborate planning and preparations that consume time, money, and effort—and is daunting to keep secret. Some less violent forms of covert action, such as forged documents for endangered persons, might help as part of a larger, multifaceted campaign against a genocide. In situations where mass killings have not yet occurred but are very possible, the early scripting of antigenocidal literature could be prepared as part of a ready-made psychological operation, or *psyop*. The most effective of *psyop* efforts, however, are those that occur on site, early in the crisis, when a worried population is most receptive to hearing any peaceful ideas on how to avoid further bloodshed. Such *psyop* efforts require the presence of their promoter on the scene.

Airpower and likewise the most long-range of so-called non-lethal weapons have domestic political advantages because they can be launched into the target country from the relative safety of the outside. Each, however, is dependent upon circumstances and tactical timing, as well as the inherent limits of any technological option. Without the combined effect of other weapons and other pressures, including international diplomatic pressure, aerial weapons of any sort are unlikely to stop a determined genocide. The NATO alliance, despite appearances to the contrary, did not prevail in the Kosovo War through airpower alone. Russia's growing displeasure with Slobodan Milosevic combined with NATO's eventual preparations for a ground invasion of Yugoslavia also helped.

Ground forces can employ expedient tactics against a genocide, but they are limited as well. Soldiers cannot stop an ongoing slaughter if there are only enough of them to escort convoys of humanitarian supplies, or even fewer soldiers than that—shortages which afflicted the UN's multinational forces in Bosnia-Herzegovina and Rwanda, respectively. The deployment of too few soldiers can render them hostages to the crisis, politically or even literally.

Safe havens were once frequently mentioned as a way to prevent genocide, that is, until the massacre at Srebrenica. Most safe havens barely qualify as forts. The havens that succeeded in the 1990s were more lucky than defensible; even Srebrenica was lucky, for years, until its last critical episode. Safe havens can save people in the narrow sense of bare existence, but the survival risk is high and most havens are appallingly unsanitary, even barbaric places. The refugees crowded within them tend to become exploited, sometimes by criminal gangs and mobs, sometimes by governments manipulating the safe havens as abstract political symbols. Sometimes both.

Safe zones are much larger than safe havens and so can provide inhabitants with a more normal existence—but only in the equivalent of an underdeveloped country with all its accompanying problems, including political instability. The foreign troops who create the safe zone tend to be withdrawn sooner or later, and without them the zone can becomes a very tenuous place. The hope that, with the pillars of international symbolism, diplomacy, and perhaps some nearby airpower, the safe zone will be respected. But these pillars depend on the active interest and will of the zone's foreign guardians, which is not always assured. A safe zone is very expensive to create, very demanding of military power, and not necessarily applicable to every case of genocide.

A FOREIGN POLICY FOR THE TWENTY-FIRST CENTURY

In the years since the Cold War's end, debates have raged over what foreign policy the United States should now pursue. Realists advocate the pursuit of strategic national interests, power politics, and *realpolitik*. Retaining a country's maximum flexibility to safeguard its sovereignty and promote its interests abroad, neither distracted nor overburdened by the internal problems of other countries, is, to the Realists, paramount. Idealists, meanwhile, advocate humanitarianism and international law, promoted by international organizations. While Realists speak of national security, Idealists speak of human security.

The United States can pursue both. In today's increasingly integrated world, the United States needs both. For if the United States pursues an exclusively Realist foreign policy, then through its own deliberate indifference it will soon discover that the "non-strategic" yet very serious "internal" problems of other countries fester into international crises. On the other hand, a foreign policy of pure Idealism would be naïve. Governments are not inherently moral entities; their behavior includes the worst atrocities of modern times. But governments still create international law and they still run international organizations. To assume that any non-governmental entity can do a better job of managing the world is to assume the unproven. Until the world achieves a utopian harmony, a powerful United States encourages international peace and stability.

Moreover, the American people, a colorful mosaic of different constituencies, will never consistently support a foreign policy that is exclusively Realist or Idealist. The U.S. political system, built upon compromise, periodic elections, and changing administrations, will not allow it. Therefore the grand strategy of the United States must be a grand compromise between Realism and Idealism, a strategy that is broadly supportable even if somewhat contradictory. The basic framework of this strategy is already in practice: A two-tier doctrine wherein the United States safeguards its national security while leaving the UN Organization to address issues of human security. This can be a complementary division of responsibilities, freeing the United States from a plague of foreign distractions while the UN addresses them with vigor and early prevention. For this two-tier doctrine to work well, however, neither tier can be neglected. Unless the United States provides the UN Organization with enough support to act with timely decisiveness instead of with tardy half-measures, today's problems of human security will become tomorrow's costlier problems involving national security. In the mid-twentieth century, when the prosperity of the United States was much less dependent upon the outside world than it is today, then-President Dwight Eisenhower nonetheless noted, "There can be no enduring peace for any nation while other nations suffer privation, oppression, and a sense of injustice and despair. In our modern world, it is madness to suppose that there could be an island of tranquility and prosperity in a sea of wretchedness and frustration."[1]

Today, there is privation more sinister, no oppression more overwhelming, no injustice and despair more horrific, than the deadly crime of genocide.

THE NEED TO SPEAK OUT

The occurrence of deadly genocide actually started to decrease in the 1990s, not worsen, at least in comparison to earlier decades of the twentieth century. In part this is because the more recent scenes of the crime, such as Rwanda and the Balkans, have generally been smaller than was Stalin's Soviet Union, or Hitler's Nazi-occupied Europe, or Mao's China, where tens of millions became victims. Genocide in the 1990s murdered about 5 million people. If the Rwandan genocide had been prevented, the toll could have been about 4 million.

But this downward trend from the 1990s is not enforced by any natural law. For it to continue downward, enough people must actively demand it. Every country on the globe with a binding signature upon at least one international humanitarian agreement—and, most particularly, upon the Convention on the Prevention and Punishment of the Crime of Genocide—is now automatically involved whenever and wherever a deadly genocide occurs. These international agreements, as well as the Information Age, have made us all involved. Since our involvement is internationally legal, and probably necessary, and indeed probably inevitable since the crime is so destructive, we should watch for its ominous signs to stop the crime sooner rather than later. And we should speak out when those signs are there.

The people with a special duty to speak out include the leaders of the world's democracies, in particular the President of the United States. For along with the obvious moral reasons, there are now tactical reasons offered by the Information Age. Unable to enforce censorship across every medium, most dictatorships can no longer keep their captive populations in total ignorance. So, to promote the Big Lie, they now employ the half-truth: They publicize one-sided news stories, leaving out whatever inconvenient facts would alter the story's moral character. One example is the half-truth promoted by Saddam Hussein's regime that the UN trade sanctions against Iraq prohibited its importation of food and medicine. The full truth is that Hussein's regime repeatedly refused those imports while demanding that the entire sanctions against Iraq, including against imports of weaponry, be lifted altogether. The UN did not try to starve Iraq's population to pressure Hussein; Hussein, by starving Iraq's population, tried to pressure the UN. His policy was so monstrous that many ordinary people in the Middle East and beyond refused to believe it, encouraged by Hussein's insidious half-truths. The President of the United States needs to loudly correct such half-truths—and thereby help to marginalize tyrants such as Hussein—through highly publicized White House speeches delivered during "prime time" television hours. To have only a President's subordinates, even as eminent as the U.S. Secretary of State, attempt to correct these half-truths is simply not sufficient: Most ordinary people will not listen carefully to any high official except the President, and only when the President speaks to them in an televised address. If the President explains why the conduct of a particular foreign policy strategy is sound, necessary, and in keeping with America's ideals, the American public will support it.

The President can also utilize the Information Age creatively—and not only with Internet websites or future technologies. During the Kosovo War, after the Chinese embassy in Belgrade was mistakenly bombed by NATO, the Chinese news media, directed by the Chinese government, truthfully reported all the facts except one: That the bombing was a mistake, instead claiming that NATO, in particular the United States, had bombed the Chinese embassy deliberately. When the U.S. government officially apologized to China, emphasizing the genuine error of the attack and that the United States had no rational reason to bomb China's embassy, that apology went unreported by the Chinese media for days, giving the regime more time to incite anti-American Chinese nationalism. But rather than allow such blatant omissions of fact, the President could have traveled to China to personally apologize to the Chinese people on live Chinese television, using that live (and therefore difficult to censor) broadcast to put forth his honest explanation for the bombing error and, moreover, explain why NATO was bombing Yugoslavia. Chinese propagandists would have disputed the President's message, of course, but by delivering it over live Chinese television he might have circumvented the regime's censors and sown some important seeds of doubt among the Chinese population about their government's own self-serving version of events.

A similar trip by the President could have been made to Russia during the second Chechen War. At that time Russia's television media was predominantly, though not completely, state-controlled, generally broadcasting only a sanitized version of the conflict, portraying only the Chechen "terrorist" side as guilty of war crimes, instead of both sides. Western criticism of Russia's disproportionate use of force was portrayed, again only half-truthfully, as criticism of Russia's military operation in general, even as support for the Chechen "terrorists." The full truth is that the West never objected to Russia preserving its own territorial integrity, by force if necessary, rooting out the genuine terrorists and criminal gangs that had plagued Chechnya for years—but that operation did not justify Russia's war crimes. As Vladimir Putin tried to sustain Russian popular support for the war and for his own coming election, so the state-controlled Russian media report only half the truth. But if the President of the United States had traveled to Russia, ostensibly for whatever reason that Moscow would accept, he could have granted interviews to Russian television, preferably broadcast live, and explained the full truth of the American position. He could have mentioned, and thus referred Russian viewers to, objective news outlets in the Russian mass media, such as the then-independent Russian television network NTV. NTV did carry news of Russian war crimes.

Tapping the full potential of the Information Age to thwart and undermine genocidal tyranny requires that the message be delivered with psychological skill, timing, and creativity, tailored to the audience's sociocultural and political circumstances. It must be delivered while the audience is still psychologically receptive as much as technically receptive, leaving enough time to be digested and accepted. The best time for active persuasion is before war hysteria or mass indifference take over. Most Serbs with access to Western news broadcasts during the Kosovo War simply refused to believe any reports of atrocities by

Serbian police and paramilitary forces in Kosovo. Most Serbs preferred to live in psychological denial and indifference, because for nearly a decade their proud nation had suffered the collective humiliation of lost wars, economic privation, political repression, and international contempt, pushing their nation (that is, their group identity) deeper and deeper into a collective inferiority complex. By 1999, after years of excruciating sacrifice and of Milosevic's propaganda, most Serbs could not accept—at least not immediately—that their nation's situation was even worse than they imagined, that their proud forces were being run by war criminals, guilty of atrocities worthy of the Nazis and the Ustashi, that their group identity as a sanctimonious nation being forced to defend itself was an enormous lie. NATO's efforts to influence the Serbs with factual news and official statements were tardy, its presentation pathetic. An earlier, broader, more sophisticated campaign of spreading the full truth was needed.

In many parts of the world, an intensive campaign of spreading the truth is needed now. Decades ago, to help combat Nazism and Communism, the United States created Voice of America (VOA) and Radio Free Europe/Radio Liberty (RFE/RL). These and similar broadcasting agencies still exist alongside the private mass media. What their original founders could not tap, but we can, is a nearly global recognition today that democratic principles and individual rights are universal values. Unfortunately, even as we recall that the Cold War was won by television as much as by tanks, even as we continue to refine our own mass marketing techniques for commercial advertising and political election campaigns, we still too frequently neglect to employ mass media technologies to proclaim and spread those universal values as a powerful means of preventing genocide.

THE ULTIMATE CURE

Restricting armaments, alleviating poverty, and promoting law and order may produce plenty of material benefits, but we should be wary of a materialist mind-set that promotes these and other materialist conceptions as cure-alls for genocide. The materialist mind-set has too frequently turned institutions of civil order into instruments of mass murder. If there is an ultimate cure for genocide, it will not be found exclusively within political arrangements and humanitarian interventions.

Rather than being compelled by our genes, genocidal behavior has its cause in the human psyche, a cause rooted in a fear so deep that this driving fear has twisted and corrupted the perpetrator's intellect, a fear arisen from his own lack of unconditional love for himself. Many of us, perhaps most of us, would rather not face our innermost feelings about ourselves, a feeling of personal self-doubt or even of self-hatred—but that is where the eventual impetus for genocidal behavior originates. If the problem of genocide had an easy solution, we would have conquered it a long time ago. It does not have an easy solution because both the problem and its solution are both, in a psychological sense, spiritual.

This is not a plea for organized religion per se. It is, rather, a recognition of our profoundly human need for our lives to have meaning. The psychoanalyst Erich Fromm asserted that there is no one without a religious need, a need to devote oneself to something larger than oneself, whether that is through money, power, a nation or ethnicity, an ideology, an organized religion, or a personal philosophy. It is why some people surrender their proverbial souls into a group identity and become its zealots. Genocide is the most perverse way that human beings try to create meaning in their lives. The perpetrators have a grand vision of the future: a society they have faithfully purged of their enemies.

Critics of religious faith rightfully note the historic complicity that so many organized religions have had in justifying the commission of atrocities even in recent times. Judaism, Christianity, Islam, Hinduism, Buddhism, Confucianism, Taoism—none of these religions, nor any organized faith, has an unblemished record among all of its claimants. And at times this complicity of religion in evil behavior has been truly ghastly, as was acknowledged in January 1995 by the Roman Catholic bishops of the Federal Republic of Germany, acknowledged in a statement they issued on fiftieth anniversary of the liberation of Auschwitz:

During the years of the Third Reich, Christians did not offer due resistance to racial anti-Semitism. . . . Not a few of them got involved in the ideology of National Socialism and remained unmoved in the face of the crimes committed against Jewish-owned property and the life of Jews. Others paved the way for crimes or even became criminals themselves.

Today the fact is weighing heavily on our minds that there were but individual initiatives to help persecuted Jews, and that even the [*Kristallnacht*] pogroms of November 1938 were not followed by public and express protest; i.e., when hundreds of synagogues were set on fire and vandalized, cemeteries were desecrated, thousands of Jewish-owned shops were demolished, innumerable dwellings of Jewish families were damaged and looted, people were ridiculed, ill-treated and even killed.[2]

Yet there is a role for even organized religion in the prevention of genocide, as the German Catholic bishops went on to emphasize:

Auschwitz faces us Christians with the question of what relationship we have with the Jews and whether this relationship corresponds to the spirit of Jesus Christ. Anti-Semitism is "a sin against God and humanity," as Pope John Paul II has said many times. In the Church there must not be any room for and consent to hostility towards Jews. Christians must not harbor aversion, dislike, and even less feelings of hatred for Jews and Judaism. Wherever such an attitude comes to light, they have the duty to offer public and express resistance.[3]

Erich Fromm, himself a Jewish refugee from Nazi Germany, once described what sort of personal spirituality actively opposes evil, at home and abroad, with the sustained determination necessary:

If you begin your resistance to a "Hitler" only after he has won his victory, then you've lost before you've even begun. For to offer resistance, you've got to have an inner core, a conviction. You have to have faith in yourself, to be able to think critically, to be an independent human being, a human being and not a sheep. To achieve that, to learn "the art of living and of dying" takes a lot of effort, practice, patience. Like any other skill, it has to be learned. Anyone whose growth takes this direction will also develop the ability to know what is good—or bad—for himself and others, good or bad for him *as a human being*, not good or bad for his success, his acquisition of power or of goods.

Widespread passivity, a lack of participation in the decisions affecting our own lives and our society's life—that is the soil in which Fascism or similar movements, for which we usually find names only after the fact, can grow.[4]

For the opposite of love is not hate, but indifference. Remembering the Holocaust, the eloquent survivor Elie Wiesel once noted:

The victims perished not only because of the killers, but also because of the bystanders. . . . What astonished us after the torment, after the tempest, was not that so many killers killed so many victims, but that so few cared about us at all.[5]

Likewise in the 1990s, in the aftermath of the Bosnian War and its siege of Sarajevo, Benazir Bhutto, the first female Prime Minister of Pakistan, observed:

Muslims could not understand why one of the great cities of Europe was reduced to rubble by a systematic destruction—and that this destruction of the city was captured nightly for all the world to see by CNN, Muslims could not understand why the West stood by, indifferent. This kind . . . of bloodshed in a Muslim city in the heart of Europe, with the West standing silently by, plays into the hands of extremists who say that, "If it were Christian Paris on fire and not Muslim Sarajevo, would the West have acquiesced?"

Because Islam is a religion that sanctifies Abraham, Moses, and Jesus as prophets, it was even more bewildering for Muslims to find that the West was suddenly suspicious of them.[6]

Aung San Suu Kyi, the devoutly Buddhist leader of the embattled democracy movement in Burma, renamed Myanmar by the country's military dictatorship, was once asked why so many atrocities were perpetrated in her native land, a nation known for its ritual devotion to Buddhism. She replied:

Well, one might as well ask how the Khmer Rouge emerged out of Cambodia. It does not mean that just because you have a good, caring religion, everyone practices it. A lot of people give lip-service to their religion. They can recite the prayers, attend the ceremonies, perform all the rites, but they may not really absorb anything into their hearts.

These things are happening because there is not enough active compassion. There is a very direct link between love and fear. It reminds me of the Biblical quotation that *Perfect Love Casts Out Fear.* I've often thought that this is a very Buddhist attitude. "Perfect Love" should be *metta,* which is not selfish or attached love. . . . Some people might think it is either idealistic or naïve to talk about *metta* in terms of politics, but to me it makes a lot of practical good sense.[7]

Most people do not concern themselves with the intricacies of international politics, because they see little reason to involve themselves. In a world where religious belief remains so common, however, most people do care about their own spiritual well-being. And in today's Information Age, only the most willfully ignorant can avoid any knowledge whatsoever of a major genocide reported somewhere on this planet. The name of the place may not sound very familiar, its victims seemingly quite different from ourselves, but we all know that mass murder is wrong, that genocide is evil.

Oscar Arias, the former President of Costa Rica and, like Elie Wiesel and Aung San Suu Kyi, a recipient of the Nobel Peace Prize, warned that "Without the principle of individual conscience, every attempt to institutionalize ethics must collapse. World leaders may see their effect in headlines, but the ultimate course of the globe will be determined by the efforts of innumerable individuals acting on their consciences." He then said this more succinctly: "The effect of one upright individual is incalculable."[8]

What can the ordinary person do? "I think you could start by convincing a friend," suggested Aung San Suu Kyi. "You have to start with a first step, and there are many ways of starting. I take heart that some big international movements have started with a letter to a newspaper, and people who read that take it up." Poignantly she added: "Every movement, ultimately, was started by one person."[9]

Around the world there are plenty of experts and even a few courageous leaders, but whatever proposals they offer us to thwart genocide will make little headway unless enough ordinary people demand that something be done. This reality was recognized in a report to the United Nations on how to better enforce the Genocide Convention:

Without a strong basis of international public support, even the most perfectly redrafted Convention will be of little value. Conventions and good governments can give a lead, but the mobilization of public awareness and vigilance is essential to guard against any recurrence of genocide and other crimes against humanity and human rights.[10]

Most of us do care. *But do we care enough?*—that is the question our elected officials rightfully ask about us. For the greatest benefit of representative democracy is also its harshest consequence: We get the government we deserve. Our elected representatives want to know whether our determination to oppose genocide is durable, willing to pay a price for our global ideals. Public activism can accomplish that. Even something as ordinary as expressing one's opinion in a public way, encouraging others to do the same, can do more than apathy ever can.

The alternative is let the passivity of the many become trampled by the zealotry of a few. And always waiting in the political shadows is some aspiring leader whose mentality has been shaped by bigotry and hatred, a person willing to incite an angry minority over a cowed majority. In the words of Adolf Hitler:

I am no friend of the *man in the street!* I match personality against the man in the street! History is made by men, not by the masses! The masses must be *led!* Great historical decisions are impracticable without stern leadership of the masses! *The people must be regimented into an authoritarian order of society!*[11]

Democratic institutions cannot prevent this destructive tyranny unless enough ordinary people actively make those institutions work. And this includes people assisting from other democracies. In Rwanda, even as illegal preparations were being made for its genocide in 1994, its government was a fragile, incomplete democracy. Tragically, its democratization was not well safeguarded, neither at home or from abroad. A preventable genocide was not prevented.

The efforts of Raoul Wallenberg saved tens of thousands of Jews during the Holocaust. The efforts of Raphael Lemkin almost single-handedly produced the Genocide Convention. Neither man was paid enough for the personal sacrifices they made. Wallenberg disappeared into the Soviet GULAG. Lemkin died in poverty and obscurity; the only so-called biography written about him during the twentieth century was produced by a group accused of being Holocaust deniers. But Wallenberg and Lemkin were both true to their consciences, and the world is now a better place because of them.

The twentieth century began with optimism. It ended in disillusionment. Whether the twenty-first century and the millennium it opens will be any better than the past is entirely up to us and to the future generations we rear. The great variety of people who have ever rescued a person persecuted by a genocide present us with a common lesson: *Do not lose faith in humanity*. Many rescuers have expressed this faith adamantly, repeatedly, urging that young people in particular be taught it. For without this faith in the basic goodness of people, life is a crushing torment to endure, no matter how well off one is materially. In the midst of a genocide the basic goodness of people may seem nonexistent, but the existence of rescuers proves otherwise. The best way we can honor rescuers, the way most of them want to be honored, is to teach this underlying faith in humanity—to teach universal values with unconditional love, naïve though it may sound.

Genocide cannot be prevented by physically eliminating "evil people" from society, for that is the flawed method the Nazis believed and tried to implement. Genocide cannot be prevented by rigidly coercing people to be good, for that is the flawed method of the Marxist-Leninists. Genocide can be prevented only when enough vigilant caring individuals, both the extraordinary and the ordinary, actively work to uphold everyone's most basic of human rights, locally and internationally. The ultimate cause and cure of genocide is more psychological than biological, more spiritual than material. We choose to murder. We choose to be indifferent. Or we choose to rescue others. The choice is ours.

The choice is yours.

NOTES

1. Quoted in Arthur Larson, *Eisenhower: The President Nobody Knew* (New York: Charles Scribner's Sons, 1968), p. 68.

2. *Statement of the German Bishops On the Occasion of the 50th Anniversary of the Liberation of the Extermination Camp of Auschwitz on January 17, 1995*, announced in Wurzburg, Germany, on January 23, 1995.

3. Ibid.

4. Erich Fromm, *For the Love of Life* (New York: The Free Press, 1986), p. 133.

5. Quoted in Carol Rittner and Sondra Myers (editors), *The Courage to Care* (New York: New York University Press, 1986), pp. 123-125.

6. From a speech by Benazir Bhutto at Harvard University, Cambridge, Massachusetts, November 1997.

7. Aung San Suu Kyi (interviewed by Alan Clements), *The Voice of Hope* (New York: Seven Stories Press, 1997), pp. 38-39 and 210.

8. Quoted in Rushworth M. Kidder, "Universal Human Values: Finding an Ethical Common Ground" *The Futurist* (July-August 1994), pp. 8-13.

9. Aung San Suu Kyi (in an interview with Ivan Suvanjieff), "You Could Start by Convincing a Friend," *Shambhala Sun* (January 1996), pp. 29-33.

10. UN Doc. E/CN.4/Sub.2/1985/6, by Special Rapporteur Benjamin C.G. Whitaker (of the United Kingdom). Quoted in the entry "Genocide" in Edward Lawson (editor), *Encyclopedia of Human Rights* (New York: Taylor & Francis, 1991), p. 668.

11. Edouard Calic (editor), *Secret Conversations with Hitler* (New York: The John Day Company, 1971), p. 40.

Index

About the Author

JOHN G. HEIDENRICH is the Senior Analyst for Genocide and Instability Warning Issues at Open Source Solutions (OSS), Inc., an international consulting firm. Formerly an analyst with the U.S. Defense Intelligence Agency (DIA), he later joined the Institute for Defense & Disarmament Studies (IDDS), a nonprofit think-tank in Cambridge, Massachusetts, where he directed its Project on Genocide Prevention. Also an Airborne-qualified officer in the U.S. Army Reserve, he has served in units associated with military police, military intelligence, Special Forces, armor, and aviation. He is a member of the Association of Genocide Scholars.